PCET

Sara Miller McCune founded SAGE Publishing in 1965 to support the dissemination of usable knowledge and educate a global community. SAGE publishes more than 1000 journals and over 800 new books each year, spanning a wide range of subject areas. Our growing selection of library products includes archives, data, case studies and video. SAGE remains majority owned by our founder and after her lifetime will become owned by a charitable trust that secures the company's continued independence.

Los Angeles | London | New Delhi | Singapore | Washington DC | Melbourne

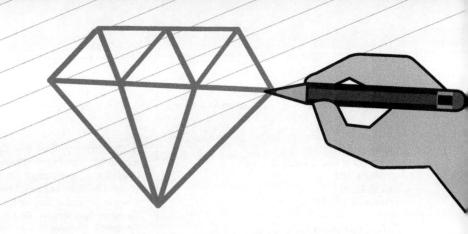

PCET

LEARNING AND TEACHING IN THE
POST COMPULSORY SECTOR

JONATHAN TUMMONS

Learning Matters
An imprint of SAGE Publications Ltd
1 Oliver's Yard
55 City Road
London EC1Y 1SP

SAGE Publications Inc.
2455 Teller Road
Thousand Oaks, California 91320

SAGE Publications India Pvt Ltd
B 1/I 1 Mohan Cooperative Industrial Area
Mathura Road
New Delhi 110 044

SAGE Publications Asia-Pacific Pte Ltd
3 Church Street
#10-04 Samsung Hub
Singapore 049483

Editor: Amy Thornton
Senior project editor: Chris Marke
Project management: Swales & Willis Ltd, Exeter, Devon
Marketing manager: Lorna Patkai
Cover design: Wendy Scott
Typeset by: C&M Digitals (P) Ltd, Chennai, India
Printed in the UK

First published 2020

Library of Congress Control Number: 2019940723

British Library Cataloguing in Publication Data

A catalogue record for this book is available from the British Library

ISBN 978-1-5264-6021-9
ISBN 978-1-5264-6022-6 (pbk)

At SAGE we take sustainability seriously. Most of our products are printed in the UK using responsibly sourced papers and boards. When we print overseas we ensure sustainable papers are used as measured by the Egmont grading system. We undertake an annual audit to monitor our sustainability.

CONTENTS

Contents

ABOUT THE EDITOR AND CONTRIBUTORS

The editor

Jonathan Tummons Associate Professor and Deputy Head of the School of Education, Durham University, UK. Research interests: learning, teaching and assessment in further, higher and adult education; learning architectures and communities of practice; actor network theory.

The contributors

Liz Atkins Professor of Vocational Education and Social Justice, Derby University. Research interests: methodological concerns and ways of working with low-attaining young people; the school-to-work transitions of young people in the context of broad vocational programmes; the professional education and identity of teachers.

Aaron Bradbury Senior Lecturer, Apprenticeships and Work-Based Learning in Education, Early Years and Children's Social Care, University College Birmingham. Research interests: widening participation (access for all), with links to apprenticeship pedagogy, Early Years and education.

Rose Cook Senior Research Fellow at the Policy Institute, King's College London. Research interests: gender, education and employment, focusing on gender differences in access to training and skill development; gender differences in STEM skills and occupations; the quality of employment; diversity and inclusion in education and employment across the life course.

Jim Crawley Visiting Teaching and Learning Fellow at Bath Spa University. Research interests: teacher education, learning technology and adult and community education. Convenor of the Teacher Education in Lifelong Learning (TELL) network, and former chair of the Post-16 Committee of the Universities' Council for the Education of Teachers (UCET).

Judith Darnell Course Leader and Lecturer for the Foundation Degree in Educational Practice, Bedford College, and Lecturer in Early Years, University of Bedfordshire. Research interests: parental involvement and attainment; primary teaching and learning, further education; Early Years; the Forest School approach; research methodology.

Carol Azumah Dennis Senior Lecturer in Education, Leadership and Management, Open University, BERA SIG Convenor. Research interests: post-compulsory education; leadership; ethics; policy; professionalism; social media.

Jane Dudeney Personal Achievement Tutor/Associate Lecturer for Teacher Education, Bedford College. Research interests: mental health and well-being of staff and students; tutoring; mentoring; student and staff satisfaction.

Roy Halpin Senior Lecturer in Lifelong Learning ITE, University of Huddersfield. Research interests: initial teacher education; use of digital technologies within education; policy and pedagogy.

Gary Husband Lecturer in Professional Education and Leadership, University of Stirling. Research interests: professional learning; governance and leadership.

Samantha Jones Advanced Practitioner Teacher Development and Scholarship, Bedford College. Research interests: vocational knowledge; continuing professional development.

Karima Kadi-Hanifi Senior Lecturer in Education, Newman University. Research interests: higher education; further education; adult and community learning (ESOL and literacy); college-based higher education; linguistics; critical pedagogy.

Annelies Kamp Head of School of Educational Studies & Leadership and Associate Professor in Leadership, University of Canterbury in Aotearoa New Zealand. Research interests: social theory and the intersection of young people, education, training and employment; critical studies of youth transition; education of sustainable development; the teenage parent and education; leadership and the 'joined-up' policy agenda.

John Keenan Senior Lecturer in Education, Newman University. Research interests: further education; college-based higher education; emotion; animation.

Nichola Kentzer Senior Lecturer Sport Psychology, Open University, UK. Research interests: teacher education; mentoring; supervision; well-being of students and staff.

Kate Lavender Senior Lecturer in Lifelong Learning ITE, University of Huddersfield. Research interests: adult education; college-based higher education; sociology of education; initial teacher education (lifelong learning); mentoring in ITE lifelong learning.

Catherine Lloyd Director of Land-Based Studies, Bedford College. Research interests: vocational knowledge; leadership and management in further education.

Janet Lord Head of Education for the Faculty of Education, Manchester Metropolitan University. Research interests: teaching and learning; assessment; identity; critical realism.

Sherene Meir Access to Higher Education Lecturer (Social Sciences), City of Bristol College. Research interests: adult learning; returning to learning; creative research methods; psychosocial theory.

Lucy Mitchell Quality Manager – Curriculum, Growth Company, Education and Skills. Research interests: quality improvement and assurance; apprenticeships, 16–19 education; teacher education; curriculum and qualification development.

Natalie Morris Lecturer (Social Science and Education), Advanced Practitioner, Bedford College. Research interests: dialogic teaching; further education; educational achievement differences.

Dale Munday Digital Learning Facilitator, Lancaster University. Research interests: further, adult and community education; teacher education; learning technology; higher education; innovative teaching and learning practices.

Lou Mycroft Nomadic researcher. Research interests: constellations of professional practice; post-human approaches to community education, social purpose leadership.

Jane Pither Researcher. Research interests: education policy; vocational education and training; further and higher education; lifelong learning.

Sasha Pleasance Lecturer, Teacher Education, South Devon College. Research interests: sociology in education (Bourdieu and Foucault in particular); policy in further, adult and community education; lesson observation; teacher education.

Cheryl Reynolds University Teaching Fellow, Department of Initial Teacher Education, University of Huddersfield. Research interests: using technology in teaching and learning, particularly around the use of social networking as a platform for the delivery of master's-level courses.

Mike Saunders Head of Quality Improvement, York College. Research interests: andragogy; social learning and situated learning; dialogue in the classroom; transnational education.

Michael Smith Learning Innovation Manager, Barking and Dagenham College. Research interests: literacy practice; assessment methodologies; professional development; learning technology.

Sharron Wilkinson Lecturer in Education, University of Hull. Research interests: teaching in prisons; prison education and policy; application of wicked theory to contemporary social issues; research skills.

Jacklyn Williams Lecturer in Education Studies, University of Plymouth. Research interests: dyslexia; language and agency; vocational–academic divide; teacher education.

Vicky Wynne Assistant Dean for Apprenticeships and Work Based Learning, University College Birmingham. Research interests: apprenticeship pedagogy, coaching and mentoring; models of learning.

Adeline Yuen Sze Goh Assistant Professor in Education, Sultan Hassanal Bolkiah Institute of Education, University Brunei Darussalam. Research interests: workplace learning; professional education; vocational education; teacher education.

ABOUT THIS BOOK

This book is for anyone who is a teacher, trainer or lecturer (different people use or prefer different titles) in what is still often referred to as the post-compulsory education and training (PCET) sector. It is not primarily a 'how-to' book about teaching, learning and assessment with apprentices, adult learners and college students – although many 'how-to' moments are in fact present. Rather, it is a book that is intended to encourage the reader to move beyond a checklist approach to understanding professional practice, to start to engage with the broader issues, themes and debates that shape the daily work of practitioners but that do not always get the attention that they deserve. Some of these are political, and others are social and economic. Some are informed by research, others by experience and reflection. Some of them are of more immediate relevance to some readers than others, but they are all interesting – and they are all important.

This book rests on three principles. The first is that both initial teacher education and ongoing professional learning and development ought to be seen as necessary elements of professionalism for all those people who teach or train in further education colleges, adult education centres, prisons and secure colleges of learning, workplaces, and so forth – all of those places that we continue to group together as PCET. This label is not used uncritically – not least as much of what the sector does is no longer 'post-compulsory', but it remains a widely used term and so I hope that a little latitude can be granted. In fact, the PCET label is challenged on more than one occasion in this book – which brings me to the second principle: both initial and ongoing teacher education and development need always to be a critical and research-informed process. A list of competences does not engender a thoughtful and self-aware, autonomous professionalism: initial teacher education is serious work that needs to embrace, amongst other things, different standpoints informed by a critical use of research. You don't have to do research to be informed by it; nor should reading research be dismissed as 'too academic', 'too difficult', or 'too removed from practice'. As such, in reading these chapters, you will find moments of respectful disagreement. As authors, we do not always agree with each other concerning everything that we wish to say – and this is as it should be. This takes us to the third principle that underpins this book, namely that the authors' voices represented within it reflect the diversity and variety of the PCET sector. All of the authors either work in the sector or used to do so (I worked as an adult education tutor for eight years and as a college tutor for six more, before getting a job in a university). As authors, we bring experience as well as expertise in offender learning, adult and community education, basic skills, apprenticeships, further education, and more.

Each chapter sets out to provide a way in to the issues discussed, a snapshot of a topic for discussion and reflection as well as action through professional practice. Key questions and theories are highlighted throughout, and suggestions for wider reading allow the reader to explore further. Each chapter is self-contained and can therefore be read in isolation – but it is hoped that readers will range far and wide, and that FE college tutors will want to learn more about offender learning, that adult education tutors will want to learn more about college based higher education, and that the provision of vocational and technical education in Aotearoa New Zealand will inspire discussions amongst teachers in England and Wales.

There isn't room for everything in one book – even a large volume such as this one. So if I have missed something, or if you want to suggest a topic for a new chapter or even a whole new book, please get in touch.

Jonathan Tummons

Acknowledgements

Many thanks are due to Amy Thornton, Tracey Cowell and Caroline Watson for their outstanding stewardship of this book, from first email to final manuscript.

1

WHAT DOES THE FURTHER AND ADULT EDUCATION SECTOR DO AND WHY DOES IT MATTER?

John Keenan and Karima Kadi-Hanifi

Key words – further education; FE; adult education; history of adult education; history of FE; purpose of adult education; purpose of FE

Introduction

We cannot give a single definition of the 'diverse, rich and ... fast changing landscape' (Duckworth, 2014, p41) of adult and further education. It is complex, changing and operates not within an insulated vacuum, but in an environment that is currently influenced by an agenda of competition, marketisation and instability (see Keep, 2013, 2018). While there is no single definition through a history of adult and further education, this chapter gives a picture of what these sectors are today and what they have been in the past, and through these draws some commonalities about their purposes.

The chapter concludes that adult and further education matters because it is accessible, because it is inclusive and because it brings the benefits of education and well-being to local communities.

A history of further education

> ### Key theory
>
> #### The development of the FE sector
>
> The development of an FE sector can be traced from the Education Act 1944. Its history and purposes are explored in the following texts:
>
> *(Continued)*

(Continued)

Hillier, Y. (2006) *Everything You Need to Know about FE Policy*. London: Continuum.

Hodgson, A. and Spours, K. (2017) *Policy and Policy Learning across the Four Countries of the UK: The Case of Further Education and Skills. An Initial Scoping Paper*, May 2017. London: UCL Institute of Education. Available at: www.ucl.ac.uk/ioe/sites/ioe/files/fe-skills-across-uk-scoping-paper.pdf

Smithers, A. and Robinson, P. (2005) *Further Education Reformed*. London: Falmer Press.

Key questions

What is further education (FE)?

When and why did FE begin?

The beginnings of the FE sector and adult education

FE has 'its roots in the Adult Education tradition' (Peart, 2013, p33) but it was created to serve a post-war industrial and academic purpose and to become a third or tertiary sector sitting between school and higher education (HE), designed to bridge the gap from school to the workplace or university. Today, institutions deemed to be FE are funded by the Education and Skills Funding Agency, and include sixth form colleges, land-based colleges, art colleges and performing arts colleges.

The Education Act 1944 raised the leaving age of pupils to 15 and charged local authorities to provide post-15 education within institutions described during parliamentary debate as 'young people's colleges' (Hansard, 1944). These colleges in turn were classified as being commercial colleges (for training in 'white-collar' skills), art colleges, and technical colleges (for training in 'blue-collar' skills). The pressure was on both local education authorities (LEAs) to find the money to ensure that training was available and on the 16–18-year-olds who would be required to attend for up to eight weeks a year (Education Act 1944). Many of the first FE colleges quickly rose to become colleges of HE (and on to becoming polytechnics, then universities of today), but those that catered for the 'lower-level qualifications ... form the core of FE today' (Simmons, 2016, p34).

Key questions

Which types of educational institution are considered to be FE?

Why does FE not have a clear identity?

What legal changes have affected FE?

Sixth form colleges came later to England and Wales in 1965 from government Circular 10/65 (Education England, n.d.b), giving instruction to local authorities to organise a comprehensive system that included post-16 provision. Initially not seen as being part of FE, they were brought under the same funding mechanism in 1992. By the 1990s, FE was carrying the 'burden of the generation', educating 50 per cent of all 16–18-year-olds, 80 per cent of whom were funded by the government (Melville and Macleaod, cited in Smithers and Robinson, 2000, p27).

What is an FE institution?

The range of institutions that come under the term 'FE', as well as the importance of the sector, is not always fully understood. Calling it the 'everything else' sector, Panchamia (2012) notes in a report for the Institute of Government: 'The further education ... sector is poorly defined and under-stood'. When Sir Michael Wilshaw (Chief Inspector of Ofsted, 2012–2016) called FE a 'mess' in which pupils 'head off towards the FE institution which is a large, amorphous institution ... and do badly' (TES, 2016), he seems to have not only made a gross generalisation, but also ignored the Further and Higher Education Act 1992, which incorporated sixth form and specialist colleges into the definition. Wilshaw's 'common sense' definition of FE as the 'local tech' can be seen in state-ments such as this: 'The main difference from school is that an FE college is a much more adult environment and students will typically call teachers by their first name and be expected to be inde-pendent' (ParentZone, 2018). HE is very much part of FE now, a fact that is often ignored: 'Further education ... includes any study after secondary education that's not part of higher education' (Gov. uk, n.d.). Notably, in both of these, FE is defined by what it is not, and compared to features of more familiar education zones – schools and HE.

Defining FE by what it is not does not give the sector an identity in its own right, nor does it recognise its role in the schooling of under-16s. Since the Tomlinson Report (Tomlinson, 1996), the 14–19 White Paper (DES, 2005) and the Leitch Review (Leitch, 2006), FE has been providing education for children as young as 14. Furthermore, what FE is in England is different from other nations in the UK. In Northern Ireland, there are only six FE and no sixth form colleges (nidirect, 2018), while Scotland retains its local authority funding system (Gov.scot, 2018).

FE in the UK today

In the UK, there are 334 FE colleges (288 of them in England), 73 sixth form colleges, 14 land-based colleges and 12 specialist designated colleges (AoC, 2017). This is an established and important sector. However, Sir Andrew Foster's review of education in 2005 stated that 'FE lacks a clearly rec-ognised and shared core purpose' as it has 'suffered from too many initiatives' (Foster, 2005, p7). If we see FE as created by government as a tertiary sector that has a particular purpose, we might see it as constantly having to respond to ever-changing political and economic policy, heavily steered by national policy levers, notably related to funding (Hodgson and Spours, 2003). New governments bring their own prejudices and ideologies, and FE can be the place where the perceived economic and societal ills might be solved. FE has had an array of funding bodies since leaving local authority control, including the Young People's Learning Agency, the Further Education Funding Council for England, the Education Funding Agency and the Skills Funding Agency (the latter two organisations were amalgamated in 2017 to form the Education and Skills Funding Agency). The changes often seem either cyclical (sometimes in the sense of 'here we go again') or just a rebranding exercise, perhaps in the hope that this time it works: 'There had been plenty of youth training schemes, none of which showed more than a very modest success' (Evans, 2003, p36). Equally, future change may bring new funding streams, in a manner similar to the way in which the Education and Skills Act 2008 increased the age for staying in compulsory education to 18 from 2015 (Gov.uk, 2018).When the European Commission declared 1996 to be the 'European Year of Lifelong Learning', the largely pro-European New Labour government appointed Dr Kim Howells as the country's first Minister of Lifelong Learning (disbanded in 2012). A White Paper created an Advisory Group for Continuing Education and Lifelong Learning in 1998 and funded an array of courses (see Field, 2006, p11). Similarly, a relaxation of laws about HE provision meant the rise of FE as a provider of university-level provision. College-based higher education (CBHE) accounts for around 10 per cent of total HE provision in England, and has done so for many years (Avis and Orr, 2016), with over 180,000 students (HESA, 2017; UUK, 2016).

Key questions

What are the main trends affecting FE today?

Current trends in FE

FE is prone to societal trends, and for education in the last few decades 'performativity' has been a key trend. Performativity is 'a drive for efficiency which assumes that it is possible to precisely gauge and make transparent the performance ... through the use of audit technologies' (Trotman et al., 2018). An example of this is the Further and Higher Education Act 1992, which charged FE institutions to increase their student numbers by 28 per cent while reducing their per capita funding. In other words, 'run faster in order to stand still' (Ball, 2006, p123), which by 1995 most institutions had failed to achieve (Ball, 2006). Central to the function of performative cultures is the emergence of 'datafication' (focusing on numbers as evidence of success; see Kitchin, 2014) and 'dataveillance' (using these numbers to monitor performance; see Mattern, 2013). The measurement of everything and the way these numbers can be used to monitor providers have meant profound changes in FE – a move towards 'gaming' the system, with a focus on the new three Rs of recruitment, retention and results. For some, such as Sir Andrew Foster, this 1992 Act was 'a defining moment of liberation' for FE. For FE, the changes meant: 'Colleges became businesses, academic principals became chief executives and ... college governors were made responsible for financial management, strategic direction and getting their institutions "competition-ready"' (AoC, 2015). It is no surprise that given the need to focus on end data, there were mergers (including additional legislative pressure to merge), and the 500+ colleges in 1992 were reduced to 334 by 2017 (AoC, 2018b). The 1992 Act meant a competitive industry ethos against schools, universities and the new private post-16 education providers that were encouraged. Colleges now bid for money from a range of sources: the Funding Council, the European Social Fund, employers, universities, training and enterprise councils (and their various guises over the decades), students and the local authority.

A history of adult education

Key theory

Researching adult education

This history of the adult and further education sectors comes from a range of sources as it emerged from industry, individuals, charities and churches. Among the main texts used in this section are:

Evans, D. (2007) *The History of Technical Education: A Short Introduction*, 2nd edn. Cambridge: T Magazine.

Kelly, T. (1992) *A History of Adult Education in Great Britain from the Middle Ages to the Twentieth Century*. Liverpool: Liverpool University Press.

Key questions

When did adult education begin?

When and why did formal adult education begin?

Adults have been formally educated in universities since the ninth century's University of Karaouine in Morocco opened its doors (UNESCO, n.d.), and in the UK at Oxford from the eleventh century onwards. For most of its history, university education has been for adults with social and economic status. For the rest, informal education for adults has always existed as relatives, friends and others in communities passed skills on to the next generation (see Wardle, 1977). From the Middle Ages, a more formalised system of apprenticeships into a craft or trade existed via guilds (associations who controlled the businesses of the day; see Epstein, 1991), with churches providing other spaces for education with spiritual and moral aims. Another motivating force for providing adult education came from the Enlightenment (Allan, 2015) with evening classes, first in Scotland in 1799 run by George Birkbeck, who was Professor of Philosophy at Glasgow's Anderson Institute. Birkbeck went on to help formalise these in a Mechanics' Institute, which then formed in other cities, such as Leicester in 1833 and Nottingham in 1837, giving 'education in the broadest possible sense, from basic instruction in literacy and numeracy to lectures on the latest scientific ideas' (Barton, 1993, p47).

The London Mechanics' Institute inspired one of its graduates, William Lovett, to help form the National Union of the Working Classes in 1831 (see Kelly, 1970), aimed at educating those on the lower strata of society in the study of science and the improvement of the mind, body and spirit. Simultaneously, companies such as the East India Company were training employees in economics (see Wagner et al., 2007) to improve their business acumen. There were also entrepreneurs who had a religious, moral or industrial purpose to setting up education for workers in the nineteenth century. In Birmingham, members of the Cadbury family both taught adult education classes and created a centre for learning (which is still in operation today; see Woodbrooke, 2018). In London, Toynbee Hall (see Briggs and Macartney, 1984) was set up in the East End of London, bringing Oxbridge undergraduates to teach and support the working class (it is still providing adult education; see Toynbee, 2018). Furthermore, out of this building came the Workers' Educational Association (WEA), dedicated to the teaching of working-class adults, and who continue to provide education for 50,397 adults on 8,082 courses with 3,000+ teaching volunteers (WEA, 2017).

While such key figures and organisations influenced adult education, the 'pathway' has also been formed by a wider range of factors, not least the creation of a 'working class' (see Thompson, 2009) that could be educated and a 'middle class' that 'became increasingly conscious of the gap between themselves and the labouring classes' (Rowe, 1967, p1). Also at this time, the Paris Exhibition of 1867 exposed a gap between the UK and elsewhere 'when it became evident that the country was beginning to lag behind France, Germany and the US' (Evans, 2007, p6). Another pressure to educate adults came from those pushing for social reform (sometimes, strangely, called 'radicals'). Minutes from the 1836 meetings of the London Working Men's Association, for example, called for education for an 'intelligent and influential portion of the working classes in town and country' (cited in Rosenblatt, 2010, p84). The combined voices calling for education reform resulted in the Education Act 1870, bringing education for all children, and the Technical Instruction Act 1889, which included adults who were to be given 'instruction in the principles of science and art applicable to industries, and in the application of special branches of science and art to specific industries or employment' (Education England, n.d.a). Surprisingly, adult education was funded further at this time by alcohol sales (or the 'whisky tax' as it became known) when the Local Taxation (Customs and Excise) Act 1890 allowed a penny tax on alcohol to be diverted to local adult education. Universities caught the zeitgeist of adult education (see Evans, 2003; Lawrie, 2014) through the University Extension Movement and provision of extra-mural education, elements of which survive today within university centres and departments of lifelong learning. Meanwhile, the City & Guilds organisation was created by the guilds in 1878 (City & Guilds, n.d.) to provide adult education, and is today one of the major awarding bodies for adult education courses.

Key questions

In the nineteenth and twentieth centuries, what were the options for adult education?

The foundations of today's adult education system, therefore, were set in the nineteenth century. By the twentieth century, an array of adult courses were available through day continuation schools, evening schools, Mechanics' Institutes, schools of art, polytechnics, university extension classes and working men's colleges (National Archives, 2018). Visionaries such as Henry Morris started the Cambridge village colleges, which acted as schools in the day and adult education centres at night, so that: 'There would be no "leaving school"! – the child would enter at three and leave the college only in extreme old age' (Morris, 1925, cited in Jeffs, 1999, p92). In literature, characters such as H.G. Wells's Mr Polly (from *The History of Mr Polly*, published in 1910) introduced working-class men searching for a place where 'there was beauty, there was delight, that somewhere – magically inaccessible perhaps, but still somewhere, were pure and easy and joyous states of body and mind'. Leonard Bast (from E.M. Forster's *Howard's End*, published in 1910), similarly from lower-class origins and given an elementary education, searched through education for something more: 'His mind and his body had been alike underfed, because he was poor, and because he was modern they were always craving better food'. We can see in the literature of the early twentieth century a somewhat romanticised (and often tragic) version of education via characters who try for self-betterment through education only to be thwarted by the harsh reality of class power.

What is adult education today?

Adult education continues today through the Open College Network, the Women's Institute, the WEA, the National Trust, the Citizens Advice Bureau, university extension courses, and a plethora of charities, churches and community centres. Local authorities still fund community education, most commonly in basic skills provision such as adult literacy, numeracy and computing. The national picture is, though, one of an ad hoc provision that seems to be 'piecemeal' (Jarvis, 2010, p49) and at a permanent 'crossroads' (Finger and Asun, 2004) and in a state of 'stasis' (Hodgson and Spours, 2003) or even 'crisis' (Tuckett, 2018). It has certainly not featured highly in government priorities of late, as the MP David Lammy pointed out in the House of Commons:

> *Since 2010 this House has discussed education on 339 occasions. There has not been a single debate on adult education – not one … Such total disregard for adult education is not good enough. It is not good to say that if someone does not go to university they cannot progress and are limited to a life of low-paid work with no prospects of change.*
>
> (Hansard, 2017)

An example of the undervalued nature of adult education is the closure, in 1982, of the Richard Hoggart Advisory Council for Adult and Continuing Education (ACACE). The final ACACE report indicated great demand for 'informal learning' (ACACE, 1982, cited in Evans, 2003, p25), with over a million students in this sector. In 1995, the National Institute of Adult Continuing Education took over a 'soft money' (Evans, 2003, p25) oversight, and since 2006 the Open College (2018) has catered for some online education for adults, but 'the adult learning which was fundable was vocational learning' (Evans, 2003, p26) and this was the province given to FE.

The purposes of adult education and FE

Key theory

Researching the purpose of adult education

For a clear review of the purposes and benefits of adult education, see:

Evans, N. (2003) *Making Sense of Lifelong Learning*. London: RoutledgeFalmer.

Finger, M. and Asun, J. (2004) *Adult Education at the Crossroads: Learning Our Way Out*. Leicester: NIACE.

Key questions

What makes adult and further education different from the rest of the education system?

What do adult and further education give to society?

As the histories show, adult education and FE have 'bridged the gap' between school and university/work, offered a lifelong community-based model of education (including HE) and enriched lives with the purpose and joy of learning. Throughout the histories of the adult and further education sectors, key purposes emerge:

- serving the local community;

- providing an adult space for learning;

- inclusion; and

- a 'second-chance' sector.

To serve the local community

The adult education and FE sectors have a 'vital role in vocational and community education' (Duckworth, 2014, p3) in meeting the needs of local communities (Rami and O'Leary, 2017) and of fostering local and regional level partnerships with employers (Hodgson and Spours, 2017). The 1956 White Paper *Technical Education* (see National Archives, 2018) determined 'meeting local needs' as a central role, while the FEFC today considers FE education to be 'within reasonable daily travelling distance from their homes' (Education Act 1996).

To provide a learning space for adults

FE and adult education provide a refreshing difference from the compulsory sector's curriculum limitations and exams system, offering subjects that were not accessible at school. With a greater focus on student choice, the sectors allow an 'ethos of support, encouragement, choice and challenge' (Pleasance, 2016, p13) for those who are part of it. The vocational nature of many courses means there should be a greater sense of purposeful study focusing on an inner drive to achieve. There should be a grown-up approach to learning not only in the amount of autonomy expected from the students, but in the dialogic and facilitative pedagogical models provided.

To provide an education space inclusive to all

Adult and further education have 'strong bonds with disadvantaged groups and communities' (Duckworth, 2014, p6). For Avis (2016), 'the heterogeneity of students' (p93) in FE is a key feature to be praised, as befits a sector that grew up out of a need to educate the poor. FE students in particular tend to be working-class (Thompson, 2009). A purpose of education for adults is therefore social justice, by 'facilitating social mobility of those drawn from disadvantaged backgrounds' (Avis, 2016, p85).

To be a second-chance sector

The adult education and FE sectors have, as part of their purpose, the support of disaffected and demo-tivated young people and adults, and for a long time have been described as the 'second-chance' sectors in which students who have been seen as being failed by the compulsory system can find an education space in which they can thrive. This can include those who enter at 14 years old and 'returners to education' who change career and/or upskill.

Other purposes of adult and further education

Of course, the purposes of education for each individual student will vary. Jenny Rogers's *Adults Learning* (2000), originally published in 1971, suggested other purposes, including dealing with isola-tion (especially for the housewives of the time) and other social motives. In 2017, Duckworth and Smith recounted narratives of 'transformed lives', each individual recounting how adult and further education had given them a new opportunity. Education brings so many benefits:

> There is powerful evidence that adults who keep learning enjoy better health, are more productive and have more secure and better-paid jobs and are more active in civic life. Equally, offenders who take up learning are less likely to re-offend. And people recover better from mental ill health if they engage in learning.

(Tuckett, 2018)

This is 'in line' with Eduard Linderman's (1895–1953) definition of education for adults as 'a co-operative venture in non-authoritarian, informal learning, the chief purpose of which is to dis-cover the meaning of experience' (cited in Finger and Asun, 2004, p37).

These ideal purposes of education for adults are not always evident in the reality of FE and adult edu-cation in the UK. In the report *Learning: The Treasure Within* (UNESCO, 1996), Jacques Delors (then President of the European Commission) called lifelong learning 'a continuous process of forming whole human beings'. In the UK, the Dearing Report of 1997 reinterpreted this report into 'individu-als and their working lives sustaining a competitive economy' (see Evans, 2003, p30). In the UK, it seems, the 'Protestant work ethic' Max Weber identified in the nineteenth century is still very much with us when it comes to education policy, as Jarvis (2010) noted: 'formal lifelong education is now regarded as something necessary for work rather than the humanity of the learner' (p45). Nevertheless, adult education and FE are very much alive in terms of variety and participation. A snapshot of adult and further education today includes publicly funded courses, privatised provision, college-based higher education, and community and work-based learning. In 2017, according to the Association of Colleges, the FE sector alone in the UK accounted for 2.2 million students, including 1.4 million 18+ and 712,000 16–18 (AoC, 2018a). In 2015–2016, FE had a £7 billion income, 50 per cent from the Department for Education's (DfE) 16–18 funds and 25 per cent from DfE funds for adult education and apprenticeships, with the final 25 per cent coming from fees, grants and other funding bodies (AoC, 2018a). The sometimes informal nature of adult education makes participation harder to gauge, but the 2016 DfE survey reported that 78 per cent of respondents were currently engaged in learning (ONS, 2016, p5).

The future for adult and further education

It is worth, here, thinking about possibilities.

Key questions

What would happen if education were fully funded and each individual could choose a course and a style of study?

This seemingly utopian vision is nearer than we think. As Tuckett (2018) summarised, there are precedents of successful adult education models across the world:

> In Europe, all the Nordic countries maintain substantial public financial support for open exploratory liberal education, where citizens can learn a wide range of subjects. In Switzerland, Austria and Germany vocational education enjoys high esteem and public investment, in stark contrast to the weakening of funding for the vocational education sector in the UK. Investment in lifelong learning, meanwhile, has attracted significant and impressive commitment, backed by legislation, in several Asian countries ... For example, the city of Suwon in South Korea guarantees a library within 10 minutes' walk and a learning centre within 20 minutes' of every citizen's home, with close co-operation with the city's universities. In Singapore, too, the combination of national investment, support for business and individual learning accounts, backed by active support from higher education, creates optimal conditions for creating a learning society – using measures many of which were introduced and too quickly dropped in the UK.

Looking for a further international perspective on adult education, we might also turn to UNESCO's recommendation of *éducation permanente*: lifelong, purposeful, humanistic, emancipatory and 'aimed at bringing out the full potential of human beings and enabling them to shape their societies' (Effert, 2018, p1). The UK should, in our view, remove from the sectors those aspects that include dataveillance, market focus, and subject and institution elitism, and focus on the promotion of education that brings a holistic sense of the self. As a starting point, policy for those educating adults could be more proactive towards a system based on the positive values of education for all for purposes of human emancipation, and less reactive (Hodgson and Spours, 2003) to the perceived shortcomings of the compulsory sector and the needs of commerce. We are not the first to call for this, nor will we be the last.

Conclusion

In this chapter, we have given a definition and history of adult education and FE and isolated some common features: local provision, adult-focused education, inclusivity and a second chance to succeed in education. Some of this history we have lived through.

As teachers of English as an additional language, we have worked with immigrants to the UK who wanted to start a new life in England.

As vocational trainers, we have provided courses for those who wanted to improve their business communication skills.

We have taught English to students over 80 years old who came to an FE college at night for no other reason than to learn more about the joy of literature and the pleasure of learning.

We have seen postmen as students in our evening class, prey to early mornings, falling asleep in our evening classes (and exams)!

As coordinators of teacher training of lifelong learning, we have witnessed adult education classes in churches, community centres and libraries on weekday evenings and Saturday mornings.

We have been present when students with mental health issues have been explaining how a dictionary could not be opened as 'the words keep coming'.

We have been in classes whose sole aim was to help a student with severe learning difficulties boil a kettle safely.

We have listened while a pupil who had a very high degree of dyslexia made his first phone call to someone to communicate something and gain a first certificate after years of failure in mainstream education, and finally learning, at age 17, to spell his name correctly.

From all of our experiences, we believe in adult education and FE, and the working woman and man of yesterday and today who walks through the doors of a place of education in order to improve their life and that of their children. From our years as students, teachers and teacher trainers in adult and further education, we have witnessed why it matters.

Chapter summary

- Adult education as we know it today in the UK grew out of the nineteenth century, when a range of providers, including industry, individuals, charities and churches, gave the working class a place and space to study. The motives behind them varied, though a desire to improve the minds of the working class, to give industrial skills and moral betterment were among them.

- During the last two centuries, adult education has fluctuated in its importance to government. Since the 1980s, its role has declined, although there are still many who are being educated today through the Open College Network, community provision from local authorities and a range of providers.

- Government financial support largely moved to FE, which was set up in 1944 as a tertiary or third sector between school and HE/work. FE is often charged to support the latest government initiative, and often whatever skills or knowledge seem to be missing from that provided by the compulsory sector.

- Key themes emerge from the history that informs the sectors' purposes: community-based, inclusive of all, dialogic and facilitative education styles, and a second chance to succeed beyond the compulsory sector.

- Education freely available for all may be a dream stance, but in different countries there are models of practice that show they see the value to society of making sure adults have access to places to develop their minds, bodies and even spirits (as many classes are provided by religious organisations).

Further recommended reading

We recommend you go to the works of Vicky Duckworth and Jonathan Tummons separately and together using this text:

Duckworth, V. and Tummons, J. (2010) *Contemporary Issues in Lifelong Learning*. Maidenhead: Open University Press.

John Lea is another key thinker and writer on the nature of adult and further education, and we recommend his work such as:

Lea, J., Hayes, D., Armitage, A., Lomas, L. and Markless, S. (2003) *Working in Post-Compulsory Education*. Maidenhead: Open University Press.

There is a comprehensive overview of the history of adult education, its purposes and the nature of learning in:

Jarvis, P. (2010) *Adult Education and Lifelong Learning: Theory and Practice*. London: Routledge.

References

Allan, D. (2015) The universities and the Scottish Enlightenment. In R. Anderson, M. Freeman and L. Paterson (eds), *The Edinburgh History of Education in Scotland*. Edinburgh: Edinburgh University Press.

AoC (2015) *70 Years of Change and Challenge in FE Colleges: 1945–1992*. Available at: www.aocjobs.com/article/history-of-further-education-1945-1992/

AoC (2017) *College Key Facts*. London: AoC.

AoC (2018a) *College Key Facts 2017/18*. Available at: www.aoc.co.uk/sites/default/files/AoC%20College%20Key%20Facts%20201718%20%28web%29.pdf

AoC (2018b) *College Mergers*. Available at: www.aoc.co.uk/about-colleges/college-mergers

Avis, J. (2016) *Social Justice, Transformation and Knowledge: Policy, Workplace Learning and Skills*. London: Routledge.

Avis, J. and Orr, K. (2016) HE in FE: vocationalism, class and social justice. *Research in Post-Compulsory Education*, 21(1–2): 49–65.

Ball, S. (2006) *Education and Social Class*. London: Routledge.

Barton, S. (1993) *The Mechanics Institutes: Pioneers of Leisure and Excursion Travel*. Available at: www.le.ac.uk/lahs/downloads/1993/1993%20(67)%2047-58%20Barton.pdf

Briggs, A. and Macartney, A. (1984) *Toynbee Hall: The First Hundred Years*. London: Routledge & Kegan Paul.

City & Guilds (n.d.) *About Us*. Available at: www.cityandguilds.com/about-us

DES (2005) *14–19 Education and Skills*. London: HMSO.

Duckworth, V. (2014) *How to Be a Brilliant FE Teacher*. Available at: www.ucl.ac.uk/ioe/departments-centres/centres/centre-for-post14-education- and-work/projects/fe-skills-four-countries-uk/pdf/FE_and_Skills_-_the_case_of_England_Final.pdf

Duckworth, V. and Smith, R. (2017) *Further Education in England: Transforming Lives and Communities*. Available at: http://transforminglives.web.ucu.org.uk

Education Act 1870. Available at: www.legislation.gov.uk/ukpga/Geo6/7-8/31/contents/enacted

Education Act 1944. Available at: www.legislation.gov.uk/ukpga/Geo6/7-8/31/section/44/enacted

Education Act 1996. Available at: www.legislation.gov.uk/ukpga/1996/56/schedules

Education England (n.d.a) *Technical Instruction Act 1889*. Available at: www.educationengland.org.uk/documents/acts/1889-technical-instruction-act.html

Education England (n.d.b) *Circular 10/65 (1965)*. Available at: www.educationengland.org.uk/documents/des/circular10-65.html

Effert, M. (2018) *UNESCO's Utopia of Lifelong Learning: An Intellectual History*. London: Routledge.

Epstein, S. (1991) *Wage Labor and Guilds in Medieval Europe*. London: University of North Carolina Press.

Evans, D. (2007) *The History of Technical Education: A Short Introduction*, 2nd edn. Cambridge: T Magazine.

Evans, N. (2003) *Making Sense of Lifelong Learning*. London: RoutledgeFalmer.

Field, J. (2006) *Lifelong Learning and the New Educational Order*. London: Trentham Books.

Finger, M. and Asun, J. (2004) *Adult Education at the Crossroads: Learning Our Way Out*. Leicester: NIACE.

Foster, A. (2005) *Realising the Potential: A Review of the Future Role of FE Colleges*. Nottingham: DfES. Available at: http://dera.ioe.ac.uk/5535/

Further and Higher Education Act (1992) Available at: www.legislation.gov.uk/ukpga/1992/13/contents

Gov.scot (2018) *Local Government Finance*. Available at: www.gov.scot/Topics/Government/Finance/spfm/locgovfin

Gov.uk (2018) *School Leaving Age*. Available at: www.gov.uk/know-when-you-can-leave-school

Gov.uk (n.d.) *Further Education Courses and Funding*. Available at: www.gov.uk/further-education-courses

Hansard (1944) *1944 Education Bill. 19 January 1944 vol 396 cc207–322*. Available at: https://api.parliament.uk/historic-hansard/commons/1944/jan/19/education-bill

Hansard (2017) *Night Schools and Education*. Available at: https://hansard.parliament.uk/commons/2017-01-13/debates/1DEF8493-7B50-479C-80FD-0F660E6FEC55/NightSchoolsAndAdultEducation

HESA (2017) *Introduction: Higher Education Statistics for the UK 2015/16*. Available at: www.hesa.ac.uk/data-and-analysis/publications/higher-education-2015-16/introduction

Hillier, Y. (2006) *Everything You Need to Know about FE Policy*. London: Continuum.

Hodgson, A and Spours, K. (2003) *Beyond A-Levels: Curriculum 2000 and the Reform of 14–19 Qualifications – Reforming the Curriculum and Qualifications System from Post 14+*. London: Kogan Page.

Hodgson, A. and Spours, K. (2017) *Policy and Policy Learning across the Four Countries of the UK: The Case of Further Education and Skills. An Initial Scoping Paper*, May 2017. London: UCL Institute of Education. Available at: www.ucl.ac.uk/ioe/sites/ioe/files/fe-skills-across-uk-scoping-paper.pdf

Jarvis, P. (2010) *Adult Education and Lifelong Learning: Theory and Practice*. London: Routledge.

Jeffs, T. (1999) *Henry Morris: Village Colleges, Community Education and the Ideal Order*. Ticknall: Educational Heretics Press.

Keep, E. (2013) The spending review: adult education and the retreat of the state. *Adults Learning*, 4: 10–17.

Keep, E. (2018) *Scripting the Future: Exploring Potential Strategic Leadership Responses to the Marketization of English FE and Vocational Provision*. Available at: http://fetl.org.uk/wp-content/uploads/2018/07/FETL_scriptingthefuture-web.pdf

Kelly, T. (1970) *A History of Adult Education in Great Britain*. Liverpool: Liverpool University Press.

Kelly, T. (1992) *A History of Adult Education in Great Britain from the Middle Ages to the Twentieth Century*. Liverpool: Liverpool University Press.

Kitchin, R. (2014) Big data, new epistemologies and paradigm shifts. *Big Data & Society*. doi. org/10.1177/2053951714528481

Lawrie, A. (2014) *The Beginnings of University English*. London: Palgrave Macmillan.

Leitch, S. (2006) *Prosperity for All in the Global Economy: World Class Skills.* London: HMSO.

Mattern, S. (2013) Methodolatry and the art of measure: the new wave of urban data science. *Places,* 5 November 2013.

National Archives (2018) *Technical Colleges and Further Education.* Available at: www.nationalarchives. gov.uk/help-with-your-research/research-guides/technical-colleges-further-education/

nidirect (2018) *Universities and Colleges in Northern Ireland.* Available at: www.nidirect.gov.uk/articles/ universities-and-colleges-northern-ireland

ONS (2016) *Adult Education Survey 2016 Research Report June 2018.* Available at: https://assets. publishing.service.gov.uk/government/uploads/system/uploads/attachment_data/file/714752/ Adult_Education_Survey_2016_research_report.pdf

Open College (2018) *UK Open College.* Available at: www.ukopencollege.co.uk

Panchamia, N. (2012) *Choice and Competition in Further Education.* London: Institute for Government. Available at: www.instituteforgovernment.org.uk/sites/default/files/publications/FE%20Briefing%20 final.pdf

ParentZone (2018) *What Is a Further Education College and What Courses Do They Offer?* Available at: http://parentzone.careerpilot.org.uk/parent/info/what-is-a-further-education-coll/?topic=5974

Peart, S. (2013) *Making Education Work: How Black Men and Boys Navigate the Further Education Sector.* London: Trentham Books/Institute of Education Press.

Pleasance, S. (2016) *Wider Professional Practice in Education and Training.* London: Sage.

Rami, J. and O'Leary, M. (2017) The impact of austerity in further education: cross-cultural perspectives from England and Ireland. In B. Bartran (ed.), *International and Comparative Education: Contemporary Issues and Debates.* London: Routledge.

Rogers, J. (2000) *Adults Learning,* 4th edn. Buckingham: Open University Press.

Rosenblatt, F. (2010) *Chartist Movement: In Its Social and Economic Aspects.* London: Routledge.

Rowe, D. (1967) The London Working Men's Association and the 'people's charter'. *Past & Present,* 36(1): 73–85.

Simmons, R. (2016) Liberal studies and critical pedagogy in further education: 'where their eyes would be opened' (sometimes). *Oxford Review of Education,* 42(6): 1–15.

Smithers, A. and Robinson, P. (2000) *Attracting Teachers: Past Patterns, Present Policies, Future Prospects.* Liverpool: The Carmichael Press.

Smithers, A. and Robinson, P. (2005) *Further Education Reformed.* London: Falmer Press.

Technical Instruction Act 1889. Available at: www.educationengland.org.uk/documents/acts/1889-technical-instruction-act.html

TES (2016) *Wilshaw: '16–19 Education Should Be Done in School'.* Available at: www.tes.com/news/wilshaw-16-19-education-should-be-done-school

Thompson, R. (2009) Social class and participation in further education: evidence from the Youth Cohort Study of England and Wales. *British Journal of Sociology of Education,* 30(1): 29–42.

Tomlinson, J. (1996) *Inclusive FE.* Available at: www.csie.org.uk/resources/tomlinson-96.pdf

Toynbee (2018) *Toynbee Hall.* Available at: www.toynbeehall.org.uk

Trotman, D., Lees, H. and Willoughby, R. (2018) *Education Studies: The Key Concepts.* London: Routledge.

Tuckett, A. (2018) The world of work is changing. We need more adult education, not less. *The Guardian,* 19 April 2018. Available at: www.theguardian.com/higher-education-network/2018/apr/19/the-world-of-work-is-changing-we-need-more-adult-education-not-less

UNESCO (1996) *Learning: The Treasure Within.* Available at: http://unesdoc.unesco.org/images/0010/ 001095/109590eo.pdf

UNESCO (n.d.) *Medina of Fez*. Available at: https://whc.unesco.org/en/list/170

UUK (2016) *Higher Education in England: Provisions, Skills and Graduates*. Available at: www.universitiesuk. ac.uk/policy-and-analysis/reports/Documents/2016/higher-education-in-england-provision-skills-and-graduates.pdf

Wagner, P., Wittrock, B. and Whitley, R. (2007) *Discourses on Society: The Shaping of the Social Science Disciplines*. London: Kluwer Academic Publishers.

Wardle, D. (1977) *English Popular Education 1780–1970*, 2nd edn. Cambridge: Cambridge University Press.

WEA (2017) *Adult Learning within Reach: WEA Impact Report 2016–17*. Available at: www.wea.org.uk/sites/ default/files/WEA_Impact_Report_2017_0502.pdf

Woodbrooke (2018) *Woodbrooke*. Available at: www.woodbrooke.org.uk

2

'KEEP AT A ROLLING BOIL': POLICY CHANGE IN THE PCET SECTOR

Mike Saunders

Key words - governance; funding methodology; curriculum change; UK government; vocational-academic divide

Introduction

This chapter deepens understanding as to how UK government policy for the post-compulsory education sector has changed over the past 30 years, and of the current position. Being in constant flux has led to a sector that is struggling to deliver the change that is required by government.

The chapter starts with a section that outlines the governance arrangements that currently apply, with a brief history of how this position was reached. It moves on to look at the ways in which funding has changed and how this has been driven by government policy rather than the requirements of the sector. It finishes with a review of the way in which curriculum has changed over the past 30 years, and how the change has been focused on those areas that are not in common with the school sector.

Policy can be seen as being framed by those who have no understanding of the sector – frequent change may have led to resources being wasted in constantly inventing the wheel. Yet the sector is one on the most efficient, responsive and lean areas of the public sector, achieving much of what is asked of it on a shoestring budget.

Governance of PCET institutions

Key questions

Is the PCET sector a model that governments aim to introduce across the education sector in the UK?

A brief history of governance

In the 1980s, the PCET sector was largely under the control of local authorities, and in many ways resembled the school sector. Staff pay and conditions were nationally negotiated and laid out in *The Silver Book* (NATFHE, 1992); among its pages, there were defined limits to the length of the working week (30 hours), the number of hours taught each week (a maximum of 21), pay scales and a defined career structure for lecturers within defined reasons for progression. The sector was dominated by further education colleges, sixth form colleges and the adult learning departments within the councils. Pay was above that of schoolteachers and the working conditions were excellent. There was little competition between providers, and a 'public service' ethos applied. The sector enjoyed small class sizes and high contact hours per student, and was not as stringently monitored as it is in 2019. Costs per student were higher than in the school sector, but this has always been the case.

In the early 1990s, the Conservative government brought forward and passed into law the Further and Higher Education Act 1992. This piece of legislation was designed to completely transform the sector and create a new model for the governance of the sector. Adult learning provision within local education authorities was not affected, but all colleges and sixth form colleges were subject to 'incorporation'. This was a process by which they were removed from the control of the local authorities and converted into separate institutions, controlled by their board of governors. National pay and condition bargaining ceased to be automatically applied as the institutions formed their own contracts of employment with their staff, institutions were placed in a situation where they would need to compete with others for students, and the new institutions immediately became subject to a greater degree of monitoring as the oversight of the local authority was no longer in place. The sector was also opened up to private companies who wished to offer training, allowing them to bid for government funding contracts.

The changes brought about by incorporation were substantial, leading to what has been called 'new managerialism' (Randle and Brady, 1997). Management were freed to take the steps needed to modernise and improve the efficiency of the sector. New contracts came into being in most institutions that increased working hours and teaching commitments while reducing pay, student contact hours and holiday allowances. The old career structure disappeared overnight, meaning that in many institutions the only way to progress was to move into management. Institutions began a transformation from operations with a public service model to operating as a business, which has continued to the present day. Government has changed the designation of PCET staff from public sector to private sector on a number of occasions, the most memorable being when Chancellor of the Exchequer George Osborne made a promise in his first budget to reduce the public sector by 2 per cent by the end of 2010. He then transferred PCET to the private sector the following day, thus reducing the public sector by that amount.

Throughout the past 30 years, there have been examples of colleges where a lack of strong governance has led to vanity projects or poor leadership choices, which have meant that institutions have become financially unstable, or so poor in teaching and learning terms, that Ofsted have graded them as 'inadequate'. Straight after incorporation, there were a number of scandals caused by management teams that took their new-found freedom to excess (Halton College in the late 1990s being an example), and action was taken by government to strengthen governance. It has become clear that successful PCET institutions have strong and effective governance, but there have been failures of governance throughout the period, including Northumberland College, learndirect, and the recent spate of principals leaving colleges that are technically 'insolvent'.

Mike Saunders

What is governance?

The Further and Higher Education Act 1992 requires all institutions to have a board of governors who are responsible for strategic oversight and operation, as well as challenging the senior management of the institution (who can be regarded as being the executive directors) on their leadership and management of the institution. Governors are drawn from the local community and are subject to strict legislative requirements, both for the individuals who are part of the board and for the board as a whole. Governors are held responsible for the financial and operational success of the institution in the same way as directors are responsible for a company.

Governance is not a paid role, and this limits the pool of people who are willing to take on the role. There are normally student and staff governors, and there may be parent governors, but most are drawn from the professions or business. They are usually chosen to reflect the make-up of the local area in terms of economic sectors and include influential individuals who have the experience to oversee the running of a large multi-million-pound organisation. There is evidence that they often do not reflect the social diversity of the local area served by the college, though this is often true of teaching staff at the institution as well.

Institutions within the sector are subject to a wide range of external influences and an extensive range of external inspections. Government departments place requirements on PCET institutions, which they use funding rules to enforce. Local communities must be consulted, involved and have their needs met. Parents, students and employers need to be satisfied with the quality and suitability of provision. Institutions need to be open to audit by funding bodies, and of course to inspection by Ofsted. If they offer higher education, they are also subject to the review process for HE institutions, and, if they have international students, to inspection by the UK Border Agency. No other sector of education is subject to this range of external inspection, and this can be seen as making PCET the most regulated sector of UK education.

In 1992, the Major government had the intention of rolling the same model of governance out into the school sector, but they backed down when it became clear that they would face strong opposition from teacher unions, including those representing head teachers. Since then, there has been a gradual move through policies of academisation and the introduction of free schools towards a similar model for schools. The reasons why government might desire this are clear. Compared to the position in 1992, PCET institutions in 2019 teach many more students per member of staff, and are more accountable and more reactive to government policy change. Indeed, it is difficult to identify a more efficient 'public service' in the UK. The current situation, where funding has been reduced more than in other sectors of the education sector, is discussed in the next section.

The 'simplified' funding methodology

Key questions

Does complexity in the funding system reflect a real need or lack of clarity in policymakers' minds?

The Education and Skills Funding Agency (ESFA) has been responsible for funding all post-compulsory education since 2017. In 2016, responsibility for the sector, as well as higher education, was transferred from the Department for Business, Innovation and Skills (BIS) to the Department for Education (DfE). The Education Funding Agency (EFA), which was responsible for school funding, amalgamated with the Skills Funding Agency (SFA), which had been responsible for the post-compulsory sector. Funding methodologies for the two sectors are still largely unaltered for the current academic year compared to those in place before the merger. The coalition government (2010–2015) made changes to the methodology with the aim of 'simplifying' it, yet it remains sufficiently complex that many staff working in the sector have no understanding of the way in which it operates.

Is this a good thing?

Funding for post-compulsory education for 16–18-year-olds

Policy insists that all young people must be in full-time education, an apprenticeship or a job that includes training. For those in full-time education, they must be undertaking a 'study programme'. This is a programme of at least 540 guided learning hours' duration in the calendar year, which must consist of:

- a main programme (e.g. three A levels, a BTEC diploma or any other main qualification listed by the agency);

- a maths GCSE if the student does not already have a GCSE grade C/4 in that subject;

- an English language GCSE if the student does not already have a GCSE grade C/4 in English language or literature;

- work-related learning if the student's intended destination is further or higher education at the end of their programme; and

- experience of the workplace if the student's intended destination is to move into employment.

Additional activity can be recorded as part of the student's hours if the above activities do not reach 540 hours. These can include enrichment activities such as educational visits and careers events.

The funding for each 16- or 17-year-old student who exceeds 540 hours is £4,000, with additional uplift for the deprivation of their home postcode and an uplift for the institution they attend. In most institutions, students exceeding 600 hours will be a cost to the organisation, so this effectively limits the hours per student to an average of 600. Students who do not reach 540 hours are funded at a proportion of the full figure. If students are 18, the funding is £3,400 (equivalent to 450–540 hours for a 16–17-year-old), with the same uplifts.

Funding for adults

For those who are 19 or greater on 1 September and are not continuing a course that they started when they were under 19, the funding rules are much more complex, as funding depends on the age of the student, the course being studied and the individual characteristics of the student. Funding is based on the qualification the student is completing, and each funded course is listed on the Learning Aims Reference Service (LARS) on the hub hosted by the Department for Education. There are a multiplicity of possible rates depending on the student's personal characteristics (e.g. whether they are unemployed or in prison), but the main one is called the matrix rate. If a course is not listed, it is not funded, and the provider can set any fee that they like but will receive no funding from the state. This type of provision is described as 'full cost recovery' (FCR).

Funding for class-based learning courses at level 2 or below

For courses below level 2, funding can be either 'fully funded', where the ESFA pays the provider the full matrix amount for a student who completes and passes the course, or 'co-funded', where the ESFA pays half the funded amount and the provider sets a fee to cover their costs beyond that value. The fee is assumed to be 50 per cent of the fully funded rate by ESFA but in actuality it is set at a value that the provider deems suitable. This creates competition on price for education courses, which is one intention of policy. In 2018/19, the individual student may be fully funded if they have never studied at level 1 or 2 before (they have 'legal entitlement' to such study), are on one of a defined list of benefits, or have an income less than £15,736.50 per annum.

Regardless of the level of funding, the provider receives 80 per cent of the monies owed over the time period of the course. They receive a double payment in the first month to reflect the cost of initial advice and guidance, and then the remainder of the 80 per cent divided equally over the remainder of the course, providing the student continues to attend. The final 20 per cent is only paid if the student achieves the learning aim for which they were studying. For example, if a course was fully funded at £200 and the provider taught it over six months, they would receive £45.72 in month 1 and £22.86 in months 2–5, then £22.84 in month 6, for a total of £160. The final £40 would be paid if the student passes the assessment for the course.

Funding for class-based learning courses at level 3 or above

The UK government has been developing a policy that the student pays for their education once they reach the age of 19 or start a higher education course. Apart from those aged 19–23 on 1 September each year but do not possess a level 3 qualification, whose courses are fully funded under legal entitlement, as for level 2 courses, all other students need to pay for their education.

To support this payment, Student Finance England (the Student Loan Company) provides loans. There are different types of loans for FE and HE students, but the repayment method for any loan that a student takes out is identical. Advanced Learner Loans (ALLs) are available for any course that is a certificate or greater in size and is at level 3 or greater. Qualifications smaller than a certificate at these levels are not funded and must be completed on an FCR basis. An ALL pays the fees for the course only, and an individual can have a total of up to four, so long as each is for a different type of qualification (e.g. a diploma, a certificate). For A levels, up to four loans are available, providing the loans are taken contemporaneously, as this counts as a single loan. ALLs are relatively easy to apply for, requiring only proof of nationality/residency, a National Insurance number and the details of the course being studied. ALLs are paid directly to the provider and repaid in the same way as higher education loans. For access to HE students, the loan is not repayable if they complete a degree programme after completing their Access diploma. Higher education (HE) loans provide payment of the fees but also a loan for maintenance. Loans for fees are available to any eligible person, but those for maintenance are means-tested based on household income.

Repayment of ALLs and HE loans is through the tax system. Nine per cent of income over £25,000 is taken directly from the individual's income to repay their debt, which is subject to interest of up to 6 per cent. After 30 years, any remaining loan is written off. The government expects only 40 per cent of the loans made to be repaid, but still favours this policy over the direct payment of fees to institutions and maintenance grants to individuals.

The move to loans funding for post-compulsory education is driven by two factors. The need to reduce the burden of FE and HE on the public purse allowed a political dogma that 'adults should pay for their education' to become the norm. The fall in the number of adult students caused by this change has had no effect in Whitehall, apart from to free up monies that can be diverted to schools as necessary. The need of the economy for 'lifelong learning' has been ignored, and adult education as it was in the 1990s has largely ceased to exist.

Funding for apprenticeships

Finally, the 'simplified' funding system has another strand. Apprenticeships are funded in a completely different way, and there are two systems. The first is for small and medium-sized enterprises (SMEs), and the second is for firms with a total payroll of £3 million or more who pay the Apprenticeship Levy.

SMEs are companies with less than 250 employees. If an SME employs an apprentice, the government provides 90 per cent of the funding for the teaching of the qualifications required by the relevant standard, with an expectation that the training provider will recover the remaining 10 per cent from the employer. Providers are not required to collect the 10 per cent, but will need to provide all the training, and ensure successful completion of all aspects, with whatever monies they receive.

Larger employers have 3 per cent of their payroll placed into their Apprenticeship Levy account. This account can only be used to pay for the training of apprentices that they employ, and if it is not used the balance is retained by the Treasury. This policy is designed to force employers to take on apprentices and thus meet the ambitious targets set by HM Government. It has led to some larger companies setting up in-house apprenticeship training providers, some of which have been found by Ofsted to be 'inadequate', and a rise in the number of existing employees being 'rebadged' as apprentices rather than new entrants to the companies. The largest rise in apprenticeship starts has been in management as companies have used their levy to pay for training for new and existing managers that would otherwise have been paid for from their training budgets.

Figure 2.1 is an attempt to provide an overview of the methodology, but does not include the criteria that decide into which category an individual student falls.

The funding crisis in the PCET sector

Since 2010, funding provided by HM Government for the education sector has been handled differently depending upon the age and stage of learning. Funding for schools has been protected in cash terms and has only recently begun to fall in terms of 'per pupil' values. Funding for higher education has risen as the number of students has risen, and income per student has risen from £7,000 per annum to £9,250 per annum.

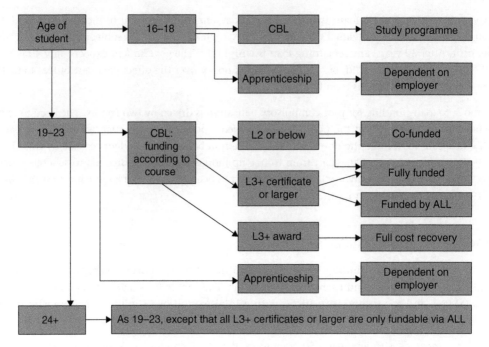

Figure 2.1 A simplified diagram of the ESFA funding methodology for PCET

Birkinshaw (2018) provided figures for the PCET sector over the period since 2010 to the Education Select Committee. She stated that:

- total funding for 16–18 education has fallen by 15 per cent, while total funding for adults has fallen by 45 per cent in the same period;

- this has led to a fall in funding for PCET of 30 per cent in 10 years and 2.5 million less adults studying in colleges than before the banking crash in 2008; and

- 16–17-year-olds receive 24 per cent less funding than those in secondary schools, with a further reduction of 17.5 per cent when they reach their 18th birthday.

Birkinshaw also made the points that schools have received additional monies to mitigate changes in National Insurance and to provide for higher pay for staff, while PCET has not. The need to teach English and maths to those who have not been successful in school costs a medium-sized college £700,000 per year, and there is no additional funding to cover this provision.

These figures are reflected in lower salaries for staff in PCET in comparison with schools, or even similar institutions in Scotland. They are also reflected in the fact that even the best managed colleges are now struggling financially, with significant numbers struggling to remain solvent. Amanda Spielman, Chief Inspector of Ofsted, has been quoted as stating in a letter to the House of Commons Public Accounts Committee 'that FE is being underfunded in comparison to other sectors, and that that underfunding is having a direct negative effect on FE provision' (Starkey, 2018). As HM Treasury seem able to find monies for every other sector of the education system but continue to fund PCET at the same level as was provided in the 1990s, it is clear that the sector is not valued by

HM Government, despite being the source of education for over 70 per cent of the UK population of 16–18-year-olds. *changing?*

Key theory

Funding terms and their meanings

- *Funded*: Any student who receives funding from the ESFA for their learning, whether directly or via a loan, is considered as 'funded'. Their achievement is recorded in official data. Any student who pays for a course themselves is not funded and excluded from the data.

- *Fully funded*: The ESFA provides 100 per cent of the funding due for the course the student is completing. Full funding may be granted on grounds of income or legal entitlement.

- *Co-funded*: The ESFA provides 50 per cent of the funding due and assumes that the provider will set a fee for the student, which will be the other 50 per cent of the funding amount.

- *CBL*: Class-based learning (i.e. learning taught in a classroom in a college).

- *WBL*: Work-based learning (i.e. taught in the workplace, even if in a training room).

- *Legal entitlement*: Students may be eligible for full funding on the basis of their previous qualifications. If they do not already have a full level 2 qualification, they can study at level 1 or 2 until they do so. If they are 19–23, those without a previous level 3 qualification have the same entitlement.

Curriculum change: the blind leading the seeing?

Key questions

Why are A levels and BTECs the only qualifications that government have allowed to continue from the 1980s to the present day?

Public policy around curriculum in the PCET sector has created and entrenched a divide between academic qualifications such as A levels and vocational qualifications such as National Vocational Qualifications (NVQs) and BTEC diplomas. This divide is entirely due to government policy as there have been a number of reports (Dearing, 1997; Wolf, 2012) that have suggested that it should be removed. A-level qualifications are taught in school sixth forms (including independent schools), sixth form colleges and general further education (GFE) colleges, so are well known to policymakers as they, and their children, have usually studied them. Vocational qualifications are taken by the majority of 16–18-year-olds but are taught mainly in GFE colleges, so are much less familiar to policymakers.

This has resulted in the format of A levels remaining much more stable over the past 30 years than the format of vocational qualifications. A levels, as a brand, have continued to exist throughout that period, though there has been change from linear to modular structures, the introduction of course-work elements, and the reversal of those changes over that period. BTEC qualifications have also survived as a brand. These are also seen as being academic courses, though more vocationally defined, and, though there has been change in the types of assessment, the structure of a 2018 course is recognisable as being a descendent of the 1980s version.

It is in vocational qualifications that there has been the greatest change. In the 1980s, vocational qualifications contained significant theoretical components (e.g. level 2 hairdressing required students to pass examinations in science and complete an art project), and in some cases were seen as progression from A-level studies (e.g. level 2 beauty therapy students were expected to have two A levels to start the course). These theoretical elements were removed in the early 1990s with the development of the National Vocational Qualification (NVQ), which focused almost entirely on the skill set needed to complete the tasks and reduced the range and depth of theoretical background substantially. NVQs continue to the present day, but are now generally part of apprenticeship standards, where a separate theory qualification may be required.

It is when looking at those subject areas where courses need to develop a blend of theoretical knowledge and practical skills that the greatest change can be observed. When NVQs were introduced, it was identified that there were subjects such as science where an NVQ was not an appropriate route, and policymakers decided to introduce an NVQ with a greater theoretical component. These were called 'General National Vocational Qualifications' (GNVQs). These courses were focused on a particular vocational area and consisted of a range of units covering theoretical (organic chemistry) and practical (organic chemistry practical techniques) elements of the subject. All students completing a GNVQ also have to complete assessment of six core skills alongside their subject-specific units. These qualifications were seen as being the vocational education equivalents of A levels, but within five years they were being discontinued. Their complexity meant that many institutions reverted to teaching the BTEC equivalent of the GNVQ, and the 'equivalence' with A levels was not reflected in the offers made by universities or the progression of students into relevant employment.

In 2008, the Advanced Diploma was introduced. This was another attempt to create a vocational course that would be seen as the equivalent of A levels, and, apart from the core skills element, was remarkably similar to GNVQs. Yet again, these qualifications were discontinued, though this time it was a policy decision by the coalition government that led to their demise. They had not been in operation long enough to become well known to the general public and had been taken by a small number of students, so their level of success is difficult to identify. The fact that government felt they could remove them from the curriculum but only reformed A levels speaks volumes as to the opinion of Advanced Diplomas in Whitehall.

Currently, all qualifications are defined as being 'academic' (A levels), 'applied general' (BTEC and some similar qualifications) or 'technical' (apprenticeships and T levels) in a series of lists produced by the Department for Education. BTEC qualifications are also recognisable as descendants of the qualifications offered in the 1980s, and their survival suggests that they hold a special place in the hearts of ministers. They are vocationally aligned but largely academic qualifications. For example, the sport and exercise science curriculum includes units in anatomy, physiology, sports psychology and biomechanics (the four theoretical pillars of the subject) and units in which these theoretical disciplines are applied to working with athletes (e.g. fitness testing). The fact that they exist in a separate category of qualification is either as a result of lobbying by the sector, or Pearson (the multinational company who own the brand), or Department of Education inertia. The fact that government policy can appear to be that all students will either study A levels or T levels means that the continued existence of applied general qualifications is unclear at this time.

Technical (T) levels are the latest attempt to create a vocational qualification that has parity of esteem with A levels. They are in the process of being introduced, and the first students will study T levels in Early Years, construction and digital technologies in 2019.

T levels consist of a study programme, with the addition of 300 hours per year of work experience with a relevant employer. There are concerns in the sector about this requirement, and it remains to be seen if employers will provide sufficient placements for students who wish to study T levels. There are also concerns about the rapidity with which these new qualifications are being introduced. In addition, there will be a single awarding organisation for each T level, which will reduce the number of available qualifications by thousands, which will reduce choice for students and may lead to some not being able to find a course that suits them. There are also significant concerns about the concurrent changes to level 2 provision as there will be a single qualification designed to prepare students to take T levels, and should they not complete that, they may be unable to progress.

An element of the whole process that is often poorly managed by government is consultation with the sector, employers and universities on changes they intend to make. In one example, the sector was given one week to respond to a document on the development of T levels at a time when most institutions were closed for at least two days due to bank holidays. In another, 'extensive' consultation with employers prior to publication of new specifications meant that almost all employer groups complained that the new specifications still did not provide them with workers with the skills they needed. It is the role of government to set policy and ensure that all stakeholder needs are met – there are many that would argue the past 30 years has been an excellent example of the failure of HM Government to achieve that within the PCET sector.

Effect of policy on the sector

Since 2010, the leaving age from compulsory education has effectively been raised to 18. Up to the age of 18, everyone is required to be in full-time education: this might involve enrolling on a college course, undertaking an apprenticeship, or being employed in the workplace with the provision of a significant level of on-the-job training. The effect of this change, along with the creation of study programmes, is still being operationalised within the sector at additional cost, for which funding has not been provided. New A-level and BTEC specifications have been introduced, apprenticeships have moved from frameworks to standards, and there has been a myriad of policy changes made by the government.

Edward et al. (2007) reported on the effects of change in the sector on teaching staff. They report that they encountered considerable flux in the teaching staff working on the courses they were following (e.g. only one course had the same tutor for the whole of the 43-month study). They found that teaching staff felt that policy change was done above them and was something they had no control over, and that they were unable to identify which policy changes were made at a national level and which were institutional. It identified that teaching staff, and their direct managers, spent time and energy shielding learners from the effects of this constant change, and also continued to innovate in the classroom, but at the cost of working well beyond their contractual obligations. In my experience, this is still true, but if anything, the pressure on staff is greater now than in 2007.

The effect of poor governance, limited funding and constant curriculum change, as outlined above, has been to reduce the stability of providers in the sector. There are examples of institutions that are coping with the situation, and overall the sector continues to provide education and training for the majority of over-16-year-olds. The critical factor in the case of those institutions that have been successful is the quality of leadership and management in those institutions. Excellent management, with strong governance, is critical to the future success of the sector, though continuous policy change means that the sector will remain fundamentally unstable.

Those that lose out most from the instability created by rolling policy change are those in learning. Whether they get caught up in the trialling of new curricula, lose out when institutions fail financially or are affected by the low morale of their teachers, it is clear that they are being failed by the system. Similar failure in schools would cause considerable political fallout, but the way in which policymakers have failed the PCET sector over the past 30 years is barely worth a mention. When a government is willing to fund pay rises and pension payment increases for schoolteachers but refuses to even acknowledge that the same is required in PCET, it is clear that policymakers do not regard PCET as being worthy of their attention. What looked like an oversight ten years ago is increasingly looking like a deliberate policy to destroy the sector in the minds of many of those who work in the sector of education charged with upskilling the workforce and giving young people the opportunity to enter the workplace with the knowledge, skills and values that will make them good citizens.

Chapter summary

- The Further and Higher Education Act 1992 created incorporated institutions that are outside the control of LEAs and can be defined as either private or public sector at the whim of government.

- Governance of these institutions has never been strong across the board, and while the major scandals of the 1990s have ceased, there are continued examples of failures of governance.

- PCET institutions offer a model for schools, which governments seem keen to implement.

- Funding is complicated, different for different types of student, and substantially less than is offered to schools and universities. This is leading to a crisis in the financial viability of PCET institutions that governments are unable, or unwilling, to resolve.

- Policy on curriculum embeds the notion of academic and vocational education as being different, and that academic education has higher value. Stability in A-level and BTEC provision can be contrasted against the continuous flux in vocational/technical education.

- The sector is highly efficient, but failures of governance, financial instability, and the introduction of inadequate provision affect some of those who are, at the time of writing, undertaking education and training. This failure to provide good education for all is a direct result of policymakers' disinterest in the sector.

Further recommended reading

FE Week: This online magazine, edited by Nick Linford, reports on all aspects of policy change in the sector and investigates issues that arise. It is a good source of information on the ways in which governance, funding and curriculum change are affecting the sector at the point of publication and is a publication all PCET professionals should follow.

References

Birkinshaw, A. (2018) Principal's news. *YC Staff News*, October 2018.

Dearing, R. (1997) *Higher Education in the Learning Society*. London: HMSO.

Edward, S., Coffield, F., Steer, R. and Gregson, M. (2007) Endless change in the learning and skills sector: the impact on teaching staff. *Journal of Vocational Education and Training*, 57(2): 155–173.

Further and Higher Education Act 1992. Available at: www.legislation.gov.uk/ukpga/1992/13/contents

NATFHE (1992) *The Silver Book*. Available at: www.lsbucu.org.uk/ewExternalFiles/Silver%20Book.doc

Randle, K. and Brady, N. (1997) Further education and the new managerialism. *Journal of Further and Higher Education*, 21(2): 229–239.

Starkey, T. (2018) *Even Ofsted Gets the FE Funding Crisis*. Available at: www.tes.com/news/even-ofsted-gets-fe-funding-crisis

Wolf, A. (2011) *Review of Vocational Education*. London: HMSO.

3

QUALITY ASSURANCE IN POST-COMPULSORY EDUCATION AND TRAINING

Lucy Mitchell

Key words – quality assurance; quality improvement; continuous improvement; total quality management; observations of teaching and learning; managerialism

Introduction

This chapter examines quality assurance in the post-compulsory education and training (PCET) sector. It will begin by exploring definitions of quality, then will move on to a brief summary of the key pieces of legislation that have influenced quality assurance in the sector over the last 20 years. There will be an examination of internal quality assurance processes, including observations of teaching, learning and assessment, and it will then look at external quality assurance. It will also include an evaluation of the impact of the teacher's involvement in quality processes.

Defining quality processes

Key questions

How do we define quality in the context of further education?

Is there a difference between quality assurance, quality improvement and quality enhancement?

How do we measure quality?

When considering the term 'quality', some keywords come to mind: excellence, standards, calibre. In order to measure the quality of education, we need to consider all aspects of the learning journey and consider how we can identify and define good-quality education. There are a number of different quality processes that can be used for this. Quality control is an audit process concerned with checking if something is missing. This has its benefits, particularly from a funding perspective, and can be used to check compliance with regulations and guidance. This is a more objective stance as it is about merely checking that something, usually documentation, is either there or not there and has been sufficiently completed. Quality assurance moves beyond this to look at the process itself and identifies how standards are being met to ensure a 'quality' result at the end. In PCET, this covers all aspects of the learner's journey and examines how each part can be improved to get the best result for the learner. This is about having good systems in place to create a good learning experience. An extension beyond this is total quality management (TQM). This is about an organisation's culture being one of continuous improvement in order to enhance the learning experience for all.

It is vital to have all of these quality processes in place. Without quality control systems in place to ensure the fundamental parts are there, an organisation couldn't move beyond this. However, quality is not just about checking what is there, but about improving systems, processes and attitudes in order to get the best results.

The concept of quality can be seen as something that is subjective. Without some underpinning standards or guidance, quality can end up being based on individual viewpoints. We will go on to examine both internal and external quality activities and identify how these are benchmarked.

In post-compulsory education and training, the quality processes within organisations should cover all aspects of the learner journey, from recruitment of the learner onto the programme to their progression onto their next step. Sallis (2002) identified 'four quality imperatives' that should underpin educational organisations' approach to quality:

- *The moral imperative*: The right for learners to have high-quality education.

- *The professional imperative*: The teachers' obligation to provide the best standards of education in line with their professional values.

- *The competitive imperative*: Organisations need to improve the quality of provision in order to compete with other providers.

- *The accountability imperative*: Providers must show they are accountable and meeting the requirements of their learners and of their funding bodies.

(pp3–4)

It is vital that these imperatives underpin all quality assurance activities conducted by providers when identifying improvements that need to be made.

The development of quality assurance in PCET: the political context

Key questions

What have been the main political influences on the PCET sector in relation to quality?

(Continued)

(Continued)

Are teachers in PCET measured in the same way as teachers in schools?

Is there parity between schools and further education providers in the way they are measured?

More accurately, the sector has worked under changing conceptions of what constitutes 'quality' since the early 1990s – especially the Further and Higher Education Act 1992. Until New Labour came into power in 1997, post-compulsory education and training was thought of as the 'Cinderella sector' (a term used by the Secretary of State for Education, Kenneth Baker, in 1989) – forgotten about and neglected. The White Paper *Learning to Succeed* outlined the new government's agenda for improving quality in the sector (Department for Education and Employment, 2000). The government established the Learning and Skills Council (LSC) in 2001 to drive these improvements forward and to set quality standards. Until this point, there were three different inspection bodies operating in the sector, and the paper identified the need to align the arrangements with the school inspection system:

> *These arrangements do not help deliver the consistent and co-ordinated approaches or the proper evidence base necessary to drive forward our agenda for raising standards. Nor do they establish the clear account-ability necessary for ensuring quality. The case for integration and harmonisation is compelling.*

> (Department for Education, 1999, p21)

This was a key turning point in the sector, and since then there have been a series of strategies and governmental acts focusing on improving the quality of the sector, supported by agencies and organisations. This was in line with the move towards new managerialism that was taking place across the public sector at the same time. Deem (1998) identified the key characteristics of new managerialism as:

> *the fostering of competition between employees, the marketisation of public sector services and the monitoring of efficiency and effectiveness through measurement of outcomes and individual staff performance. Other features include attempting to change the regimes and cultures of organisations and to alter the values of public sector employees to more closely resemble those found in the private 'for profit' sector.*

> (p50)

In 1999, the Moser Report, *Improving Literacy and Numeracy: A Fresh Start*, identified significant issues with the English and maths skills of adults in England and noted that the quality of teaching and learning was inconsistent (Moser, 1999). This led to a move to professionalise the sector through the development of specific teaching qualifications and the introduction of regulatory requirements to ensure that teaching staff held such qualifications – Further Education Teachers' Qualifications (England) Regulations 2001 and 2007. In 2006, the Leitch Review recommended that 'the UK commit to becoming a world leader in skills by 2020' (Leitch, 2006, p3) and set out clear targets relating to the development of adult literacy and numeracy skills (following on from the Moser Report) and level 3 and 4 qualifications. It also identified that there should be an increased investment in funding from individuals, employers and the government. This is in line with the neoliberal view that the focus of support from government should be to enable people to become 'employable' by developing 'skills' for work (Simmons, 2010).

Further action to improve standards in the sector was taken through the introduction of the Framework for Excellence in 2007, the main aim of which was 'to provide a single, unified framework for assessing and reporting achievement in all key areas of performance' (Learning and Skills Council, 2007, p3). This was to be used by Ofsted alongside the provider's self-assessment as a tool for measuring performance (see Figure 3.1).

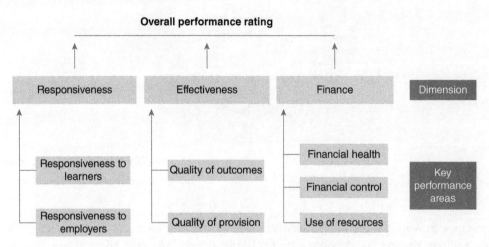

Figure 3.1   Derivation of Framework for Excellence overall performance rating

This can be seen as a move to introduce a business model of quality improvement into the sector, in the form of a 'balanced scorecard'.

The LSC closed in 2010 to be replaced by the Education Funding Agency (EFA) and the Skills Funding Agency (SFA) to preside over funding responsibilities for the sector. Further changes have taken place since then, and funding for the sector is now held by the Education and Skills Funding Agency (ESFA).

In 2008, the Institute for Learning (IfL) introduced Qualified Teacher Learning and Skills (QTLS) professional status, which was a move towards parity with secondary and primary education. QTLS is equivalent to qualified teacher status (QTS), meaning that staff with QTLS can work in schools as a teacher. Membership of the Society for Education and Training (SET) is also needed for employment in schools – remembering that academies and free schools can employ whoever they like. This was a significant change as up until this point, post-16 teaching qualifications had never been accepted by schools.

In 2012, the Lingfield Report, *Professionalism in Further Education*, pronounced that it was no longer a requirement for teachers in the further education sector to be qualified; it was now up to employers to decide which qualifications they would accept (Department for Business, Innovation and Skills, 2012). In addition, another set of new qualifications were introduced into the sector: the award, certificate and diploma in education and training. In 2013, the Education and Training Foundation (ETF) was established to replace the IfL. The following year, the ETF developed a set of professional standards for teachers, covering professional values and attributes, professional skills, and professional knowledge and understanding. This represented another move towards parity with other sectors within education (see Figure 3.2).

Figure 3.2   The professional standards
Source: Education and Training Foundation (2014)

In just over 20 years, the post-compulsory education and training sector has gone through numerous and significant changes and development. It is clear that steps have been taken to raise standards in the sector and to improve the quality of provision, and more stringent regulations are in place, comparative to schools.

Internal quality assurance/self-assessment

Key questions

What is the value to the organisation, to tutors and lecturers and to the learner?

Are internal quality assurance activities conducted for Ofsted, or for staff and learners?

PCET providers are required to self-assess their performance and develop quality improvement plans. Ofsted measures the effectiveness of this activity during their inspections, and the outcome contributes to the grading that providers receive in the leadership and management domain. The current inspection handbook (at the time of writing) states that:

The lead inspector's pre-inspection analysis of evidence may include, but will not be restricted to:

- *the provider's current self-assessment report or equivalent evaluation report*

- *the provider's development/quality improvement plan, including any plans for subcontractors.*

(Office for Standards in Education, Children's Services and Skills, 2018a, p16)

There are clear links to external quality assurance, but what about the value to the organisation, to tutors and lecturers, and to the learner? Are internal quality assurance activities conducted for Ofsted, or for staff and learners?

There are various different quality assurance mechanisms and sources of information that organisations use to inform the self-assessment. There is no single prescribed method for undertaking self-assessment and there are no requirements to present this in a particular format. The senior management team (SMT) at an organisation will decide on the process and format for their self-assessment activities. These will be conducted in a variety of different ways according to the setting and the decisions of the SMT.

In some organisations, a top-down approach is taken. The senior management team will identify overall strengths and areas for development and these will be passed down to department managers.

Other organisations start at the team level. Departments meet and evaluate their own provision through various activities (e.g. SWOT analysis) and identify their own strengths and areas for development. This is fed upwards to the SMT, who then identify organisation-wide trends.

A wide range of data sources should be used to inform self-assessment activities. These can include data/outcomes, observations of teaching and learning, learner surveys and feedback, employer feedback, staff surveys, tutors' evaluations, and reflections. Many organisations now are using a 'balanced scorecard' approach, outlined earlier in the chapter, which has developed from the traditional quality background of manufacturing and business. A wide range of sources are then used to evaluate provision and inform judgements. Some organisations carry out 'mocksted' inspections to validate the judgements within the self-assessment reports. This is usually carried out by staff within the organisation using Ofsted guidance as a framework.

Example

The quality team and senior management decide on key indicators to include on the scorecard. Data and quality teams compile the scorecard, and this is provided to department managers. The managers then work with their teams to produce a self-assessment report based on these data, including a grade for the department. Managers are then required to attend a panel meeting, where they are questioned about their data and self-assessment report to validate their judgements and grades. At the team level, improvement plans are developed to identify any areas for improvement and actions are monitored throughout the year.

It is vital that providers ensure the validity of their data, as this will come under scrutiny during an actual inspection. They need to ensure that their judgements are robust and that they can provide evidence to support them.

It is also important to engage teachers in the process. Not doing so can create an environment where teachers perceive quality assurance as something that is done *to* them, and not something that they are part of. Quality assurance and improvement activities can include observations, learning walks, audits, learner work checks, sampling and questionnaires, among other things, which, in the absence of staff buy-in, can result in teachers feeling as though they are being monitored.

All staff must take ownership of the quality improvement process to ensure it is successful. Staff will be unlikely to embrace unwanted changes or address actions that they see as unnecessary (Lumby, 2001, p79). Quality is everyone's responsibility, and everyone must play a part in the internal quality processes in order for it to be effective and accurate.

A prominent debate in this context is between what Randle and Brady term the 'professional' and 'managerialist' paradigms. The 'professionals' view education in terms of its worth to the participants, whereas 'managerialists' are inclined to recognise value in terms of income generated and impact on success rates (Randle and Brady, 1997, pp128–130). The teacher can feel that teaching and learning at the heart of the process are getting lost in a sea of data and monitoring.

Internal quality assurance: beyond the use of data

Overall provider success is measured in outcomes and achievements, but there are more valuable success stories evident in the impact that education has on the individual's life, which are not always measurable through outcomes. Teachers have the learners at the heart of the process and want to make improvements for themselves and for the learners.

Effective self-assessment needs to use both quantitative and qualitative information; numerical data do not tell the whole story. Measures are needed for comparisons and judgements, but this needs to be enhanced and expanded through the use of meaningful examples and evidence. As discussed, there is no prescriptive way to complete self-assessment, so it is up to providers to decide how they do this. Ofsted will look at certain sets of data and will use the common inspection framework and inspection handbooks as the basis for their inspection, but they do not enforce a set way of carrying this out. Providers will also have to use these documents to make their own judgements, but they can do this in their own way.

Where self-assessment is most ineffective is when it becomes a paper exercise with no involvement of learner-facing staff. In a sector where time is scarce and there is immense pressure on managers and staff, self-assessment activities can slide down the list of priorities. There may not be time to complete this effectively, and managers end up completing this themselves, which then gives the team no involvement or ownership of the process. Teachers need to be involved in this as those with the closest involvement with what is routinely happening in the classroom.

Quality assurance processes should also involve the learners. This could be through internal or external surveys (such as the FE Choices Learner Satisfaction Survey), learner forums or councils, or informal learner feedback. One of the main issues with learner surveys is the typically poor response rates. The response rate for the 2017/18 FE Choices Survey was 19 per cent (341,627 respondents out of 1,821,629 eligible learners) (Department for Education, 2018).

There is also a significant focus on employer involvement (particularly for apprenticeship providers), from ensuring the curriculum meets employer needs to validating self-assessment judgements. The ESFA has recently implemented a process to gather employer feedback about apprenticeship provision by training providers in the form of a 'smiley face' review, measured from 'very poor' to 'excellent' (FE Week, 2018). This feedback needs to be included in self-assessment activities.

The question is also how reflective and self-critical can providers be? They will use the data and sources of information, but will their interpretation be accurate? Ofsted will measure this during inspections; ultimately, they will judge how effective the self-assessment process is.

Following self-assessment activities where strengths and areas for improvement are identified, improvement planning should take place. Actions should be set with clear measurable targets and these should be reviewed on a regular basis. In order for improvements to be truly effective, double-loop learning needs to take place. Providers should examine the reasons behind their areas of weakness, question this, and then set targets to address them (Argyris, 1977). This will inform the improvement plan, which should then be monitored and reviewed on a regular basis. The provider must then evaluate the impact that the changes have had on the quality of provision and the learner's experience.

Providers have to make this a process of continuous learning and improvement. Quality assurance activities should be ongoing and regularly reviewed and monitored. Providers must continuously monitor and validate their internal quality assurance processes and monitor improvements or declines in any areas.

Where quality improvement activities are most effective is when all staff buy into the process, and this is managed well at the team level. It should not be seen as an additional burden or administrative duty, but a vital part of improving the learner experience.

Teaching observations

Key questions

Should lesson observations be graded?

What is the value of grading lesson observations?

How can observations be used as a tool for continuing professional development?

During external inspections, Ofsted will conduct observations of teaching and learning (OTLA) and learning walks. PCET providers are required to monitor the quality of the teaching and learning in their organisations by conducting their own observations, and Ofsted then validate their judgements during inspection. In recent years, this has become a contentious issue in the education sector, as such initiatives can be perceived by teachers as being a mechanism to check up on, monitor and performance-manage staff.

The main purpose of the observation process is to gather a picture of the teaching and learning that is taking place in an organisation. Providers are responsible for developing their own processes for evaluating the quality of teaching, but Ofsted will monitor this during inspection. Observations are an integral part of teacher development. At the very beginning of a teaching training programme, trainee teachers are observed, given feedback and set actions for development in order to improve their own practice. Observations help to identify good and bad practice but also, more importantly, are about raising standards of teaching within organisations (Ewens, 2001, p1).

There are many benefits of observations; they help organisations measure the quality of teaching and they can identify areas of good practice to be shared across the organisation, as well as high-lighting areas for targeted development. Although observations can help teachers to develop their own practice, there are suggestions that some teachers can also be intimidated by them (Armitage et al., 2016, p52). Many teachers cite observations as a cause of stress within their role; they can be used by managers as a performance management tool and a 'stick to beat teachers with' (O'Leary, 2013, p6).

Observations: graded or ungraded?

The current debate about observations is whether they should be graded. Ofsted has now moved away from grading individual lessons and many providers are also doing the same. Matt O'Leary's extensive research into teaching observations identifies that graded teaching sessions have not been used as a tool for improving the quality of teaching, but for identifying issues with performance (O'Leary, 2013, p18). The question, then, is how do we make an overall judgement about the quality of teaching if we don't grade the sessions? Although Ofsted doesn't grade teaching observations, they do grade overall teaching and learning standards. Providers will have to use qualitative data to analyse trends and iden-tify overall strengths and areas for development.

O'Leary (2006) describes Ofsted's observation model as a 'deficit', one that identifies the 'missing' pieces and faults in a lesson (p197), and therefore makes the teacher passive in this process. Teachers are given feedback and told what was good and what needs to be improved. There is also the issue of subjectivity given the unilateral nature of an observation, even if a framework is used. Observations need to move beyond this model. They should be focused on the development of the teacher and their continuous improvement. O'Leary (2013) states:

> Observation is at its most effective as a form of intervention when it prioritises the growth of tutors' pro-fessional learning and skills and empowers them to become active agents in the construction of their own professional identity, learning and development.

> (p9)

However, it is important for providers to identify poor practice too, especially where this is to the det-riment of the quality of education provision. Observations are a vital part of this process, and poor practice needs to be identified and addressed as a priority.

For providers using graded teaching observations, the aim is that all teaching staff are good or out-standing. The driver for this is that organisations want to achieve at least a 'good' grade on their Ofsted inspections. This would support an Ofsted grade 2 for teaching, learning and assessment. The exter-nal assessment by Ofsted informs the internal quality assurance practices. Many staff are happy with achieving a grade 2 as it means they won't be observed again that year. Staff do not want to be graded as outstanding, as they think they will be given additional responsibilities (peer observations, sharing good practice, etc.) that will add to their workload. Providers should be establishing a culture of learn-ing in their organisation where teachers continually want to develop and improve.

A significant issue with the observation process is the follow-up of actions and the closing of the loop. Every session will have some actions or areas for development (even an outstanding session is not a perfect session) that will be detailed on the action plan, but these are not always followed up and signed off. Progress towards these actions will usually be monitored at the next observation, but this might not be for another year. Providers need to ensure that staff take some ownership of their own development and managers follow this up. This links the process back to performance management again as these actions could feed into the appraisal process.

Introducing ungraded observations will result in all staff having actions relating to their areas of improvement. They will need to take ownership of these and show progress towards meeting them. Everyone will have areas for improvement, and the removal of grades means that staff may not develop that complacency that comes with achieving a grade 2. They become active in the process as they have to evidence their development (O'Leary, 2006, p18).

Most organisations have a core team of staff who carry out observations, but they may be observing teaching in a different subject to their own specialism, which can lead to challenges from those being observed. O'Leary's (2013) research identified two key issues that teachers had with people who were conducting their observations: 'the extent to which they were appropriately trained to carry out their role and ... whether they had experience and/or knowledge of the subject areas they were responsible for observing' (p77). In particular, this was identified as an issue in vocational subjects where sessions are mainly practical. To address this, it is vital that observers are formulating judgements about the quality of the learning taking place in line with set guidance (Ofsted and/or internal criteria) and that ongoing training and development takes place, as well as regular moderation activities. Observers can also benefit from the observation processes as they witness a range of different sessions and teaching styles and can identify ideas to inform their own practice.

Providers will carry out standardisation and moderation of their observations. Standardisation exercises are often carried out on observation paperwork, but this approach can be somewhat flawed given the focus on the standardisation of the report rather than the judgement itself. Another method is to carry out joint observations. By doing this, judgements can be moderated as there are two people in the session. This is a method that Ofsted will use in inspections to validate provider judgements. However, this could create additional pressure for staff, with two people observing them.

Another issue with observations is that they are only a snapshot of that teacher's performance and it can be questioned if this is a valid judgement. Some teachers also have an 'observation lesson' that they have already prepared and is something that they deliver year after year for their annual observation. Alternatives to formal OTLA are peer observations, good practice groups and mentoring, which are more informal than observations but still promote continuous improvement.

Teaching observations should be about the quality of the teaching and learning that is taking place. The learner should be at the heart of this process and it is important that observers talk to the learners who are in the session. Observations should be concerned with ensuring learners have the best possible experience. Teachers need to take ownership of their own professional development and improve their own practice. The ETF professional standards state that teachers and trainers should reflect on and evaluate their professional practice in relation to the impact that they have on learners (Education and Training Foundation, 2014). It is clear that teachers need to reflect and improve on their own practice, and observations can be a useful tool to do this, but the way they are conducted can impact on their effectiveness.

External quality assurance

Key questions

Are Ofsted measuring the right things?

Is there too much focus on outcomes?

How else can we measure the quality of teaching, learning and assessment in PCET?

The White Paper *Learning to Succeed* identified a need to improve standards in post-16 education and proposed that further education should be inspected in the same way as schools (Department for Education and Employment, 2000). In 2007, the Adult Learning Inspectorate (ALI) was amalgamated into Ofsted, which has resulted in a more standardised approach across all education providers in England.

Ofsted's purpose is to measure and regulate the quality of education, and will grade providers on:

- effectiveness of leadership and management;

- quality of teaching, learning and assessment;

- personal development and welfare; and

- outcomes for learners.

In further education, Ofsted will inspect each type of provision: 16–19 study programmes, adult learning programmes, apprenticeships, traineeships, provision for learners with high needs, and full-time provision for 14–16 learners (Office for Standards in Education, Children's Services and Skills, 2018a, pp14–15).

Coffield (2017) identified some key benefits of inspection:

- monitoring the quality of education nationally;

- regionally and institutionally;

- reporting on general themes such as the quality of maths teaching;

- setting and raising expectations;

- providing feedback and checking to see if it is acted on;

- involving parents, governors and the local community in the process; and

- challenging unquestioned assumptions, poor practices and incompetent teachers in the search for improvement.

(pxii)

Inspections can be a useful tool. They can highlight good practice and focus on what providers are doing well. Identification of areas for development is useful for providers as they can target these to improve the quality of their provision. It is necessary to identify poor practice, as it is not acceptable for organisations to be providing inadequate education and to be failing learners (Harfold, 2015). Inspections can also highlight issues within providers not necessarily related to teaching, learning and assessment, such as financial misconduct or management/leadership issues.

The benefits of a standardised approach for measuring the quality of education are clear, but Ofsted has been criticised for an over-reliance on data to measure performance (Coffield, 2017, p4). Prior to an inspection taking place, Ofsted examines the provider's outcomes and arrives with key lines of inquiry linked to these and the organisation's self-assessment report. Key judgements are made using outcome data, which, if not satisfactory, means providers will find it difficult to argue a case that their provision is good. National average data are used to benchmark; however, good providers are expected to perform above these rates. Outcomes should be more objective than other data sources, such as lesson observations. Observations can be seen as subjective as they are an individual's judgement made against a framework. Although outcomes may be objective, Coffield (2017) states that 'much of the data is unreliable and invalid' and can be manipulated (p22).

There can be a climate of fear within organisations in regard to Ofsted inspections. The attitude of senior management teams can also perpetuate this with their own behaviour and put additional pressure onto teaching staff. Many staff feel that inspections are something that are done to them, not something in which they can take an active part. Teachers are doing their jobs day in, day out, but Ofsted only see a snapshot. Additional evidence is provided during inspection, but in terms of teaching, judgements are made on walk-throughs and observations that may only be 20 minutes long. Teachers may perceive this to be unfair and feel pressure to 'perform'. Conversely, this can also be put to the teacher's advantage; teachers can 'showcase' a lesson that ticks all the Ofsted boxes, but which is not typical of their usual delivery. However, inspectors validate their findings by talking to learners, and they can be quick to identify to visitors when sessions are not of their usual quality!

The extensive work done by Frank Coffield (2017) on Ofsted inspections identifies the need to expand the inspection regime beyond the measurement of outcomes to include a wider examination of the development of the learner and the quality of teaching. Inspectors measure outcomes, make judgements and identify areas for improvement, but don't support providers on how to improve, unless they are underperforming, when this is done through the support and challenge process (Hodgkinson, 1997, p74).

Amanda Spielman, Ofsted's Chief Inspector, spoke in October 2018 about upcoming changes to the common inspection, moving away from outcomes and focusing more on the quality of provision:

> We want to know what is being taught and how schools are achieving a good education, not just what the results are looking like … A new focus on substance should change that, bringing the inspection conversation back to the substance of young people's learning and treating teachers like the experts in their field, not just data managers.

> (Spielman, 2018)

This is a significant shift for Ofsted, and one that has been welcomed by managers and teachers in the sector. The question is how will performance be measured if outcomes are not considered?

If the curriculum is excellent but outcomes are not, what will the judgement be? Curriculum and outcomes are inextricably linked. There needs to be a process for measuring the quality of education and providers need to be benchmarked against others. It is important that providers are held accountable as they are in receipt of public funding, but is Ofsted the right way to do this, and are they measuring the right things?

The next steps after an inspection are as important as what happens during it. Providers will be measured at their next inspection on how they have addressed their areas for improvements. This is particularly important from providers rated as inadequate or requiring improvement. Support and challenge programmes are provided by Ofsted, and providers are expected to make rapid and significant progress towards their areas of weakness.

The culture and leadership and management within the provider is key to its improvement. Internal quality improvement must be led by the provider, not by external inspectors (Sallis, 2002, pvii). It is vital that organisations are 'reflective' so that meaningful analysis and action can take place.

To instigate and effectively implement significant transformation, a change of culture may also be necessary within the organisation. Staff need to be on board with the changes in order for them to be successful. Following the inspection, the provider would be expected to create an improvement plan and the cycle of continuous improvement would continue.

Other forms of external quality assurance

There are also other forms of external quality assurance. Qualifications are assessed by external quality assurers from awarding bodies or by the completion of exams. The new apprenticeship standards now require all learners to be externally assessed through the End Point Assessment process. This is carried out by an independent assessor from an End Point Assessment organisation. Feedback from employers had been that apprentices didn't always have the skills they needed for the workplace, so the introduction of the End Point Assessment means that the apprentice's competence is measured by an independent expert who validates the quality of their skills. In addition to this, Investors in People, a non-departmental public body, provides benchmarks for people management that rest on employee feedback and the measuring of support and guidance services within workplaces.

External quality assurance works in conjunction with the internal processes; it is about validating the judgements made with organisations and benchmarking performance with other providers and national standards. Internal quality assurance activities should be accurate in order for external quality assurance to be successful.

Conclusion

Ensuring learners have access to good-quality education is at the heart of all quality assurance and improvement activities within PCET. All providers need to show that they are continually moving forward and identifying how they can improve their provision. In 2017/18, only 4 per cent of further education providers were graded as outstanding (Office for Standards in Education, Children's Services and Skills, 2018b). The question is: Should this be the ultimate goal for all providers in the sector? Is this realistic or achievable? As outlined at the start of the chapter, over the last 20 years, a range of government initiatives have been introduced to drive the 'constant forward progression' (Coffield and Edward, 2009, p373) of quality in the sector. However, this means that benchmarks for quality are constantly shifting; is this to improve quality in the sector, or to control the workforce and the sector?

Ofsted grades are important for providers as they can affect contracts, funding and reputation, but Ofsted are not the only measurement of good practice; the learner experience should be central to all improvement activities. There will always be new standards and benchmarks being developed, and providers have to be responsive to those. Teachers and managers should work together in 'communities of practice' where they identify how they can improve their practice and the quality of provision (Wenger, 2006).

Chapter summary

- Definitions of quality control, improvement, assurance and total quality management.

- A summary of the development of quality assurance activities in PCET since the 1990s.

- Internal quality assurance and the involvement of teachers.

- A discussion on observations of teaching and learning.

- How quality is measured by external agencies.

Recommended further reading

O'Leary, M. (ed.) (2017) *Reclaiming Lesson Observation: Supporting Excellence in Teacher Learning*. London: Routledge.

This book examines the latest thinking in lesson observation and how to put this into practice in your organisation.

References

Argyris, C. (1977) Double loop learning in organizations. *Harvard Business Review*, September–October: 115–125.

Armitage, A., Evershed, J., Hayes, D., Hudson, A., Kent, J., Lawes, S., Poma, S. and Renwick, M. (2016) *Teaching and Training in Lifelong Learning*. Maidenhead: Open University Press.

Coffield, F. (2017) *Will the Leopard Change its Spots? A New Model of Inspection for Ofsted*. London: UCL Institution of Education Press.

Coffield, F. and Edward, S. (2009) Rolling out 'good', 'best' and 'excellent' practice. What next? Perfect practice? *British Educational Research Journal*, 35(3): 371–390.

Deem, R. (1998) 'New managerialism' and higher education: the management of performances and cultures in universities in the United Kingdom. *International Studies in Sociology of Education*, 8(1): 44–70.

Department for Business, Innovation and Skills (2012) *Professionalism in Further Education: Final Report of the Independent Review Panel*. London: Department for Business, Innovation and Skills.

Department for Education (1999) *Learning to Succeed: Raising Standards in Post-16 Learning*. Nottingham: Department for Education and Employment.

Department for Education (2018) *FE Choices Learner Satisfaction Survey 2017 to 2018 19 July 2018*. Available at: www.gov.uk/government/statistics/fe-choices-learner-satisfaction-survey-2017-to-2018

Department for Education and Employment (2000) *Learning to Succeed: A New Framework for Post-16 Learning*. London: Department for Education and Employment.

Education and Training Foundation (2014) *Achieving Professional Potential*. Available at: www.et-foundation.co.uk/wp-content/uploads/2014/05/ETF_Professional_Standards_Digital_FINAL.pdf

Ewens, D. (2001) *Observation of Teaching and Learning in Adult Education: How to Prepare for It, How to Do It and How to Manage It*. London: Learning and Skills Development Agency.

FE Week (2018) *ESFA Ready to Roll Out TripAdvisor-Style Review Feature for Apprenticeship Programmes*. Available at: https://feweek.co.uk/2018/09/28/esfa-ready-to-roll-out-trip-advisor-style-review-feature-for-apprenticeship-programmes/

Harfold, S. (2015) *Speech to Association of School and College Leaders Conference*. Available at: www.gov.uk/government/speeches/speech-to-association-of-school-and-college-leaders-conference-2015

Hodgkinson, P. (1997) Neo-Fordism and teacher professionalism. *Teacher Development*, 1(1): 69–82.

Learning and Skills Council (2007) *Framework for Excellence: Raising Standards and Informing Choices*. Coventry: Learning and Skills Council.

Leitch, S. (2006) *Prosperity for All in the Global Economy: World Class Skills*. London: The Stationery Office.

Lumby, J. (2001) *Managing Further Education: Learning Enterprise*. London: Paul Chapman.

Moser, C. (1999) *Improving Literacy and Numeracy: A Fresh Start*. London: Department for Education and Employment.

Office for Standards in Education, Children's Services and Skills (2018a) *Further Education and Skills Inspection Handbook*. Available at: https://assets.publishing.service.gov.uk/government/uploads/system/uploads/attachment_data/file/753634/Further_education_and_skills_inspection_handbook_051118.pdf

Office for Standards in Education, Children's Services and Skills (2018b) *The Annual Report of Her Majesty's Chief Inspector of Education, Children's Services and Skills 2017/18*. London: Ofsted.

O'Leary, M. (2006) Can inspectors really improve the quality of teaching in the PCE sector? Classroom observations under the microscope. *Research in Post-Compulsory Education*, 11(2): 191–198.

O'Leary, M. (2013) *Developing a National Framework for the Effective Use of Lesson Observation in Further Education*. London: University and College Union.

Randle, K. and Brady, N. (1997) Managerialism and professionalism in the 'cinderella service'. *Journal of Vocational Education and Training*, 49(1): 121–139.

Sallis, E. (2002) *Total Quality Management in Education*. London: Routledge.

Simmons, R. (2010) Globalisation, neo-liberalism and vocational learning: the case of English further education. *Research in Post-Compulsory Education*, 15(4): 363–376.

Spielman, A. (2018) *HMCI Commentary: Curriculum and the New Education Inspection Framework*. Available at: www.gov.uk/government/speeches/hmci-commentary-curriculum-and-the-new-education-inspection-framework

Wenger, E. (2006) *Communities of Practice: A Brief Introduction*. Available at: http://wenger-trayner.com/introduction-to-communities-of-practice/

4

SOCIAL JUSTICE AND EDUCATION

Liz Atkins

Key words - social; justice; education; inclusion; pedagogy; inequality; equality; learner; ideology; fairness; individual; society; policy

Introduction

This chapter explores social justice and what that means in further and adult education (FAE). This is not straightforward, because social justice is a 'slippery' term, which means that it is understood and interpreted differently by different groups of people. This is because social justice is a value, and is therefore related to individual people's belief systems and what they understand to be right and wrong. We will begin with a discussion about what social justice means (and where the definitions used in this chapter come from). Broadly speaking, social justice is concerned with in/equalities and creating a more equitable state of society (and education). This means it should be of concern to any-one working in education, but particularly those of us working in FAE, since FAE caters for many of the most marginalised and excluded learners. However, it is a term that has also been taken up by groups with different ideological positions, such as politicians of opposing parties, and we will discuss how their ideas – and understanding of social justice – can conflict with one another, and with the values and beliefs that are held by professionals working in FAE. The chapter will also explore some of the in/equalities in education and society, and ways in which some of those in/equalities could be addressed. It concludes with some ideas for changes and developments that practitioners can make in their own classrooms in order to contribute to a more socially just FAE sector.

What is social justice?

The idea of social justice that underpins this chapter is generally considered to be the key under-pinning value of FAE. However, it is a problematic concept, not least because it is a 'slippery term', meaning that different people interpret and understand it in different ways. Indeed, I have put the question 'What does social justice mean to you?' to many groups of teachers, all of whom arrive at varied and sometimes conflicting definitions (e.g. 'British values', 'the rule of law', 'inclusion'). This means that it is important to begin by providing a definition of social justice. This is more difficult than it sounds, since there are so many different ways of understanding it. For example, some writers see it as 'reciprocal' (e.g. where help is given in return for something, such as in *benefits for work* programmes), while others see it as being concerned with the 'common good', an idea that can be traced back to Greek philosophers such as Aristotle and Plato, and the original teachings of the Abrahamic religions. For example, Aristotle (1988) argued that 'the greatest good ... is justice, in other words, the common interest' (*Politics* III, II. 1282b 15). Some present-day writers use the same ideas: these include John Rawls' (1999) debates on 'fairness' (pp301, 308), and Amartya Sen's (1985) work on welfare and 'capabilities'. Other writers have also tried to define social justice. For example, Morwenna Griffiths (2003) argues that social justice is 'a dynamic state of affairs that is good for the common interest, where that is taken to include both the good of each and the good of all' (p54), and also (paraphrasing Gandhi) that 'social justice is not the end, it is the way' (Griffiths, 1998, p12). Griffiths' idea of 'the way' suggests a journey, and this is how social justice is seen by many people – as a gradual process during which education and wider society become more equitable. It is also important to note that equity has quite a different meaning to equality. Equity is about ensuring *fairness*, which is not necessarily the same as equality. For example, if a class was given an examination in which they all had one hour to answer the same question, and they all had the same preparation, they could be seen as having an equal chance to do well. However, if one of those students was dyslexic and could not read the questions, they would do badly, however knowledgeable they were about the subject. Social justice is concerned with trying to promote equity in situations of inequality, such as that described above, and involves individuals and wider society.

Like Morwenna Griffiths, I believe that social justice is something we have to work towards. It is about taking action as well as having ideas, so that means we must 'walk the walk' as well as 'talk the talk'. Drawing on these ideas, social justice can be defined as being *concerned with the common good, and referring to particular social and human values about equity and the way in which they are enacted by individuals and society*. Because social justice is concerned with inequalities, this means that it is also related to politics, to understanding how different people have more (or less) educational opportunities depending on characteristics such as social class, race, disability and gender, and the way in which these intersect (act together to increase or compound social in/exclusion), and the *actions* we can take to address this. This means that social justice itself is not only a form of politics, but also a guiding philosophy (Atkins and Duckworth, 2019).

Because social justice is grounded in values and belief systems, it is also concerned with morality. Indeed, at his trial, Socrates is reputed to have debated the meaning of living a good life. This may seem slightly odd at face value, but the Greek word for justice, on which most debates around social justice are based, has a wider meaning than the English translation, and can be interpreted as implying, among other things, morality and 'right conduct' (Lee, in Plato, 1987). Ideas about morality and 'right conduct' form the basis of two (related) core concepts – both with differing interpretations – that arise from the debates around justice. Those concepts are *reciprocity* and the notion of the *common good*, which might also be considered to relate to understandings of equity, as well as to the concerns around in/equalities and marginalisation that characterise FAE.

Ideas about reciprocity appear throughout time; for example, appearing in the Old and New Testaments, as well as in work by philosophers during the Enlightenment period and in the twentieth century. This idea was particularly prevalent in Victorian times, in discussions about the 'deserving' and 'undeserving' poor. We can see it now in policies such as those around the eligibility requirements for Jobseeker's Allowance and some other benefits. This distinction between social justice as being reciprocal and social justice as being for the common good is important, since the way social justice is understood by practitioners in FAE is closely related to ideas of the common good – of caring for the less advantaged, and promoting a more just and equitable education system. In contrast, politicians and policymakers tend to draw on ideas of reciprocity and of being 'deserving' or 'undeserving'.

Over the past generation, social justice has been adopted as a 'cause' by a variety of political and activist groups, and has come to be widely regarded as something to which all reasonable people should subscribe. This helps to explain why both major UK political parties (Labour and Conservative) have used the term as part of their policy aims for FAE: the term can be found in policy documents in 2003, then as recently as 2016. Clearly, different ideological and political beliefs influence the understandings of social justice used to justify particular policies developed by different governments. Policy documents do not define what they mean by social justice, but do use it in relation to ideas of 'deserving' and 'undeserving'. In other words, if the policy documents did define social justice, they would probably say something about reciprocity.

FAE as a vehicle for promoting social justice and equity

'Academic' education has traditionally been seen as the pursuit of knowledge as a social good. It has historically been associated with the 'liberal arts', which include subjects such as literature and history, and which have their origins in the writings of Plato. In contrast, vocational education has its origins in the apprenticeship systems of the medieval guilds and the Mechanics' Institutes of the nineteenth century. Historically, each form of education took a different approach, with the liberal arts being focused on reading and debate, and the different forms of vocational education emphasising practical skills and the knowledge associated with those skills. Apprenticeships utilised an approach in which the master personally taught the apprentice and was also responsible for the board and moral well-being of the apprentice.

Due to their different historical and social origins, these different forms of education have, over time, come to be seen in different ways. In England and Wales, which follow a Platonic model of education, academic education has traditionally been seen as 'elite', while vocational education has been seen as being for 'practical' or 'non-academic' young people. This has been the case for over a century. The Taunton Commission (1868) noted that there were tensions between the liberal and vocational curricula, and that these were related to social class, then Whitehead (1929) argued that 'the antithesis between a technical and a liberal education is fallacious' (p74). This lack of parity of esteem has been a concern for practitioners, researchers and politicians who are concerned with developing a more socially just education system; as early as 1916, John Dewey (2011) argued that a society must make 'provision for participation in [education and society] of all its members on *equal terms*' (p56, emphasis added) and that being able to do what you are good at is 'the key to happiness' (p169).

In relation to this, educational researchers and philosophers have attempted to understand what the *purpose* of education should be in contemporary civil society, and how this might help to create a more socially just society. For example, Richard Pring and others involved in the Nuffield Review of 14–19 education asked, 'What counts as an educated 19-year-old today?' and, 'Are the models of education we have inherited from the past sufficient to meet the needs of young people [and the community]?' (Pring et al., 2009). A focus of this work, as well as other educational research, has been the social inequalities that result in young people from different social classes (broadly speaking, working class and middle class) pursuing different forms of education (vocational versus academic), which result in very different life chances in terms of potential income and security of employment. These concerns have led to questions about the differences in the way the academic and vocational curricula are designed and structured.

The key difference in curriculum is in the way in which the academic curriculum is structured relatively broadly in comparison to the competence-based approach that is used for vocational and skills education. Many writers (e.g. see Bloomer, 1996, 1997) have been critical of the competence-based curriculum we are familiar with in FAE. Key arguments against competence-based approaches are focused around the use of knowledge criteria for learning and assessment, suggesting that by limiting knowledge in a certain area to a list, it becomes fragmented and less valuable and useful (Bathmaker, 2013; Ecclestone, 2011). This is important in terms of social justice, as most vocational and competence-based programmes are mainly accessed by working-class young people. These arguments suggest that working-class young people are effectively denied access to the more valuable, less fragmented, academic curriculum associated with A levels, university attendance, and then professional occupations, which, in general terms, are better paid than craft and technical roles. An education system where children and young people follow particular routes, with different outcomes, according to their social class is clearly unequal and inequitable, whatever their individual outcomes. Making changes to the curriculum and to the structure of the education system to make it more socially just is hugely challenging, and is a job for government. However, there is still a great deal that can be done at the practitioner level in order to help create a more socially just environment at the individual classroom level.

The FAE practitioner and social justice

Key questions

What does social justice mean for the FAE practitioner and how can it be enacted at classroom level?

The answer is that every teacher's personal values associated with social justice will influence their actions. This means their pedagogy, the approach they take to supporting their students, their personal approach to inclusion, to differentiation, and how they approach the assessment procedures on the courses they teach.

A good place to start thinking about these issues is to consider your own values in relation to FAE. What do you think about students' differences and individual challenges, and the barriers to education that these might create? What can/do you do about this? What concerns you most about your students and their circumstances? Why do you choose to teach here? What are the key life experiences that informed your values and the way you think about your students? What are the likely implications of adopting a more socially just approach for you and your students?

Your reasons for teaching in the sector will be value-based and may well be related to ideas about wanting to give something back and/or particular concerns about specific groups of students. For example, my own story, which led to my concerns about level 1 students, is typical of many others, and yours may be similar. At 16, I spectacularly failed my exams and went to a further education (FE) college to do what was then a pre-nursing course, which eventually generated the five O-level (GCSE) passes then necessary to enter nurse training. I became a psychiatric nurse, eventually leaving for health reasons and finding my way into FE as a health and social care teacher, where I was naturally drawn to 'failures' like myself.

From a social justice perspective, it is important to understand why those 'failures' occur, why we see them as 'failures', and how and why students come to enrol on particular courses. In/equality is part of the reason behind each of those issues. For example, 'failure' or 'success' is determined by government policy at age 16, in relation to the number of GCSE 'passes' an individual attains. Five or above equals success, and below five equals 'failure'. However, the statistics on this can never tell the whole story, and issues around inequalities and their impact on individuals can be a large part of the reason why many young people attain at levels below their potential. There is a world of difference between the chances available to a non-disabled young person from a comfortable home with educated, supportive parents, and to a similar young person with a learning disability. But what if the young person with the disability grew up in care, or in poverty, or in an area beset with knife crime, and had brothers already in prison? What if a young person had been consistently bullied for their sexuality, was an asylum seeker, or was continually exposed to domestic violence? What if their parents just did not have the education or time to support them? These examples illustrate just a few of the inequalities (sometimes also referred to as *exclusionary characteristics*) faced by FAE students, and you are likely to be familiar with many of them. They also highlight some of the challenges that can result in students being labelled as 'successes' or 'failures' at 16, as well as issues related to intersectionality. Intersectionality refers to the fact that some people have more (or less) opportunities depending on characteristics such as social class, race, disability and gender, and the way in which these *intersect* or act together to increase or compound social in/exclusion.

You will probably recognise some of the issues of intersectionality and the way in which these can contribute to the barriers individual students can face in terms of education. For example, think of Calvin, a level 1 black student who is disruptive in class. Calvin has been thrown out by parents who reject his sexuality, and he is 'sofa surfing' at his auntie's. He has no benefits entitlement and just happens to also have a minor form of epilepsy. Because so many students have so many different exclusionary characteristics and face so many challenges, it is a matter of social justice that we are aware of students' needs at an individual level.

Importantly, this means we must not think of students as groups (e.g. as 'level 1 learners', 'ethnic minority learners' or 'dyslexic learners') because this leads us to see all members of a group in terms of a single shared characteristic, something that is not equitable (because those members of that group are individuals with individual lives, interests, experiences, strengths and weaknesses), and therefore contrary to social justice. In addition, it means we focus on one characteristic rather than all those issues facing the student. In Calvin's example above, thinking of him as underachieving and disengaged because he is black (and research shows that these are, for a variety of reasons, persistent problems with black Caribbean boys) would be a mistake. He is likely to be exhausted (no one sleeps well on a sofa), stress may be exacerbating his epilepsy, which may be another factor in his disengagement, and emotionally he will be dealing with family rejection. Lack of money may mean that he is hungry. He will certainly be fearing for the future. Trying to create an equitable learning environment for Calvin means looking at him as an individual and trying to find ways of supporting his many needs. Faced with complex situations such as this, it is easy to feel that there is little that you can do in your role as a classroom practitioner. In fact, there is a lot that can be done beyond actions such as referral to student support and external services such as social workers and charitable organisations. Just recognising Calvin's difficulties – perhaps by acknowledging that he looks tired, for example – is a start. This places a specific value on him, his needs and his importance as an individual human being. It shows him that his teacher is concerned about him and is part of generating a 'safe space' for him. Other strategies might be:

- talking to him about why he thinks he is disruptive, and working together to plan how to deal with it;

- giving him a responsibility in the group;

- identifying a quiet space where he can have time out;

- getting friends to remind him when his medication is due and/or to alert an appropriate person if he has a seizure; and

- involving him in initiatives that might be close to his heart (such as Pride or other awareness-raising initiatives).

You may be able to think of other interventions that will help Calvin. Each of those suggested above is designed to consider Calvin as a whole person rather than addressing individual characteristics. For example, discussing the reasons for his disruption with him opens up opportunities to put wider support mechanisms in place and gives Calvin a sense of responsibility. It is also a way of dealing with stereotypes. It is easy for teachers to stereotype students as disruptive and ascribe it to particular characteristics (e.g. all level 1 students are disruptive and difficult), but this just becomes a self-fulfilling prophecy, and so is contrary to social justice. If you have a student who, like Calvin, has multiple barriers to learning in the form of exclusionary characteristics, it may be useful to spend a few minutes thinking about what the cumulative effect of all those barriers or characteristics might be, and to come up with a list of interventions that could help to make your classroom a more equitable place for that student.

Inclusion and social justice

All FAE institutions have policies and procedures on inclusion, and this is something we now see as a standard part of everyday practice. However, this was not always the case. Philosophies and policies around inclusion emerged as mainstream educational practice around a generation ago, probably initiated by the 1989 United Nations Convention on the Rights of the Child (United Nations, 1989) and the Salamanca Statement and Framework for Action on Special Needs Education (UNESCO, 1994). These philosophies and practices have also become enshrined in law in many countries, including those making up the UK.

Broadly speaking, inclusive practice is intended to ensure that every individual has the opportunity to succeed, regardless of characteristics such as disability, race, gender, sexuality or language. As such, it seems obvious that any practitioner with a concern about social justice would also be committed to inclusive practice. However, like social justice, inclusion is a problematic idea. First of all, the list of characteristics that can cause *exclusion* is potentially infinite, and goes way beyond those characteristics (such as disability, race or gender) that are protected in law (see Equality Act 2010). So, if you are a female teacher whose class includes a man who has been a long-term victim of domestic violence and who becomes anxious around women, you will have to consider his particular needs and concerns to include him and provide an equitable experience for him in the context of your class.

Second, some ideas and practices about inclusion can be exclusionary. A good example is sitting a deaf or hearing-impaired student at the front of the class so they can see/hear what is happening, but not acknowledging how exhausting it is to see/hear for an extended period when this takes maximum concentration (something most hearing people are unaware of). Recognising this and building in breaks would be much more inclusive. In an example from a research project I undertook (Atkins, 2016), a student who used a wheelchair and the accessibility routes around the buildings explained that while they enabled him to attend and to learn, the fact that his friends all used the 'quick routes' meant that he missed out on conversations and ended up on the 'margins' of the group. As learning is a social activity, this was an important aspect to exclusion. In the same study, another student complained that his support worker sometimes joined in group learning discussions, making him feel that he couldn't have his own ideas. Therefore, in terms of social justice, it is important to think of inclusion in its widest sense, and to consider all the implications of an individual student's circumstances, rather than just implementing a particular policy approach.

Pedagogies for social justice

The fact that you are reading this book means that you are someone who wants to learn and who is striving to be the best teacher they can be. You probably already try to make your teaching interesting and engaging and think of different strategies to help students learn. In this section, we will explore a few common approaches used in FAE, and consider how they might be adapted or developed in a social justice context.

First, most FAE courses are outcomes-based, and many lessons begin with a statement of learning outcomes that is revisited at the end of the session. It is useful to think about learning outcomes, and the way in which we build on them, in the context of the student and their life experiences. For example, on a typical social care programme, a learning outcome might be to *describe a range of leisure activities suitable for elderly people*, and that lesson might begin with a group activity which involves students discussing and recording potential activities before those are shared and the teacher uses the information to develop learning. However, many FAE students, because of their poor socio-economic backgrounds, do not have access to a range of leisure activities and are likely to have very limited experience of them. In the course of some research, I recently met an 18-year-old student who had never eaten out (including fast-food outlets) until his college included him in a Christmas meal, and others who had never been to the cinema. These students would be unable to contribute ideas in the same way, and could only think of activities such as the cinema in abstract as the teacher developed the session.

So, how can the same outcome be used in a way that is inclusive of all students and promotes social justice? A learning activity that is potentially more socially just would be to plan in advance, and ask students to interview an older person about their preferred leisure activities, how and why they enjoyed them, and what barriers might occur. This activity would generate more meaningful examples (because they came from the older people), would provide some intergenerational learning, and would be real rather than abstract examples. Another useful strategy can be to use learning outcomes at an individual level, rather than as a group, so students have the opportunity to indicate whether they are confident/not confident in their knowledge and learning can be more effectively differentiated. This can be achieved by using individual handouts or individual space on a virtual learning environment (VLE), rather than listing them on a PowerPoint or similar presentation, and is also a useful way of differentiating learning.

In relation to pedagogy and social justice, a key point is that social justice is about communicating respect. This means acknowledging that students have valuable knowledge and learning beyond this class, but which might be valuable to it. A good example of this is using students' experience of placement and their learning in that environment in the classroom. This can be achieved by asking students for examples of particular issues they have faced and how they were dealt with at placement, something that can be built on so that a whole group can learn from a single experience. Similarly, students' life experience can contribute to learning; for example, the literacy student who is a refugee from Mali might share different forms of oral tradition that reflect different kinds of literacy, and an engineering student might have a Saturday job helping his mechanic uncle. Understanding and recognising students' knowledge and experience, and integrating it into your teaching through discussion and use of examples, respects and values the contributors and generates a richer learning environment.

Assessment and social justice

As I have noted earlier in this chapter, FAE uses a competence-based curriculum. This is then assessed according to whether or not the student meets certain assessment criteria. This approach to assessment is widely believed to be a valid and reliable way of assessing learning, and therefore 'fairer' than other methods, such as norm-referencing (assessment has changed over time, and norm-referencing was a system that allocated a 'quota' to each grade, based on the assumption that some would do very well and some would do very badly but most would get an average mark). However, from a social justice perspective, there are difficulties with ideas of validity and reliability. To begin with, the resources and people conducting the assessment for the same qualification will be different in different places, and this may impact on an assessment outcome. In addition, although criterion-referencing is intended to be objective, complete objectivity is never really possible – there are always fine judgements to be made about the extent to which a criterion has been made, and these rely on the professional judgement of the assessor, and in some cases assessors will interpret criteria differently. This means that some students will potentially have better opportunities to gain higher grades than others. Similarly, inconsistencies such as those outlined here can affect the reliability of assessment.

Social justice is, to a great extent, about *fairness*, and these examples illustrate the fact that no assessment process can ever be completely 'fair'. In addition, in many cases, you are constrained by what the awarding body will, or will not, allow as part of an assessment process. So, what can you, as an FAE practitioner, do to try to make sure that you are giving every student a fair chance in an assessment situation? First, as with pedagogy and your wider practice, it is important to know each student and their particular needs and circumstances intimately. This enables you to take a wider view of the assessment and any potential barriers or difficulties that individual students might face. Second, as a professional in FAE, you need to understand the concept of assessment and the problems that might arise with different forms of assessment. For example, are you conducting a formative assessment? A summative assessment? Is this an AP(E)L or an ipsative assessment? What processes are you using to conduct that assessment, and are they fair – and so socially just – in respect of all your students? In most of these cases, there is a degree of flexibility which can enable you to take different approaches that better meet the needs of different students.

It is important to state here that different does not – and should not – mean easier. It simply means giving people who face particular challenges a more appropriate – and so a more equitable and socially just – way of demonstrating their knowledge and/or skills. To illustrate this, think about Connor, a basic skills numeracy teacher working in adult education. As a means of formative assessment, and to check learning, Connor ends most of his lessons with a 'quick-fire' round of questions. Sometimes these are directed at the whole class, and sometimes at individuals. However, both these approaches have the potential to be exclusive, and so contrary to social justice. Most adult learners lack confidence in the classroom, and being 'put on the spot' can be frightening. This also means that some students will 'opt out' of general questions, and Connor may miss the fact that they do not fully understand the concepts he is teaching. Other students may be unable to process verbal questions well. To make his formative assessment fairer, and more inclusive, Connor could write the questions on the board/ PowerPoint, as well as calling them out, and rather than giving verbal responses, students could be given the opportunity to write down some answers, or share their answers with a colleague, which would include an element of peer assessment. Using a wider variety of approaches in this way would mean that Connor's assessment was more inclusive and fairer to those involved.

In relation to summative assessment, the options might be more constrained, but providing the awarding body requirements are met, there is still always a little flexibility. This might involve a written exercise instead of a presentation for a student with anxiety, additional time, or a practical test with a mentor in the workplace rather than an assessment in college for a student who is excellent in placement but lacks confidence in the college environment. Students with specific needs will often also need flexible approaches to assessment. These are usually described as part of a support plan, but sometimes tiny actions taken by the tutor can be just as effective. This was the case in relation to Jack, who was a health and social care student in the final year of a BTEC national. He had a mild form of ADHD, was easily distracted in class and behind on his assessed coursework. Final deadlines were looming, and this put his dream of becoming a nurse into question. In negotiation with him, his tutor and his placement, he went into college on three placement days and worked alone under the supervision of a tutor. He completed his work successfully and went on to train as a nurse. In this situation, the assessment undertaken by the student was exactly the same as that undertaken by his peers. However, offering him the flexibility to work alone with a tutor on call created an assessment context in which he could independently, and successfully, complete his work.

There are many other potential examples, and you probably have some of your own. The key to conducting assessment that is socially just is to bear in mind that students who share particular characteristics do not necessarily have the same needs, and that intersectional issues may be relevant. Finally, consider exactly what challenges an individual student faces, and how that student could best be enabled to demonstrate their knowledge and skills, then, using your knowledge of the assessment process, make a plan for an assessment which offers that individual the best possible opportunity to achieve.

Chapter summary

This chapter has explored the meaning of social justice, its origins, and its implications for practitioners in FAE. This chapter has also considered some of the inequalities and exclusionary
characteristics that affect many of the students in FAE, and it is to offer them a more equitable education and better opportunities that we need to work towards a more socially just education system.
Key features of social justice are respect for the individual, consideration of individual needs, thinking about the implications of intersectionality, and *action*. As we have seen, there are many actions
that the FAE teacher can take to make the classroom a more socially just space that promotes equity
for all students while also recognising that there are some issues, such as the way the education system and the curriculum are structured, that are the business of politicians. In respect of those, it is
important that rigorous and credible research continues to come out of the sector, which can inform
policymakers and, over time, potentially contribute to more socially just policymaking.

References

Aristotle (1988) *The Politics*, ed. S Everson. Cambridge: Cambridge University Press.

Atkins, L. (2016) Dis(en)abled: legitimating discriminatory practice in the name of inclusion? *British Journal of Special Education*, 43(1): 6–21.

Atkins, L. and Duckworth, V. (2019) *Research Methods for Social Justice and Equity*. London: Bloomsbury.

Bathmaker, A.-M. (2013) Defining 'knowledge' in vocational education qualifications in England: an analysis of key stakeholders, and their constructions of knowledge, purposes and content. *Journal of Vocational Education and Training*, 65(1): 87–107.

Bloomer, M. (1996) Education for studentship. In J. Avis et al. (eds), *Knowledge and Nationhood: Education, Politics and Work*. London: Cassell.

Bloomer, M. (1997) *Curriculum Making in Post-16 Education: The Social Conditions of Studentship*. London: Routledge.

Dewey, J. (2011) *Democracy and Education*. New York: Free Press.

Ecclestone, K. (2011) Emotionally-vulnerable subjects and new inequalities: the educational implications of an 'epistemology of the emotions'. *International Studies in Sociology of Education*, 21(2): 91–113.

Equality Act 2010. Available at: www.legislation.gov.uk/ukpga/2010/15/contents

Griffiths, M. (1998) *Educational Research for Social Justice: Getting Off the Fence*. Buckingham: Open University Press.

Griffiths, M. (2003) *Action Research for Social Justice in Education: Fairly Different*. Buckingham: Open University Press.

Plato (1987) *The Republic*, ed. D. Lee. London: Penguin.

Pring, R. et al. (2009) *Education for All: The Future of Education and Training for 14–19 Year Olds*. London: Routledge.

Rawls, J. (1999) *A Theory of Justice*, rev. edn. Oxford: Oxford University Press.

Sen, A. (1985) *Commodities and Capabilities*. Amsterdam: Elsevier.

Taunton Commission (1868) *Schools Enquiry Commission*. London: HMSO.

UNESCO (1994) *The Salamanca Statement and Framework for Action on Special Needs Education*. Salamanca: UNESCO.

United Nations (1989) *The Convention on the Rights of the Child*. Geneva: United Nations Children's Fund.

Whitehead, A.N. (1929) *The Aims of Education and Other Essays*. London: Ernest Benn.

5

DIVERSITY IN THE PCET SECTOR

Dale Munday

Key words – diversity; inclusion; quality; widened; participation; gender; disability; policy; legislation; education; demographic; LGBT; barriers; learning

Introduction

The further and adult education (FAE) sector is highly complex and one of great diversity, welcoming a wide cross section of the population, from pre-entry to degree-level programmes, and anyone over the age of 14 (with no upper age limit). Embedding equality and diversity into everyday practice in further education and work-based learning provision has never been more important, with increasing prosperity in the UK, as well as delivering considerable benefits to society as a whole, directly linked to improving our skills base. The focus on equality and diversity in the sector has implications for managers, teachers (and support staff) and students, whether that be professional competence or affordance of opportunity, with the consequences having powerful ramifications.

This chapter will highlight the role of policy and legislative changes, from the inception of the Education Act 1902 to the Children and Families Act 2014, with crucial changes discussed and their impact on the FAE sector equality and diversity evaluated. The Equality Act 2010, the Disability Amendment Act 2005 and the 2004 14–19 Curriculum and Qualifications Reform will be given prominence, and will be addressed as to whether we have successfully achieved what governments have set out to. Furthermore, a focus on economic, social, political and cultural marginalisation in the sector will be emphasised, addressing whether labelling has become the norm and a subsequent issue for inclusive design. The chapter will end with a look at education or segregation, analysing the relationship with both the medical and social models of disability.

Current developments in the sector

Currently, the further education (FE) sector is undergoing significant reforms. Apprenticeships 2020, the Report of the Independent Panel on Technical Education, usually referred to as the Sainsbury Review (Department for Education, 2017), and the subsequent Post-16 Skills Plan provide a framework under which the Department for Education (DfE) will reform the skills landscape. The specific immediate challenges to which teachers in the sector must rise are those relating to the new technical education routes, the delivery of high-quality apprenticeships and raising standards in English and mathematics, while dealing with an ever-changing student demographic. Tensions between lecturers in FE being both occupational professionals passing on their expertise and teachers with access to pedagogical theories and techniques (dual professionalism) is identified as a challenge in the literature, which can lead to a dereliction of requirements in regard to preparation to deal with diverse students. Prior to this, the deregulation of FE teaching in 2010 saw the removal of mandatory membership of a professional body, minimum CPD entitlements and the requirement to hold or be working towards a teaching qualification, which can be seen as a dereliction of the need to be constantly updating teaching skills and practical application. Most recent government and sector data demonstrate the diverse learner base and range of differences that must be considered to meet various laws and legislation. With the inception of the Equality Act 2010, additional expectations and duties have been placed on organisations and those individuals who work within them. This Act brings together over 116 separate pieces of legislation and provides a legal framework to protect the rights of individuals and advance equality of opportunity for all (Equality and Human Rights Commission, 2017).

Equality and diversity policy landscape in the UK and impact on FAE

Key questions

Are policy changes positively influencing the quality of provision in the sector?

Since the Education Act 1902, there have been numerous iterations along with supplementary policy changes and Acts focused on equality and diversity. In 2013, the Department for Business, Innovation and Skills (BIS) undertook a detailed analysis of the benefits associated with further education (FE) and skills, paying particular attention to the economic impact and wider benefits associated with learning and qualification attainment. The DfE's vision is a highly educated society in which opportunity is more equal for children and young people, no matter what their background or family circumstances. Education has always been a source of social vitality, and the more people we can include in the community of learning, the greater the benefits to us all. Over the years, the concept of embracing equality and diversity has assumed greater significance (Kennedy, 1997). The Kennedy Report sought to address and review current approaches to widening participation with further education. The report recommended:

- redistribution of public resources 'towards those with less success in earlier learning';

- the establishment of 'a lifetime entitlement to education ... which is free for young people and those who are socially and economically deprived';

- the creation of 'a national network of strategic partnerships to identify local need, stimulate demand, respond creatively and promote learning';

- encouraging employers to provide learning centres linked to a 'university for industry';

- reform of financial support to students to promote equity and 'welfare to work through learning'; and

- the setting of new national learning targets and local targets for participation.

(Kennedy, 1997, pp13–14)

Associated legislation, statutory and non-statutory requirements, education policy and guidance have been produced – each making its own demands on further education and post-compulsory learning providers. However, having a written policy and communicating it is only one step. Is this enough to enact real progress and change in the sector? It must be accompanied by actions to implement it to help people flourish in learning and work, prevent discrimination, harassment and bullying, and deal with it effectively when it occurs. A selection of key and influential policy and legislative changes can be seen in the timeline below.

- The Education (Handicapped Children) Act 1970 made the provision for discontinuing the classification of handicapped children as unsuitable for education at school.

- The 1978 Warnock Report (Oxford Reference, n.d.) was to change the educational picture for children with disabilities as most of the recommendations became enshrined in law in the Education Act 1981.

- The Education Act 1981 was a pathway for the integration of children with 'special needs' and gave parents new rights in relation to special needs.

- The Disabled Persons Act 1986 aimed to provide for the improvement of the effectiveness of, and the coordination of resources in, the provision of services for people with a mental or physical handicap and for people with mental illness.

- The Disability Discrimination Act 1995 made it unlawful to discriminate against disabled persons in connection with employment, the provision of goods, facilities and services, or the disposal or management of premises.

- The 1997 Green Paper *Excellence for All* (Parliament UK, n.d.) supported the 1994 UN statement on special educational needs (SEN), which 'calls on governments to adopt the principle of inclusive education' and 'implies a progressive extension of the capacity of mainstream schools to provide for children with a wide range of needs'.

- The Special Educational Needs and Disability Act 2001 (SENDA) amended Part 4 of the Education Act 1996 to make further provision against discrimination, on the grounds of disability, in schools and other educational establishments, and for connected purposes.

- The Disability Amendment Act 2005 (Shepherd & Wedderburn, 2005) introduced a duty on the public sector to promote disability equality.

- The Equality Act 2010 brought together over 116 separate pieces of legislation into one single Act. Combined, they made up a new Act that provided a legal framework to protect the rights of individuals and advance equality of opportunity for all.

- The Children and Families Act 2014 set a new legislative framework for children and young people (aged 0–25) with special educational needs and disabilities. General FE and sixth form colleges must now use their best endeavours to secure the special educational provision that the young person needs.

So, are these policy changes positively influencing the quality for provision in the sector? All of the Acts and legislative changes have shaped and augmented the post-compulsory education sector to varying degrees, both with the workforce and student base. The DfE's vision of lifelong inclusive learning has become increasingly difficult to achieve with additional expectations and increased budgetary demands. The number of adults reporting they are learning is at the lowest level in more than two decades. Recent adult learning participation rates released by the Learning and Work Institute (2018) reveal a steady decline in participation rates from the high point of 2001, when 46 per cent of respondents reported taking part in some form of learning, to a record low of just 36 per cent in 2018.

So, legislative changes to increase the opportunity of education, on the face of it, have yet to yield success. In a 2017 survey, the most common barrier to learning identified was work or other time pressures, mentioned by roughly one in seven adults (14 per cent). Other common barriers included feeling too old (10 per cent), a lack of interest (10 per cent), childcare or other caring responsibilities (9 per cent), cost (8 per cent), an illness or disability (7 per cent) or simply feeling no need to learn (6 per cent). Surely, we must be doing more to dispel myths as to who can and who can't learn, focusing on practical steps to improve accessibility across a broad demographic, including the provision of childcare facilities, flexible provision, distance learning or the use of bursaries to support individuals financially.

Key questions

Do we have a diverse workforce in the post-compulsory sector to match the student demographic?

The introduction of the Disability Amendment Act 2005 and the Children and Families Act 2014 placed further education and sixth form providers with the requirement of further supporting students with SEN, whether they had an education healthcare plan (EHP) or not. Figure 5.1 visualises an overall increase in students who identify as having a learning disability/difficulty (2002/03 7.9 per cent, 2005/06 11.5 per cent, 2014/15 17.0 per cent, 2015/16 24.4 per cent, 2016/17 17.9 per cent) and a decrease in those who do not know (2002/03 19.1 per cent, 2005/06 8.6 per cent, 2014/15 4.7 per cent, 2015/16 4.3 per cent). One could argue that the legislative changes are positively impacting on the identification and planned support for these students, with a more focused approach to the support and curriculum offer required.

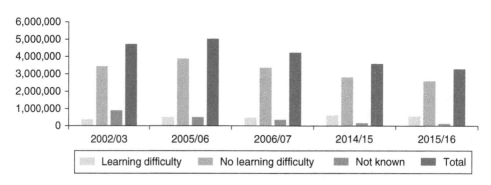

Figure 5.1   FE and skills student demographic

The Equality Act 2010 also shows signs of impact in the FE and skills sector workforce when comparing data from workforce data and SIR Data Insights from 2005/06, 2006/07 and 2012/13–2016/17. In the further education workforce data for England for 2004/05 (Lifelong Learning UK, 2005), sexuality was not recorded, along with age, gender, region, etc. However, the most recent publication of the 2016/17 data (Education and Training Foundation, 2018) addresses this and sheds light on the changing demographic in the FE and skills workforce and approaches therein. The report shows the sexual orientation of the FE workforce: 82 per cent self-report as heterosexual, and 16 per cent state that they prefer not to answer the question, which could intimate that more work is required for confidence to disclose. When the sector is becoming increasingly more diverse, surely the workforce must reflect this too?

In 2008/09, 89 per cent of the workforce were white British (Lifelong Learning UK, 2011), while in 2017 the workforce in FE colleges is primarily white British. In detail, white British represent 93 per cent of the workforce of independent providers, 84 per cent of colleges and 87 per cent of other providers.

In 2008/09, 2.9 per cent of all further education staff and 2.8 per cent of teaching staff in England disclosed having a disability. This has increased slightly since 2004/05; however, the rate of staff disclosure remains extremely low for a sector that is mainly represented by older staff, where the likelihood of acquiring an impairment increases with age. In 2017, close to 6 per cent of staff in FE reported having some form of disability. However, over half of these staff members chose not to disclose the nature of their disability. Of those indicating their disability, the most common was a physical impairment (2 per cent of all staff across provider types).

Inclusive curriculum

'We believe that learning can only be fully effective if it is inclusive' (Centre for Studies on Inclusive Education, 1996, p1). The concept of curriculum is not new; however, with all the legislative changes and shifts in educational policy aimed at providing inclusive education, the idea of an inclusive curriculum has emerged in more recent years. An inclusive curriculum seeks to expose and overcome exclusion 'in all its forms, the language we use, the teaching methods we adopt, the curriculum we transmit' (Slee and Allan, 2001). There should be a clear connection between the design of an inclusive curriculum, considering the choice of assessment and feedback methods, the types of course materials that will be used, and the classroom environment that can be fostered. Inclusive practice or inclusive teaching and learning should draw on the strengths and differences of students and colleagues.

Key questions

Have we achieved an inclusive curriculum across the sector?

The report *Inclusive FE* (Centre for Studies on Inclusive Education, 1996) was the result of a three-year enquiry into the educational needs of and provision for adults with disabilities and/or learning difficulties in England. The core of John Tomlinson's report was the view of 'inclusive learning', which placed the responsibility for providing suitable education with the teachers, the managers and the

exploring the 'inclusive' curriculum

system, which took a social model of disability, rather than problematising the student as one with a deficit. Tomlinson aimed to improve educational opportunities for those already attending education and training, projecting a five- to ten-year timescale to extend the opportunity for those currently unable to attend due to equality and diversity issues (Centre for Studies on Inclusive Education, 1996). The move towards an inclusive model of education presents teachers with the difficulty of differentiating the curriculum, but also opportunities to harness the individual differences that can enrich the learning experience of all involved. Inclusive education perceives diversity as part of human nature, and as such the educational institution (and not the student) has to adapt in order to provide quality education for all. Within this context, an inclusive education approach demands an inclusive curriculum and learning processes based on the philosophy of embedded accessibility and universal design for learning. An extensive, but not exhaustive, overview of the scope of diversity and examples can be seen in Figure 5.2, and how they all need consideration in curriculum design. Transposing the diversity characteristics from HE to FE possibly fails to exemplify the scale and impact of many considerations across the two, yet they give a clear idea of the considerations and challenges faced when designing an inclusive curriculum.

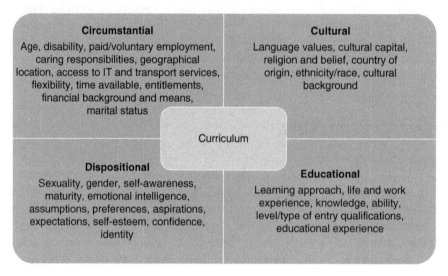

Figure 5.2   Student diversity
Source: Adapted from Thomas and May (2010)

positive progress

At a time when the educational landscape is rapidly changing, with institutions having to provide for learners of increasingly diverse needs, there is an increased onus on providers to meet these demands, with SEN a key factor. Recent FE and skills participation data released by the government highlight in 2002/03 a total of 4,719,400 learners attended, with 371,920 disclosing or diagnosed with a learning difficulty/disability (equating to 7.9 per cent of the total). From this, 900,080 were not known to either have disclosed or diagnosed learning difficulties/disabilities. Comparing this with recent 2016/17 data from the government displays a 10 per cent increase (563,100 in total) in students attending with a learning difficulty/disability and a reduction in not known by 22.3 per cent to just 102,150 students. This can be seen as a positive step in the identification of students' needs and a starting point for the creation of an inclusive curriculum, but is it enough? Figure 5.3 highlights the changes between 2002/03 and 2016/17.

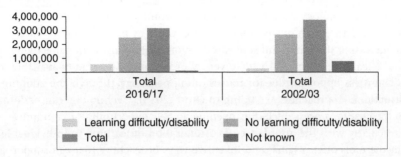

Figure 5.3   FE and skills participation comparison

Case study

Engaging and supporting learners by improving curriculum accessibility through use of assistive technologies

Teachers, trainers and assessors at Runshaw College received training on the concepts and use of digital accessibility software to enhance the student experience. This was offered as mainstream provision for all students at the college rather than for discrete groups. Empowering students to confidently use assistive technologies can have a transformative effect on engagement, participation and learning. The college focussed on ensuring staff were confident using text-to-speech software and have access to a range of materials to support their use. With the effective integration of assistive technologies into the classroom, students have multiple means to complete their work, with greater independence in performing tasks previously troublesome. Subsequently, the range of teaching and assessment approaches can be extended and developed to offer greater variety and inclusion too.

(JISC, 2015)

This case study represents a development in modern curriculum design from the traditional curriculum design models (Biggs, 2003; Taba, 1962; Tyler, 1949). Instead of adapting the approach for the minority, the focus is on encompassing all in the approaches taken. Fletcher and Munoz (cited in Chiappe, 2013) stated dyslexia as the fastest growing learning difficulty in FE in terms of increase in number of self-reported learning difficulties. This exacerbates the need to take a more innovative approach to curriculum design, with variety in teaching methods, resources, assessment and feedback approaches. Developing a curriculum with an awareness of assistive technologies and inclusive practices allows for equality and inclusion from the outset. The Skills Funding Agency found that the greatest barrier to learning for LGBT students was 'insensitive curriculum content', particularly on vocational or professional courses that suffer from gender stereotyping (explored further in the subsequent section).

As educational participation has a range of economic benefits and the impact of non-economic benefits extend beyond the classroom into personal life and into the community, it can be transformative for individuals and communities (Schuller et al., 2002). In addition, a very general but crucial conclusion from some of the academic literature was cited by the Department for Business, Innovation and Skills (2015), which hypothesises that education has a sustaining effect on people's lives.

Rapid advances in technology have provided the opportunity to create entirely new learning environments, extending the reach of education to those who may previously have felt marginalised, by significantly increasing the range and sophistication of possible instructional activities in both conventional and e-learning settings. A wide diversity of powerful and readily available technological tools offers countless opportunities for transforming pedagogy through the adoption of learner-centred instructional approaches. According to Groff (2013), 'Technology can perform several key functions in the change process, including opening up new opportunities that improve teaching and learning, particularly with the affordance of customisation of learning to individual learner needs' (p2). Multimedia tools offer original and inventive ways of teaching that can support and enhance learning opportunities and inspire innovative teaching methods that stimulate collaboration among learners. In addition to this, new technologies support the creation and sharing of information and the development of online learning communities to shape and develop the curriculum, removing physical and locational barriers.

Case study

Using audio feedback to improve engagement and performance

Tutors at Kingston College used a free screen casting app called Jing to provide responsive audio feedback to students on their progress and performance. This offered teachers greater opportunities to develop more inclusive feedback practices, enabling screen capture and recording feedback on a range of assignment formats. The flexibility of the software provided the ability to feedback on practical activities, written as well as graphical work and to provide commentary to support student use and understanding of their personal performance data. Timely feedback can play an integral role in affecting learning, along with being explicit, identifying what they have yet to achieve and how they can improve their performance or complete their course assignments. An example of tutor feedback for a hairdressing apprentice illustrates how this can provide detailed and encouraging feedback. Jing was used to help learners to take ownership of their learning and making it easier for them to understand and use their performance data more effectively. Staff found that using Jing reduced the amount of time taken to assess and give detailed feedback to learners and that it also reduced duplication of paper-based records.

(JISC, 2015)

Other benefits are that audio feedback can be easier for students to assimilate than written feedback; when combined with video recordings of practical tasks, it can be used to give detailed feedback to individuals participating in group work. Hard-to-reach learners can receive a personal response, helping them to maintain their links to the college. Soden (2017), drawing on prior research, explained the value in developing new modes of feedback in addition to written text, which might then be received by the reader in a tone incongruent to what was intended. He also addressed the danger of repeated negative or critical feedback serving to reinforce low self-esteem and low motivation in poorly performing students, which could be highly detrimental to traditional further education and skills students.

The advancement of technology brought forward a huge range of opportunities in the education of learners with disabilities and learning difficulties aiming to reinforce the efforts for inclusive education and inclusive curriculum. These advancements have the ability to be transformative and shift the paradigm of what it means to learn, but it is not the overall solution. The extensive elements of student diversity make technology only one possible development in a myriad of requirements.

Economic, social, political and cultural marginalisation in the sector

'Little makes more difference to people's lives than the empowerment they receive from education' (John Hayes MP, cited in Wolf, 2011, p6). Accounts from FE learners demonstrate that further education courses are pathways to overcoming economic, social, political and cultural marginalisation. Labelling is experienced at school, and for some students this stemmed from undiagnosed learning difficulties and disabilities, but in others it relates to other aspects of perceived identity – such as originating from a housing estate with a negative reputation. Labelling contributes to a lack of aspirations, as well as underachievement, self-doubt and anger. Labelling theory can be defined as the process by which society comes up with descriptors to identify people who vary significantly from the norm (Hardman et al., 1999). There are at least two elements in the definition by Hardman et al. (1999) that are worth noting. First, it is the role of society in coming up with 'names' that denote certain behaviours within society. In that respect, society creates 'names' and expects the individuals to behave as characterised by the name, which can be a type of self-fulfilling prophecy, where an individual accepts their label and the label becomes true in practice. In that regard, labels are a societal construction that can have severe detrimental implications for students. Second, the definition brings in the importance of norms and the role they play in assessing behaviour. Norms suggest orthodoxy, and failure to meet the expected norms contributes to labelling.

Key questions

With the requirement placed on institutions to create inclusive environments, has this led to labelling, and if so, positively or negatively?

The views of women and men, and the roles appropriate to each, can stem from the political, social and cultural climate, and relates to social power structures (Lynch and Feeley, 2009). The lasting culture of subjects that have developed traditions and identities, rooted in wider gendered social contexts, are difficult to change, especially in the more traditional sense of vocational education. However, this is something that the post-compulsory education sector can work towards and should aspire to overcome. Those who attempt crossing into non-traditional areas of study and work for their gender have not always found the experience tolerable. The small numbers of women in engineering, construction, science or technology training can find themselves having to conform into a male-dominated culture where they are viewed merely as tokens. Research in the construction field has found that women's arrival polarises attitudes and results in misogynistic behaviour to the newcomer, who faces risk and isolation if they challenge the existing state of affairs. Lynch and Feeley (2009) draw upon prior research to address how subject cultures can change within traditional male-dominated fields, so long as there is a concerted effort to ensure that they do. The research cited below highlights the efforts being made within the sector to challenge the more traditional/restrictive outlook on educational routes and employment, and how they can shift paradigms of expectation and aspiration.

Following the Equality Act 2010, an increased awareness and focus on the importance of diversity has led to more emphasis being placed on the reduction of bullying, harassment and discrimination. The Equality Act 2010 says you must not be discriminated against because:

- you are heterosexual, gay, lesbian or bisexual;

- someone thinks you have a particular sexual orientation (this is known as discrimination by perception); or

- you are connected to someone who has a particular sexual orientation (this is known as discrimination by association).

However lesbian, gay, bisexual and transgender (LGBT) students entering college are likely to have experienced bullying at school previously, with the School Report (University of Cambridge Centre for Family Research, 2017) finding that more than half of LGBT young people who were bullied feel that homophobic, biphobic and transphobic bullying has had a negative effect on their plans for future education (e.g. by deciding not to go to university or college). Student accounts of bullying can take many forms, but the sector needs to do more to limit these occurrences and educate staff and students around difference and acceptance. Numerous examples of bullying and harassment across the FE sector can be sought to highlight the need for engagement in LGBT issues from both a staff and student perspective.

Two student quotes highlight the issues faced:

> I didn't know much about LGBT people at the time and I was only exposed to the negative connotations that people sometimes associate with being gay, so I just saw being called a lesbian as an insult and was too embarrassed to admit to anyone that I had been called that. Olivia, 16, sixth form college (South West)

> Because the teachers made fun of trans people I was too scared to tell anyone about it. Jesse, 17, FE college (Scotland)

(University of Cambridge Centre for Family Research, 2017, p17)

A crucial aspect of reducing such marginalisation in the sector is to ensure staff have the required skills and training to deal with such occurrences and be appropriately equipped to deal positively with the situation and plan an inclusive curriculum. The drivers of social mobility have been defined as those factors that tackle the 'opportunity deficit' and counteract patterns of advantage and disadvantage (Department for Business, Innovation and Skills, 2015). They encompass improvements in income, employment and educational attainment. These drivers operate within a wider context of the structure of the labour market and the income distribution. Recent data show a reduction in the number of adults accessing 'second chances', as measured by the number achieving qualifications at level 3.

The further education sector offers new opportunities for individuals whose lives have been adversely affected by the linearity of our compulsory education system. According to the evidence from this project, further education can enhance social integration, social mobility and the agency of these learners, with consequent knock-on effects in their families and communities. Recognition of further education's role in strengthening social integration, social mobility and social equality extends beyond the provision of apprenticeships to the large groups of young people and adults who access further education in order to change their place in our society, and to benefit themselves, their families and their communities. To do this, a shift in approach is required at all levels, as well as a commitment to have a sector ready to meet the needs of its intended learner group.

Medical and social models of disability in the sector and their impact

Education or segregation?

Two of the most widely used models of disability are the 'medical' and 'social' models, which differ greatly and can have a lasting impact in both an educational and societal setting. According to Scope (2018), the medical model of disability focuses on disabled people by their impairments and differences. It highlights what is 'wrong' with the person and can create low expectations and lead to a loss of independence, choice and control in their lives. Negative attitudes based on prejudice or stereotypes (sometimes called disablism) can stop disabled people from having equal opportunities. In contrast, the social model of disability is a way of viewing the world from the disabled person's point of view. The model suggests that people are disabled by barriers created in society, not by their impairment or difference. Barriers can be physical or attitudinal, with both having a detrimental impact on disabled people. The social model promotes the recognition of these various barriers, which can make life harder for disabled people, with a view to removing the barriers to create equality and offering disabled people more independence, choice and control. Inclusion London (2018) visualise the difference between both clearly in Figure 5.4.

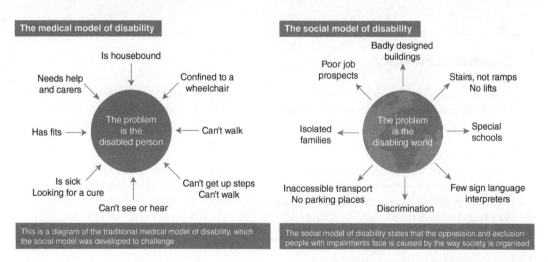

Figure 5.4   Medical and social models of disability

The medical model of disability rests on assumptions of what a disabled person cannot do as a result of their physical or cognitive impairment, whereas the social model of disability is focused on the restrictions placed on a person by the ways in which everyday life is organised.

Case study

City of Westminster College

At the City of Westminster College in London, an example of the social model of disability and inclusion can be seen in the way that students overcome limiting factors in the educational setting, demonstrating the ability to limit the disadvantages that a student may face and facilitate an inclusive environment for all. In a computer science course, one student with a hearing impairment was accompanied by a sign language interpreter. Yet neither the teacher, nor most of the other students, were versed in British Sign Language (BSL). A technological solution (Microsoft Teams) was used to help bridge this communication gap, allowing students to collaborate more effectively. The impact on the classroom and students was immediate. They all had the ability to communicate clearly and quickly, without the barrier of the spoken word.

(Microsoft Education Team, 2018)

This case study demonstrates a social model approach to overcoming the limiting factors in the educational setting, demonstrating the ability to limit disadvantages a student may face and facilitate an inclusive environment for all to flourish. Inclusive design not only relates to the curriculum, but the physical environment too. Without a clear and strategic focus on inclusive education as a sector, as well as at an institutional and individual level, we could fail hundreds of thousands of current and potential learners in the sector. For any institution or provider taking the medical model of disability, it will be failing to provide the opportunity for any disabled person to enhance their opportunities and quality of life (Alliance for Inclusive Education, n.d.).

Chapter summary

If we are to create a truly inclusive sector, where the vast array of diversity is catered for and welcomed, appropriate funding and professionalisation of the roles must be a focus. Ensuring educators are given the space to develop as dual professionals is key, with a focus on inclusive practice a top priority. The tendency to limit professional development opportunities around inclusive practice is not intentional, but is far from a priority. Raising awareness of the range of inclusive and assistive technologies widely available, often within currently used resources, can be transformative. During the planning and designing of curriculum, more emphasis on the demographic of learners, the language projected, and the potential impact of the labelling and stereotyping that has become ingrained in modern society must be addressed.

Additional factors to consider when designing a curriculum must include:

• the background and experiences of the teacher/student;

• the ethos and culture of the classroom;

• the inclusion of assistive technology for all;

- the language of the content (gender, age, sexuality, faith, culture, etc.);

- the physical environment, and how this can impinge or enhance the teaching; and

- assessments, and how they can be inclusive for all and limit the need for adjustments.

References

Alliance for Inclusive Education (n.d.) *The Medical Model of Disability*. Available at: www.allfie.org.uk/definitions/models-of-disability/medical-model-disability/

Biggs, J. (2003) *Aligning Teaching for Constructing Learning*. s.l.: Higher Education Academy.

Centre for Studies on Inclusive Education (1996) *Inclusive FE: The Report of the Further Education Funding Council Learning Difficulties and/or Disabilities Committee Chaired by Professor John Tomlinson*. s.l.: Centre for Studies on Inclusive Education.

Chiappe, B.T. (2013) *Modelling Provision for Learners with Dyslexia in General Further Education Colleges in Yorkshire and Humberside*. Leeds: University of Leeds.

Children and Families Act 2014. Available at: www.legislation.gov.uk/ukpga/2014/6/introduction/enacted

Department for Business, Innovation and Skills (2015) *The Contribution of Further Education and Skills to Social Mobility*. London: Institute for Employment Studies.

Department for Education (2017) *Post-16 Technical Education Reforms*. London: DfE.

Disability Discrimination Act 1995. Available at: www.legislation.gov.uk/ukpga/1995/50/introduction

Disabled Persons Act 1986. Available at: www.legislation.gov.uk/ukpga/1986/33/introduction

Education Act 1981. Available at: www.legislation.gov.uk/ukpga/1981/60/enacted

Education and Training Foundation (2018) *Workforce Data and SIR Data Insights*. s.l.: SIR Data Insights.

Education (Handicapped Children) Act 1970. Available at: www.legislation.gov.uk/ukpga/1970/52/enacted

Equality Act 2010. Available at: www.legislation.gov.uk/ukpga/2010/15/introduction

Equality and Human Rights Commission (2017) *What is the Equality Act?* Available at: www.equalityhumanrights.com/en/equality-act-2010/what-equality-act

Groff, J. (2013) *Technology-Rich Learning Environments*. Paris: OECD.

Hardman, M.L., Egan, W.M. and Drew, C.J. (1999) *Human Exceptionality: Society, School, and Family*, 6th edn. Boston, MA: Allyn & Bacon.

Inclusion London (2018) *The Social Model of Disability*. Available at: www.inclusionlondon.org.uk/disability-in-london/social-model/the-social-model-of-disability-and-the-cultural-model-of-deafness/

JISC (2015) *Digital Student Exemplars*. Available at: https://digitalstudent.jiscinvolve.org/wp/files/2015/09/FE22_3_Environment_-_Kingston_FINAL.pdf

Kennedy, H. (1997) *Learning Works: Widening Participation in Further Education*. London: Further Education Funding Council.

Learning and Work Institute (2018) *Rates of Adult Participation in Learning*. Available at: www.learningandwork.org.uk/our-work/promoting-learning-and-skills/participation-survey/rates-of-adult-participation-in-learning/

Lifelong Learning UK (2005) *Further Education Workforce Data for England: An Analysis of Staff Individualised Record (SIR) Data 2004/2005*. s.l.: Skills for Business.

Lifelong Learning UK (2011) *Further Education College Workforce Data for England: An Analysis of the Staff Individualised Record Data 2008–2009*. s.l.: s.n.

Lynch, K. and Feeley, M. (2009) *Gender and Education: Lessons from Research and Policy*. s.l.: European Commission's Directorate.

Microsoft Education Team (2018) *London College Gives Every Student a Voice with Teams*. Available at: https://educationblog.microsoft.com/2018/03/london-westminster-college-teams-student-voice/

Oxford Reference (n.d.) *Warnock Report (1978)*. Available at: www.oxfordreference.com/view/10.1093/oi/authority.20110803121057612

Parliament UK (n.d.) *Education and Skills: Third Report*. Available at: https://publications.parliament.uk/pa/cm200506/cmselect/cmeduski/478/47805.htm

Scope (2018) *The Social Model of Disability*. Available at: www.scope.org.uk/about-us/our-brand/social-model-of-disability

Shepherd & Wedderburn (2005) *A New Definition of Disability: The Discrimination Act 2005*. Available at: https://shepwedd.com/knowledge/new-definition-disability-discrimination-act-2005

Slee, R. and Allan, J. (2001) Excluding the included: a reconsideration of inclusive education. *International Studies in Sociology of Education*, 11(2): 173–192.

Soden, B. (2017) The case of Screencast feedback: barriers to the use of learning technology. *Innovative Practice in Higher Education*, 3(1): 1–21.

Special Educational Needs and Disability Act 2001. Available at: www.legislation.gov.uk/ukpga/2001/10/introduction

Taba, H. (1962) *Curriculum Development: Theory and Practice*. New York: Harcourt, Brace & World.

Thomas, L. and May, H. (2010) *Inclusive Learning and Teaching in Higher Education*. London: Higher Education Academy.

Tyler, R. (1949) *Basic Principles of Curriculum and Instruction*. Chicago, IL: University of Chicago Press.

University of Cambridge Centre for Family Research (2017) *School Report: The Experience of Lesbian, Gay, Bi and Trans Young People in Britain's Schools 2017*. Cambridge: Stonewall.

Wolf, A. (2011) *Review of Vocational Education*. London: DfE.

6
LITERACY AND NUMERACY IN THE POST-COMPULSORY SECTOR

Michael Smith

Key words – employability; situated learning; discourse; problem-solving; engagement

Introduction

This chapter explores what is understood by the terms literacy and numeracy. It looks at how they are positioned in the context of the post-compulsory sector, with reference to policy and curriculum documents. The chapter includes links to wider research and theoretical models that offer multiple interpretations of literacy and numeracy. Throughout the chapter, you will find 'key questions' and examples of 'good practice' in literacy and numeracy pedagogy.

Literacy

> ### Key questions
>
> What is meant by the term literacy?

At its core, literacy is concerned with language and understanding. To describe someone as literate is to infer they have the capacity to access, process and derive meaning from information coded in words, figures and symbols. Many definitions position literacy as relating to language comprehension (reading) and language production (writing and speaking). Within this, there are varying schools of thought; some view literacy as a set of skills that can be acquired step by step, whereas others argue that literacy cannot be detached from the context in which it operates, and that these contexts shape what literacy is, depending on to which purposes, settings and participants it can be located.

A logical place to start is the Adult Literacy Core Curriculum (DfES, 2001a), which defines the standards that learners in the post-compulsory education phase work towards when developing their literacy skills through study of functional skills English. The curriculum adopts the view that literacy exists as a discrete set of skills, and differentiates between three dimensions in the process of reading and writing:

- text focus addresses the overall meaning of the text, the ability to read critically and flexibly and write in different styles and forms;

- sentence focus deals with grammar and sentence structure; and

- word focus looks at the individual words themselves, their structure, spelling and individual character.

(DfES, 2001a, p7)

This definition charts the scope and scale of literacy skill development in a technical paradigm, spanning whole-text through to word-level understanding. The curriculum notes that educators should 'draw simultaneously on all three in their work on reading and writing' (DfES, 2001a, pp7–8) and encourages a holistic approach to how these foundation concepts are taught. In spite of this, by positioning literacy as a list of technical skills that span a range of competency levels, the curriculum, perhaps unintentionally, stirs the notion that literacy is no more than a set of atomised criteria that exists separate from any context in which it might be located.

In a broader tradition, the International Adult Literacy Survey (IALS) (OECD, 2000) determines literacy to be 'the ability to understand and employ printed information in daily activities at home, at work and in the community, to achieve one's goals and to develop one's knowledge and potential' (px). Here, we see an acknowledgement of literacy as a socially situated skill, albeit one grounded in understanding more prominently than production. There is a recognition that literacy has a socially situated purpose. Strikingly, the survey observes that many international studies concerned with determining literacy rates have in the past treated it as a binary condition that adults either have or do not have, and that the IALS themselves used to define literacy in terms of an arbitrary standard of reading performance alone (OECD, 2000, px). In its place now, there is a recognition that standards of proficiency in literacy exist on a continuum pertaining to the above broader definition (see Figure 6.1).

What is the importance of literacy for the lifelong learner?

As seen above, there exists much debate about what literacy is, what skills it comprises and how it can be understood in evolving contexts. This section will explore some of the definitions that see literacy as a set of skills that can be learnt independently of social context, what Street (1984) terms 'autonomous literacy', in greater depth. With this backdrop, we will consider the importance of literacy for the lifelong learner.

The Adult Literacy Core Curriculum describes the remit of its standards as to 'provide a map of the range of skills and capabilities that adults are expected to need in order to function and progress at work in society' (DfES, 2001a, p3). These standards are uniquely positioned in the UK education sector as they span a huge age range of potential learners, from 14 upwards with no determinable upper limit. Despite the wide age range, the focus remains predominantly on readying people for employment. When it was published, the Core Curriculum stated that:

over 7 million adults in England have difficulties with literacy … Three attainment groups make up the 7 million:

- *a higher-level group (just over 4 million) who need fairly modest help to 'brush up' their skills to the required level;*
- *a middle-level group (just under 1.5 million adults) who have greater difficulty and need more specific and in-depth help;*
- *a lower-level group (just under 1.5 million adults) who require intensive teaching by specialist teachers.*

(DfES, 2001a, p5)

The impact of low literacy rates has far-reaching consequences, including on employability. A 1993 survey that determined people with pre-entry-level skills had access to only 1 in 50 of lower-level jobs, those with entry-level skills had access to 50 per cent, and those with level 1 skills had access to 75 per cent (Institute for Employment Studies, 1993). More recently, the National Literacy Trust (2011) determined that '1 in 7 (14.9%/5.1 million people) adults in England lack basic literacy skills', suggesting that despite a slight improvement in the decade since the publication of the Core Curriculum, much work is still needed.

Brynner (2002) examined the relationship between literacy and employability by analysing data on basic skills that were collected in large-scale birth cohort studies undertaken in 1970. Brynner studied the functional literacy of samples of 10 per cent of the participants in each study through the use of a half-hour testing session at the end of a 45-minute interview. The results showed 'striking evidence of the significance of literacy and numeracy skills both in gaining employment on leaving school, but also in retaining it and progressing in it' (Brynner, 2002, p25). He concluded by noting that 'not succeeding in this area is the phenomenon that poses perhaps the biggest threat to cohesive society, social exclusion' (Brynner, 2002, p26).

These figures hold wider implications for the post-compulsory sector here; they infer that even after completing compulsory education to the age of 16, many are still lacking in their literacy skills and require further support. This is made all the more significant when considering that a command of literacy can provide agency and empowerment for individuals that can enable successful integration into employment and wider society. It is here the post-compulsory institutions – private training providers, offender learning providers, further education colleges, community colleges – provide access points for adults that are looking to engage in literacy learning.

What is meant by literacy as a social practice?

Those that subscribe to the idea that literacy is a socially situated practice believe that the fundamental skills of reading, writing and communicating, both verbally and in written form, cannot be detached from the context in which they function. Scribner and Cole (1981) observe that 'literacy is not simply knowing how to read and write a particular script, but applying this knowledge for specific purposes in specific contexts of use' (p236). This tradition is not concerned with standardised criteria that define what literacy is in universal terms, and instead champions an appreciation of the multitude of ways that we participate in the exchange of information with one another, in formal and informal scenarios, in the workplace and at home, and through face-to-face and digital mediums. This section will examine this idea further and consider implications for practitioners in post-compulsory settings.

In a call for greater appreciation of socially situated forms of literacy, Hamilton (2010) argues:

> *Something as basic as writing down the bare facts of your life is never done in a vacuum. These facts are written in a CV, a diary or an autobiography. They may be written by another person in medical case notes, given as a speech at a funeral or other ceremonial event, or reported in a police statement. In each situation, the form and process of the writing will be different … In other words, literacy is situated and embedded in local activities, and can never be pulled out and captured as a separate and unvarying thing.*

> (pp7–8)

As practitioners in the post-compulsory sector, we have to appreciate the experiences our learners arrive with at the beginning of their learning journeys, and the communities and cultures to which they belong. Moreover, in appreciating these, we need to also be aware that their command of literacy that has been forged through participation in these social situations does not always correlate with those that they are required to adopt in order to succeed in formal assessment tasks (Smith, 2016).

The idea of recognising and certificating achievement in socially situated forms of literacy was explored by Stewart (2011). Stewart drew from Ireland's Further Education Training Awards Council (FETAC) standards as an accreditation system that offers what Derrick et al. (2007) term 'local freedom' in the assessment of performance that 'provides flexibility, without undermining the rigour of summative assessment processes' (Stewart, 2011, p47). He goes on to cite examples of community-led activities that his learners have participated in, and how they can be designed so as to best capture the literacy practices naturally occurring in these. It remains to be seen if such an approach might be applied successfully to a vocational programme of study, which itself would offer practitioners a contextually rich foundation on which to build a similar model, but the model does appear to lend itself to adaptation. Stewart (2011) maintains that 'while the practitioner may be the expert in terms of teaching methodology and assessment procedures, the student is the expert in their use of literacy' (p52), and that by forging opportunities for learners to develop and demonstrate their command of literacy in contextually familiar scenarios, practitioners are more effectively meeting the needs of their learners.

What might effective practice in the development of students' literacy skills look like?

This section features a good practice example that will draw from and make reference to the definitions, theories and research above in considering an example of effective practice in developing learners' command of literacy. This example is situated within the context of a large London-based FE college. The learners mentioned are all between the ages of 16 and 18 on full-time vocational programmes spanning a range of curriculum areas, and are working towards completing a functional skills English qualification. The example details the approach taken by a teacher in getting to know their learners in the first few sessions of the programme so as best to support their development throughout the academic year.

Identifying learning needs: why the first sessions matter

The first few weeks with new learners is a crucial time. It is where learners' learning and support needs can be identified, where the learners' interests and goals become apparent, and where norms of behaviour and expectations are set and established. In post-compulsory settings, where time with learners is often shorter than in other phases of education, this is even more critical. On identifying and agreeing learning goals, Crowley (2008) suggests:

> *If we accept the importance of prior learning and experience, then the trajectory of learning must be shaped by both the teacher and the learner; the teacher can be the source of ideas to consider, but the informed decision must be owned by the learner.*
>
> (cited in Coffield, 2008, p12)

This is effective practice, in that it encourages teachers to collaborate with their learners when shaping their targets and goals, rather than adopting a one-way transactional relationship. Such interactions will foster greater agency in the learner's ownership of their learning. Moreover, this approach can be reconciled with Stewart's (2011) claim that the learner is the expert in their own literacy, with the practitioner an expert in teaching methodologies. The practitioner can influence the aims and goals that are agreed with knowledge of the curriculum, 'beneficial' secondary discourses and desirable forms of literacy, and identified learning needs, while at the same time appreciating the learner's socially situated literacy skills.

Supporting literacy development and shaping learning trajectories

Current orthodoxy in the post-compulsory sector typifies that learners undertake a computer-based assessment of their English skills to establish their learning needs at the beginning of their study programme. The shortcomings of these systems have been well documented (Roberts and Smith, 2014), namely that they supplant practitioners' professional judgements (Clarke, 2001) and fail to take into account what Coffield (2008) notes as the 'importance of prior learning and experience' that responds to the 'personal and cultural experiences of different groups' (p12).

Rather, what makes for a more effective start to a new programme for learners are sessions that holistically incorporate all elements of the literacy curriculum. These sessions might draw from topics such as music, storytelling, communication, comedy and other socially situated contexts from which literacy-rich content can be found. This has the benefit of inducting and engaging learners into the programme in a more humanised manner. Through these sessions, an initial approximation of learners' skills, needs, interests and behaviours can be gleaned by the practitioner. The judgements they make from these can then inform the discussions with learners when agreeing their learning aims and goals, and ensure that an individual's command of literacy, through whatever form this takes, is shaping their future learning trajectory.

Numeracy

Key questions

What is meant by the term numeracy?

Michael Smith

The term numeracy has multiple meanings, ranging from some that comprise basic skills of computation to those that emphasise broader skills, knowledge and understanding (UNESCO, 2016). Some understandings of numeracy characterise it as being a less prestigious equivalent to mathematics because it is only considered to be relating to basic arithmetic operations (Tout and Schmitt, 2002). In some public discourses, it is thought to represent the foundation skills acquired at a young age by schoolchildren, on which more complex mathematical knowledge can be later built. But in other schools of thought, numeracy is recognised as a crucial body of skills, knowledge and understanding that provides the lifelong learner a way of better understanding and engaging with the world around them. Steen (1997) refers to the five different dimensions of numeracy as follows:

practical, for the immediate use in the routine tasks of life; civic, to understand major public policy issues; professional, to provide skills necessary for employment; recreational, to appreciate games, sports, lotteries; and cultural, as part of the tapestry of civilization.

(pxxii)

These 'dimensions' outline the scale and breadth of numeracy as a concept. The implications for practitioners are pronounced, in that many of these 'dimensions' cannot be taught in rote fashion. Instead, there is a need to develop in learners a transferability in the underpinning skills and strategies that can enable them to address new, unfolding and emerging problems as they are encountered. As stated by the OECD (2012b), 'mathematical knowledge is developed in many situations and not only through formal education' (p39).

The relationship between numeracy and mathematics is a divergent one depending on the definition of numeracy that is adopted. Coben (2006) observes that some conceptualisations of numeracy regard it as being contained within mathematics (DfES, 2001b; Wedege et al., 1999), while some see numeracy as 'not less than maths but more' (Johnston and Tout, 1995). Here, O'Donoghue (2003) notes that 'mathematical skills alone do not constitute numeracy' (p8). On the international stage, Maguire and

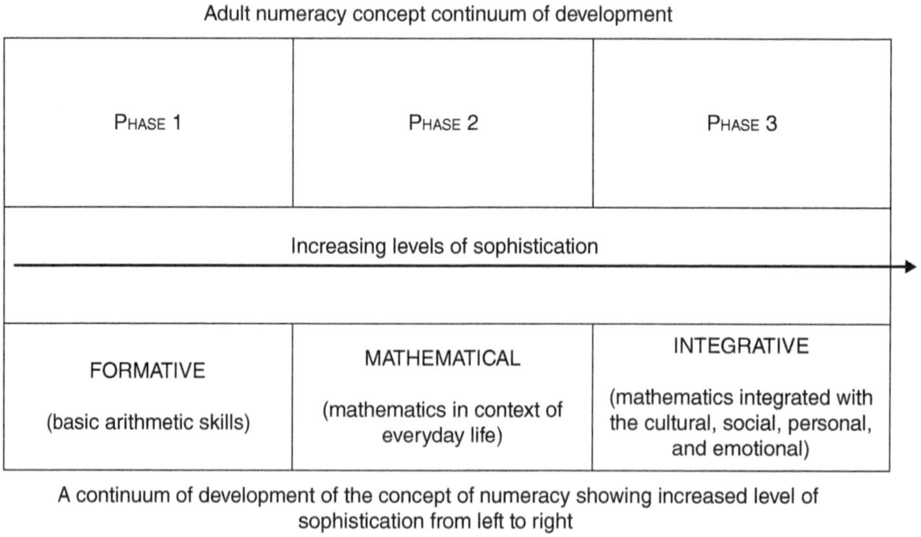

Adult numeracy concept continuum of development

PHASE 1	PHASE 2	PHASE 3
Increasing levels of sophistication		
FORMATIVE (basic arithmetic skills)	MATHEMATICAL (mathematics in context of everyday life)	INTEGRATIVE (mathematics integrated with the cultural, social, personal, and emotional)

A continuum of development of the concept of numeracy showing increased level of sophistication from left to right

Figure 6.1   Adult numeracy concept continuum of development

O'Donoghue (2002) propose a framework for gauging increasing sophistication in how numeracy is conceptualised in policy terms along a continuum.

The *formative phase* here represents the view that numeracy is a basic skill acquired in childhood, and one that presupposes that all adults need is simple arithmetic. The *mathematical phase* accounts for mathematics in context, in which the importance of mathematics in everyday life is recognised. The *integrative phase* views numeracy as 'a complex multifaceted sophisticated construct incorporating the mathematics, cultural, social, emotional and personal aspects of each individual in a particular context' (O'Donoghue, 2003, pp155–156). When the framework was published, Maguire and O'Donoghue situated the development of the concept of numeracy in policy terms in the UK as being in the mathematical phase, with only Denmark and Australia being located in the integrative phase.

It is perhaps pertinent to explore the mathematical phase in greater detail here, considering the role of policy in defining and governing the form and function of numeracy in the post-compulsory sector. In this definition, numeracy can be understood as the 'ability to use mathematics in everyday life' (National Numeracy, 2011). Subsumed in this are mathematical ideas of interpreting numbers and figures, processing information, solving problems, and applying logic and reasoning in specific scenarios. Numeracy is positioned as being grounded in specific contexts and scenarios, with reference to users of numeracy who apply it in practical ways, rather than operating solely in abstracted forms of mathematics. Parallels can be drawn between numeracy and literacy, both of which are useful and necessary in helping individuals to function in modern life.

From a UK policy stance, the Adult Numeracy Core Curriculum defines numeracy as 'the ability to use mathematics at a level necessary to function at work and in society in general [i.e.] to: understand and use mathematical information; calculate and manipulate mathematical information; interpret results and communicate mathematical information' (DfES, 2001b, p3). The Core Curriculum became the basis for the development of functional skills mathematics qualifications, first proposed in the Tomlinson Report (DfES, 2004), and subsequently given key roles in later policy documents (*14–19 Education and Skills*, DfES, 2005; *Implementing the Leitch Review of Skills in England*, DfES, 2007), that emphasised the need for more robust qualifications that could help get unemployed adults back into work. Functional skills maths can be studied across a range of levels, spanning from entry level to level 2, with level 2 seen as the 'benchmark' standard that lifelong learners work towards achieving.

The relationship between 'functional maths' and practical definitions of numeracy are closely aligned, in that functional skills qualifications aim to equip learners 'with the knowledge, skills and attributes needed to succeed in adult life, further learning and employment' (DfES, 2004, p4). Despite this, the decision to use *mathematics* in the qualification title rather than numeracy is perhaps indicative of the desire to separate these qualifications from conceptions of numeracy that portray it solely as a set of basic skills. This trend is one that continues to pervade the sector; in more recent times, we have seen the introduction of Core Maths, a level 3 qualification intended to complement academic and technical programmes and designed to prepare learners for the varied contexts they are likely to encounter in future employment and life – for example, financial modelling and analysis of data trends. Regardless, it is clear that numeracy still has an important role to play in post-compulsory sector policy. In his *Review of Post-16 Maths*, Sir Adrian Smith observed that 'Everyone needs good numeracy ... Such skills are necessary elements of citizenship, for example to participate in or follow public debate individuals need the ability to understand and potentially challenge arguments based on quantitative evidence' (DfE, 2017, p20).

Overall, we can see that numeracy is understood to mean different things in different contexts, and that it shares a complex and integral relationship with broader mathematics. In policy terms, we can recognise clear and consistent evidence of numeracy being positioned as a set of skills that, once attained, underpin mathematical faculties that are important for functioning in employment and wider society.

Problem-solving

Key questions

What is the relationship between numeracy and problem-solving?

This section will explore the relationship held between numeracy and problem-solving. With numeracy often positioned as being concerned with interpreting, understanding and applying numbers and figures in context, we can observe how this relationship is an important one. This union of ideas carries significant implications for practitioners in the post-compulsory sector; it is common convention for maths and numeracy assessments to require learners to problem-solve hypothetical scenarios that have been designed in a way to assess the application of skills rather than just the skills themselves. This is not solely restricted to the post-compulsory sector, but the explicit links between qualifications such as functional skills maths and the development of readiness for employment contribute to the prominence of contextualised problem-solving.

Let us first establish the domains of numeracy that an individual must navigate when problem-solving. In accounting for this, the Programme for the International Assessment of Adult Competencies (OECD, 2012a) draws a parallel between numeracy and what they term 'numerate behaviour', through which an individual can problem-solve. This numerate behaviour 'involves managing a situation or solving a problem in a real context, by responding to mathematical content/information/ ideas represented in multiple ways' (OECD, 2012b, p34). Each of these facets are elaborated thus:

1. *In a real-life context*: These are presented as including everyday life, work-related, society or community, and further learning. It is argued that performance in any one of these contexts require a combination of cognitive and non-cognitive elements and accordingly numeracy needs to be considered as a competency and not just a set of technical skills.

2. *By responding*: Responses are grouped under three headings: identify, locate and access; act upon or use; and interpret, evaluate/analyse and communicate. It is proposed that problem-solving is not a separate response to each of these, but rather comes about as a result of the demands of the scenario.

3. *To mathematical content/information/ideas*: This includes quantity and number; dimension and shape; pattern, relationships and change; and data and chance.

4. *Represented in multiple ways*: The representation of mathematical information can take many forms including: pictures, symbolic notation, formulae, visual displays including diagrams, charts, graphs and tables, maps, and texts where words and phrases carry mathematical meaning.

(OECD, 2012b, pp34–38)

Problem-solving is recognised as an 'enabling process' that negotiates with each of these facets of numerate behaviour when attempting to reason a solution. It is stated that in order to solve problems, individuals have to reconstruct reality in a mathematical way. Strategies that an individual might employ in doing this include 'extracting relevant information from a task, rewriting the task, drawing pictures, diagrams or sketches, guessing and checking, making a table, and/or generating a concrete model or representation' (OECD, 2012b, p38). In summary, we can take problem-solving to be a soft skill that can be learned and improved on, as with other skills, through guidance and purposeful practice.

How might we teach problem-solving skills in numeracy effectively?

With the dimensions of numerate behaviour and a broader understanding of problem-solving alongside this now identified, we can consider approaches to developing the problem-solving skills of our learners.

George Pólya's *How to Solve It* (1945) provides a four-step procedure for solving mathematical problems:

1. Understand the problem.

2. Devise a plan.

3. Carry out the plan.

4. Reflect on what has been done.

The first two steps detail activity that will inform how to find the solution, the third is to test this out, and the fourth involves reflecting and learning from the process to enable the user to predict what strategy to use to solve future problems.

Mathematics Education Innovation's *Mathematical Problem Solving* (MEI, 2017) builds on this. Each step of the procedure is expanded on, with considerations made into the kinds of support that might be provided to help progress learners along. They highlight the potential difficulty in learners 'understanding the problem' in the very first step, and suggest framing questions to assist with this:

•   Do the final stages of the problem indicate where the problem is trying to take you?

•   Are there some clear 'target' expressions you have to find?

•   Does the form of what you have to find (what it looks like) indicate the skills that you need to use?

(MEI, 2017, p13)

These questions are designed to get learners thinking about possible solutions to the problem, and to get them moving on from any initial apprehension they might be feeling.

At the second stage, devising a plan is reframed as 'engaging with the problem'. Techniques to assist at this stage comprise looking for patterns, looking for a visual representation, working backwards when the solution is part known or estimated, listing all of the possibilities, and making educated guesses and testing them (MEI, 2017, pp15–16).

In the third stage, it is recommended that learners reflect in the moment as they execute their plan and aim to solve the problem. They note that it 'feels good to string some mathematical processes together and this can give the an illusion of progress', and that as such it is 'vitally important for students to reflect on what they are achieving when they are running through calculations' (MEI, 2017, p16) to ensure that progress is made even if the correct solution is not reached. Similarly, the fourth stage recommends reflection, only this time after the event. It is noted that this is often the most neglected of the four steps, but also the one that can have the greatest impact in developing problem-solving skills that are transferrable across scenarios and contexts.

We can take that these steps to problem-solving can be shared with learners to help them as they work through the process. It would be wrong to assume, however, that these alone will ensure all learners are always able to successfully and independently reach correct solutions to problems. MEI's (2017) assertion is that these steps engender an active and self-directed approach to problem-solving, but that the importance of a teacher to guide this process remains crucial. Preceding MEI's report, Pólya (1945) notes that problems should be proportionate to learners' current knowledge, and that they should be based around skills that are already embedded. Even in the capacity as a facilitator, in which their learners adopt a self-directed approach, it is argued that the teacher plays a key role in challenging curiosity, selecting suitable problems and posing stimulating questions that help the learners solve the problem themselves.

Learner engagement: a common theme

Engagement is a fundamental component of learning. It is synonymous with ideas of participation, involvement and being active in the moment. The benefits of being engaged in learning is demonstrable; Brophy and Good (1986) identify the relationship between 'academic engaged time' and student achievement as one of the 'most consistently replicated findings' in the literature (p360). Moreover, the risks in not being engaged in learning are well documented too (Claxton, 2007; Gilbert, 2007; Prensky, 2001). Engaging learners in developing their command of literacy and numeracy is crucial in post-compulsory settings. Learners are required to study these subjects up to the age of 18, but often view literacy and numeracy as optional additional components to their main vocational programme, rather than core skills that underpin all of their disciplines.

Key questions

How can we engage students in becoming more literate and numerate in post-compulsory settings?

The following section features project findings from a National Institute of Adult Continuing Education (NIACE) research project (NIACE, 2015) into how learners can be effectively engaged in their learning of GCSE English and mathematics. Forty-eight learners aged between 16 and 24 contributed to the report through interviews and focus groups that included questions on their attitudes towards learning and how they felt they could be more effectively supported. The questions asked learners to reflect on their experiences of learning in schools and post-compulsory settings as a means of comparison. The responses from learners are summarised below.

On teaching and learning

The majority of learners felt that the teaching of English and maths was better post-16 than it had been at school. This was attributed to teachers providing better explanations of topics and employing more engaging teaching methods such as in-class discussions. The importance of assessment and feedback was also noted, with learners highlighting how regular assessment allowed them to see their progress (NIACE, 2015, p17).

On their peers

Learners spoke positively about their peers, stating that many of their peers were very supportive of each other. They recognised that peer collaboration helped to create an environment in which confidence could be built and easier ways of tackling problems were learnt (NIACE, 2015, p23).

On attitudes towards English and maths

Many learners spoke about feeling more motivated to engage with English and maths in post-compulsory settings, which was largely attributed to them seeing the value of these subjects in relation to their progression in education and employment. In contrast, very few learners suggested they were motivated to engage in learning solely as a result of enjoyment in the subject, suggesting that external factors around progression are more powerful than intrinsic motivators (NIACE, 2015, p25).

Key messages for the sector

The findings of the report were compiled into a series of key messages for the sector that span each of the themes identified above:

Learners are more likely to engage and have positive attitudes to maths and English when:

1. *Learning is fun, interactive and practical.*

2. *There is a strong understanding of the purpose and importance of holding these qualifications, relating them to real life situations.*

3. *Learning has a personal relevance which is explained to learners and feedback on their performance relates the activities to the qualification they are studying for.*

4. *Appropriate time and support is given to individuals to practise challenging topics, in and out of the classroom.*

5. *There is a clear assessment process with clarity on marking schemes, enabling learners to adequately prepare for exams and coursework assignments.*

6. *Timely initial assessments are carried out to identify support needs, and any additional support learners require is put in place as soon as possible.*

7. *Class sizes are kept small, enabling teachers to have sufficient time to support all learners. Larger classes are perceived by learners as a barrier to effective teaching and learning.*

Michael Smith

8. *Teachers have strong behaviour management skills to reduce the impact of peers distracting learners during lessons.*

9. *A supportive environment is fostered in the classroom and learners are encouraged to ask for help from teachers and peers. Embarrassment can be a strong factor in learners not asking for support when they need it.*

10. *Practitioners listen to learners' needs and tailor support and learning accordingly. Practitioner research is an effective way to gather learner voice to inform future work and delivery. It can enable practitioners to gain a deeper understanding of learners' individual needs, allowing them to tailor support and learning programmes accordingly.*

(NIACE, 2015, pp28–29)

In the above recommendations, we can recognise some similar themes to those already discussed in the above sections, including the importance in placing literacy and numeracy within a specific and relevant context, and employing timely initial assessments that can accurately identify support needs. In addition to this, many of the suggestions relate to fostering a nurturing environment in which learners feel comfortable with their peers and their teacher, receive individualised support, and are actively involved in owning their learning, through knowledge of assessment processes.

Chapter summary

Literacy

- Literacy is a complex and fluid concept, and is recognised as being more than just basic technical skills in reading, writing and speaking.
- A good command of literacy can provide agency and empowerment for individuals that can enable successful integration into employment and wider society.
- Initial assessment is crucial when working with learners to develop their command of literacy, and should unearth and draw from the literacies in which the learner is already proficient.

Numeracy

- Definitions and understandings of numeracy differ in what this comprises; some position it as being concerned with basic arithmetic, while others assert it underpins cultural, social, emotional and personal aspects of each individual.
- Problem-solving can play a valuable role in resolving mathematical operations.
- Problem-solving is a skill that can be taught, practised and improved upon.

Literacy and numeracy

- Engagement in learning enhances the rate at which learning occurs.
- A supportive environment for learners of literacy and numeracy can help to foster engagement in learning these subjects.

References

Brophy, J. and Good, T. (1986) Teacher behavior and student achievement. In M. Wittrock (ed.), *Handbook of Research on Teaching*. New York: Macmillian.

Brynner, J. (2002) *Literacy, Numeracy and Employability*. Queensland: Adult Literacy and Numeracy Australian Research Consortium, Nathan Queensland Centre.

Clarke, S. (2001) *Unlocking Formative Assessment: Practical Strategies for Enhancing Pupils' Learning in the Primary Classroom*. London: Hodder Education.

Claxton, G. (2007) Expanding young people's capacity to learn. *British Journal of Educational Studies*, 55(2): 1–20.

Coben, D. (2006) What is specific about research in adult numeracy and mathematics education? *Adults Learning Mathematics: An International Journal*, 2(1): 18–33.

Coffield, F. (2008) *Just Suppose Teaching and Learning Became the First Priority*. London: Learning and Skills Network.

DfE (2017) *Review of Post-16 Maths*. London: DfE.

DfES (2001a) *Adult Literacy Core Curriculum*. London: DfES.

DfES (2001b) *Adult Numeracy Core Curriculum*. London: DfES.

DfES (2004) *14–19 Curriculum and Qualification Reform: Final Report of the Working Group on 14–19 Reform*. London: DfES.

DfES (2005) *14–19 Education and Skills*. London: DfES.

DfES (2007) *World Class Skills: Implementing the Leitch Review of Skills in England*. London: DfES.

Derrick, J., Ecclestone, K. and Merrifield, J. (2007) A balancing act? The English and Welsh model of assessment in adult basic education. In P. Campbell (ed.), *Measures Success: Assessment and Accountability in Adult Basic Education*. Edmonton, AB: Grass Roots Press.

Gilbert, J. (2007) Catching the knowledge wave: redefining knowledge for the post-industrial age. *Education Canada*, 47(3): 4–8.

Hamilton, M. (2010) Literacy in social context. In N. Hughes and I. Schwab (eds), *Teaching Adult Literacy: Principles and Practice*. Milton Keynes: Open University Press.

Institute for Employment Studies (1993) *Basic Skills and Jobs*. London: Adult Literacy and Basic Skills Unit.

Johnston, B. and Tout, D. (1995) *Adult Numeracy Teaching: Making Meaning in Mathematics*. Melbourne: National Staff Development Committee for Vocational Education and Training.

Maguire, T. and O'Donoghue, J. (2002) A grounded approach to practitioner training in Ireland: some findings from a national survey of practitioners in adult basic education. In L.Ø. Johansen and T. Wedege (eds), *Numeracy for Empowerment and Democracy? Proceedings of the 8th International Conference of Adults Learning Mathematics – A Research Forum (ALM8)*. Roskilde, Denmark: Centre for Research in Learning Mathematics, Roskilde University, in association with Adults Learning Mathematics – A Research Forum.

MEI (2017) *Mathematical Problem Solving: A Guide for Teachers*. Available at: http://mei.org.uk/problem-solving-guide

National Literacy Trust (2011) *What Is Literacy?* Available at: https://literacytrust.org.uk/information/what-is-literacy/

National Numeracy (2011) *What Is Numeracy?* Available at: www.nationalnumeracy.org.uk/what-numeracy

NIACE (2015) *Engaging Learners in GCSE Maths and English*. Available at: www.learningandwork.org.uk/wp-content/uploads/2017/01/Engaging-learners-in-GCSE-maths-and-English.pdf

O'Donoghue, J. (2003) Mathematics or numeracy: does it really matter? In J. Evans, P. Healy, D. Kaye, V. Seabright and A. Tomlin (eds), *Policies and Practices for Adults Learning Mathematics: Opportunities and Risks. Proceedings of the 9th International Conference of Adults Learning Mathematics (ALM9) – A Research Forum*. London: ALM and King's College, London.

OECD (2000) *Literacy in the Information Age: Final Report of the International Adult Literacy Survey*. Paris: OECD.

OECD (2012a) *About PIAAC*. Available at: www.oecd.org/skills/piaac/

OECD (2012b) *Literacy, Numeracy and Problem Solving in Technology-Rich Environments: Framework for the OECD Survey of Adult Skills*. Paris: OECD.

Pólya, G. (1945) *How to Solve It*. Princeton, NJ: Princeton University Press.

Prensky, M. (2001) Digital natives, digital immigrants. *On the Horizon*, 9(5): 1–6.

Roberts, P. and Smith, M. (2014) *Make Them Laugh, Make Them Cry: Re-Imagining the Initial Assessment Process for GCSE English Students in the Further Adult and Vocational Education Sector in England*. Available at: www.excellencegateway.org.uk/content/etf2596

Scribner, S. and Cole, M. (1981) *The Psychology of Literacy*. Cambridge, MA: Harvard University Press.

Smith, M. (2016) Exploring the role of literacy in students' writing development in the further education and vocational education sector. *Teaching in Lifelong Learning: A Journal to Inform and Improve Practice*, 7(1): 25–35.

Steen, L.A. (ed.) (1997) *Why Numbers Count: Quantitative Literacy for Tomorrow's America*. New York: College Entrance Examination Board.

Stewart, J. (2011) *Extending the Assessment of Literacy as Social Practice*. Dublin: National Adult Literacy Agency.

Street, B.V. (1984) *Literacy in Theory and Practice*. Cambridge: Cambridge University Press.

Tout, D. and Schmitt, M.J. (2002) The inclusion of numeracy in adult basic education. In J. Comings, B. Garner and C. Smith (eds), *Annual Review of Adult Learning and Literacy: Volume 3*. San Francisco, CA: Jossey-Bass.

UNESCO (2016) *Assessment of Adult Numeracy Skills*. Available at: http://unesdoc.unesco.org/images/0024/002455/245573E.pdf

Wedege, T., Benn, R. and Maaß, J. (1999) 'Adults learning mathematics' as a community of practice and research. In M. van Groenestijn and D. Coben (eds), *Mathematics as Part of Lifelong Learning: The Fifth International Conference of Adults Learning Maths – A Research Forum (ALM-5)*. London: Goldsmiths College, University of London.

7

PARENTAL INVOLVEMENT, STUDENT MOTIVATION AND ATTAINMENT IN FE

Judith Darnell

Key words – parental involvement behaviours; parenting styles; student attainment; intrinsic motivation; student autonomy; ownership

Introduction

Anyone involved in teaching and training in FE is likely to have an interest in the different extrinsic and intrinsic factors that may relate to attainment for students. These factors range, for example, from classroom-based teaching styles, student aspirations and socio-economic background to the effects of peers, siblings and day-to-day family home life. This chapter will discuss different external influences for student motivation and attainment but will specifically critique the idea of parental involvement for FE students. Gaining an understanding of the potential influences of parental involvement (both positive and negative) is important for educators in FE in order to understand the varied backgrounds that FE learners can experience. Learner perceptions of parental involvement as a potential external influence on student outcomes is a vastly under-represented area of research in PCET, and hence the chapter will discuss my recent research project, which focused on this important topic.

The chapter begins by reviewing current literature regarding aspects of motivation for FE learners and the ways in which parents are seen to be most likely involved with college. It presents some visual supports to aid understanding of the different kinds of parental involvement strategies that parents of FE students can employ, and explains what the term 'parental/carer involvement' can look like from the student perspective. It then critiques the common perception that parental involvement in any form can directly result in higher student attainment. It reviews home–college communication strategies and policy and explores the delicate balance between catering for both the Ofsted requirement for parents to be kept informed of learners' progress and the drive for student autonomy and ownership in student learning. Finally, the chapter then reports on a research project investigating students' perceptions of their 'parental involvement behaviours' (PIBs) within the home and explores associations between these and student outcomes. It argues that parental involvement behaviours are reactive to student needs, and so are also likely to be affected by previous student performance and not influential in their own right. This section also offers a reflection on the specific kinds of involvement that are likely to be most helpful for adolescent learners (i.e. post-16), since parents are likely to be limited to emotional – rather than academic – support techniques. A theory that developed from the research is explained. Specifically, these models are presented in order to highlight the need for more investigation into the range of student experiences that are reported by students in FE and are tentatively used to make suggestions for lecturers, tutors and policymakers in FE institutions in the key summary section, keeping in mind that findings for this particular study are limited to one institution, and that more research is needed in this area.

Motivation for FE learners

Student motivation for learning and high aspirations are commonly acknowledged as being important in driving students to perform well within education (Bolkan and Goodboy, 2015; Goldman et al., 2017; Rothon et al., 2011; Ryan and Deci, 2002; Wallace, 2014). Indeed, Goldman et al. (2017) note that students who are intrinsically motivated view academic activities to be worthwhile and meaningful, which drives students to work hard and perform highly, and Bolkan and Goodboy (2015) argue that support for autonomy is likely to increase motivation for adolescent students specifically. Despite this, Wallace (2014, p346) notes that a general lack of motivation is a 'common phenomenon' in FE specifically. She recognises that there are benefits for student learning and motivation where teachers have positive, cheerful interactions with students, but that in the long run this is limited to a superficial level. She concludes that the root causes of student motivation levels lie beyond their control. Interestingly, Ryan and Deci (2002) link motivation to self-determination theory and suggest that motivation is a natural human process but that it can be discouraged or enhanced by the students' social environment. Likewise, Koshkin et al. (2018) recognise that motivation is affected by a complex array of beliefs, motives and external pressure factors, which includes social class and family expectations. Social environment is therefore important in securing the optimum supports for student engagement and can be heavily influenced by parental attitudes. Indeed, Curzon and Tummons (2013) note that parental attitude has the ability to effect intrinsic motivation for students. They suggest that for some parents, college may be a symbol of failure as a second-best option because it may reflect their child's lack of ability to obtain full-time employment. If this parental view is shared with students, it is likely to diminish intrinsic motivation. Indeed, the introduction of the RPA (raising of the participation age) is likely to affect the attitudes of students enrolled at FE colleges and their motivations for or rejections of an imposed further programme of learning. However, the particular benefits of different types and attitudes of parental involvement for college-aged students has not been widely recognised within FE literature.

What is parental involvement?

Key questions

Can parental involvement in any form directly result in higher student attainment?

During my research, I developed an understanding of in-home parental involvement behaviours that have been researched worldwide during the past two decades. In Figure 7.1, I present a mind map that sets out these behaviours (Darnell, 2019).

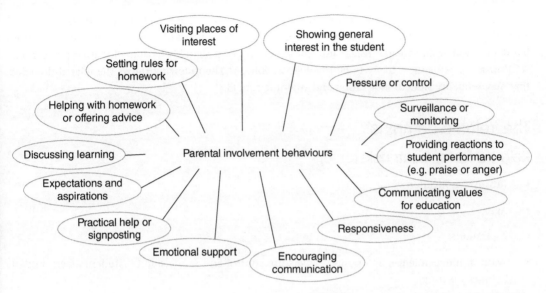

Figure 7.1   Parental involvement behaviours

Please note that this group of behaviours is not exhaustive, but offers a range of behaviours that can be considered to demonstrate parental involvement. As can be expected, and as a general rule, the *amount* of involvement is not identified to be the most influential factor, and *quality* of interactions with parents appears to be more important for learners than quantity. However, once children reach the stage of adolescence, the *types* of parental involvement that are viewed by students as helpful in regard to attainment are limited to a few particular behaviours that are related more closely to emotional support than practical 'hands-on' support or surveillance. Additionally, it is worth noting here that the idea of 'parental involvement' encompasses behaviours, feelings and attitudes that are not 'fixed' and are often based within and developing from a historical context where the relationship between learner and parent is constantly evolving. It is therefore nonsense to suggest that one style (i.e. a group of positive behaviours) will *result* in high attainment, although *associations* between learner experiences and attainment may be apparent.

The way in which parents are involved in college students' education has been reported minimally in literature and extends mainly to the parental role in the choice of educational pathway for learners (Daley et al., 2015; Huddleston and Unwin, 2013). There is a reported growth in consumerism within education, where parents and their children are 'consumers' who have the power to choose educational providers. Indeed, Huddleston and Unwin (2013) discuss the idea that previous governments have introduced an element of parental choice in education that should close the social class attainment gap, but their explanation of the benefits of parental involvement do not move beyond this idea. Similarly, when reviewing the idea of democratic professionalism of FE teaching staff, Daley et al. (2015) suggest that parents have a role in education because links between educational professionals and stakeholders are formed. They do not, however, probe the role that parents hold or how best FE parents can support the learning of their children. Curzon and Tummons (2013) offer more insight into the influences of parental behaviours, where they discuss that parental models are likely to influence student behaviours within college but also that some students may be attending college primarily in response to parental pressure or in response to a threat of having to leave the parental home, which challenges the popular assumption that students in FE have chosen freely to attend. Additionally, Spenceley (2014) mentions that parents are likely to use the language of values surrounding education but does not offer any greater insight into the influences of parental behaviours for attainment in FE. So, how are parents most likely to be involved at college? The following shows the related domains that may influence student motivation and attainment in FE.

The 'related domains'

Related factor 1: intrinsic factors

- Intrinsic motivations.

- Age.

- Aspirations.

- Want of independence, autonomy, ownership, control and responsibility (student assertion and boundary-setting).

- Personality traits (which may affect subsequent relationships).

Related factor 2: internal family factors

- Emotional PIB: support, encouragement, reassurance, advice, interest, praise, prompts, safety net.

- Practical PIB: signposting, resource-finding, timekeeping, proofreading, transport, food, clothes, accommodation.

- DAPSS: parental pressure, mistrust, top-down, forceful, controlling (for minority of students).

- Economic and social capital: resources, space, contacts, signposting, opportunities.

- Siblings/family structure: nuclear/single-parent family, close extended family, positive and negative effect of siblings, relationships between parents and child.

- Parental competence/abilities/available time to help/parental tiredness or stress.

- Parental aspirations and expectations.

- Responsiveness.

Related factor 3: external factors

- Peers.

- Earning money.

- Casual work.

- Travel to college.

- College course – level 3 content.

- College staff – knowledge and support (safety net).

What evidence is there that parental involvement has an impact on outcomes in FE?

The notion of 'parental involvement' is widely presumed to initiate or encourage higher grades for learners of all ages. Therefore, most people may be likely to presume that parental involvement is almost certainly an 'enhancer' when referring to its effects on attainment. A majority of studies from different parts of the world have indicated that, for younger children of preschool and primary school age, practical and emotional support, demonstration, surveillance (i.e. observing children doing their homework) and role modelling, interest shown through extensive engagement and communication of expectations, aspirations and values for education, are all positively associated with attainment.

Studies into parental involvement are generally difficult to compare and contrast, since they have focused on different age groups of students, different choices of participants or respondents (i.e. teachers, parents or learners), different measures of parental involvement, different measurement of outcomes, and different geographical locations that may influence findings or interpretation of findings due to culture or ethnicity.

Key theory

Theorising parental behaviour

Boonk et al. (2018) reviewed 75 parental involvement studies that have been published since 2003 and found that different parental behaviours appear to be influential for learners at different ages. The team looked at early childhood (0-6 years), elementary school (6-12 years) and middle school and beyond (12-18 years). Their main finding was a shift through the ages in relation to types of support where a reduction in practical support such as checking homework was associated with higher academic performance for older (adolescent) learners. This study is primarily based on school-aged children but is presented here in the absence of any similar work completed in FE colleges. Table 7.1 shows the different kinds of parental behaviours that related positively to attainment specifically for the age group 12-18 years.

Table 7.1 Parental influences and associations with attainment for adolescent students

Positive relation with attainment for ages 12-18	Negative relation with/not related to attainment for ages 12-18
High parental expectations and aspirations	Academic pressure
Valuing academic attainment and reinforcing learning at home	Parental control
	Interference with homework
Academic encouragement and support	Homework-related conflict
Parent-child educational discussions	Checking homework
	Controlling homework
	Helping with homework

Source: Adapted from Boonk et al. (2018, p33)

Key theory

The negative outcomes of parental involvement

Interestingly, a study by Robinson and Harris (2013) claimed to find that when looking at 63 measures of involvement with students aged 18, parental involvement in general was negatively associated with outcomes, and so this study concluded that some elements of parental involvement can actually be harmful in relation to attainment. This piece of research has, however, been criticised for suggesting that one set of behaviours directly causes a 'negative result' in student performance. Instead, a suggestion is that students who are performing poorly have responsive parents who recognise their struggles, and so become involved to try to help them, and this is the reason for the association (Greene, 2015). This idea has previously been referred to as the 'reactive hypothesis' (Hampden-Thompson et al., 2013).

Another important concept to highlight here is the idea of an 'academic trajectory', which Sy et al. (2013) argue is created in the home at the age of 3 or 4, where some parents plan a route for their children on their educational journey. This journey is encouraged through communicating the idea of high expectations, aspirations and values for education and for children's future success. This suggests that performance during adolescence is related more closely to previous learner experiences rather than being affected by individual parental influences and behaviours at age 16+.

Key questions

Is intrinsic motivation more influential in relation to student grades than extrinsic factors for college-aged students?

Although there is some research based on parental involvement for adolescent students in the UK and abroad, at present there is no published research into student perception of parental involvement in FE and attainment in the UK college context. However, my current research, which is seeking to 'fill this gap', investigates the complex associations between student perception of PIB and attainment, and will be referred to in the subsequent paragraphs. For the moment, the important question to ponder relates to whether the relationship between parental involvement and attainment is more complex than initially presumed.

Key questions

Is parental involvement an enhancer or an inhibitor in relation to attainment?

In short, there is no simple answer, but parent–student relationships need to be viewed in a context that is nuanced, flexible and based on reciprocity, which means it is incredibly difficult to decipher a 'one-style-fits-all' philosophy. Parental involvement has many facets, but for college-aged students it appears that one particular set of behaviours relating to homework/coursework help and surveillance associates negatively with attainment. This has been discovered by Boonk et al. (2018), Darnell (2019) and Hampden-Thompson et al. (2013). Reasons for this may relate to the 'reactive hypothesis', as mentioned above, where parents become actively involved because they perceive their child to be struggling.

Links between parents and college

In the FE college context, many lecturers and managers have undoubtedly experienced frustration at the lack of parental attendance at parents' evenings and, from experience, many note the distinct differences in perceived parental interest for college learners opposed to the parents of learners who attend a school or college sixth form. However, let us not presume that this lack of contact/interest is solely due to resistance from parents. Indeed, many college learners will have based the decision to study at college both on the choice of course and on the notions of autonomy and independence that is promised by an FE college educational experience. For parents who are aware of this element, which may have directed their child's decision-making process, this is likely to be reflected in their respect for student desire to have ownership for their learning and autonomy in decisions relating to their college course. Most colleges have a prospectus that communicates an expectation that students are encouraged to become mature and independent learners. Likewise, many FE staff fail to receive communication from parents on receipt of their child's course report, which lecturers are likely to have spent many hours producing. Again, this should not necessarily be viewed as parental resistance, but is more likely to be a response to learner request to respect freedom of study within the FE context.

My research project found that parental behaviours that related to respect for student autonomy, independence, ownership, pride and aspirations were noted as most important to students when discussing their perception of parental involvement behaviours, as shown in the examples below:

> Don't get me wrong, I love Mum and Dad to bits … but I don't need them to be involved with my work and education any more. College should be an independent place to be. I chose this route because I know I am capable, I am driven, I don't want them watching my every move. It makes it too much like school. I'm doing this course for me, not them.

> I am older so I need to make my own decisions about working hard. Even though my parents can guide me, it is my decision.

> I made the decision to come here and do this course and I feel like I'm more motivated to actually do well and I'm enjoying it, so I think it's good that I'm in control of my future.

> (Darnell, 2019)

Additionally, prior to the start of the research project when I was both teacher and personal tutor for a group of health and social care students, I explained to the students that parents would receive student reports. On hearing this, one student looked at me disbelievingly and said, 'Really? A *parent* report? Woooah, this is too much like *school* …'. Your first thought on reading this might be that this student was a poor performer and did not want her parents to have her progress revealed to them. However, as it happens, this student was very able in her work but had a firm view of independence and wanted to be proud of her accomplishments and to be treated like an adult. However, in contrast to this, the view of Ofsted in particular is that parents at FE level must be kept informed:

Ofsted's *Further Education and Skills Inspection Handbook* states an expectation that parents:

> *are engaged in planning learner's development; they are kept informed by the provider of each learner's attendance, progress and improvement ... Where appropriate, parents are provided with clear and timely information that details the extent of learners' progress in relation to the standards expected.*

> (Ofsted, 2016, pp42, 44)

Although Ofsted do not state an expectation for parents to be involved in supporting their child directly in the home, they do expect some form of communication/link between college and parents. Clearly, it may be difficult for colleges to get the balance right between allowing FE learners complete autonomy and ownership but adhering to guidance published by Ofsted for which colleges are judged against.

Key questions

How do you view this need for the college to balance catering for both student and Ofsted?

How might these requirements of the different parties work together, and what might this look like in your setting?

The value of parental involvement: perception complexity

Clearly, there are more complexities within the idea of parental involvement and its influence on student attainment than might be first realised. In light of the above, it is interesting to note that many colleges do have a parental involvement strategy where they view parents to be:

- crucial in supporting students in their studies;
- important in influencing students in regard to retention and attendance; and
- able to directly increase attainment for students.

Indeed, in line with the requirements of Ofsted (above), college policies often suggest that they seek clear and strong channels of communication with parents/guardians and recognise the value of the support of parents/guardians to enable students to realise student success and maximise achievement. It is not surprising, then, that many colleges attempt to encourage parents to remind their children how many hours they should spend studying outside of college hours, and if assignments are due then parents might help by checking with the students that this work is under completion. Although this sounds very positive and supportive (and more importantly, it appears from first glance that these parental behaviours are very likely to result in higher grades for students), the links between parental involvement and grades, as reported by students themselves, are more complex. Students largely do not report finding surveillance a helpful strategy. The majority of students like to feel a sense of freedom but acknowledge the occasional requirement for a 'safety net' provided by parents in times of need *at the student's request*. This safety net may take the form of a conversation around the student's work, a question about subject content, or even just an encouragement or boost that the end is in sight during hard times. The crucial distinction here is that from the perspective of students, support from parents ought to be sought by the students and delivered by the parent rather than forced or instigated by the parent.

To be clear, I am not suggesting that parental involvement at FE level is not at all necessary, but I am attempting to highlight that the relationship between parental involvement and attainment for adolescent students is not straightforward and it cannot be presumed that parental involvement will cause or influence students in a particular way. Every learner–parent relationship and exchange will be rooted in a context that has been developed over time and can, at times, be sensitive and fragile. It is also crucial to note that this chapter is not suggesting that learners' parents should not be contacted at all. Indeed, when appropriate, any safeguarding concerns should involve parents and other multi-agencies in order to protect vulnerable learners. However, when a concern does not relate to safeguarding, but lack of student motivation or drive, it might be worth approaching the student as the first port of call rather than the parent since extrinsic factors are less likely to change attainment.

Parental involvement behaviours: the associations with attainment and the issues surrounding parental 'capabilities'

Four parental/carer behaviours that associate positively with attainment are:

1. Lifelong high parental expectations.

2. Parental aspirations in relation to student's hard work and future career accomplishments.

3. Parental trust.

4. Parental respect.

(Darnell, 2019)

However, this is not to suggest that these parental behaviours/attitudes/factors will always *induce* high grades for students, and when investigating parental involvement, we must keep in mind that they do not *cause* students to gain more UCAS points, but that they *associate* with more UCAS points. These two relationships are very different, and in this instance the above factors appear to associate together due to the responsiveness of the parent–child relationship. Responsiveness is a key aspect when looking at the social relationships surrounding parental involvement.

Case study

Parental capability

To explain the idea of parental responsiveness, let's take an example student and call her Hayley. Hayley is academically gifted and has always had a drive to do well in her education. In her primary school education, she was always above average, even in the reception class. She worked hard through primary and secondary school and made her college choices based on her interests and career prospects. At college, her parents trusted that she would succeed as they had always had high expectations of her since she was a young child and could see that she was doing well. They knew that she would go on to have a successful career because she was able and hard-working, and subsequently they respected her decisions in regard to her education. Hayley achieved very highly in her college course and gained high UCAS points. During her course, she was asked to respond to a questionnaire on her parental involvement. She reported within the document that her parents had always expected her to do well, had always inspired her to work hard and to pursue her dream career, and that they fully trusted and respected her decisions.

Here, we see an example of parental responsiveness. At college, Hayley's parents never felt the need to engage in surveillance techniques for Hayley. They did not need to stick the assessment schedule to the fridge door and to constantly ask her about her deadlines. Their trust, expectations and aspirations resulted in respect for Hayley's autonomy with her work, and hence the association is apparent between these four factors and a high level of UCAS points.

The importance of intrinsic motivation

Intrinsic motivation has been found to be more influential for student grades than external factors, including individual parental involvement behaviours. I developed the 'elements of motivation' (EoM) diagram (see Figure 7.2), and it reflects student perceptions relating to the influences for motivation in regard to college work and attainment.

The EoM diagram indicates the most influential factors in regard to student attainment, as reported by students themselves.

Key questions

Why is student motivation placed centrally?

Student motivation is placed centrally because it can be influenced by/associated with other factors and is seen as the principal focus for the diagram. The inner layer shows the 'intrinsic drivers' for motivation, which are 'age', 'student pride', 'student aspirations', 'responsibility and ownership for learning' and 'freedom and choices'. These can associate with each other as well as directly relating to student motivation (e.g. student pride has links with responsibility, ownership for learning, and success).

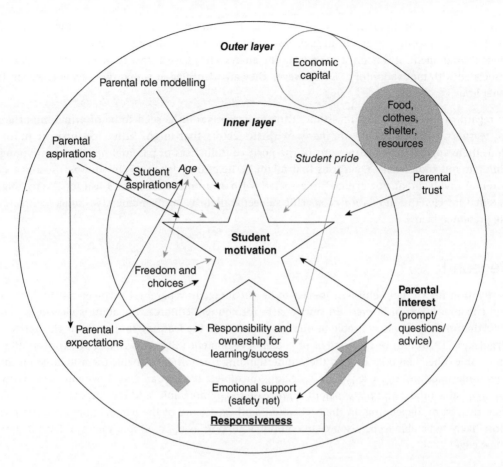

Figure 7.2   The elements of motivation

The outer layer holds 'extrinsic drivers' for motivation that associate with PIB. These are reported as parental trust, parental expectation, parental role modelling, parental aspiration, parental interest and emotional support. As well as directly affecting student motivation, these extrinsic drivers may also influence or associate with the intrinsic drivers for motivation (e.g. parental aspirations can often be reflected in student aspirations; see arrows). They can also link with more than one aspect (e.g. parental expectations can link to student age and responsibility/ownership for learning). As is seen for parental expectations and parental aspirations, there can also be links between extrinsic drivers (shown by the double-ended arrow between the two).

Emotional support is placed in such a way as to underpin the inner layer, which is additionally reinforced by responsiveness (i.e. the idea that PIB is fluid and responsive to student need or situation and is best understood through deep relationships and understanding). A key feature of emotional support was seen to be offered through parental interest (seen by asking questions, prompts, or offering advice or help), and this is shown by the arrow that connects the two within the outer layer. This idea of emotional support can also be perceived by students as non-specific, such as parents enquiring how students are (and not specifically relating to their studies). Therefore, emotional support remains separate from parental interest.

Economic capital and practical support in terms of accommodation, food and clothes are aspects positioned in the outer layer within their own spheres because, although necessary in some ways for student attainment, it was not clear during the analysis in phase 1 how these directly or indirectly associated with motivation, if at all. However, they are identified as supportive elements within the outer layer.

In regard to the above diagram, student intrinsic motivation is seen to be of prime importance for learners. Although there are many extrinsic factors that might influence intrinsic motivation, there appear to be distinctions in the positive influences of parental help between younger children and adolescents. Questions that might be helpful to ask are: Why are specific aspects of parental involvement not deemed to associate with attainment for level 3 learners? Why might parental interference in relation to specific subject content be problematic? Two suggested reasons are presented below.

Reason 1

Motivation for younger children is seen to be encouraged by parental involvement for learning and encouragement of interest. In simple tasks for younger children, the adult is viewed as 'more able' than the child and so is able to nurture and scaffold the learning for the child. This relates to Vygotsky's (1978) idea of the zone of proximal development (ZPD), where through conversation a 'more able other' can offer or lend their understanding to another to enable them to build on their own understanding. However, when reflecting on subject content at level 3, we must ask: Who is the more able other? Might the parent/carer cease to be 'more able' and the student be 'more able' than the parent, depending on the background and experience of the parent? Might the parent be more likely to be able to be a source of emotional support as opposed to a source of level 3 course knowledge?

Reason 2

Shulman (1986) discusses the idea of 'pedagogical content knowledge', which relates to the idea that teachers and trainers not only have subject knowledge in order to teach at level 3, but also reflect pedagogical knowledge, which ensures that the information is absorbed and understood by the learner effectively. He stated that these two areas should not exist as mutually exclusive of each other, but should be combined within teacher training programmes, as they are inextricably linked and form the foundation for specialist teacher knowledge. Although some parents may have studied in the same academic field as their child (and so may have some subject/content knowledge), Shulman (1986) would argue that they are at a disadvantage in teaching that information to their child due to a lack of combining their understanding of the pedagogy in relaying that knowledge.

The above examples have hopefully unpicked some of the reasons why parents are less likely to be able to support their children holistically, and indicates that their emotional support may be more useful to students than offering their practical/subject knowledge support or surveillance methods. The majority of students reported that parents had not acquired the skills and knowledge to be able to help them with their studies at level 3. Indeed, when asked about practical help at home, one young man replied in a frustrated tone, 'Mum can't help me with anything. I think that if I did have her involvement, I would end up with worse grades than I am currently getting!'

A new theory: the six main models of FE students' experiences

The six main models of student experiences have been segregated into three separate tables (see Figures 7.3–7.5). Each table contains two models of student experience within it, as shown below:

1. Absent parental interest ('dismissed' and 'headstrong').

2. Independence ('clarified independence' and 'supposed independence').

3. Authoritised parenting ('positive expectations, aspirations and values' and 'negative expectations, positive aspirations and values').

The tables include the model names and a percentage for the proportion of students who are believed to experience these parental behaviours.

Model name	Absent parental interest	
	Dismissed (4%)	Headstrong (3%)
Independence	Student may not feel independent/ responsible or may be forced into independence through no offer of support, confused motivation	Students are intrinsically motivated to be independent, have responsibility and ownership
Trust	Trust not openly communicated	
Support and interest	Absent interest and no safety net	
	Student wants parent to show interest, but doubts it would happen	
Parental competence	Low parental competence	
Support offered	Practical home support: accommodation, services, food	
	In some cases, student may live independently	
Outcomes	Lower outcomes	Higher outcomes
Motivation	Motivation is absent, weak or forced by external aspects, may be driven/supported by teachers at college or peers	Motivation is intrinsic
Autonomy, choices and freedom	Age-related expectations: autonomy, choices and freedom due to lack of care or interest	

Figure 7.3   Absent parental interest

Students in the above models report that parents fail to have an interest in them or their work. Additionally, parents fail to provide any kind of support (either practical or emotional). However, some students who face this situation, and are naturally determined, focused and driven to succeed, take responsibility and ownership for learning, and are intrisically motivated and hence perform highly. Those that do not have the intrinsic motivation feel dismissed and perform poorly.

My research found that students report two main kinds of independence. Those with 'clarified independence' are highly trusted by their parents and receive no practical work-related support at all because they are highly motivated and enjoy a sense of freedom and autonomy. However, they are

Model name	Independence	
	Clarified independence (35%)	*Supposed independence (47%)*
Independence	Strong intrinsic motivation Responsibility Ownership	Motivation either newly formed in recent years or in the process of forming, possibly from parental aspirations or expectations/discussions about the future
Trust	High trust	High/moderate trust
Support and interest	◄──────────── Responsiveness ────────────►	
	Safety net rarely needed	Safety net always available Help usually requested
Parental competence	Mix of parental competence	
Support offered	Parents may use economic capital to support student No practical support provided	Practical home support: resources, accommodation, services, food, economic capital Practical educational support: proofreading, signposting, guidance Emotional support: encouragement via communication: questions/prompts/interest/reassurance (student is likely to appreciate this support)
Outcomes	Mainly a mix of average to high outcomes, depending on other factors	
Motivation	Motivation formed through communication of high values for education, parental aspirations/inspirations and expectations over time	
Autonomy, choices and freedom	Age expectations: choices, freedom Autonomy	
	Very high	Slightly lower

Figure 7.4   Independence

aware that their parents will be there for them if they ever needed it. Those in the 'supposed independence' model enjoy a sense of freedom and autonomy, but are fully willing to ask for help from parents when they need it and feel a sense of emotional support from parents. Parents can help practically, economically and emotionally.

Students who report parental behaviours that are controlling and based on surveillance measures experience 'authoritised' parenting. Students report feeling little independence and speak of control or pressure to work in order to satisfy parental wishes/requests. Students report that parents are frequently involved despite whether they have low or high academic competence, but parents usually assume high competence and believe they know more than their children about college work, which makes students frustrated. In this way, the students are authoritised (i.e. someone assumes authority over them). Students in this model are likely to receive practical home support (i.e. accommodation/food), practical educational support (help with essay writing and researching course/subject content) and possibly some emotional support (through encouragement). Importantly, the main difference between the two categories is whether the behaviours are coupled with positive or negative communication of expectations. Here, we see that where parents have high expectations, students attain more highly. However, this is most likely to be based on previous student achievement, rather than high expectations in themselves being an influencing factor for student attainment at this level.

Dismissed (4%)	Headstrong (3%)	Clarified independence (35%)	Supposed independence (47%)	Authorised (positive expectations, aspirations and values) (6%)	Authoritised (negative expectations – positive aspirations and values) (5%)
				Little independence	
Student may not feel independent/responsible or may be forced into independence through no offer of support, confused motivation	Intrinsically motivated to be independent, responsibility and ownership	Strong intrinsic motivation Responsibility Ownership	Motivation either newly formed in recent years or in the process of forming, possibly from parental aspirations or expectations/ discussions about the future	Motivation is driven by parent but internalised	May lack own intrinsic motivation
Trust not openly communicated		High trust	High/moderate trust	Low trust	
Absent interest No safety net		← Responsiveness → Safety net rarely needed	Safety net always available Help usually requested	Parental support feels overpowering, surveillance can be high	
Low parental competence Student wants parent to show interest, but doubts it would happen		Mix of parental competence		Parent assumes they have high competence and can be helpful	
Practical home support: accommodation, services, food In some cases, student may live independently		Parents may use economic capital to support student No practical support provided	Practical home support: resources, accommodation, services, food, economic capital Practical educational support: proofreading, signposting, guidance Emotional support: encouragement via communication: questions/ prompts/interest/reassurance (student is likely to appreciate this support)	Practical home support: resources, accommodation, services, food, economic capital Practical educational support and emotional support through encouragement	
Lower outcomes	Higher outcomes	Mainly a mix of average to high outcomes, depending on other factors		High outcome	Low outcomes
Motivation is absent, weak or forced by external aspects, may be driven/supported by teachers at college or peers	Motivation is intrinsic	Motivation formed through communication of high values for education, parental aspirations/ inspirations and expectations over time		Motivation driven by parent through DAPSS and parental aspirations	Intrinsic motivation is likely to be weak
Age-related expectations: autonomy, choices and freedom Forced (absent parental interest)	Natural	Age expectations: choices, freedom Autonomy Very high	Slightly lower	Control, pressure Parental satisfaction Little respect for student choices	

Figure 7.5   Authoritised parenting

So, what can we learn from this new theory?

The 'six main models of students' experiences' diagram generated from gathering student experiences suggests that there are six main categories through which student experiences can be viewed. Some of these categories are starkly different from one another and, particularly for the 'dismissed' group, can expose a worrying sense of neglect. Students should and must remain the focus in relation to college performance. Students' independence and feeling of autonomy should be supported to enable intrinsic motivation to drive attainment and interest.

Key questions

Could college staff organise more students' evenings/meetings as opposed to parents' evenings?

Could college staff write reports relating to performance and direct it to/discuss it with the student as well as send it to the parent?

Individuals working in FE should consider this idea carefully, including whether they can create any strategies that offer students a chance to celebrate ownership of work and encourage autonomy, as student drive has been found to relate to intrinsic motivation rather than external (parent) motivation. Students who experience the 'dismissed' model of parenting seek tutor support, both for practical and emotional support, and, although they may not perform highly, positive attention and understanding from college staff may make them more likely to gain a pass for their course.

Chapter summary

- Parental involvement is multifaceted and built on fluid and ever-changing dynamic relationships and historical/cultural aspects, and is responsive to student need and past student attainment.

- Intrinsic motivation underpins student performance, and PIB does not associate (other than those behaviours that are based on prior student attainment).

- FE college staff should focus on the students in relation to care, respect and attention, and refrain from going straight to the parents unless there is a safeguarding issue. Students seek autonomy and ownership in relation to their studies.

- Parents are limited in their understanding of specific learning techniques and subject content knowledge at level 3, but the majority are reported to be able to offer general emotional support if sought by the student.

- Students who report being 'dismissed' have given up on their parents, and, although they are not happy, they generally do not want their parents to change. They appreciate and strive to gain support from college staff through one-to-one tutorials and need patience and understanding since they report lacking love and positive attention at home.

- Findings suggest that PIB choices are immersed within the relationships between parent and student that are based on reciprocity and responsiveness. This idea of responsiveness suggests that parent-student relations are both fluid and nuanced, and change depending on factors such as current exam results or feedback and student intrinsic motivation, but importantly are primarily based on prior student educational performance.

References

Bolkan, S. and Goodboy, A.K. (2015) Exploratory theoretical tests of the instructor humor–student learning link. *Communication Education*, 64: 45–64.

Boonk, L., Gijselaers, H.J.M., Ritzen, H. and Brand-Gruwel, S. (2018) A review of the relationship between parental involvement indicators and academic achievement. *Educational Research Review*, 24: 10–30.

Curzon, L.B. and Tummons, J. (2013) *Teaching in Further Education: An Outline of Principles and Practice*, 7th edn. London: Bloomsbury.

Daley, M., Orr, K. and Petrie, J. (2015) *Further Education and the Twelve Dancing Princesses*. London: IOE Press.

Darnell, J.A. (2019) *Parental Involvement Behaviours and Attainment: Student Perceptions in FE*. Unpublished PhD thesis, University of Bedfordshire.

Goldman, Z.W., Goodboy, A.K. and Weber, K. (2017) College students' psychological needs and intrinsic motivation to learn: an examination of self-determination theory. *Communication Quarterly*, 65(2): 167–191.

Greene, J.P. (2015) Wrong diagnosis on homework help from parents. *Education Next*, 15(2): 72–73.

Hampden-Thompson, G., Guzman, L. and Lippman, L. (2013) A cross-national analysis of parental involvement and student literacy. *International Journal of Comparative Sociology*, 54(3): 246–266.

Huddleston, P. and Unwin, L. (2013) *Teaching and Learning in Further Education: Diversity and Change*, 4th edn. London: Routledge.

Koshkin, A.P., Abramov, R., Rozhina, E. and Novikov, A. (2018) Role of social representatives in student motivation for acquiring further education. *Interchange*, 49(3): 313–341.

Ofsted (2016) *Further Education and Skills Inspection Handbook*. Available at: www.gov.uk/government/publications/further-education-and-skills-inspection-handbook

Robinson, K. and Harris, A.L. (2013) *The Broken Compass: Parental Involvement with Children's Education*. Cambridge, MA: Harvard University Press.

Rothon, C., Arephin, M., Klineberg, E., Cattell, V. and Stansfeld, S. (2011) Structural and socio-psychological influences on adolescents' educational aspirations and subsequent academic achievement. *Social Psychology of Education*, 14(2): 209–231.

Ryan, R.M. and Deci, E.L. (2002) An overview of self-determination theory: an organismic dialectical perspective. In E.L. Deci and R.M. Ryan (eds), *Handbook of Self-Determination Research*. Rochester, NY: University of Rochester Press.

Shulman, L. (1986) Those who understand: knowledge growth in teaching. *Educational Researcher*, 15(2): 4–14.

Spenceley, L. (2014) *Inclusion in Further Education*. Northwich: Critical Publishing.

Sy, R., Gottfried, A.W. and Gottfried, A.E. (2013) A transactional model of parental involvement and children's achievement from early childhood through adolescence. *Parenting: Science & Practice*, 13(2): 133–152.

Vygotsky, L.S. (1978) *Mind in Society: The Development of Higher Psychological Processes*. London: Harvard University Press.

Wallace, S. (2014) When you're smiling: exploring how teachers motivate and engage learners in the further education sector. *Journal of Further and Higher Education*, 38(3): 346–360.

8

MOTIVATING STUDENTS: WHY WOULD THEY WANT TO LEARN?

Jonathan Tummons and Jacklyn Williams

Key words – attribution theory; attachment theory; benefits of learning; curiosity; engagement; motivation theory; relevance

Introduction

Many teachers and trainers in colleges or adult and community education centres continue to find aspects of their own students' behaviour surprising, challenging and unpredictable, specifically in relation to motivation, and hence to behaviour. This is not to say that as teachers in the PCET sector, we do not expect to encounter challenges to motivation or consequent difficult behaviour – far from it. A lack of motivation, and hence engagement, can lead to occasional low-level behavioural issues of the kind that are frequently made reference to in textbooks: students chatting to each other instead of getting on with their work, and perhaps distracting others, using their phones, or asking inappropriate or perhaps embarrassing questions. By contrast, for other groups of students, a college environment can be motivating and engaging, especially in comparison to a school environment; many students enjoy 'not being at school' and instead being in a more grown-up environment. In turn, those teachers and trainers who demonstrate a conspicuous engagement with the course and with their students might prove to be infectious, and enthusiasm for teaching in turn can act as an additional motivator.

Simply put, the variety of student behaviours in further education colleges can be a challenge for new as well as experienced college lecturers. One student might work hard throughout her programme of study; a second may drift in and out, producing work of variable quality; and a third may view her course as of no value in her plans for the future, and therefore disengage from her studies. For some students, outside factors will undoubtedly impact on motivation and engagement. In such situations, it is always the first responsibility of the trainer or teacher to help students access appropriate support from elsewhere in the college: colleges invariably provide very good support for students who have to deal with difficult or time-consuming issues, ranging from organising childcare to managing unseen disabilities or mental health problems. At the same time, for those students who do not have such pressures impacting on their engagement with their studies, it seems right to think about the extent to which they are motivated to participate. We might argue, therefore, that motivating a group of students is in some ways the single most important task for the trainer or teacher. No matter how well designed our activities are, how well prepared our workshops are, how up to date our materials and resources, how creative our assessments and constructive our feedback, without motivation we will not be able to engage our students in learning.

Of course, this is not to say that these pedagogic activities can only ever come after motivation has been either established or encouraged. Well-designed activities can spark enthusiasm and engagement. Formative and summative assessment, augmented with constructive and meaningful feedback, can encourage students to try harder and to try new things. Motivating our students, making them want to take part and therefore to learn, is an ongoing process that is entirely bound up within our wider professional practice. But we need our students to walk through the door in the first place. And assuming that they have done so – more or less willingly, as we shall go on to discuss later in this chapter – we need to maintain that motivation and provide our students with, among other things, a sense that they have made a more or less right choice in deciding to come to college or attend our evening class, or whatever other model of provision that we might be involved with.

Key questions

What is motivation? What is engagement?

What do motivation and engagement look like in pedagogic practice?

How can different theories of motivation help us reflect on our pedagogic practice?

What is motivation?

Motivation can signify reasons for acting or behaving in a particular way, the desire or willingness to do something, with a degree of enthusiasm. It can refer to engagement, perhaps even to enjoyment. Certainly, it is not unusual – if not as common as we might hope, as practitioners – for our students to demonstrate a conspicuous enjoyment of their studies. Both psychological and sociological theories of motivation are plentiful, and while it is beyond the scope of a single chapter to consider such theories in depth, a brief account of some of the more well-known and widely used approaches seems appropriate, encompassing physiological mechanisms, to conscious and unconscious mental processes, and responses to actions and perceived actions and motivations of others. And we shall discuss one very well-known approach that, we suggest, requires a more critical perspective. Psychologists tend to speak of the concept of motive in terms of that which accounts for a student's energy, direction and persistence of behaviour. As such, it becomes possible to infer the student's motives from observation of her or his use of learned behaviour, from the direction of that behaviour, and from their persistence in pursuing and attaining their goals, which might relate to an entire programme of study – the award of a qualification – or to finishing a specific task within a single session.

Research focus

Theories of motivation

Herzberg's two-factor theory of motivation

Motivator factors are the factors directly associated with the content of an activity, and examples include positive recognition for the work being done, a sense of responsibility, and feelings of accomplishment. By extension, if these factors are present in the workshop or classroom, motivation will be enhanced, having a positive effect on learning.

Hygiene factors are the factors directly associated with the context of an activity. As applied to a workshop or classroom setting, examples of such factors include teaching style, the extent to which students feel welcome, and peer relationships. When met, hygiene factors such as these prevent dissatisfaction, but do not necessarily lead to satisfaction.

Heider's attribution theory

Internal attribution involves explaining a person's behaviour through reference to internal factors such as attitude or effort. *External attribution* involves explaining behaviour through reference to external factors such as environmental conditions. Students who are highly motivated equate success with their own effort (internal attribution), and equate difficulties with external factors that are beyond their control such as 'a difficult question' or 'bad luck' (external attribution). Students with lower motivation equate success with 'good luck' (external attribution) rather than their own effort or ability, which they perceive as being insufficient, leading in turn to disengagement from study (internal attribution).

Bowlby's attachment theory

Attachment theory initially focused on relationships between parents and young children, but has been extended to explore wider relations between adults and young people. According to this theory, the relationship that students have with their teacher is central to how the students behave in the workshop or classroom environment. Students with positive and secure relations with their teacher are more likely to feel motivated to explore and work in this environment with confidence, and be willing to take risks and make mistakes. Students with insecure relations with their teacher will lack the motivation to engage.

Berlyne's curiosity theory

Berlyne explored why people display curiosity, why they explore their environments, and why they seek out information and knowledge. He theorised that if people encountered situations that led to discrepancies between what the current situation might mean and what people already knew and could do, then a particular form of motivation would result, so long as the new situation was not so challenging that it might become overwhelming. In the workshop and classroom, this theory is best seen at work when students are given challenges to work through or tasks to accomplish that are not too simple (otherwise not much can be learned) and also not too difficult (because these will be off-putting).

As is the case with many other theories, whether derived from psychology or from sociology (Chapters 10 and 11 provide further good examples of both in relation to learning more generally, rather than motivation and engagement specifically), it is not always the case that a specific or single theory is immediately applicable to every pedagogic context. So long as theories have been established through appropriate and robust research, then they can be usefully considered as ways to help us explore and then make sense of our experiences in the workshop or classroom. But what happens when a theory is widely used but not based on serious empirical research?

Key theory

Myth-busting: Maslow's hierarchy of needs

In his research, Maslow produced a hierarchy of human needs that affects the motivation designed to achieve a goal. Maslow visualised these as a pyramid (easily found online) consisting of:

- fundamental physiological needs such as thirst and hunger;

- safety needs such as a desire for protection and physical and psychological security;

- belonging needs or social needs such as friendship or affiliation;

- self-esteem needs such as a desire for competence, attention and prestige; and

- self-actualisation needs such as internal cognitive growth - to which education contributes.

However, Maslow's theorising appears to be based on insubstantial speculation rather than thorough and robust research. Simply put, the hierarchy of needs is not based on research evidence (Child, 2007, p242). Arguably, his theory relies for its underpinnings on colourful anecdotes, selective case reporting and inconclusive observations (Illeris, 2007).

Nonetheless, there are many examples of Maslow's theory being used to explore pedagogic practice. At one level, it seems right to say that if a student is very hungry, then they might not be engaged with their learning, or if a workshop is too cold, then students will not be motivated to participate. The caveat is that it is not too difficult to find examples from practice that refute Maslow's strictures: apprentices working outdoors will still be learning, whatever the weather. Moreover, there is a tendency to use Maslow's hierarchy of needs in a very deterministic manner – to assume that these needs always apply, with no concern for context or for individuality. For these reasons, while the careful use of theories is to be encouraged, we suggest that the theories of Herzberg, Heider, Bowlby and Berlyne (as well as others) are of at least as much value as those of Maslow.

Different types of motivation

A number of categories of motivation have therefore been proposed over time. Four such categories are easily identified in current and recent literature: instrumental motivation, social motivation, achievement motivation and intrinsic motivation. We outline these briefly here, mindful of the fact that it is important to remember that they are not mutually exclusive. That is, more than one category may be seen as influencing learner motivation at any given time (Biggs and Telfer, 1987).

1. *Instrumental motivation.* This type of motivation, which is purely external or *extrinsic*, is in evidence where students perform tasks solely because of the consequences likely to ensue (e.g. the chance to obtain some tangible reward or to avoid a reprimand). It is in complete contrast to intrinsic motivation (see below). In the face of motivation of this nature, trainers and teachers should ensure that the task to be performed is placed in a context perceived as constructive and meaningful to the students.

2. *Social motivation.* Students influenced by this type of motivation tend to perform tasks so as to please those they respect, admire, or whose opinions are of some importance to them. Rewards are of limited significance even if tangible; the reward here is non-material and is related in direct measure to the perceived relationship between the student and the person whose reinforcement activity (e.g. praise or approval) is considered important.

3. *Achievement motivation.* This is involved where students learn 'in the hope of success' (Ausubel, 1968). This consists of three interrelated elements: *cognitive drive*, where the student is attempting to satisfy a perceived need to know; *self-enhancement*, where the student is satisfying the need for self-esteem; and *affiliation*, where the student is seeking the approval of others.

4. *Intrinsic motivation.* In this case, there are no external rewards; the task is undertaken for the pleasure and satisfaction it brings to the student. It seems to be central to high-quality involvement in a task and to be self-maintaining and self-terminating. Curiosity and a desire to meet challenges may characterise the attitude and approach to learning of students motivated in this style.

From theories of motivation to pedagogic practice

It used to be thought that the motivation to study among students in further education colleges could be taken for granted (Wallace, 2002). If young people had chosen to come to college after leaving school at 16, after their GCSEs, they surely would be motivated to attend, having chosen their new course of study? Particularly for those students who did not enjoy school, who prefer technical and practical subjects to academic subjects, attending college could be seen as the obvious next step, not to mention that they would be working towards qualifications that would have real-world application, linked to future employment or perhaps further study. Many students welcome the different culture or 'feel' of the FE college, in comparison to school, and thrive in an atmosphere that affords them more autonomy and agency. We might also find mature learners enrolling on other programmes, at colleges or at adult education centres offering local education authority courses or courses run by the Workers' Educational Association (WEA), seeking personal and/or professional development opportunities. This might be this industry-standard training, or it might be a way to fulfil a personal desire to change employment status, or perhaps work towards promotion in an increasingly competitive working environment that requires constant upskilling and reskilling. Other students learn for reasons of self-fulfilment, or simply to start or develop a hobby in a safe and affordable space. And a further explanation for participation among both young people and adults can be found in the construction of PCET as the 'second-chance sector'. Colleges in particular have long been seen as providing a second chance for many students who, for whatever reason, were unable or unwilling to benefit from the school system.

However, if we apply a more critical perspective and begin to unpack the reasons why students enrol at college, we can see how these unproblematic notions of PCET students as 'wanting to be here and therefore motivated' do not in fact provide a robust account:

- Many young people, eager to throw off the shackles of school and often simultaneously of the academic curriculum, do indeed enrol on college courses to learn a future career – and a significant attraction of many such courses is their vocational nature. However, many students will quickly discover that many programmes impose a requirement for English and/or maths for students aged 17–18 and aged 19–25 if they have not previously achieved GCSE grade 9 to 4/A*–C, or equivalent. For students who have already experienced failure in these areas of the academic curriculum, the requirement to retake these examinations can be a significant barrier to participation.

- Other young people and adults who do not want to study within an institution, but want to enter the workplace instead, take up apprenticeships. Apprenticeships too bring with them the need to achieve English and maths qualifications prior to or during the programme – a factor that is at best treated with reluctance, and at worst has deleterious effects on learner motivation.

- For some young people, enrolling at their local FE college is simply the last viable option available to them. They do not have sufficiently strong GCSE grades to stay on at school (and probably do not wish to). Nor can they find an apprenticeship or other appropriate employment with work-based training. And yet they are now legally obliged to remain in education, employment or training until they reach 18. At worst, no aspect of their programmes of study provides motivation for these students; at best, they are attending more or less entirely due to the fact that they have to, and not because they want to.

- Other students are enrolled onto a variety of short courses at college, in order that they can complete qualifications that are considered mandatory to secure or retain employment. This might be due to policy on the part of their employers, or due to national or sector-wide wider legislation. Examples include Construction Skills Certification Scheme (CSCS) cards, basic food hygiene courses and safeguarding courses. Such courses are sometimes treated in a perfunctory manner, lacking any inherent worth, and for which, once again, there might be little motivation.

Motivation and engagement: critical perspectives

By now, it should be becoming clear that motivation and engagement are complex notions that rest on a number of factors: the individual student, the course being offered, the social and economic context within which the course is being studied, and so forth. It would be a mistake to assume that motivation and engagement can be 'fixed' or 'improved' in isolation, no matter how often FE teachers and trainers might be told that they need to find ways to motivate their students. An interested and enthusiastic teacher is always to be preferred over a teacher who is disengaged and lacking application. At the same time, it can be difficult to motivate students who feel more or less compelled to attend an English resit class, who have to attend college because they lost out on their first choice for post-16 education, or who are enrolled on a programme with little chance of leading to meaningful employment or opportunity for further study (Atkins, 2009). Participation in education and training has over time been widened through the provision of new courses and programmes, the construction of new forms or models of participation, and the establishment of new training partners and institutions; what might be termed the further education and training landscape has arguably never been as diverse as is currently the case. Within such a landscape of choice and flexibility, it might be argued that since opportunities for young people are so plentiful, motivation and engagement need not concern us too much. But these opportunities are limited in all kinds of ways: by compulsory attendance, by the need for prerequisite qualifications that not everyone will have, by only limited employment opportunities post-qualification, by familial or other social background factors, and so on.

Irrespective of the ways in which motivation might be understood – as internal, based on enthusiasm, or as external, based on rewards and possibly punishments – engagement with the curriculum can be seen as resting on just two factors, but it is important to note that these are intertwined:

- *Confidence in the value of the course or programme of study.* If the programme itself is valued (by parents, by employers, by government ministers and by professional endorsement, as well as by the students themselves), then the value of the certification that the course provides can be established. Simply put, what does the piece of paper give to the student?

- *The inherent value or importance of the skills and knowledge that the course provides.* If the topics, skills, content or capacities that the course rests on and gives to students (assuming successful completion) are perceived as being inherently worthwhile, valuable or important, then the value of the field of study can be established. Simply put, to what extent is the course considered, at an individual and societal level, as being 'worthwhile', as being a 'proper subject'?

In this way, we can see how our earlier four types of motivation overlap, demonstrating how some theories need to be considered as complementing each other, not conflicting with each other. The *instrumental* motivation comes through gaining a qualification. The *social* motivation comes through being seen to be studying for a 'proper', worthwhile qualification, but at the same time through gaining a qualification, which is an important form of social capital. The *achievement* motivation comes through gaining certification. And the *intrinsic* motivation comes through the interest or curiosity generated by the inherent value or quality of the course being followed.

Making things relevant

What should we do when students regard course content as irrelevant and lacking meaning? There will surely be little motivation to participate in the learning and teaching process if the course lacks relevance. Students working towards a level 2 certificate in basic plumbing studies may not at first understand why they have to learn how to work with sheet lead, but as it is a component of the syllabus, it is required that they do so. Students working towards a level 3 certificate in childcare and education may not at first understand why one of the compulsory units of their programme requires them to have to learn some of the outline details of current legislation that applies in settings such as nurseries. If learning requires engagement, and engagement requires the course to be meaningful, then relevance needs to be established:

- To begin, there must be a full explanation to students of the *significance* of those subject areas that are perceived to be redundant, meaningless or otherwise unacceptable, in terms of content, its relationship with the course subject as a whole, and its contribution to the skills and/or knowledge being worked towards. At the same time, short-term goals, such as the successful completion of assessed tasks, the acquisition of professional skills or the final award of a certificate, must not be overlooked. For students, these ought to be of equal importance.

- Trying to motivate students by telling them that they need to 'broaden their outlook' or 'not just focus on the end test' are likely to be ignored at best and resented at worst. It is not sufficient simply to state that students *ought* to do or know something; they always need to be told *why* they need to do or know something.

For our plumbing students, an explanation of the use of lead flashing on boiler flues would be of benefit for those members of the group who question why they have to learn how to work with lead. The childcare students who do not understand why they have to learn about government legislation could be helped to make sense of what might be seen as an abstract theoretical subject through a discussion of the impact of the Early Years Foundation Stage on the day-to-day working lives of nursery staff – especially if linked to inspections. In this way, the engagement of the students – and consequently a *deeper* approach to their learning – can be established.

Case study

Policy focus: the Wolf Report

The Review of Vocational Education conducted by Professor Alison Wolf of King's College London, and hence known as the Wolf Report, was commissioned by Michael Gove, the then Secretary of State for Education, in 2010 and published in the following year. The Wolf Report provided a comprehensive and arresting account of the current and recent state of 14-19 vocational education provision, perhaps best summarised by the central message that although the vocational education system contains many examples of excellent practice (the examples given in the report included companies such as Rolls-Royce and Airbus, and further education colleges such as Macclesfield and Westminster Kingsway), the vocational education system as a whole was wildly variable in quality. Specifically, she argued that the vocational education system was in several key ways failing the students that it purported to serve. Too many young people failed to achieve good grades in English and mathematics at GCSE - positioned as essential key skills for all students aged 14-19, irrespective of whether they follow the 'vocational' curriculum or the 'academic curriculum'. The vocational education system was rigid and unresponsive and overly centralised.

However, from the point of view of this chapter, the key finding of the report related to the range and quality of the qualifications being offered. According to Wolf, too many awarding bodies were offering too many qualifications. Moreover, the real-world value of too many qualifications was inflated. This could be seen in terms of equivalences (the ways in which a certain number of vocational qualifications are deemed to be 'worth' a particular number of GCSEs according to a predetermined tariff). This could also be seen in the proliferation of vocational qualifications at levels 1 and 2 (which are delivered in both schools and in FE colleges), which failed to help young people gain meaningful employment and also failed to help them progress to higher education. The recommendations made by the report included reducing the number of vocational qualifications, requiring all school/college leavers to obtain maths and English GCSEs (or equivalent), and changing the tariff attached to qualifications so that institutions will not be encouraged to enter students for qualifications that will not lead to progression (to either employment or higher education), and to make improvements to work experience (for full-time students, not for apprentices).

Establishing motivation and engagement in the workshop or classroom

What, then, does an engaging and motivating approach to teaching look like? In what ways might our pedagogic choices help to generate motivation and engagement – or at the very least work to prevent demotivation – among our students? Mindful of the fact that several of these themes will overlap with issues raised elsewhere in this book, a number of possible strategies are briefly presented here:

- *Pre-course contact, initial assessment and comprehensive advice.* Providers should always offer pre-course contact, initial assessment, and comprehensive information, advice and guidance (IAG) on individual courses and employment and opportunities routes, to enable students to make informed and meaningful decisions about enrolment. Colleges and teaching teams need to create templates to facilitate high-quality course information that is consistent across provision, and easy to compare, and where possible offer realistic tasters and workshops to introduce applicants to the course content and working level.

- *Help students to set their own goals during their course.* Students supported to set their own goals and/or manage their own progress are more likely to experience personal success, regardless of their overall grade or the performance of their peers (Ormrod et al., 2016). Colleges and teachers should provide learners with an overview of the nature and structure of the information they will be learning, and encourage them to make links to their goals. Hattie and Yates (2014) recommend the use of advance organisers, which can also assist students with planning and organisation, as well as making connections between different pieces of information.

- *Encourage 'real-time' reflection on distance travelled.* Teachers and trainers need to ensure that students and colleagues alike continually monitor individual students' current strengths and gaps. They should make sure the student 'owns' their tracking and monitoring records, which should not only visibly show distance travelled towards competency and other goals, but also refer to internalised personal values of goal achievement. *Diagnostic* and *ipsative assessment* through an individual learning plan or similar should be used to help students engage meaningfully with these processes.

- *Recognise and reward interim achievements and quick wins.* Students exert effort to perform at a high level when they are confident of achieving worthwhile goals in the short term (Hattie and Yates, 2014). Constructive feedback and positive encouragement need not be restricted to summative assessments, but should be part of the ongoing workshop or classroom practice of the teacher/trainer.

- *Create an environment of autonomy, ownership and pride.* Teachers need to create an environment that clearly establishes values and expectations of learner autonomy, ownership, and pride in their own work and the work of the peer group/organisation. Where appropriate, teachers should involve students in planning and negotiating objectives and behaviours. Students are much more likely to accept an outcome, whether positive or negative, if they have been fully involved in its development and feel that the process was fair and transparent.

- *Balance challenges with current skills.* There are few things as demotivating for students as stumbling over tasks or activities that are beyond their grasp. Instead, teachers need to plan carefully to push their students to progress, without asking them to do too much too soon. Scaffolding new activities from a Vygotskian perspective (as discussed in Chapter 11) allows both the teacher and the student to arrive at an optimal level of challenge, which is essential to the enjoyment and effectiveness of intrinsically motivated, goal-directed activities (Abuhamdeh and Csikszentmihalyi, 2012).

- *Eradicate external pressures but involve significant others.* It can be difficult to shut out distractions from outside. Nonetheless, as far as possible, it is important to try to eradicate excessive external pressure and controls, and try to involve parents and guardians (where appropriate), employers and other members of the wider community to create an atmosphere that lends a sense of realism and purpose, as well as support, to activities.

- *Build opportunities for pastoral support.* Building good teacher–student relationships is important if we are to foster significant and enduring, if not necessarily immediate, improvements in student motivation (Hattie and Yates, 2014). Where appropriate, teachers should be present and available to listen to students and afford them the chance to share their authentic selves, their hopes and their problems. Teachers and trainers should not be social workers, but they should be able to act as a first point of contact while remembering that their main responsibilities are vocational/academic, not pastoral (Ecclestone, 2007).

- *Focus on course structure.* Teachers can build a supportive environment by communicating clear, concrete and realistic expectations for performance, through focussing on how (process), not what (product), in order to encourage students to keep working, accepting challenges as opportunities rather than threats of failure.

- *Make the most of different methods of assessment and feedback.* Assessment and feedback (the two are always interlinked) provide a powerful venue for motivation. To generate motivation, assessment feedback needs to be timely, relevant and practicable. Many teachers and trainers use learner peer and self-assessment processes to encourage groups of students (as discussed in more depth in Chapter 12).

- *Praise technique and effort, rather than skill or intelligence.* Notwithstanding the ways in which skill or intelligence might be seen as being fixed, changeable or something in between, it is important for praise (as distinct from feedback, which is an element of the assessment process) to focus on aspects of student behaviour that can, unambiguously, be seen as being able to be improved or practised.

- *Prepare learners to overcome passivity by learning control.* Students' beliefs in their capabilities can be usefully increased in order to foster efficient self-regulation and thereby enhance motivation. It can be useful to help students to be aware of, interpret, and adapt their own physical and emotional states prior to beginning an activity (Schwarz and Clore, 2007).

- *Choose and design learning materials and equipment thoughtfully.* Few things are as off-putting for students as being given a series of tasks to complete that are difficult to understand because the instructions are poorly written or the diagrams are reproduced in such a way that they cannot be understood. Instead, it is important to prepare learning materials thoughtfully to ensure clarity and easy assimilation.

- *Find equity and tolerance in the workshop or classroom.* It is important to find ways for students to know that they've been heard, understood and treated with dignity as an individual, and with equity in relation to others around them.

- *Invoke prosocial motivation.* There is more to college than 'just' the qualification being worked towards. It is important for teachers and trainers to expand conceptions of worthwhile learning outcomes to develop students as active citizens who see beyond the instrumental attainment of academic qualifications (Coffield, 2008).

Key theory

Theory focus: the wider benefits of learning

Research carried out by the Centre for Research on the Wider Benefits of Learning has identified a number of benefits of learning beyond the immediate goals of qualifications and employment (Feinstein et al., 2008):

- Adult education can increase civic participation and increase the likelihood of voting in local and national elections.

- Further education can increase self-esteem – with consequent benefits for mental health – and facilitate social networking.

- People with better qualifications are more likely to have a healthy lifestyle, with benefits for both them and for their children (if they have any). They are less likely to smoke and less likely to commit crimes.

- Adult education can increase people's social networks and work to prevent social isolation, with consequent benefits for both physical and mental health.

- Further education can increase participation in community-based activities and promote citizenship.

- Further education colleges can act as catalysts for local and regional civic pride.

Chapter summary

Motivation and engagement are complex issues, and oftentimes outside the control of the individual teacher or trainer. We cannot control for what happens outside the colleges and community centres where we work, but we can take steps within our own professional practice to encourage meaningful engagement for all of our students through:

- pre-course contact, initial assessment and comprehensive guidance;

- helping students to set their own goals and reflect on them;

- encouraging an environment of autonomy, ownership and pride;

(Continued)

(Continued)

- balancing challenges with current skills;

- eradicating external pressures but involving significant others;

- offering relevant pastoral support;

- making the most of assessment and feedback, particularly formative assessment; and

- choosing and designing learning materials and equipment thoughtfully.

Wanting to engage and motivate all students is not the same thing as making everyone be students, in some form, as a consequence of raising the age at which a young person can choose to leave education or training voluntarily. At some point, we may need to reconsider the extent to which it is appropriate to make the assumption that all young people, up to and including age 18, should be in formal education or training; if a young person does not want to be in formal education or training, she or he no longer has the right to say so. Vocational and technical education and training remains underfunded and undervalued in relation to the academic curriculum – a form of provision for 'other people's children'. Unless this attitude can be changed, educational inequalities will persist. And so long as some forms of education and training are seen as being second best, then can it be any wonder that, whatever the age of the student, there is resistance to engagement, and hence to motivation and to learning?

References

Abuhamdeh, S. and Csikszentmihalyi, M. (2012) The importance of challenge for the enjoyment of intrinsically motivated, goal-directed activities. *Personality and Social Psychology Bulletin*, 38(3): 317–330.

Atkins, L. (2009) *Invisible Students, Impossible Dreams: Experiencing Vocational Education 14–19*. Stoke-on-Trent: Trentham Books.

Ausubel, D. (1968) *Educational Psychology: A Cognitive View*. New York: Holt, Rinehart & Winston.

Biggs, J. and Telfer, R. (1987) *The Process of Learning*. Upper Saddle River, NJ: Prentice Hall.

Child, D. (2007) *Psychology and the Teacher*, 7th edn. London: Continuum.

Coffield, F. (2008) *Just Suppose Teaching and Learning Became the First Priority*. London: Learning and Skills Network.

Ecclestone, K. (2007) Resisting images of the 'diminished self': the implications of emotional well-being and emotional engagement in education policy. *Journal of Education Policy*, 22(4): 455–470.

Feinstein, L., Budge, D., Vorhaus, J. and Duckworth, K. (eds) (2008) *The Social and Personal Benefits of Learning*. London: Institute of Education.

Hattie, J. and Yates, G.C.R. (2014) *Visible Learning and the Science of How We Learn*. London: Routledge.

Illeris, K. (2007) *How We Learn: Learning and Non-Learning in School and Beyond*. London: Routledge.

Ormrod, J.E., Anderman, E.M. and Anderman, L. (2016) *Educational Psychology: Developing Learners*, 9th edn. Harlow: Pearson Education.

Schwarz, N. and Clore, G.L. (2007) Feelings and phenomenal experiences. In A. Kruglanski and E.T. Higgins (eds), *Social Psychology: Handbook of Basic Principles*, 2nd edn. New York: Guilford.

Wallace, S. (2002) *Managing Behaviour and Motivating Students in Further Education*. Exeter: Learning Matters.

Wolf, A. (2011) *Review of Vocational Education*. Available at: www.gov.uk/government/publications/review-of-vocational-education-the-wolf-report

9

HOW SHOULD WE TEACH IN FE?

Sasha Pleasance

Key words – transformative education; disjuncture; resilience; radicalisation; discourse; evidence-based practice

Introduction

Further education (FE) has a long-standing role in the English education system to address inadequacies in the school system by offering a second chance to both young people and adults; it offers an important alternative to mainstream education; and it offers the opportunity to retrain and pursue aspirations in a diverse range of educational opportunities and career pathways provided by a wide-ranging curriculum offer encompassing pre-entry-level qualifications right up to degree level, with a student population ranging from 14-year-olds all the way up to those who could be well into their retirement.

This chapter explores different ways of thinking about the practice of teaching within the PCET sector. It considers the ways in which pedagogies for the vocational curriculum can be seen as distinct from pedagogies for the academic curriculum, how knowledge and content within the vocational curriculum can be understood, and ways in which different philosophies of education can inform pedagogical practice in the PCET sector.

The purpose and remit of FE

FE provision has three essential roles, and its curriculum offer accordingly provides pathways to:

- enter and progress in the workplace;

- transition to higher-level study; and

- support social mobility.

Persistent government intervention in both FE policy and practice to overcome socio-economic problems and failures by schools has seen its provision return to a more singular emphasis on economic imperatives since mid-2000. In pursuit of trying to regain a sense of the overall purpose of FE amidst a fragmented and disconnected policy arena, the Nuffield Review of 14–19 Education and Training (Pring et al., 2009) addressed the lack of clarity about its purpose.

Key questions

What counts as an educated 19-year-old in this day and age?

Since publication, successive governments have ignored the recommendations from the Nuffield Review; however, one of the five key recommendations that is significant to discussion in this chapter was:

> The re-assertion of a broader vision of education *in which there is a profound respect for the whole person (not just the narrowly conceived 'intellectual excellence' or 'skills for economic prosperity'), irrespective of ability or cultural and social background, in which there is a broader vision of learning and in which the learning contributes to a more just and cohesive society.*

> (Pring et al., 2009, p4, emphasis in original)

Given its diversity in curriculum, student population and purpose, it seems therefore unreasonable to assume that how we 'should' teach in FE is a fixed and stable entity. However, in a sector that is increasingly driven by a managerialist and inspection-driven agenda, it is important for us to critically examine models of teaching in FE, and in so doing generate discussion around notions of knowledge and learning within teaching. Trends in teaching are thus critiqued as discussion on teaching in this chapter unpicks the purpose of FE within the UK education system.

A theory of vocational pedagogy

Key questions

Does teaching in vocational education require a different theory of pedagogy to academic education?

This debate draws upon the continuing failure to obtain parity of esteem between vocational and academic education in the UK. Subsequently, this failure has weakened the status of vocational education, and its constant review and reform among policymakers and employers in the UK has emphasised skills for workplace performance that are separate from a knowledge base in a competency-oriented curriculum (Clarke and Winch, 2006). According to Bathmaker (2013), the danger is that the teaching of vocational skills then becomes procedural with its restricted access to certain types of knowledge, so:

the issue of knowledge is not just a technical question, but relates to questions of equity and justice. If vocational education qualifications are to enable people to gain valuable knowledge and skills, and are to open up opportunities rather than constrain and limit futures, then questions of knowledge in these qualifications, and how these questions are decided, are crucial.

(p88)

Vocational education within the current policy context of FE has a clear line of sight: work. As such, it seems the issue is whether this requires, or even deserves, its own theory of pedagogy. Lucas et al. (2012), in their report, work towards an agreed theory of vocational pedagogy. In, summary they assert that 'the best vocational education is broadly hands-on, practical, experiential, real world as well as, and often at the same time as, something which involves feedback, questioning, application and reflection and, when required, theoretical models and explanations' (p9). Lucas et al. (2012) categorise vocational education into three types:

1. Working with practical materials – for example, bricklaying, plumbing, hairdressing, professional make-up.

2. Working with people – for example, financial advice, nursing, hospitality, retail, care industries.

3. Working with abstract concepts (symbols) – for example, accountancy, journalism, software development, graphic design.

(p35)

It is understood by Lucas et al. that these are not mutually exclusive categories, and indeed they assert that occupations involve each of these three types to varying extents. These three types of vocational education can help teachers make decisions about which methods to use in their practice. The first two categories may adopt methods such as simulation, watching and imitating, trial and error (when possible), and feedback. The third category may use visual representations/models, critical thinking and worked examples. Many of the methods referred to by Lucas et al. are already an essential part of many vocational teachers' repertoires.

In the categorisation of vocational education by Lucas et al. (2012), we see a clear distinction between teaching methods for practical learning experiences and practical skills and methods for theoretical learning. According to Lucas et al. (2010), vocational education 'concerns the development of practical competence within, or for, a defined work "domain"' (p21).

How can we differentiate work-based education and training and work-related education and training? We can consider the former to be credentialised skills needed for specific workplace performance such as apprenticeships, and the latter a broad general education embedded within a vocational area. This distinction brings us back to the overriding question concerning the purpose of FE, and therefore its conflicting demands from various stakeholders that continue to pull its desired outcomes in different directions.

Key questions

Can teaching open up the possibility of knowledge that is situated within a vocational area while also allowing students 'to participate in "society's conversation"' (Wheelahan, 2010, p1)?

The summary report of the Commission on Adult Vocational Teaching and Learning (CAVTL), *It's about Work*, posits that:

> The best vocational teaching and learning combines theoretical knowledge from the underpinning disciplines (for example, maths, psychology, human sciences, economics) with the occupational knowledge of practice (for example, how to cut hair, build circuit boards, administer medicines). To do this, teachers, trainers and learners have to recontextualise theoretical and occupational knowledge to suit specific situations.

(McLoughlin, 2013, p15)

So, whether Lucas et al. (2010) are right to argue for a theory of vocational pedagogy as something separate and distinct from academic pedagogy or not, what their report has done is bring attention to vocational education and an opportunity to consider the distinction between training and education whereby 'training is inculcation into a set of usually rigid routines, while education develops the whole person' (Clarke and Winch, 2007, p9).

The importance of both the practical and the theoretical

McLoughlin (2013) identified eight distinctive features of vocational pedagogy that emphasise the importance of both practical and theoretical elements in the development of occupational expertise:

1. that through the combination of sustained practice and the understanding of theory, occupational expertise is developed;

2. that *work-related attributes* are central to the development of occupational expertise;

3. that *practical problem-solving and reflection on experience*, including learning from mistakes in 'real' and simulated settings, is central to effective vocational teaching and learning;

4. that it is most effective when it is *collaborative and contextualised*, taking place through *communities of practice* that involve different types of 'teacher' and capitalise on the experience and knowledge of all learners;

5. that *technology* plays a key role because keeping on top of technological advances is an essential part of the occupational expertise required in any workplace;

6. that it requires *a range of assessment and feedback methods* that involve both 'teachers' and 'learners';

7. that it often benefits from operating across *more than one setting*, to develop the capacity to learn and apply that learning in different settings just as at work; and

8. that occupational *standards are dynamic*, evolving to reflect advances in work, and that through collective learning *transformation* in quality and efficiency is achieved.

Teaching should situate theory in practical examples, and wherever possible embrace and put to use what McLoughlin (2013) refers to as 'the "live" knowledge' that students bring from their workplaces. Emphasis is, however, placed on the importance of contextualised practice in real or simulated workplace settings advocating teaching methods such as problem-solving and critical reflection on practical experience. The recommended teaching approach is therefore practical and experiential.

One of the eight key features identified by McLoughlin (2013) is that vocational teaching benefits 'from operating across more than one setting ... to develop the capacity to learn and apply that learning in different settings just as at work' (p9).

The capacity to learn and apply that learning

Vocational teachers are required to prepare students for work predominantly, although not exclusively, in settings outside of the workplace. The demand on vocational teachers is to take the skills and knowledge of the occupational workplace and reformulate it in a teaching and learning environment so it is not only comprehensible, but also then transferable back into the workplace. The notion of transferability negates the context-bound character of skills and qualities currently bound up in the term 'employability' and its assumptions about generalised skills and qualities independent of context.

While there may be some transfer of skills and knowledge from the teaching and learning environment to the workplace, the notion of transferability is relatively limited, yet vocational education is endowed with the requirement to produce students who possess an array of transferable skills for future employment as policymakers persist that they:

> hold out the promise of producing a flexible and adaptable workforce, and of solving problems associated with training people for an uncertain future ... [but] on the basis of the available evidence ... we believe that the pursuit of such skills is a chimera-hunt, an expensive and disastrous exercise in futility.

> (Hyland and Johnson, 1998, p170)

Is a broader conceptualisation of knowledge needed?

Perhaps the real issue for discussion is less about a theory of vocational pedagogy and more about academic snobbery in the UK, societal attitudes towards the hands-on pedagogy of much vocational education, attitudes that degrade vocational occupations, and thereby perpetuate the hierarchal labour market in the UK, which is increasingly characterised as high-skill and low-wage. Perhaps, as a sector, we need to focus more on the development of vocational education as more expansive, which therefore offers 'a broader conceptualisation of knowledge than the "useful knowledge" normally associated with the workplace' (Avis, 2014, p47). 'At its best, vocational teaching and learning also results in multiple outcomes including the building of identity – people learn to "become" (occupational name) and to grow (as responsible adults/citizens)' (McLoughlin, 2013, p16).

According to Avis (2014), the tendency towards a narrow emphasis on outcomes and standards in vocational education to meet the interests of employers not only reduces the complexity of occupational practice, but also leads to anti-educative consequences that deny the opportunity for vocational students to interrogate and develop a deeper understanding of the political and democratic structures of wider society, something that is particularly relevant in the current era of austerity and the ongoing struggle for social justice for marginalised groups. If vocational education is just about work as the line of sight, then we need to consider whether it is in danger of reproducing the structural relations of inequality in the ever-increasing austere conditions of social formation in which we are currently living and working.

Critical, participative and emancipatory pedagogies

The power of FE is how it can transform people's lives, improve their life chances and increase their democratic participation in society. The true power of FE is emancipation. This emancipatory approach to pedagogy is exemplified in Freire's book *Pedagogy of the Oppressed* (1970) and the work of Mezirow (1978, 1998, 2000), and his emphasis on strengthening teachers' and students' knowledge of social and political realities. Furthermore, this approach emphasises dialogue to critically challenge and assess students' (and teachers') underlying assumptions and beliefs about the world, so dialogue is not only a tool for teaching, but also a means to evaluate learning. Learning is more than a cognitive process, and knowledge is not a static entity within the transformative approach to pedagogy.

Transformation comes through disjuncture, whereby taken-for-granted assumptions are challenged and our experience, or life history, is reinterpreted or reconstructed, and so learning brings about change not only in thinking, but in action. These moments of disequilibrium, where what is thought and understood about the world is challenged, can lead to discomfort for students.

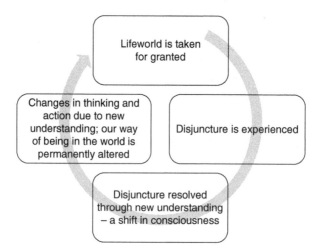

Figure 9.1   Transformation through disjuncture
Source: Adapted from Jarvis (2009, p26)

Key questions

Is disjuncture a useful basis for dialogue in teaching?

A dialogic approach to teaching

Teaching in a dialogic approach means using dialogue between you and your students. It means moving away from the teacher presentation model. Furthermore, it means moving away from an objective-driven model of lesson preparation, and therefore teaching. Using talk means your students are your resource: their perspectives, their developing ideas, their limits of understanding. Student–teacher interactions are more than simple recall in question/answer routines. Instead, student contributions are extended rather than received, challenged and justified rather than accepted to deepen lines of enquiry, but this requires the teacher to accept uncertainty in outcome as this approach moves away from the safe and conventional certainty of an objective-driven lesson where its ends are a preordained given.

The implementation of this teaching approach in FE may, however, rely more on the commitment and thinking of individual teachers due to the emphasis on measurable outcomes in vocational education, which favours skills over other less measurable outcomes of education.

FE has a pivotal role in overcoming economic, social, political and cultural marginalisation, and is therefore crucial in challenging inequality and transforming lives and communities (Duckworth and Smith, 2016). Sadly, the transformative contribution of FE is overlooked as it has become increasingly central to successive governments' economic imperatives. As such, its remit has become progressively more pressured, both for its teachers and managers, making the space for transformation more challenging.

Teaching resilience

Since the publication of the Wolf Report (Wolf, 2011), FE has become accountable for the compulsory maths and English resit policy. Despite opposition to the policy, students are required to continue to study each subject until they achieve at least a grade 4 as a condition of funding for colleges. While the policy intent may be right (i.e. help young people achieve the standard grade 4 in both subjects because it helps them to progress in life, learning and work), in practice the policy is surely failing if the facts show that of students aged 17-plus taking GCSE maths, 22.7 per cent achieved a grade 4 or higher, and of those taking GCSE English, 33.1 per cent achieved a grade 4 or higher (JCQ, 2018).

Since the introduction of this policy in FE, college CPD events have focused more on ideas stemming from the psychology of Dweck's growth mindset theory, in particular the notion of resilience. These ideas are being promoted to encourage teachers to adopt methods to cope with the affective barriers so many resit students face in maths and English lessons. Resilience is defined as the 'capacity to continue to "bounce back", to recover strengths or spirit quickly and efficiently in the face of adversity' (Gu and Day, 2007, p1302). In the 1970s, resilience was the domain of psychiatry and complex trauma; now it has shifted to being a social norm for both teachers and students to cope with negative aspects within the education system. Successive government papers from 2009 onwards have stated that developing character and resilience is a central part of their plan for education: to create a generation of confident, resilient young people to help them succeed academically, improve their job prospects and 'bounce back' from setbacks. It is also one of the key attributes that comprises the components of employability (Yorke and Knight, cited in Pleasance, 2016).

According to Dweck et al. (2014), the key ingredients to build resilience are:

1. *Challenge*: high teacher expectations and promoting a growth mindset.

2. *Scaffolding*: cognitive scaffolding to support intellectual growth; motivational scaffolding, including approaches such as goal-setting.

3. *Belonging*: creating an environment where there is a sense of fellowship between peers and teachers.

The concept of resilience also appears in policy and practice around radicalisation as part of the Prevent Strategy (HM Government, 2011). Here, in this context, resilience is defined as 'the capability of people, groups and communities to rebut and reject proponents of terrorism and the ideology they promote' (HM Government, 2011, p108). If we are to truly tackle issues such as radicalisation in ways that are transformative rather than punitive, we need to create safe spaces for dialogue in our teaching. How to teach in the face of such divisive and complex times is not included in CPD events on radicalisation; the focus is often more on the reporting of incidents that may be a cause for concern. As such, fear is perpetuated on the part of both teachers and students in discussing controversial issues in an environment where they could be reported for saying the wrong thing.

Research by the DfE (2011) identified three key ingredients to build resilience in young people:

1. making a connection through good design and a young-person-centred approach;

2. facilitating a safe space for dialogue and positive interaction; and

3. equipping young people with appropriate capabilities – skills, knowledge, understanding and awareness.

Transformative approaches to teaching in FE

As FE teachers, we are teaching the future generation of makers, thinkers and doers, and therefore our role as teachers needs to shift away from transmission models of teaching to more transformative approaches that help students engage creatively and purposefully in their learning.

Within a transformative approach, the teacher becomes catalyst, mentor, provocateur and peer. This approach to teaching requires teachers to build trust with students, thereby facilitating positive spaces where the social and emotional aspects of learning are nurtured alongside vocational learning. Here, the primary role of the teacher shifts from being a transmitter of a fixed body of knowledge to being a facilitator. A facilitator helps students engage creatively and intelligently in their sense-making enquiries.

Evidence-Based Practice

What is considered evidence in teaching has shifted over time, and today we are in an era that prioritises quantitative evidence stemming from randomised controlled trials (RCTs) over other types of evidence, especially evidence from teachers' own practical knowledge gained through experience. Current educational research emphasises the impact of interventions on students' learning outcomes, irrespective of any contextual factors such as socio-economic background, ethnicity, disability and gender (see Snook et al., 2009, 2010). All teachers want their students to succeed, 'if not within the system and the world they would ideally choose, then within the system and the world that exists' (Moore and Clarke, 2016, p9).

Key questions

What is best practice?

The leading proponents of evidence-based practice in education are Hattie (1999, 2003, 2009, 2017) and Marzano et al. (2001), who you may well have come across in your own teacher education programme.

Debates about direct instruction as opposed to experiential, discovery, problem-based or enquiry-based pedagogical approaches are ongoing, but as we see from Hattie's research, direct instruction is reported to significantly effect student achievement (Hattie, 2003, 2009, 2017). According to Hattie (2009), direct instruction is not didactic; it is intensive deliberate practice, and he advises that direct instruction involves the following seven steps:

1. communicate goals to help orient students to the content;

2. assess students' knowledge and skills needed to understand the new content;

3. present key principles of the new content through clear instruction;

4. check student mastery and understanding by posing questions, providing worked examples and correcting misconceptions;

5. provide opportunities for guided practice;

6. assess performance and provide feedback on guided practice; and

7. provide opportunities for independent practice through group or individual work.

In summary, Hattie's work suggests that the most powerful effects come from approaches where the teacher acts as an activator rather than a facilitator. A facilitator assists students; they do not control the activities of the learners. A facilitator of learning, therefore, is a teacher who does not operate under the traditional concept of teaching, but rather is meant to guide and assist students in learning for themselves – picking apart ideas, forming their own thoughts, and owning material through self-exploration and dialogue.

Marzano et al. (2001) have also identified nine specific teaching strategies that have significant impact on student outcomes (see Table 9.1).

Table 9.1 Nine essential teaching strategies

Identifying similarities and differences	Helps students understand more complex problems by analysing them in a simpler way.
Summarising and note-taking	Promotes comprehension because students have to analyse what is important and what is not important and put it in their own words.
Reinforcing effort and providing recognition	Showing the connection between effort and achievement helps students see the importance of effort. Note: Recognition is more effective if it is contingent on achieving some specified standard.
Homework and practice	Provides opportunities to extend learning but should be assigned based on relevant grade level. All homework should have a purpose that is readily evident to the students. Additionally, feedback should be given for all homework assignments.
Non-linguistic representations	Has recently been proven to stimulate and increase brain activity.

(Continued)

Table 9.1   (Continued)

Cooperative learning	Has been proven to have a positive impact on overall learning. *Note:* Groups should be small enough to be effective and the strategy should be used in a systematic and consistent manner.
Setting objectives and providing feedback	Provides students with a direction. Objectives should not be too specific and should be adaptable to students' individual objectives. There is no such thing as too much positive feedback; however, the method in which you give that feedback should be varied.
Generating and testing hypotheses	Research shows that a deductive approach works best, but both inductive and deductive reasoning can help students understand and relate to the material.
Cues, questions and advanced organisers	Helps students use what they already know to enhance what they are about to learn. These are usually most effective when used before a specific lesson.

Source: Adapted from Marzano et al. (2001)

In particular, Hattie's work has been very influential in policymaking in the UK and the development of research evidence to inform the education system about 'what works'. The Education Endowment Foundation (EEF), an independent body in receipt of a funding grant from the DfE, leads the way on evidence-based research to find the most effective approaches and interventions for improving educational attainment: 'It shows that they [teachers] can make a difference and that they are the most important people in the education system who are able make that difference to children and young people's learning' (EEF, 2011, p3).

Key questions

Are there any dangers in an emphasis on evidence in teaching?

Is the government right to favour the work of Hattie?

The danger is that the privileging of this type of evidence base in education may limit research only to what is measurable at the expense of other ways of knowing, such as teachers' professional experience and judgement. Biesta (2010) argues that the privileging of evidence-based research in professional practice restricts the opportunities for democratic participation in educational decision-making, and further argues that:

> questions about the effectiveness of educational actions are always secondary to questions of purpose ... [and] ... only in light of decisions about the aims and ends of educational practices that questions about evidence and effectiveness begin to have any meaning at all.
>
> (pp500–501)

Decisions about teaching approaches are based on value judgements made within specific contexts, and these value judgements about actions to achieve the aims and ends of education is what ultimately constitutes educational practice.

'Best practice' teaching approaches

It is important for us, as teachers, to critically examine what influences our own teaching approaches and to interrogate what is promoted as 'best practice'. Currently, cognitive load theory along with mastery learning and mindset theory are being promoted, and perhaps before these learning styles were the most influential 'best practice' strategy. Of course, it is important to bear in mind that 'best practice' is part of the dominant educational discourse that conceptualises knowledge, learning and therefore teaching in very specific ways.

Educational theories have long drawn on psychology, and learning has therefore been traditionally understood as a psychological matter, and thus primarily researched as a cognitive process of acquisition. As such, knowledge is assumed to be a stable entity that is acquired by individuals through the interaction of teaching. However, as teachers, I think we fully realise that learning is a complex matter to which there is no quick fix. Individuals learn in very different ways, and therefore how we teach needs to take account of this. As the principle of inclusion in education rose to prominence in the 1990s, so too did the promotion of 'best practice' strategies to drive up standards of educational achievement, but which equally specified the range of teacher behaviours that could then be managed to improve the performance of individual teachers. Evidence is needed to make practical decisions about teaching, as the legacy of learning styles proves; however, as teachers we need to question the increasing reliance on effect sizes from RCT and meta-analyses research and the role this evidence plays in decisions made by policymakers about how we should teach.

Mastery learning or cognitive load theory

Both mastery learning and cognitive load theory are based on the idea that as students become increasingly familiar with the content, cognitive processing is altered so that content can be handled more efficiently by working memory to meet learning outcomes. In this way, it is believed that students can master complex or technically challenging content through deliberate and repeated practice. With cognitive load theory specifically, the aim is to keep the cognitive load of students at a minimum during the learning process to develop long-term memory (Sweller, 1988, 1999). The three approaches recommended to reduce cognitive load are:

1.   Present material that aligns with the prior knowledge of students (intrinsic load).

2.   Avoid non-essential and confusing information (extraneous load).

3.   Stimulate processes that lead to conceptually rich and deep knowledge (germane load).

Learning outcomes are constant but the time needed for students to become proficient or competent in these outcomes is varied. Both terms are connected to a concept known as 'overlearning', which I first came across many years ago in my own teacher training for working with students with dyslexia – it is interesting that if you are in education long enough, ideas are recycled and reinterpreted as new. Indeed, Ayres (2006) asserts that 'describing [cognitive load theory] as a "recent" approach denies much of the history of instructional design' (p288). For example, we only have to look at Bloom's taxonomy (Bloom, 1956) in the cognitive domain, which has long been a component of the teacher-training curriculum for the PCET sector, to see the reference to prior learning assessment. Bloom categorised cognitive processes he considered essential for learning and critical thinking.

By establishing what students already know, teachers can plan and adjust teaching in lessons accordingly, and Bloom's taxonomy provides a useful strategy for formulating effective questions, which moves learning beyond factual recall of knowledge to cognitive processes such as analysis and evaluation, thus promoting critical thinking.

The key criticism levelled at these approaches is principally based on empirically establishing the extent to which working memory is in fact required for learning. Understanding is undoubtedly an important part of the teaching and learning process, but even here there is the recurrence of the assumption that knowledge is a fixed and stable entity. In addition, further evidence is required to establish whether, and how, the different kinds of cognitive load constrain each other, how they relate to the process of learning and, last but not least, clarification as to how they can indeed be measured (de Jong, 2010; Schnotz and Kurschner, 2007). So, here we see the prominence of teaching approaches being propelled into professional practice based on their statistical appeal and their instrumental value. Teaching approaches that foster dialogue and collaborative enquiry offer broader outcomes that are less procedural, and thus more difficult to measure:

> *Nothing has brought pedagogical theory into greater dispute than the belief that it is handing out to teachers recipes and models to be followed in teaching ... Education must be conceived as a continuing reconstruction of experience ... the teacher is engaged not just in the training of individuals, but in the formation of the proper social life.*
>
> (Dewey, 1897, p79)

Mindset theory

When it was first introduced, mindset theory was anticipated to be a major influence on educational attainment and ability, and caught on and spread like wildfire through the education system. The theory stems from Dweck's work on intelligence and the tension between conceptions of intelligence deriving from nature or nurture. From her original research base, Dweck has come up with the theory of mindset whereby she categorises people into two types: fixed mindset or growth mindset. A teaching approach that promotes a growth mindset is believed to improve learning outcomes for individuals through the development of self-belief and resilience. This theory suggests that those with a fixed mindset are more vulnerable to challenge in their learning due to the belief that intelligence is something you are born with, as opposed to a growth mindset, which suggests that intelligence is malleable and comes from effort and hard work. While there seems to be much anecdotal evidence about the efficacy of mindset theory on educational attainment, there is little empirical evidence to support its claim to improve outcomes. There is also a silent correlation between the idea of a growth mindset and failure; it is the responsibility of the individual student if they fail as they did not try hard enough, or the individual teacher did not do enough to instil a growth mindset in their students.

Lately, there has been some work carried out into mindset theory and its implications for practice. Replications of Dweck's research have proven inconclusive about its effects on learning attainment: 'Fixed beliefs about basic ability appear to be unrelated to ability, and we found no support for mindset-effects on cognitive ability, response to challenge, or educational progress' (Li and Bates, 2017, p2). It does seem difficult to conceive that human psychology can be simply categorised into two types.

Teacher knowledge in teaching

We have begun to examine influences on professional practice and the implications this has for us as professionals working in FE. The sector is subject to ever-higher stakes in terms of accountability, and therefore affects how teachers are managed within colleges. In turn, this has incrementally encroached on what teachers teach through externally imposed curricula, and increasingly how they should teach through the use of 'best practice' standards. Here, teacher knowledge will be explored in light of previous discussion on the contested evidential hierarchy of RCTs and meta-analyses over other types of evidence that may inform policymaking and pedagogical decision-making, such as teacher expertise gained from practical experience of teaching.

Key questions

Should teachers themselves have the freedom to choose the teaching approaches they use, or is it the choice of the organisation they work for?

The FE sector has fought long and hard to raise the professional status of its teachers and to gain the professional recognition its teachers so rightly deserve. The introduction of ITE qualifications for the sector, a professional body and QTLS as a professional formation process are all important factors in the professionalism of the sector. Reflective practice is a central tenet of ITE qualifications, and in most colleges reflection plays a role in professional development of teachers through the observation process. Schön's (1983) concept of 'knowing in action' draws upon consideration of knowledge *how* as an active and reciprocal process between the self and the situational context to comprise expertise of knowledge *how* and knowledge *what* to inform what Schön terms 'professional artistry' in teaching. Schön's disillusionment with technical rationality, which discounted the role of experience in teacher knowledge, is expressed in his concern for teacher knowledge being interpreted as a fixed entity, as a possession of individuals and as independent of context. Instead, he argued that it is situative, and as such entails a 'continual interweaving of thinking and doing' (Schön, 1983, p280), which involves all participants in professional practice (i.e. students as well as teachers). In short, teaching expertise is based on knowledge of key principles and procedures, but their use is determined by teachers in relation to the situational context of their practice.

Currently, output-based measures of successful teaching and learning are used to judge teacher effectiveness. Professionalism and its identification of what makes a 'good' teacher is a shifting concept in educational discourse. According to Hargreaves (2000) and Ozga (2000), this reflects the policy churn in education, and in turn the changing relationship between teachers and the government over time. Dominant educational discourses, such as 'best practice' currently, conceptualise teacher effectiveness in ways that tend to emphasise the individual teacher's accountability for the success or failure of their students, and as such underplay the role of wider society and the education system in such successes and failures.

Chapter summary

This chapter has explored the question of how we should teach in FE, and in so doing has raised a few questions for consideration regarding vocational pedagogy and the current educational discourses that increasingly govern how teachers should teach. Much policy work in FE is done to teachers rather than in collaboration with them, at the expense of the professions' judgement and experience in the pursuit of a means/end conceptualisation of teaching and learning. Acknowledgement of FE teachers' contribution within the broader educational context is essential because, ultimately, we are educating students for an uncertain future, with many threats at a local, national and global level. Hence, as professionals, we need the opportunity to interrogate our own pedagogy, as well as what has shaped it, and question whether it is adequate to help students face this uncertain future: 'We educators need to reclaim our professional freedom of thought and action; to introduce a curriculum that deals with the threats we face; and to renew both our educational "system" and our society through democratic values and practices' (Coffield and Williamson, 2011, p76).

Today, we are not only being told what to teach in prescriptive curricula, but increasingly being told how to teach. The word 'should' implies that there is a right way to teach and a wrong way to teach, and therefore has very real effects on the decisions we make as teachers in the classroom, workshop or other spaces we use for teaching in FE. The notion of a 'right' and a 'wrong' way to teach is most recently endorsed by evidence-based research in education that underpins what is understood as 'best practice' strategies currently promulgated by external agencies, policymakers and college management teams.

Teaching approaches that provide experiential and practical learning are sadly stigmatised by societal attitudes that favour academic education over vocational education, and evidence-based research has seemingly contributed to this lack of parity of esteem. Perhaps the introduction of the new 'T-level' qualifications in 2020 will help to challenge these attitudes; we will have to wait and see. As educators working in FE, there is an expectation to teach 'useful knowledge' to meet labour market needs and to give students as much real-world learning as is possible, but importantly the reassertion of a broader vision of education requires us to teach much more than this if we are to develop not only a skilled workforce, but active and compassionate citizens - citizens who can participate in democratic society and challenge some of the issues, such as inequality, environmental degradation, low pay, job insecurity and other socio-economic conditions created by the austerity and divisiveness of these current times to create a more just and cohesive society.

Recommended further reading

Illeris, K. (2014) *Transformative Learning and Identity*. London: Routledge.

For further information, resources and techniques on radicalisation, see *Teaching Approaches That Help to Build Resilience to Extremism among Young People* (DfE, 2011) and *Teaching Approaches for Building Pupils' Resilience to Extremist Narratives* (Educate Against Hate, 2017).

References

Avis, P. (2014) Workplace learning, VET and vocational pedagogy: the transformation of practice. *Research in Post-Compulsory Education*, 19(1): 45–53.

Ayres, P. (2006) Impact of reducing intrinsic cognitive load on learning in a mathematical domain. *Applied Cognitive Psychology*, 20(3): 287–298.

Bathmaker, A.-M. (2013) Defining 'knowledge' in vocational education qualifications in England: an analysis of key stakeholders and their constructions of knowledge, purposes and content. *Journal of Vocational Education and Training*, 65(1): 87–107.

Biesta, G. (2010) Why what works still won't work: from evidence-based education to value-based education. *Studies in Philosophy and Education*, 29(5): 491–503.

Bloom, B. (ed.) (1956) *Taxonomy of Educational Objectives: Handbook I – The Cognitive Domain*. London: Longman.

Clarke, L. and Winch, C. (2006) A European skills framework – but what are skills? Anglo-Saxon versus German concepts. *Journal of Education and Work*, 19(3): 255–269.

Clarke, L. and Winch, C. (2007) *Vocational Education: International Approaches, Developments and Systems*. London: Routledge.

Coffield, F. and Williamson, B. (2011) *Exam Factories to Communities of Discovery: The Democratic Route*. London: Institute of Education.

de Jong, T. (2010) Cognitive load theory, educational research, and instructional design: some food for thought. *Instructional Science*, 38(2): 105–134.

Dewey, J. (1897) My pedagogical creed. *School Journal*, 54: 77–80.

DfE (2011) *Teaching Approaches That Help to Build Resilience to Extremism among Young People*. London: DfE.

Duckworth, V. and Smith, R. (2016) *Transformative Further Education: Empowering People and Communities*. London: UCU.

Dweck, C., Walton, G. and Cohen, G. (2014) *Academic Tenacity Mindsets and Skills That Promote Long-Term Learning*. Seattle, WA: Bill & Melinda Gates Foundation.

EEF (2011) *EEF Toolkit Report*. Available at: https://educationendowmentfoundation.org.uk/evidence-summaries/teaching-learning-toolkit/mastery-learning/

Freire, P. (1970) *Pedagogy of the Oppressed*. New York: Continuum Books.

Gu, Q. and Day, C. (2007) Teachers resilience: a necessary condition for effectiveness. *Teaching and Teacher Education: An International Journal of Research and Studies*, 23(8): 1302–1316.

Hargreaves, A. (2000) Four ages of professionalism and professional learning. *Teachers and Teaching: Theory and Practice*, 6(2): 151–182.

Hattie, J. (1999) *Influences of Student Learning*. Inaugural Lecture, Professor of Education, University of Auckland, 2 August 1999.

Hattie, J. (2003) *Teachers Make a Difference: What Is the Research Evidence*. University of Auckland Australian Council for Educational Research.

Hattie, J. (2009) *Visible Learning: A Synthesis of Over 800 Meta-Analyses Relating to Achievement*. London: Routledge.

Hattie, J. (2017) Educators are not uncritical believers of a cult figure. *School Leadership and Management*, 37(4): 427–430.

HM Government (2011) *Prevent Strategy*. London: HMG.

Hyland, T. and Johnson, S. (1998) Of cabbages and key skills: exploding the mythology of core transferable skills in post-school education. *Journal of Further and Higher Education*, 22(2): 163–172.

Jarvis, P. (2009) Learning how to be a person in society: learning to be me. In K. Illeris (ed.), *Contemporary Theories of Learning*. London: Routledge.

JCQ (2018) *GCSE (Full Course) Outcomes for All Grade Sets and Age Breakdowns for UK Candidates Results Summer 2018*. Available at: www.jcq.org.uk/examination-results/gcses/2018

Li, Y. and Bates, T. (2017) *Does Growth Mindset Improve Children's IQ, Educational Attainment or Response to Setbacks? Active-Control Interventions and Data on Children's Own Mindsets*. Working Paper, SocArXiv, 7 July 2017: 1–27. Available at: https://osf.io/preprints/socarxiv/tsdwy

Lucas, B., Spencer, E. and Claxton, G. (2012) *How to Teach Vocational Education: A Theory of Vocational Pedagogy*. London: City & Guilds.

Marzano, R., Pickering, D. and Pollock, J. (2001) *Classroom Instruction That Works: Research-Based Strategies for Increasing Student Achievement*. Alexandria, VA: ASCD.

McLoughlin, F. (2013) *It's about Work: Excellent Adult Vocational Teaching and Learning*. London: Learning and Skills Improvement Service. Available at: https://api.excellencegateway.org.uk/resource/eg:5937

Mezirow, J. (1978) *Education for Perspective Transformation: Women's Re-Entry Programs in Community Colleges*. New York: Teacher's College, Columbia University.

Mezirow, J. (1998) On critical reflection. *Adult Learning Quarterly*, 48(3): 185–198.

Mezirow, J. (2000) *Learning as Transformation: Critical Perspectives on a Theory in Progress*. San Francisco, CA: Jossey-Bass.

Moore, A. and Clarke, M. (2016) 'Cruel optimism': teacher attachment to professionalism in an era of performativity. *Journal of Education Policy*, 31(5): 666–677.

Ozga, J. (2000) *Policy Research in Educational Settings*. Maidenhead: Open University Press.

Pleasance, S. (2016) *Wider Professional Practice in Education and Training*. London: Sage.

Pring, R., Hayward, G., Hodgson, A., Spours, K., Johnson, J., Keep, E. and Rees, G. (2009) *Education for All: Nuffield Review of 14–19 Education and Training, England and Wales*. London: Routledge.

Schnotz, W. and Kurschner, C. (2007) A reconsideration of cognitive load theory. *Educational Psychology Review*, 19(4): 469–508.

Schön, D. (1983) *The Reflective Practitioner: How Professionals Think in Action*. New York: Basic Books.

Snook, I., Clark, J., Harker, R. and O'Neill, A.M. (2009) Invisible learnings: a commentary of John Hattie's book *Visible Learning: A Synthesis of Over 800 Meta-Analyses Relating to Achievement*. *New Zealand Journal of Educational Studies*, 44(1): 93–106.

Snook, I., Clark, J., Harker, R. and O'Neill, A.M. (2010) Critic and conscience of society: a reply to John Hattie. *New Zealand Journal of Educational Studies*, 45(2): 93–98.

Sweller, J. (1988) Cognitive load during problem solving: effects on learning. *Cognitive Science*, 12: 257–285.

Sweller, J. (1999) *Instructional Design in Technical Areas*. Victoria, Australia: Australian Council for Educational Research.

Wheelahan, L. (2010) *Why Knowledge Matters in Curriculum: A Social Realist Argument*. London: Routledge.

Wolf, A. (2011) *Review of Vocational Education: The Wolf Report*. London: DfE.

10

IT'S ALL IN THE MIND … OR IS IT? CAN AN UNDERSTANDING OF PSYCHOLOGICAL APPROACHES TO LEARNING ENHANCE TEACHING?

Janet Lord

Key words – learning; approaches; evidence; psychology; behaviourism; constructivism; humanism; neuroscience

Introduction

This chapter introduces ideas about how people learn and of some of the different processes involved, and of different ways of thinking about these processes. It will consider constructivist, behaviourist, humanist and neuroscientific approaches to learning. The chapter will also discuss how best to use these understandings of learning in further and adult education settings.

What are psychological theories of learning?

Psychological theories of learning are theories that explain how individuals learn; they are rooted in psychology. Many psychologists would explain learning as being a relatively permanent change in behaviour. Psychological theories of learning are theories that focus on the individual and the learning processes that the individual engages with or goes through in learning. Such theories comprise an organised set of principles explaining how individuals acquire, retain and recall knowledge.

In this chapter we will look at four main theories:

1. *Behaviourism* emphasises the role of environmental factors in influencing behaviour. We learn new behaviour in various ways – learning through associating two stimuli or events; or through being reinforced for our behaviours; or by watching, imitating and learning from other people.

2. *Constructivism* states that people construct their own understanding and knowledge of the world, through experiencing things and reflecting on those experiences.

3. *Humanism* sees learning as a personal act to fulfil potential, and that learning is student-centred and personal.

4. The *neuroscientific approach* is that the learning process involves working memory, long-term memory and associated control processes. The mental processes involved in learning are key, and learning involves changing the brain.

Behaviourist approaches to learning

Basic assumptions of the behaviourist approach

The behaviourist approach considers that learning (which behaviourists consider to be changes in behaviour) results from an individual's direct experience of their environment. Behaviourists take a scientific approach to learning, and do not consider or discuss that mental processes are involved in learning – these processes are not observable and so cannot be studied objectively.

Behaviourists use the principles of *classical* and *operant* conditioning (conditioning is another word for learning) to explain how learning happens.

Classical conditioning is sometimes called Pavlovian conditioning after the Russian physiologist Pavlov, who first described the processes involved. In classical conditioning, learning happens by association between an involuntary behaviour and a response. Two stimuli are linked together to produce a new learned response. For example, students sometimes associate doing examinations with anxiety and pressure. This response might be as a result of a primary school experience, where a child was given a timed examination and felt anxious – the child associated the nervous feeling with the examination. When the student is older, this association may affect their behaviour in college (e.g. when they have to sit an examination or undergo a practical assessment). Teachers in colleges can be aware of these negative associations that may have been built up over time, and try to create a calm, low-pressure assessment environment to help the student deal with the effects of the association between tests and anxiety.

Operant conditioning, or learning by reinforcement, was developed by the neo-behaviourists. Neo-behaviourism was the second phase of behaviourism, and developed in the period from about 1930 to 1955. This approach is associated particularly with the work of Skinner. Neo-behaviourists suggested that learning and scientific ethos were important to psychological theories of learning, and they also tried to formalise the laws governing behaviour. The theory of operant conditioning is based on the work of the famous psychologist Skinner, whose work with rats showed that animals make associations between a behaviour and its consequence. This work was extended to humans, and operant conditioning is now a key part of learning theory. In operant conditioning, behaviour is affected by its consequences. Learning happens as a result of reinforcement or punishment. These two are frequently confused, so Table 10.1 will help to explain the differences.

Table 10.1   Operant conditioning

Reinforcement or punishment		Explanation	Example
Reinforcement - makes a behaviour *more* likely to happen.	Positive reinforcement - called positive because something (a stimulus) is added to the situation to increase the likelihood of the behaviour happening.	This is when a stimulus, a pleasurable one, is given after a particular behaviour is exhibited (e.g. giving praise or a reward to increase the likelihood of the behaviour occurring again).	A teacher gives positive feedback to a student for submitting an excellent assignment.
	Negative reinforcement - called negative because something (a stimulus) is taken away from the situation to increase the likelihood of the behaviour happening.	This is when a stimulus, usually something unpleasant, is *removed* after a particular behaviour is exhibited. The likelihood of the particular behaviour occurring again in the future is increased because of removing/avoiding the negative consequence.	The teacher gives a student an exemption from a test because they have attended every timetabled learning session.
Punishment - makes the behaviour *less* likely to happen.	Positive punishment - adding an aversive or unpleasant stimulus to reduce the likelihood of the behaviour occurring.	The individual experiences something unpleasant as a result of performing the behaviour, and so is less likely to repeat the behaviour.	A student is criticised for doing a poor presentation in a class assessment.
	Negative punishment - removing a pleasant stimulus to reduce the likelihood of the behaviour happening.	Something that the individual likes is removed as a result of them performing a particular behaviour, and so the individual is less likely to repeat the behaviour.	A student is always late for class, so loses the privilege of having a five-minute break to get a snack.

In the classroom, if a student has to give a presentation in front of the whole class, then if the other students laugh (positive punishment) at the student, the student may get nervous and not want to give a presentation again (as a result of the laughter, they are less likely to repeat the behaviour). On the other hand, if the audience clap and cheer the student (positive reinforcement), they will be more likely to repeat the behaviour and do a presentation again.

Table 10.2 shows the differences between operant conditioning and classical conditioning.

Table 10.2   Operant conditioning and classical conditioning

	Type of learning	
	Operant conditioning	Classical conditioning
Learning process	Learning is through reinforcement/punishment. Reinforcement and punishment affect the frequency of behaviours.	Learning is through association. Involves forming an association between two stimuli, resulting in a learned response.
Key names	Skinner	Pavlov
Features	Focuses on voluntary behaviours.	Focuses on involuntary behaviours.

Key questions

What are the challenges of using the principles of behaviourism in teaching in the FE and skills sector?

Robert Gagné: the application of behaviourism to online learning environments

Robert Gagné (1985) emphasised the use of operant conditioning and, in particular, positive reinforcement in learning. His initial work was rooted in behaviourism, and he combined this with a more cognitive information-processing approach. He originally worked on military instruction and the ideas that apply to that – drill, practice and order – are also seen in the way that instructional online computer programmes are designed to work. In an online learning environment, behaviourism involves dividing the content into smaller steps. These smaller, more manageable steps can then be repeated with ongoing monitoring of student learning.

Gagné suggests that the most essential ingredients of teaching, which are mainly drawn from behaviourism, are:

- presenting the knowledge or demonstrating the skill;

- providing practice with feedback; and

- providing learner guidance.

These basic principles are still used in the design of learning courses. Miner et al. (2015) reported that in nurse education, student evaluations were positive and indicated increased effectiveness and enthusiasm. Overall, the student nurses' final grades increased as a result of using Gagné's methods.

Impact of behaviourism on curriculum design

Some curricula are based on behaviourism. The principles of curriculum design in this model are to specify goals and objectives, and then to link specific content and activities to the goals. Everything the students do must be observable as this is the evidence that the student has achieved the goals and objectives, which are also based on observable behaviours. All activities lead to students being able to do whatever the goals and objectives specify. The principles of behaviourism, and specifically social learning theory, are also seen in a teaching method known as 'sitting with Nellie', which is still used

Key questions

Are there dangers of seeing students as passive recipients of knowledge in using behaviourism in the classroom?

If so, how might these dangers be mitigated?

in some jobs/apprenticeships – it means at first just watching an experienced member of staff do a job, then helping a little bit, and then moving, using simple steps, to doing the job yourself.

Constructivism
Basic assumptions of the constructivist approach

In contrast to behaviourists, constructivists believe that learning is an active, constructive process where individuals actively construct or create their own representations of reality.

The work of Piaget

Piaget's theory of constructivist learning (e.g. Piaget, 1936, 1952) has been very influential in education. Piaget sees cognitive development as a process that occurs due to biological maturation and interaction with the environment. He suggested that children and adults learn in very different ways. In this section, we will focus on adult learners, but Piagetian ideas about children's cognitive development will help to set the context.

According to Piaget, schemas are the basic building blocks of cognitive models. A schema is a cognitive structure that represents the knowledge relating to everything that we know about the world, including ourselves, other people and events. They enable us to form mental representations of the world. According to Piaget, the development of an individual's mental processes happens through increases in the number and complexity of the individual's schemas.

As we grow, we adapt to the world. Piaget suggested that adaption comprised two key processes: assimilation and accommodation. Assimilation is when people use an existing schema to deal with something new (e.g. using a schema for making a chocolate cake and altering it to make a lemon drizzle cake). Accommodation is when an existing schema (knowledge) does not work and needs to be changed to deal with a new object or situation. For example, when a person first sees an analogue clock or watch with hands, they won't be able to use their 'digital clock or phone' schema to help them to tell the time, and they will have to develop a new schema for telling the time – one that includes an analogue watch or clock.

Equilibration is the force that moves development along. Equilibrium occurs when an individual's schemas can deal with most new information, through assimilation. However, an uncomfortable state, disequilibrium, occurs if schemas cannot be assimilated to deal with a new situation. Equilibration is the force that drives the learning process in this situation as we accommodate our schemas to deal with new information. Once we are back in equilibrium, then the discomfort of disequilibrium is over.

Piaget proposed four stages of cognitive development that reflect the increasing sophistication of children's thought:

1. sensorimotor stage (birth to age 2);

2. preoperational stage (from about age 2 to age 7);

3. concrete operational stage (from about age 7 to age 11); and

4. formal operational stage (age 11+ to adolescence and adulthood).

In further and adult education, we can normally assume that all our learners are in Piaget's formal operational stage. Operational thinking means thinking that is logical, and the term 'formal' means that individuals can understand the 'form' of an argument; they do not need ideas to be represented concretely and they can think abstractly and manipulate ideas in their head. For example, take a question such as 'Harry is taller than Martha, and Martha is taller than Zainab. Who is the shortest?' Individuals using *concrete* thinking processes, if they are thinking operationally (logically), might be able to solve this problem, but perhaps only if they are allowed dolls to represent the people in the problem. An individual who has reached the formal operational stage of thinking would be able to do the problem in their head without representing it in a concrete fashion.

Bruner and discovery learning

Although Piaget established the foundations of the theory of constructivist learning, Jerome Bruner contributed important ideas; his theory concerns 'discovery learning', a method of enquiry-based learning. This approach encourages learners to build on past experiences and knowledge and to use their intuition and creativity. Learning is not simply about absorbing information, but comprises actively seeking for answers and solutions. Some important ideas suggested by Bruner were:

- the goal of education should be cognitive and intellectual development, not just rote learning of facts;

- the development of problem-solving skills through the processes of enquiry and discovery is important; and

- the curriculum should be designed so that the mastery of skills leads to the mastery of still more advanced ones.

An important part of discovery learning is the notion of the 'spiral curriculum'. Bruner (1966) believed that 'any subject can be taught effectively in some intellectually honest form to any child at any stage of development' (p33). In other words, teaching starts off with basic ideas and then revisits these ideas, building and developing them.

The work of Bruner has had a significant effect on education and on the ways that teachers work with learners.

Constructivism in the classroom

Constructivism feels like a very natural fit for the further and adult education sector because of its focus on continuous learning and the emphasis on the value that learners bring to their learning experiences.

If you were to work with this kind of approach, you would be likely to work using these assumptions:

1. The students' current beliefs are important, even if they might not be correct.

2. Every individual is different and will have a different learning experience based on their own understandings of the world.

3. Understanding and the construction of meaning are active, ongoing processes.

4. Learning may involve some significant changes to what individuals think.

5. As learning is an active process, this means that it depends partly on the learners taking responsibility for their own learning.

Key questions

Is a teacher a 'sage on the stage' or a 'guide on the side'?

In typical constructivist classrooms, teachers act more as a guide than as the source of all knowledge, and they aim to provide students with the opportunity to test out their own ideas and understandings of the world and of the material they are learning (see Table 10.3).

Table 10.3 Constructivism in practice

What might you be like if you were a constructivist teacher in further and adult education?
You believe that learners actively construct their knowledge through a process of active enquiry and discovery.
You want to facilitate learning by providing the necessary resources, and by creating learning sessions where learners are encouraged to reflect on and question their own learning processes.
You will work with learners by helping them to assimilate their new knowledge with their old knowledge and experiences.
Your curriculum/scheme of work/lesson plan is flexible enough to allow for students' own experiences and areas of interest to be included.
You are happy to work with the knowledge that students will always interpret information in their own individual ways.
You think that it is a good idea to work by encouraging learners to think about real-world situations.
You like your students to work together, rather than to compete with each other (on the whole), and you are keen to provide opportunities for peer learning and support, where learners can learn from each other.
You want to support your learners by scaffolding their learning when appropriate and by helping them to develop knowledge and skills.

Humanism

Basic assumptions of the humanist approach: learning as a personal act to fulfil potential

Humanism is a philosophical and pedagogical approach that views learning as a personal act to fulfil an individual's potential. One of its key ideas is that the individual is seen as a whole person who grows and develops over their lifespan. So, for humanists, the self, motivation and goals are important ideas.

At the end of the twentieth century, this approach was very popular in further and adult education, mainly because of its emphasis on lifelong development and personal growth. The value-driven humanist approach fitted with the ethos of many further education colleges. At the same time, in psychology, there was a move away from the 'scientific' approach to understanding human behaviour, and so humanism fitted well with this move. Increasingly, people were seen as individuals, and personal choice and freedom, agency and motivations were emphasised.

If you look back at the previous sections of this chapter, you will see that humanism is a very different approach to either the constructivist or the behaviourist approach to learning and pedagogy.

The work of Carl Rogers and Abraham Maslow

Two humanist theorists who focus on learning as growth are Abraham Maslow (1943) and Carl Rogers (1946).

Carl Rogers, often seen as one of the founders of the humanist approach, felt that education involved the whole person; their individual experiences were key. Feelings and intuitions were seen as important as logic and intellectual thinking.

He saw the following features as being significant:

- The idea of the whole person is important in learning – both feelings and cognitions are taken into account.

- The motivation for learning comes from within the individual and is self-initiated.

- Learning makes a difference to people's lives, including to an individual's behaviour and attitudes.

- Learners think about and reflect on their own learning and whether it is fulfilling their needs.

Maslow is another humanist theorist, probably most famous for his 'hierarchy of needs'. The hierarchy of needs, often represented as a pyramid with five levels of need, is a psychological theory about motivation. At the lowest level of the pyramid are physiological needs, and at the highest level is self-actualisation. Only when the lower needs are met is it possible to fully move on to the next level. Once physiological needs such as hunger, thirst and sleep are met, then the individual strives to meet safety needs, such as somewhere secure to live; belongingness needs include needs for warm and satisfying relationships; and self-esteem needs are about independence, recognition and mastery. At the final, top level of the pyramid is self-actualisation – the achievement of being the best person you can be. Self-actualisation is about morality, creativity, psychological growth, fulfilment and satisfaction.

The focus on learning and growth suggested by Maslow and Rogers was attractive to educators in the twentieth century and continues to be so now. This is interesting in view of the fact that there is only limited evidence for the ideas in the hierarchy of needs. For example, Wahba and Bridwell (1976) suggest that there is a lack of empirical evidence for the Maslovian approach, and Tay and Diener (2011) have demonstrated that the ranking of needs varies substantially between individuals. Nonetheless, the use of Maslow in college classrooms is widespread. A recent paper by Compton (2018) acknowledges the lack of scientific evidence for some of the ideas, although he does suggest that there is in fact a good deal of relevant empirical research. Even if Maslow's ideas about the hierarchy of needs are sometimes misinterpreted, and even though Maslow did alter them in various of his papers, Compton suggests that the rich insights that Maslow's work may provide are valuable and relevant.

One theory of learning that utilises a humanist approach together with a constructivist one is that of Jack Mezirow.

Mezirow and transformational learning

Mezirow (1994) described transformational learning theory as being 'constructivist, an orientation which holds that the way learners interpret and reinterpret their sense experience is, central to making meaning and hence learning' (p222).

Mezirow described how individuals use their reflections on life to change the ways in which they see the world. One of the main ideas in his theory is that what is called a 'disorienting dilemma' can result in people changing their worldview. Disorienting dilemmas are experiences that don't fit into a person's current understandings of the world (e.g. witnessing a serious accident or being challenged about your beliefs concerning the existence of a deity). When faced with a disorienting dilemma, people are put into a situation where they have to rethink their beliefs to fit the new experience into the rest of their worldview. The resulting learning is transformative; by this, Mezirow (2003) means 'learning that transforms problematic frames of reference to make them more inclusive, discriminating, reflective, open, and emotionally able to change' (p58). In other words, it is transformational.

Personalised and student-centred learning: what does this mean in practice?

The overall aim of education, according to the humanist philosophy, is to encourage individuals to be open-minded, active and thoughtful; people who are motivated to learn, who know how to learn, and who want to continue to learn. In the FAE classroom, the learner is at the centre of the learning, and their individuality is respected. Learners are given the autonomy to make decisions about their own learning, and ideally should choose what they want to learn. Lessons are not rigidly prescribed, but flow according to the needs, styles and goals of each learner. Each student is respected as an individual and is responsible for making decisions about her or his learning. In the FAE classroom, both feelings and knowledge are important to the learning process.

Key questions

Are there any learners for which this approach could be particularly useful?

Approaches from neuroscience

Basic principles of the approach

Neuroscience is to do with the biology of the nervous system, including how the brain works, at the anatomical level such as neurons. For neuroscientists, the learning process involves changing the brain, and includes working memory, long-term memory and associated control processes. The approach has been discussed by psychologists and educators such as Sarah-Jayne Blakemore and Uta Frith (Blakemore and Frith, 2005).

The role of neuroscience in considering how students learn

Over the last few years, the neuroscientific approach to learning has been very much in the news. The basic premise is that when learning occurs, the brain changes. For educational neuroscientists, it is important to ensure that the optimal conditions for this learning to happen are in place. These might include sleep, nutrition and exercise; these factors are thought to be good for what is called neuroplasticity (changes in the brain due to stimuli) and neurogenesis (the production of new neurons). There are various ways in which this may happen; for example, sleep, good nutrition and exercise may keep chemicals such as dopamine and cortisol, two important hormones that may affect learning, in balance.

Some approaches to the neuroscience of learning suggest that a moderate amount of stress, sometimes called physiological arousal, is good for learning, while both too much and too little stress are not. So, if you are feeling very laid back and chilled, or incredibly stressed, then optimal neural conditions for learning might not be met; for instance, high stress is associated with the 'fight or flight' mechanism and less activity in the parts of the brain's cortex where higher-level learning happens. But a moderate amount of stress (e.g. that experienced when a student is asked to take part in a small group activity) may stimulate the brain in the right ways to induce learning.

Active learning is also emphasised in the neuroscientific approach. The more complex the thought processes, the more activation there is in the brain, and the more brain areas will be stimulated by the activity.

It is worth pointing out that some researchers in this area (e.g. Bishop, 2014) have advised caution in regard to the neuroscientific approach in education, suggesting that it is not as useful as some people may think.

Differences between adults and children as learners

There are differences between children's and adults' brains. As individuals age, structural and functional changes mean that learning may take place differently in adults than in the ways it does in children, and/or that it may be difficult for adults to learn at all. We know that adult learning can be transformational for adults – it can affect their quality of life and life chances – and so it is important that as educators we think about how learning might be different for adults. We have already seen how many adult learners are working and/or have family and caring responsibilities. We know that the brain changes as we age, and so we also need to consider the implications for teachers and teaching of these changes. Some of these are shown below.

Implications of neuroscience for adult curriculum design and delivery

Some principles for adult learning based on neuroscience have been identified by Knowland and Thomas (2014). Of course, further research is on-going in this area, but there are some well-established principles:

1. Practice is important to learning, and so is long-term commitment from teachers and learners. Also, long-term investment in education is important for successful learning to take place.

2. Motivation and attention are important. This is true for both children and adults, but possibly more so for adults.

3.   The role of effective feedback is possibly even more important for adult learners than it is for children.

4.   The role of active learning may be more significant for adults than for children – engagement with a tutor and with the materials is important.

5.   Working on fundamental cognitive and study skills, such as attention, say, will help to support learning of higher-order skills and materials.

Key questions

Are adult learners sometimes too stressed to learn?

If so, what can teachers do about this?

Although there is a relatively large amount of public interest in neuroscience, accessible high-quality empirical information is relatively hard to find. As a result, educators and researchers in this field often urge caution in the rush to apply approaches that are based on neuroscience, many of which do not yet have a sound basis in science.

Myth-busting

Learning styles: introduction to the controversy

The idea that we learn better when taught in such a way that we can use our 'preferred learning style' is one that is very pervasive in education. In classrooms throughout the Western world, learners are assessed on their learning style and teachers use the ideas in planning lessons and activities. There are more than 70 different instruments or tests for classifying learning styles (Coffield et al., 2004). These tests try to assess individual differences between learners by classifying them as having 'styles' such as 'visual' or 'kinaesthetic', or along dimensions such as 'active/reflective' and 'abstract/concrete'. According to most interpretations of learning styles theory, teaching learners in ways that match their assessed 'learning style' will result in improved learning. It is relatively simple to check whether this is in fact the case, and as a result of this checking it is generally agreed that there is no evidence to support the use of learning styles in this way (e.g. Rohrer and Pashler, 2012). This has led to learning styles being widely classified as a 'myth' (e.g. Howard-Jones, 2014).

Examples of learning styles in practice

One learning styles inventory that is widely used is Kolb's learning styles inventory, based on the theoretical work of Kolb (1984). Kolb's learning styles are based on two dimensions: active/reflective and abstract/concrete. The test can be done online, and when a learner completes the test, recommendations for teachers are provided too.

Another common test is the VARK test, based on the work of Fleming and Mills (1992). In this test, learners are identified as being either visual, auditory, reading/writing or kinaesthetic types of learners.

These kinds of questionnaires and inventories are still widely used (Newton and Miah, 2017). Sadly, they also found that 32 per cent of academics in UK universities said that they would continue to use learning styles inventories despite the lack of an evidence base to support the idea and the lack of a strong theoretical framework.

Evidence base and evidence-based practice: what do these challenges mean for practice in FAE more generally?

When we read about the fact that learning styles seem to be seductive, yet they may be of little use in learning, this leads us to think about the nature of evidence in education, and to think about evidence-based practice. We could think more seriously about making education an evidence-based profession, with teachers as action researchers, researching their own practice, and basing their future practice on this research. This certainly seems to be the way that medical practice is going. However, on the whole, educational outcomes are different from medical ones. We know that with adult learners, there are complexities in the ways that their learning is situated. Learners are not the same as patients, and the outcomes are not necessarily measurable in a useful way. We know that any research into learning has to take account of a myriad of factors: those at the individual level, then the immediate context of the learning (e.g. the learner's college or workplace), and the more macro-level factors such as discourses about the nature of education and its funding. We are not always sure of what needs to be measured (or indeed what ought to be measured), so we perhaps need to be wary about calling for 'evidence-based education' in an oversimplified way, which may not reflect the realities of educating adult learners.

Chapter summary

There are a variety of theories about how learners learn. Some of the theories are:

- *behaviourism*, a focus on stimulus response and the behaviour of learners;

- *constructivism*, a focus on the construction of meaning and active learning; and

- *humanism*, a focus on personal growth and self-fulfilment.

This chapter has also looked at a relative newcomer to the field - that of neuroscience.

The chapter has considered the value - or otherwise - of learning styles in education.

So, in answer to our chapter title, 'Can an understanding of psychological approaches to learning enhance teaching?' it seems that we can reply with a resounding 'yes'. But to think a bit more deeply, this chapter has led us to think about the nature of and need for evidence-based education, and the complexities that that might involve. Perhaps our thinking should take us back to the fundamental question, 'What is the purpose of education?'

If we start from this, and start to unpick our ideas and beliefs about the ways in which individuals learn, and the reasons for them wanting to learn, we may well find that we want to change our practice and our education system, but we will also have a clear idea of the beliefs about learning and education that drive what we do in helping learners to learn.

Further recommended reading

This is a great website that summarises a huge number of learning theories and is free to use: www.learning-theories.com/

Behaviourist approach to learning

This is a TED-Ed Talk on classical and operant conditioning that is clear to understand: www.youtube.com/watch?v=H6LEcM0E0io

This is a BBC 4 *The Brain* programme about the Bandura et al. (1961) Bobo doll experiment – it is only a few minutes long, but has some great footage and a clear explanation: www.youtube.com/watch?v=zerCK0lRjp8

Constructivism

This website will give you a clear explanation of Piaget's work; it also provides a more detailed explanation of the Piagetian stages of development than is provided in this chapter: www.verywellmind.com/piagets-stages-of-cognitive-development-2795457

This video shows Jerome Bruner talking about discovery learning and what kinds of learning environments he creates for students – well worth watching: www.youtube.com/watch?v=pZuHz49CYOA

This is a useful website about Bruner, constructivism and discovery learning. It's also got some useful references and video material: http://mile.mmu.edu.my/orion/1711/bruner-discovery-learning/

Humanism

This is an overview of humanistic psychology in general, with hyperlinks to some of the most important ideas: www.verywellmind.com/what-is-humanistic-psychology-2795242

This website includes the theory and key terms about humanism and also talks about Mezirow and the work of Carl Rogers: www.learning-theories.org/doku.php?id=learning_paradigms:humanism

If you want to read more about Maslow, this is a brief useful guide that includes links to other resources: www.studentguide.org/an-introduction-to-maslows-hierarchy-of-needs/

Neuroscience and learning

This article looks at how our understanding of the human brain can be useful in relation to the decisions about curriculum, pedagogy and assessment that we make. It's a useful starting point: www.teachermagazine.com.au/articles/brainy-teaching-educational-neuroscience-and-classroom-practice

Learning styles

You can find a basic introduction to the idea of learning styles here: www.verywellmind.com/what-is-a-learning-style-inventory-2795159

If you'd like to explore the learning styles 'controversy' a bit further, this is a good place to start: https://digest.bps.org.uk/2018/04/03/another-nail-in-the-coffin-for-learning-styles-students-did-not-benefit-from-studying-according-to-their-supposed-learning-style/

For an overview of VARK learning styles, see here: www.verywellmind.com/vark-learning-styles-2795156

An overview of Kolb's learning styles inventory is here: www.verywellmind.com/kolbs-learning-styles-2795155

References

Bandura, A., Ross, D. and Ross, S.A. (1961) Transmission of aggression through the imitation of aggressive models. *Journal of Abnormal and Social Psychology*, 63: 575–582.

Bishop, D. (2014) What is educational neuroscience? *BishopBlog*, 24 January 2014. Available at: http://deevybee.blogspot.com/2014/01/what-is-educational-neuroscience.html

Blakemore, S.-J. and Frith, U. (2005) *The Learning Brain: Lessons for Education*. Malden, MA: Blackwell.

Bruner, J.S. (1966) *Toward a Theory of Instruction*. Cambridge, MA: Belknap Press.

Coffield, F., Moseley, D., Hall, E. and Ecclestone, K. (2004) *Learning Styles and Pedagogy in Post 16 Learning: A Systematic and Critical Review*. London: Learning and Skills Research Centre.

Compton, W.C. (2018) Self-actualization myths: what did Maslow really say? *Journal of Humanistic Psychology*. doi:10.1177/0022167818761929.

Fleming, N.D. and Mills, C. (1992) Not another inventory, rather a catalyst for reflection. *To Improve the Academy*, 11: 137–155.

Gagné, R.M. (1985) *The Conditions of Learning and Theory of Instruction*, 4th edn. New York: Holt, Rinehart & Winston.

Howard-Jones, P.A. (2014) Neuroscience and education: myths and messages. *Nature Reviews: Neuroscience*, 15: 817–824.

Knowland, V.C.P. and Thomas, M.S.C. (2014) Educating the adult brain: how the neuroscience of learning can inform educational policy. *International Review of Education*, 60: 99–122.

Kolb, D.A. (1984) *Experiential Learning: Experience as the Source of Learning and Development* (Vol. 1). Englewood Cliffs, NJ: Prentice Hall.

Maslow, A.H. (1943) A theory of human motivation. *Psychological Review*, 50: 370–396.

Mezirow, J. (1994) Understanding transformation theory. *Adult Education Quarterly*, 44(4): 222–232.

Mezirow, J. (2003) Transformative learning as discourse. *Journal of Transformative Education*, 1(1): 58–63.

Miner, A., Mallow, J.M., Theeks, L. and Barnes, E. (2015) Using Gagne's 9 events of instruction to enhance student performance and course evaluations in undergraduate nursing course. *Nurse Educator*, 40(3): 152–154.

Newton P.M. and Miah, M. (2017) Evidence-based higher education: is the learning styles 'myth' important? *Frontiers in Psychology*, 8(444). doi:10.3389/fpsyg.2017.00444

Piaget, J. (1936) *Origins of Intelligence in the Child*. London: Routledge & Kegan Paul.

Piaget, J. (1952) *The Origins of Intelligence in Children*, trans. M. Cook. New York: W.W. Norton & Co.

Rogers, C.R. (1946) Significant aspects of client-centered therapy. *American Psychologist*, 1: 415–422.

Rohrer, D. and Pashler, H. (2012) Learning styles: where's the evidence? *Medical Education*, 46: 634–635.

Tay, L. and Diener, E. (2011) Needs and subjective well-being around the world. *Journal of Personality and Social Psychology*, 101(2): 354–365.

Wahba, M. and Bridwell, L. (1976) Maslow reconsidered: a review of research on the need hierarchy theory. *Organizational Behavior and Human Performance*, 15(2): 212–240.

11

TALK! TALK! DIALOGUE IN THE CLASSROOM: A SOCIAL LEARNING PERSPECTIVE

Mike Saunders

Key words – social learning; situated learning; dialogic learning; Vygotsky; Bandura; Alexander; Wells; Wiliam

Introduction

This chapter shows how dialogic learning, which champions the place of talking in the classroom, is built upon the work of social learning theorists. The work of Albert Bandura, who developed a theory of social learning which suggests that learning involves the observation of models, is linked to the work of Vygotsky, on the way in which learning requires social interaction mediated by language. These theories are placed in context and linked to the dialogic theories proposed by Alexander and Wells, before a discussion of the concept of situated learning. The idea that 'classroom talk' is the key to good teaching, learning and assessment will be interrogated, and the chapter will end with an evaluation of this area of educational thought using the work of Dylan Wiliam.

'Learning is linked to what we observe' (Albert Bandura, born 1925)

Key questions

How does what we see affect what we learn?

Bandura, a social cognitivist psychologist, posited a model of behaviour in which three factors determine how an individual behaves in a particular situation. Bandura (1986) called this model the 'triadic model of reciprocal determinism'. The three factors are the 'environment influences' created by the situation in which the behaviour takes place, the observed 'overt behaviour', and the 'personal factors' that are internal to the individual, such as beliefs and self-perceptions. The model involves the way in which these factors interact with each other. Thus, a student in a classroom will exhibit overt behaviours that are affected by the environment they are in, their beliefs as to what is expected of them, and the behaviours of those around them. This model offers an explanation for why students behave differently in class and outside, and why the same class will behave differently with different teachers. It also suggests that there are mediating factors that mean the behaviours are not learned by humans in the same way as they are learned by rats.

Bandura felt that classical behaviourists, such as Pavlov and Skinner, missed an important point in their emphasis on learning through reinforcement. Earlier behaviourists posited that any behaviour that was reinforced (either by positive reward or negative punishment) would become learned. Bandura moved the theory on by suggesting that learning through observation was an important process. He had the idea that new patterns of behaviour can be acquired in the absence of physical reinforcement through observation of the behaviour of others, reactions to that behaviour, and then that this would lead to repetition of the observed behaviour.

Key theory

Albert Bandura: social learning

Bandura's 'Bobo' doll experiments offer empirical evidence of the existence of observational learning. Bandura et al. (1963) reported on the last of a series of experiments in which children were exposed to differing behaviours towards a doll that was able to stand itself up after being knocked down. At first, children observed an adult playing with the doll in an aggressive or non-aggressive way. They were then placed into a situation where they were left alone with the doll and their behaviour was observed. In the second experiment, they observed the model being praised, punished or ignored for their behaviour towards the doll, and the final experiment introduced filmed behaviour rather than observation of real situations. In all cases, their behaviour towards the doll was affected by the behaviour of the model they had observed earlier. There was also evidence that models who were more like them (e.g. of the same gender) had a greater effect on their behaviour.

He investigated the process through a series of studies making use of a 'Bobo' doll in which children observed the behaviours of adults towards the doll, and were then given unsupervised, but observed, access to the doll. The nature of their interaction with the doll was influenced by the behaviour of the adults they had observed (see key theory box).

The behaviour of the adult in the Bobo doll experiments is the model of behaviour that is learned by the observing child. Bandura's contribution to learning theory is the idea that what is seen is as important as what is being taught in the classroom. He posits that we learn by observing and copying others, and that those we perceive as being powerful are used as role models whose behaviour we copy and thus learn. So, a teacher who says that they are interested in their subject, but appears bored when teaching it, is going to find that students will also be bored by the subject. If a teacher is concerned that the use of the word 'algebra' will worry students and calls it 'the "A" word', they are reinforcing the very thing they are trying to avoid.

Bandura (1997) explains that self-regulation is the psychological process by which we are able to overcome the biological urges that affect our bodies. For example, addicts have limited ability to self-regulate their behaviour with respect to the subject of their addiction. This process is a learned behaviour and there is a link between the efficacy of our self-regulation and the behaviours we observe in childhood. Bandura makes the point that self-regulation is 'domain-specific', which links back to the 'environmental influences' part of the triadic model. He also found that those who were able to delay gratification at the age of 5 (i.e. wait before they took a biscuit) were less likely to display addictive behaviour when they were adults. Those individuals who have strong self-regulation can also be described as having high self-efficacy.

Table 11.1 The observational learning process

Stage 1: attentional processes	Observe and accurately identify the behaviour of a role model
Stage 2: retention processes	Remember the model's behaviour
Stage 3: motor reproduction processes	Translate the memories of the model's behaviour into own behaviour patterns
Stage 4: motivation processes	When positive reinforcement is available, use learned behaviour patterns that mimic the model's

Table 11.1 shows the four stages that Bandura suggested were involved when an individual is learning by observing others. Once the behaviour has been identified, it is memorised, integrated into the individual's own behaviours, and then enacted when the time seems appropriate. This is when the individual feels that behaving in this way will produce a positive reaction from others. Reinforcement that will lead to the enaction of the learned behaviour can be either vicarious positive reinforcement or self-reinforcement. The individual either feels that they are acting in a way that matches the experience of the model or has assimilated the behaviour so thoroughly that they feel good when they enact the behaviour.

'It is through others that we become ourselves' (Lev Vygotsky, 1896–1934)

Key questions

How does the work of a dead Russian sociologist affect the classroom in the PCET sector?

Lev Vygotsky was a social constructivist whose work was discovered by the West in the 1960s and 1970s. In his seminal work (Vygotsky, 1978), there are six 'big ideas' that are introduced to learning theory:

1. The most significant idea he introduces is that all learning comes from social development mediated by language. He posits that for a human being to learn, they must be involved in some form of social interaction that develops them socially and that all learning relates to the

acquisition of language. His ideas are supported by the fact that children who are brought up in total isolation often have reduced vocabulary and also learning delay.

2. The idea of 'guided participation' is that learning can happen when the learner's activity is guided by another more experienced person. The learner takes part in an activity (e.g. building an arch of bricks), supervised by someone who knows how to do the task. The person who knows how to complete the task ensures that the learner completes the task successfully by showing them what to do or helping them to work out what to do. For instance, they start part of the task to show the learner what to do and then let them take over to complete the task.

3. The 'more knowledgeable other' (MKO) is the name that Vygotsky gives to the person who is guiding the learner. This person does not have to be in a position of power or even an adult. If a teenage child is showing an older person how to use an aspect of a mobile phone, they are the 'MKO', and not the adult. The MKO can, in the modern world, even be accessed electronically through the internet, and the way in which online video is used to learn new skills by millions each day is evidence of this. This individual takes the role of the 'model' in Bandura's theory.

4. The 'zone of proximal development' (ZPD) is explained as being that area of knowledge that an individual can access with the aid of an MKO. The individual's current knowledge can be extended out towards the limits of human knowledge with the assistance of the MKO, but only within their ZPD. This explains why teachers need to ensure that students have knowledge securely before building upon it. The teacher is acting as the MKO, and if they do not work within the ZPD of their students, learning will not take place.

5. Vygotsky suggests that MKOs who are successful in bringing about learning use scaffolding to help the learner they are guiding. Scaffolding is any technique or resource used to present information to the learner to allow them to gain new understanding or skills. In the classroom, scaffolding is found in the teaching methods and materials used by the teacher, and in the activities that teachers use to guide the learning of their students. It is clear that scaffolded, guided participation by an MKO to help a learner to gain new knowledge or skills that are within their ZPD is the principal way in which learning occurs in the view of Vygotsky. This implies that all learning requires interaction between people and interaction between people inevitably requires the use of language. This leads to the next 'big idea'.

6. Vygotsky posits that all learning occurs by the acquisition of language. The primacy of language means that new information is only learned when the relevant word has been linked to the real-world action, or idea, that it means. For example, 'red' is a name given in English for the colour seen when our eyes look at radiation with a wavelength of 700–635 nm. Using the word brings the colour into our mind's eye. If we had been taught to call this colour of light 'fon', we would identify UK postboxes by their fon colour. The word is simply a tag for a reality we encounter, and by learning the word we make sense of our reality. If all our reality is linked to the words we know, the acquisition of greater vocabulary is the primary result of education, and a larger vocabulary will give a greater grasp of the knowledge we have of our environment. The continuing debate around the 'word gap' evidenced by children from deprived backgrounds when compared with those from middle-class homes (Fernald et al., 2013) is evidence that Vygotsky's ideas about the primacy of language are being supported by current reality.

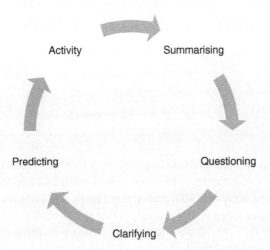

Figure 11.1 *The 'reciprocal teaching' cycle*
Source: Adapted from Palincsar and Brown (1986)

Reciprocal teaching (see Figure 11.1) is a modern application of Vygotsky's theories developed in the 1980s. The teacher and student engage in dialogue around a text in order to improve the student's ability to learn from text through the practice of four skills: summarising, questioning, clarifying and predicting (Palincsar and Brown, 1986). The student needs to be able to summarise what they have been reading, then question their own understanding of the meaning of the text through the identification of areas of the text that are not yet clearly understood, before clarifying the answers to these questions. This allows the student to predict what the next section of text will be about or where the evidence provided so far is leading. The teacher is acting as MKO, guiding the participation of the learners to make sure that they remain within their ZPD, scaffolding their learning so that they are able to absorb the new language in the text and thus learn the new information. This cycle has been applied to many other subjects since its inception.

Key theory

Links between the primacy of language and schema theories

Bartlett (1932) first suggested that human beings create a mental framework into which they insert new information so that they can organise information and make it available to them in the future. This framework is known as a schema (plural: schemata). There is evidence from later work by Brewer and Treyens (1981), Mandler (1984) and Rumelhart (1980), among others, that schemata are generally robust and resistant to change. New information is checked against the existing schema and is less likely to be remembered if it does not match with the existing schema. There is also evidence that stories are particularly powerful in the formation of schemata and that schemata about the self are an edited version of the individual's true history. There is also evidence that schemata are built around language - the brain remembers the word (what it looks and sounds like) and links it to an object or idea. For example, a tree has a particular shape and colour, and individuals' brains are able to link visual knowledge of that information to the word to identify the tree when they see it.

Situated learning: learning in context

Key questions

How has social learning theory developed in the past 20 years?

Since the 1980s, the ideas of social constructivist theorists such as Vygotsky and Bandura have been developed into a range of social models of learning. These models build on the Vygotskian idea around all learning being social to posit that all learning takes place in a local and social context. Situated learning is one of these, and suggests that learning is best understood as placed into a context that is found within the 'real world'. This would suggest that someone learning skills in the workplace will learn them better than someone learning them in a classroom (i.e. an apprentice will learn skills faster than a full-time student) as they can understand how the skills are used in work. Learning in this way – situated in a real-world context – creates meaning from the activities of everyday living.

Situated learning theory was elucidated by Brown et al. (1989) and Lave and Wenger (1991). The theory emphasises the development of higher-order thinking rather than the acquisition of facts by focusing on the application rather than retention of knowledge. It encourages reflection on learning, and is aimed at enhancing the wider skills, ability to think analytically, and employability of those whose teachers use it. Above all, it posits that learning takes place through dialogue within what is called a 'community of practice'.

Communities of practice

Communities of practice exist when a group of people with common goals are learning together over a sustained period of time. A class of students can also be considered a community of practice, especially if they are studying a vocationally focused course such as an apprenticeship or other course that leads to a 'licence to practise' and they engage in discussion about their learning outside of the classroom (Wenger-Trayner and Wenger-Trayner, 2015). All the members have common goals and are learning together about their profession, and they meet together to discuss issues of interest and share best practice. Engagement within a community of practice occurs according to the ideas of legitimate peripheral participation. An individual must be a member of the community of practice to engage at all. They begin on the periphery of the group, and can remain there if they wish, but over time can participate more in the group and move towards the centre of the group, possibly taking up a leadership role, so long as their opportunities for learning are legitimate (i.e. authentic).

Figure 11.2 shows one way in which communities of practice exclude those who do not have a legitimate reason to be part of the group. Brown et al. (1989) suggest that this relates to the way in which individuals are able to deal with the subject matter to which the group relates. The practitioners (full members of the community of practice) are able to operate at a high cognitive level and use subject-specific language that is not in common parlance. They have mastery – they are fully fluent with all the ideas and are aware of their limitations within the subject area. Students (peripheral members of the community of practice) understand some of the language and concepts but do not have sufficient fluency with them to deal with them in the same way. All these individuals have greater understanding of the subject than members of the general public, who Brown et al. (1989) call 'Just Plain Folk'.

	Just Plain Folk (JPF)	Students	Practitioners
Reasoning with	Causal stories	Laws	Causal models
Acting on	Situations	Symbols	Conceptual situations
Resolving	Emergent problems and dilemmas	Well-defined problems	Ill-defined problems
Producing	Negotiable meaning and socially constructed understanding	Fixed meaning and immutable concepts	Negotiable meaning and socially constructed understanding

Figure 11.2   JPF, students and practitioners

Source: Brown et al. (1989, p35)

Herrington and Oliver (2000) explain that for situated learning to be successful, there are nine critical characteristics that must be built into the learning situation:

1. *Provide authentic contexts that reflect the way the knowledge will be used in real life.* The context in which learning takes place must be as real as possible. One of the advantages of learning as an apprentice is that the knowledge and skills taught in, for example, a college workshop are put into practice in the workplace in the presence of skilled members of the community of practice that the student is aiming to join. The skills are honed in the performance of real tasks that are meeting the needs of the business and its customers.

2. *Provide authentic activities.* As above, but it reminds teachers whose students do not have access to external real-life examples to use activities that are as realistic as possible and, where possible, to find authentic needs to be met by the activity. An example would be using a charity event to teach enterprise skills.

3. *Provide access to expert performances and the modelling of processes.* All teachers should be able to provide this for their specialist subject area, but it is important for them to maintain their subject currency in order to do so. This also emphasises the importance of guest speakers who can provide expert performances for the students to observe and expert talk for them to learn from.

4. *Provide multiple roles and perspectives.* Courses of instruction that are led by a single teacher are inherently less successful at developing situated learning as they only provide a single model for students to observe. Watching a range of people perform a task they are highly skilled at provides the observer with evidence of a variety of ways in which the task can be performed. Some elements will be common to all performances but each individual will introduce variations. The observer can choose the best elements from all performances to form their own method of doing the task.

5. *Support collaborative construction of knowledge.* As this is a development of the theories of Vygotsky, it is not surprising to see that working collaboratively to construct knowledge is a critical characteristic of this learning theory.

6. *Provide coaching and scaffolding at critical times.* The link between coaching, which is a skill that too few teachers are truly masters at, and scaffolding is made clear by this statement. Coaching is

only one way in which scaffolding can be provided, but it is a powerful one as it involves an MKO working with the learner to help them find their own way to some knowledge that is within their ZPD. It is Vygotskian theory in action. Note also that the support is only needed at certain times, and the skill to support when necessary but back off and allow self-development is another one that all teachers need to develop.

7. *Promote reflection to enable abstractions to be formed.* Reflection is one process by which all the knowledge learned in a day can be built into the schema of the individual who is learning. Focusing time and effort on identifying what knowledge, skills, etc. have been learned, what areas need more work, and possible next steps is never wasted, and allows the development of the mastery required to be a full member of the community of practice.

8. *Promote articulation to enable tacit knowledge to be made explicit.* The process of regularly reflecting on, and then returning to, learning allows the individual to articulate aspects of their knowledge together. This development of articulation between areas helps the learner to gain a level of understanding that allows them to explain the issue to another person rather than just being able to do the task well. All new teachers have to go through this process when they first teach their subject, which accounts for the need to read up on some areas of what they are expected to teach.

9. *Provide for integrated assessment of learning within the tasks.* Situated learning requires the course to integrate the assessment within the learning activities. An example of this in an Initial Teacher Training course is how the observations of teaching and learning are an activity that helps develop teaching skills but also an assessment tool.

Dialogic learning (talking the talk)

Key questions

How does dialogic learning work in the classroom?

Dialogic learning builds on the work of the previous theorists around the importance of language and of students being able to express their own views as 'legitimate practitioners' in the classroom. The idea that the development of students' ability to use dialogue to learn has been developed over the past 30 years by a variety of researchers. Wells (2000) clearly explains how the idea of dialogic inquiry (investigation of a topic through discussion in the classroom) is based on the ideas of Vygotsky. In the UK, dialogic teaching is an idea first elucidated by Robin Alexander (2003, 2005a, 2005b, 2017), though he draws on a range of existing theoretical ideas and applies them to the contemporary classroom. He was working as an adviser based in primary schools in North Yorkshire when he first suggested ways in which teachers could develop dialogue in their classroom.

The idea that the most effective way to ensure learning was to ensure that there was talk in the classroom is not new, but the idea that that talk should involve teacher–student and student–student interactions is. In many classrooms, the students only respond when asked questions, and Alexander, Wells and others suggested that learning would be greater if all the individuals in the classroom were initiating communication as well as responding to the teacher. Dialogic learning requires teachers to develop methods of classroom instruction that promote discussion and encourage every individual in the room to feel that they can initiate a conversation. This is something that takes a great deal of courage for many teachers as it means allowing students to have more autonomy and thus more freedom from teacher control.

Alexander (2017) identifies five principles of dialogic learning that need to be used if the technique is to be successful. These are that classroom dialogue should be:

1. *Collective.* All participants should take part. This includes the learners as well as the teacher, whose role is to help the learners discuss the topic in question and to use questioning to draw those who are not contributing into the conversation. The use of techniques such as 'pose, pause, pounce, bounce' (PPPB) and Socratic questioning are essential to develop dialogue within the classroom.

2. *Reciprocal.* Participants should listen to others, share ideas and be open to alternative viewpoints. Teachers need to ensure that they have given the learners appropriate metacognitive training in discursive talk before they can be expected to challenge each other without causing excessive friction, or be able to argue a position without becoming aggressive towards those who take different ones. Thus, the dialogic classroom may need to be carefully developed over a period of time with younger FE students, while adults may be more easily persuaded to take part in the dialogue.

3. *Supportive.* Participants should feel free to speak freely, without any fear of a 'wrong' answer, and be willing to help others seek out a common understanding. Teachers need to create a 'safe' environment in which all questions are perceived as being a good thing, all answers as helping to develop the group's understanding of the subject, and everyone's opinion is valued. This requires the teacher to take the position of 'lead learner' in the classroom and accept challenges from students, which takes competence and confidence on their part.

4. *Cumulative.* Participants build on each other's answers and contributions to develop coherent thinking and understanding about the subject. The dialogue develops the initial contribution, through the addition of others' perspectives, knowledge and opinion, into a well-developed position on the topic that all agree upon. The teacher's skill in drawing out contributions from all and helping learners to find the links between their ideas is critical in the process.

5. *Purposive.* Classroom talk must be planned to achieve defined learning goals while remaining open and dialogic. The teacher will maintain the focus of the dialogue, though they will allow on-topic conversations between learners until they cease to be effective in developing the ideas of the class. The teacher starts the topic and guides the conversation, but also ensures that everyone contributes and is learning from the discussion.

There are a number of simple techniques that can be used to develop classroom talk. Socratic questioning and 'PPPB' have already been mentioned, but another is the use of structures within the classroom to support dialogue. Talk partners are pairs of students who are asked to speak to each other about a topic; they can then be asked to feed back to the class directly. By building these pairs into larger buzz groups, before moving to a full-class dialogue, the teacher can provide support for the development of students' ability to have successful dialogue. Dialogic teaching works well with other social constructivist approaches, and the following case study illustrates one way in which this technique can be used.

Case study

Dialogic learning in action: the classroom full of talk

Students have been working on an assessed piece of work. They have had a briefing on the require-ments of the assessment and have been given time to develop a draft of the piece.

The teacher then chooses to use a lesson to promote dialogue around the drafts. Students are reminded of the requirements of the assessment. They are then asked to spend five minutes com-paring their draft against the outcomes and grading criteria.

When this self-assessment is complete, they are placed into pairs. The first student in each pair has 10 minutes to explain their response to the brief to their peer, who can ask questions but not make comments. The peer then has five minutes to provide feedback to the first student. The pair then swap roles.

Two pairs are then put together to discuss the lesson learned. For example, they are given 10 min-utes to find two things that have gone well, two things that need to be improved and two areas that need more investigation based on the experience of all those in the buzz group.

During all this activity, the tutor is setting and monitoring the timings, walking the room and asking questions to keep students on track, to help them develop their ideas and to help them think through the issues. When the group activity is over, they lead a full-class discussion and produce a whole-group critique of the piece in a format that can be shared with the group to enable them to use it when redrafting their work.

The combination of peer and self-assessment required by the 'upwards cascade' of talk in the classroom has been found to be effective in maximising progress and the quality of student work by me in my teaching practice.

Engineering discussion

Dylan Wiliam is one of the foremost researchers into assessment for learning in the classroom (known as formative assessment), and his description of the role of the teacher in the classroom to 'elicit evi-dence of learning' (Wiliam, 2018, p52) needs careful consideration. This statement makes it clear that the purpose of the teacher is to ensure that learning is taking place, and the discussion that follows shows that Wiliam expects that the classroom will be full of dialogue, both teacher–student and student–student. This encapsulates all the previous theories laid out in this chapter and adds in an important new facet. Based on the social learning theories of Bandura and Vygotsky, the importance of social interaction lead-ing to talking is emphasised and, in addition, the importance of teachers using techniques which allow them to see that learning is taking place. In my own practice, this is achieved both by the use of a range of questioning techniques, observation of students at work and the discussion they are having about a topic, and the product of tasks and activities that students carry out. This understanding of the place of formative assessment suggests that the teacher's role is to ensure that their classroom is a place in which students take part in discussion (dialogic learning), activities and tasks (social constructivism) that provide evidence of learning through embedded formative assessment that is relevant to the context (situated learning). While it is clear that behaviourist learning theories help us to manage behaviour in the classroom more effectively, cognitivist learning theories provide a useful explanation of how we actually learn new things, and neuroscience is starting to provide a biological understanding of brain function, social constructivist learning theory appears to provide a strong explanation of how classrooms should function. Wiliam's description of the role of the teacher is supported by years of research and is one that all teachers should consider when developing their courses.

Chapter summary

- Albert Bandura is a social cognitivist psychologist who has developed the idea that learning requires social activity and that language is the medium through which learning occurs.

- Lev Vygotsky is a social constructivist whose work provides six 'big ideas'. He posits that all learning occurs first as social development, and that language is the prime method of learning.

- Reciprocal teaching is a technique developed in the 1980s that provides evidence of Vygotsky's ideas in action.

- Situated learning defines learning as taking place in communities of practice and being subject to legitimate peripheral participation.

- Herrington and Oliver (2000) define nine critical characteristics of situated learning.

- Dialogic learning (Alexander, 2003; Wells, 2000) develops Vygotsky's ideas.

- There are five principles of dialogic learning that need to be followed.

- Wiliam's (2018) definition of the role of teachers as being to 'engineer discussions' is the conclusion of years of research.

Recommended further reading

Alexander, R.J. (2017) *Towards Dialogic Teaching: Rethinking Classroom Talk*, 5th edn. York: Dialogos.

This book looks in more detail at the way in which dialogic teaching works in the classroom. It is useful reading, especially if you are interested in using this teaching method in practice.

Wiliam, D. (2018) *Embedded Formative Assessment*, 2nd edn. Bloomington, IN: Solution Tree Press.

This book looks in more detail at the way in which assessment is linked to teaching and learning, and explores the ways in which language is used in the classroom to assess learning. It is useful reading, especially if you are completing an assignment on assessment.

References

Alexander, R.J. (2003) *Talk for Learning: The First Year*. Available at: www.robinalexander.org.uk/docs/NYorks_EVAL_REP_03.pdf

Alexander, R.J. (2005a) *Teaching through Dialogue: The First Year*. Available at: www.robinalexander.org.uk/bardagreport05.pdf

Alexander, R.J. (2005b) *Talk for Learning: The Second Year*. Available at: www.robinalexander.org.uk/docs/TLP_Eval_Report_04.pdf

Alexander, R.J. (2017) *Towards Dialogic Teaching: Rethinking Classroom Talk*, 5th edn. York: Dialogos.

Bandura, A. (1986) *Social Foundations of Thought and Action: A Social Cognitive Theory*. Englewood Cliffs, NJ: Prentice Hall.

Bandura, A. (1997) *Self-Efficacy: The Exercise of Control*. New York: Freeman.

Bandura, A., Ross, D. and Ross, S.A. (1963) Imitation of film-mediated aggressive models. *Journal of Abnormal and Social Psychology*, 66(1): 3–11.

Bartlett, F.C. (1932) *Remembering: A Study in Experimental and Social Psychology*. Cambridge: Cambridge University Press.

Brewer, W.F. and Treyens, J.C. (1981) Role of schemata in memory for places. *Cognitive Psychology*, 13(2): 207–230.

Brown, J.S., Collins, A. and Duguid, P. (1989) Situated cognition and the culture of learning. *Educational Researcher*, 18(1): 32–42.

Fernald, A., Marchman, V.A. and Weisleder, A. (2013) SES differences in language processing skill and vocabulary are evident at 18 months. *Developmental Science*, 16(2): 234–248.

Herrington, J. and Oliver, R. (2000) An instructional design framework for authentic learning environments. *Educational Technology Research and Development*, 48(3): 23–48.

Lave, J. and Wenger, E. (1991) *Situated Learning: Legitimate Peripheral Participation*. Cambridge: Cambridge University Press.

Mandler, J.M. (1984) *Stories, Scripts, and Scenes: Aspects of Schema Theory*. Hillsdale, NJ: Lawrence Erlbaum Associates.

Palincsar, A.S. and Brown, A.L. (1986) Interactive teaching to promote independent learning from text. *The Reading Teacher*, 39: 771–777.

Rumelhart, D.E. (1980) Schemata: the building blocks of cognition. In R. Spiro, B. Bruce and W. Brewer (eds), *Theoretical Issues in Reading Comprehension*. Hillsdale, NJ: Lawrence Erlbaum.

Vygotsky, L.S. (1978) *Mind in Society: The Development of Higher Psychological Processes*, ed. M. Cole, V. John-Steiner, S. Scribner and E. Souberman, trans. A.R. Luria, M. Lopez-Morillas and M. Cole, with J.V. Wertsch. Cambridge, MA: Harvard University Press (original manuscripts *c.*1930–1934).

Wells, G. (2000) Dialogic inquiry in education: building on the legacy of Vygotsky. In C.D. Lee and P. Smagorinsky (eds), *Vygotskian Perspectives on Literacy Research*. New York: Cambridge University Press.

Wenger-Trayner, E. and Wenger-Trayner, B. (2015) *Introduction to Communities of Practice*. Available at: http://wenger-trayner.com/introduction-to-communities-of-practice

Wiliam, D. (2018) *Embedded Formative Assessment*, 2nd edn. Bloomington, IN: Solution Tree Press.

12
ASSESSMENT
Jonathan Tummons

Key words – diagnostic assessment; feedback; feedforward; reliability; self-assessment; summative assessment; validity

Introduction

Assessing learning is a process that is always bound up in broader processes of learning and teaching. It is difficult, if not impossible, to imagine a session in a motor vehicle workshop, a health and social care seminar room or a basic skills tutorial that does not, at some point, involve the teacher or trainer making a decision regarding how much the students have learned, whether or not they have demonstrated competence in performing a specified task or whether they have shown that they understand the topics being discussed. In order to help make the process of assessment more understandable, it is possible to identify a number of distinct types or modes of assessment according to the stage or moment at which they tend to occur and the purposes for which they are being carried out. This is not to say that these types of assessment always have to be treated separately; there is often some overlap between them. Nonetheless, being able to explore them in turn allows for a meaningful as well as convenient method of analysing assessment more broadly.

> ## Key questions
>
> What are the different modes of assessment and how are they related?
>
> What are the challenges to robust and fair assessment practice?

Diagnostic assessment

Many of the programmes of study that are offered in colleges or workplaces – apprenticeships, short block-release courses, part-time programmes – use diagnostic assessment. It is not uncommon for students to have to go through some kind of formal selection process to ensure that they have, for example, the necessary prior qualifications or experience. This is to ensure that the course that has been chosen is appropriate to the student. If a student has been allowed to enrol on a programme for which she or he is not suited (either through interest, capability, or prior qualifications or experience), there is a risk that they will be *set up to fail*. Other forms of diagnostic assessment occur after the students have begun their programmes. Sometimes these diagnostic assessments are formally embedded into the curriculum; for example, the assessment of a student's literacy or numeracy levels (if the student does not have a GCSE or other equivalent level 2 qualification). Normally the results from diagnostic assessments such as these will be recorded in the student's individual learning plan (ILP) or similar.

A third type of diagnostic is the assessment of specific learning needs or disabilities. This is a complex form of assessment that will be carried out by suitably qualified professionals; a proper needs assessment for a student with a disability (this might be a seen disability such as impaired mobility, or an unseen disability such as a mental health issue) would be beyond the competence of the majority of teachers and trainers in the sector. But as teachers, we all need to be aware of the issues; it is only upon entering the further education sector that previously undiagnosed learning difficulties or disabilities might be noticed and then properly diagnosed for the first time, and any teacher or trainer may need to refer new and existing students to appropriate colleagues in learning support departments (Powell and Tummons, 2011).

Key theory

The literacy demands of assessment

Many of us, as trainers and teachers, are sensitive to the fact that our trainees and students might require support for their literacy skills, or even be required to undertake formal literacy qualifications in addition to their main programme of study. But something that often goes unnoticed is that specific areas of the curriculum have their own ways of writing and reading that students will need to acquire if they are to succeed. In their research into the reading and writing requirements of hospitality courses, Richard Edwards, Sarah Minty and Kate Miller found that for hospitality students, the specific ways in which they needed to be able to read and write within the hospitality curriculum constituted a potential barrier to progress, and that these context-specific or *situated literacy practices* were not only often invisible, but also more demanding than the literacy requirements for functional skills courses (Edwards et al., 2013).

Self-assessment

Self-assessment similarly can be used in several ways. Here, I suggest that three main functions of self-assessment are:

1. The identification of the student's own initial entry behaviours relating to prior knowledge, experience and qualifications, thereby allowing the student to consider and then identify any specific areas that require development or particular attention.

2. The establishment of targets against which future progress can be assessed. These targets will need to refer to curriculum requirements and/or professional or occupational standards, as appropriate to the programme of study being followed.

3. The assessment of needs independently of the student's teacher or trainer.

Capturing these processes usually involves an individual learning plan (ILP) that would be updated by the trainee, candidate or student throughout their programme of learning or study, and which in turn may build up to be a portfolio for summative assessment. In this sense, self-assessment takes on a formative function because the process is intended as an activity that can encourage learning and that provides feedback. Self-assessment can also have a diagnostic aspect (e.g. in the assessment of specific aptitudes such as basic or key skills, or specific learning difficulties or disabilities). For the process to be a meaningful one for the student, however, she or he will need a very clear understanding of the direction or purpose of the assessment. But this is far from straightforward. ILPs can be bulky, awkward documents that demand much of the trainee or student. The use of ILPs can often seem to be a barrier to learning and participation because of the complexity of their construction. At another level, ILPs can be responded to in an *instrumental* manner, as an exercise in form-filling and nothing more, where the bureaucratic burden of completing the paperwork gets in the way of meaningful assessment and feedback.

Formative assessment

Formative assessment, or assessment for learning (AfL), is invariably discussed in terms of the influential research of Paul Black (Emeritus Professor of Science Education at King's College London) and Dylan Wiliam (Professor of Educational Assessment at the Institute of Education, University of London). Formative assessment has been defined in various ways by different authors, and there is arguably no single definition that everybody would agree with (Ecclestone et al., 2010).

Key theory

Defining assessment for learning

One of the most comprehensive definitions of assessment for learning (AfL) was published by the Assessment Reform Group at the University of Cambridge:

1. AfL should be part of the planning process, including feedback, with a focus on the progress being made towards the goals set by the course or programme of study.

2. AfL should focus on how students learn as well as what they learn.

3. AfL should be seen as central to all pedagogic practice, such as demonstrations, question-and-answer sessions, observing learners and so on.

4. AfL should be seen as a professional skill requiring training.

5. AfL should encourage motivation through positive reinforcement (e.g. emphasising achievements) rather than negative reinforcement (e.g. emphasising failure).

6. Students should be encouraged to work with assessment criteria as part of AfL in order to plan their own learning.

7. Constructive feedback that focuses on how students can improve should always be part of AfL.

(Continued)

(Continued)

8. AfL should encourage students to reflect on their own learning.

9. AfL should recognise that learners will achieve at differential levels.

10. AfL should embody an ethic of care to the student as a whole person and not simply focus on results.

Lots of different activities, in a workshop or a classroom or over the internet, have the potential to be used for formative assessment: case studies, quizzes, presentations, short-answer tests, multiple-choice tests, practical tasks, simulations. These may be designed solely by the tutor, or adapted from resources supplied by a colleague, or other open sources. It is clear that many, if not all, of the learning and teaching strategies employed by teachers and trainers within a PCET setting have a formative assessment aspect to them. It is in the methodical manner of their employment within a classroom or workshop that the five key characteristics of formative assessment are found (Tummons, 2011):

1. to facilitate learning;

2. to see whether learning has taken place;

3. to provide feedback to teachers and trainers on how students are progressing;

4. to provide feedback to students concerning their own progress; and

5. to diagnose students' needs or barriers to learning.

Summative assessment

Summative assessment is the term used to describe the mode of assessment that seeks to establish and record what has been learned through taking part in a course or programme of study. It is always a formal process, and it is used to see if students have acquired the habits, skills, knowledge, aptitude or understanding that the programme they have been following set out to provide them with. Historically, the majority of summative assessments are found at the end of a programme of study, but over time patterns of course delivery have changed, and summative elements might also be completed during the programme. Some programmes of study require students to submit small elements of summative work on an ongoing basis; this is referred to as continuous assessment. The completion of an assessment portfolio (which might contain written work, photographs, testimonies, evidence of work-based learning or engagement, etc.) provides a common example of continuous assessment. Sometimes trainers and teachers design and mark summative assessments, with responsibility for making sure that the activities that they design are compatible with the requirements of the awarding body. On other occasions, the awarding body provides very specific guidance as to how the summative assessment is to be carried out.

Summative assessment leads to the award of qualifications: grades, diplomas and certificates. For some students, a qualification will lead to new employment or changes to existing employment. For others, a qualification may be needed in order to progress to the next level of educational provision.

Employers rely on qualifications and records of achievement to ascertain the skills and abilities of their new employees. Award bodies need to make sure that their qualifications and assessments are being uniformly carried out across the country. Funding agencies want to know that they are receiving value for money. Summative assessment therefore has four key characteristics (Tummons, 2011):

1.   to record achievement through the award of certificates and diplomas;

2.   to anticipate future achievement;

3.   to allow students to progress to higher-level study; and

4.   to allow students to enter or progress within the workplace.

Doing assessment *with* students, not *on* students

It is increasingly common for trainers and teachers to involve their trainees and students in the assessment process from the start of their programme. Students are encouraged to think about the tasks that they are completing and the criteria that they are working towards, or the ways in which their work can improve and go from being a 'pass' to a 'merit', or from a 'merit' to a 'distinction'. Whatever the context, the benefits of involving students in their own assessment can be considered as follows:

1.   Through involving students as active participants in, as opposed to passive recipients of, the assessment process, teachers can encourage a higher level of motivation.

2.   If it is accepted that such engagement can lead to higher levels of motivation among students, it follows that a deep, as opposed to surface, approach to learning will be encouraged. For those trainers and teachers who subscribe to cognitivist, constructivist or social practice theories of learning, such a deep approach will be understood as being necessary for meaningful learning.

Blurring the boundaries between assessment modes

It is important to remember that the different functions or modes of assessment that have been explored here are not mutually exclusive – and I have already indicated how they can be seen as overlapping. That is to say, depending on the ways in which the programme of learning being studied has been structured, summative assessment tasks can have a formative function, and formative tasks can be diagnostic. In these matters, the role of *feedback* (discussed more fully below) is crucial. When thinking about the mode of an assessment activity, therefore, it is important to remember that a particular kind of activity – a short-answer quiz, an observation of practical skills, or a simulation – is not *inherently* formative or summative. It is in the use of the activity – is it to accredit past learning or to provide a space for future learning through feedback? – that the formative and/or summative aspects of the assessment task can be located. Similarly, a diagnostic assessment might have a formative function, and a formative assessment might be used for self-assessment.

Validity and reliability in assessment

For an assessment to be fair and to stand up to scrutiny from employers, government departments, inspectors and funding bodies, it has to be both valid and reliable. *Validity* can be seen as being made up of a number of different elements. First, the assessment must assess the actual body of knowledge or skill that the course set out to deliver and assess in the first place; second, there must be adequate coverage of the content of the course; third, the assessment methods should be appropriate to the subjects being studied and assessed; and fourth, the assessment needs to be able to predict the future performance of the student. Validity can be encouraged through a number of strategies (Tummons, 2011):

1. wording the question, explaining the task or defining the activity correctly, to prevent students performing activities that do not correctly match up to the course outcomes;

2. setting assessments that do not miss out one or more of the outcomes or content areas of the course;

3. taking care not to unintentionally include something that was not part of the course content; and

4. ensuring sufficient resources to allow for authentic assessment.

Reliability of assessment is all about consistency, about ensuring that personal or environmental factors do not affect the assessment process. In an educational environment where assessment systems are imposed on a national basis across many hundreds of sites, which employ many thousands of teachers and trainers, the need to prevent local or personal factors from affecting assessment practice is self-evident. To establish reliability within summative assessment, we need to take account of several factors (Tummons, 2011):

1. Assessors or examiners will agree on the mark or grade to be awarded to a given piece of work.

2. There will be consistency between the students' work and the markers' or examiners' grades.

3. There will be consistency between students' grades or marks irrespective of where or when they completed the examination or test.

4. The language used during the assessment process is clear, unambiguous and inclusive.

5. The environment in which the assessment will be carried out will not affect the process.

6. Students or candidates will not have been coached.

Formative assessment draws on the concept of reliability in a rather different fashion, however. It goes without saying that teachers always have to ensure fairness and consistency in the assessment decisions that they make. Even an informal formative assessment such as a quiz needs to be worded and structured in such a way that it can provide reliable results. However, the potential for formative assessment to be used to encourage as well as measure learning means that in order to account for the differing levels of ability or progression or understanding that may be exhibited by a group of students, a teacher may quite legitimately decide to concentrate more attention on one student or group of students rather than another. This is a form of bias, admittedly, but it is an entirely well-intentioned and correct approach. If formative assessment is assessment for learning, then it follows that some students may find themselves under closer scrutiny, or spending more time with their teacher discussing the outcomes of the assessment, compared to others.

Validity and reliability: critical perspectives

Both validity and reliability can be seen to be key concepts when contemplating the objectivity of any assessment process. To some extent, they intertwine with each other and also with ipsative assessment. The quality assurance procedures that surround assessment are considerable, and the maintenance of validity and reliability can be seen as being the responsibility of external verifiers and examiners, and awarding bodies, as well as a responsibility of those tutors who design and administer summative assessment. A variety of procedures and tools are used to maintain validity and reliability, therefore, including:

1. the creation of detailed written criteria for assessment activities;

2. the use of marking and/or feedback pro forma;

3. the establishment of internal verification, second marking, and external verification and examination procedures; and

4. the positioning of assessment as a focus for quality assurance and inspection, most conspicuously by Ofsted.

And yet despite the growth of many different systems and procedures to manage assessment processes, and to ensure that assessment decisions are always impartial and objective, the fact remains that subjectivity can and does find its way. This might be at the level of individual interpretations of assessment criteria, or of differences of opinion relating to the extent to which students may or may not have met the learning outcomes of a particular course or programme of study. Another factor that has to be considered is the extent to which an assessor might take a view of the progress made by a trainee that might lead to an assessment decision based on an overall judgement, rather than based on scrupulous examination of each criterion in turn.

Key theory

Assessing motor vehicle apprentices

In a research paper published a decade ago, Helen Colley and Janis Jarvis discussed their research into assessment within the motor vehicle industry (Colley and Jarvis, 2007). Through carrying out observations, conducting interviews with both employers and apprentices, and reading course documentation, they found that the ways in which assessment decisions were being made in the workplace relied on informal as well as formal processes. Formal assessment judgements were indeed being made according to official criteria, but informal decisions were also being made based on the extent to which the assessors thought that an apprentice might or might not be a 'good fit' in the workplace, and whether they were a 'good bloke' or not. On other occasions, assessors would provide informal mentoring, even coaching an apprentice during an assessed observation if they felt that the apprentice was the 'right kind of person' for the job.

Quality assurance and evaluation

Summative assessment practices are subject to rigorous systems of checks and balances, all designed to assure that assessment is 'fit for purpose'. For all of the stakeholders involved (students, employers, funding agencies, professional bodies and awarding bodies) to have confidence in assessment, and particularly in the certificates and qualifications that formally accredit the successful completion of the programme of study, a number of processes have been established over time. These are all of immediate relevance and importance to both the newly appointed trainer or teacher, as well as to more experienced colleagues (however, it is unlikely that a trainee teacher on placement would be asked to be involved in these processes).

There are several processes by which assessment is quality-assured, and these are described below. It is important to note that the ways in which these quality assurance procedures are used varies according to the specifications of the awarding body in question, in the case of summative assessment, and according to local departmental or college policies, in the case of formative assessment.

Second marking

The simplest process by which the reliability of an assessment decision can be established is through second marking. If a dispute arises between a first and second marker (e.g. if one argues that the student has met the required competence but the other argues that she or he has not), then a third marker will be asked to assess the work involved. If two of the three markers agree, this will usually be recorded as the final assessment decision. By checking each other's marking, we can spot discrepancies and obtain support for our own assessment decisions.

Internal moderation

Internal moderation is a process by which assessment decisions made within the college are scrutinised by another member of staff (who may need to hold specialist qualifications if assessing NVQs). The purpose of internal moderation is not to mark work again, but to examine the process by which the work has already been marked. For example, after a set of assignments has been first and second marked, the entire set would then go forward for internal moderation. The role of the internal moderator would be to ensure that the first and the second marker have both followed the correct assessment procedures that have been specified by the awarding body.

External examination or validation

As well as ensuring the quality of assessment decisions within teaching teams in colleges, awarding bodies and funding agencies also need to be confident that assessment decisions are reliable and valid across the sector as a whole. The function of external examination or validation (different awarding bodies tend to use different terms, but the function is the same) is to scrutinise assessment practices across a number of different colleges, often on a regional basis. The role of the external examiner/validator varies according to the specifications of the awarding body in question. Some externals monitor assessment processes and others may have the authority to overturn assessment decisions that have been made at one of the colleges under their purview (although this is a very rare occurrence).

Inspection and observation

Coverage of the ways in which Ofsted inspects further and adult education provision is well known, and I do not intend to discuss it here, not least as it is such a big subject. However, it is worth mentioning that assessment constitutes a significant aspect of learning and teaching activity, and therefore comes under the purview of Ofsted inspectors. In preparing for Ofsted, it is common practice for colleges to compile self-assessment reports. This college-wide process of evaluation is normally used to identify current areas of good practice, and also areas that require improvement. Assessment of and for learning may be an area for concern. Within these processes, observations of teaching and learning are commonplace and may also focus on assessment and feedback practices.

Exploring different assessment activities

Portfolio-based assessment

A portfolio is a collection of documents, materials or other work produced by an individual student during her or his time on a course, consisting of a variety of different types of evidence to demonstrate those areas of knowledge, skill and understanding that are relevant for the qualification in question. Assuming that the different components of the portfolio are carefully linked to specific objectives, assessment validity is high. For work-based or work-related qualifications, the generation of materials for the portfolio is very often drawn directly from, or modelled on, workplace practice, thereby ensuring authenticity (a key component of validity). It is a form of continuous, summative assessment: continuous because they are collected over a period of time, summative because they assess learning on a programme or module against the criteria. However, portfolios can also have a formative function: as tasks are completed, feedback from the trainer or teacher can be designed so as to offer developmental, forward-looking comments designed to improve future performance. Portfolio compilation and assessment can be time-consuming and bureaucratic, however. For some qualifications, the sheer volume of evidence required and the time taken to organise it can be off-putting. There is also a danger that the search for sufficient evidence can lead to a mechanistic approach to portfolio-building, where the physical collection of evidence takes precedence over learning and the quality assurance requirements take precedence over the developmental needs of the student (Hamilton, 2009).

Simulation

Many further education colleges provide real-world environments where students can learn and work; common examples include motor vehicle workshops, hair and beauty salons, stonemasonry yards, restaurants, and travel agencies. Working environments relating to other areas of the curriculum are not so straightforwardly recreated within the college environment, however. Students on counselling courses or hospitality, catering and tourism courses, for example, might not be able to access authentic working environments. In these cases, the teacher might choose to establish a simulation, normally based around a specified theme, in order to allow students to generate evidence for a portfolio. A typical example would be a role play (e.g. relating to managing customer complaints and expectations) that can be recorded and written up. For some programmes of study, however, simulation is not permitted, and authentic working practices have to be assessed, reflecting the distinction between work-based programmes and work-related programmes (courses that do not require the student to be in employment). However, simulations can be awkward, even embarrassing, and should be negotiated carefully with the students in order to ensure a good level of engagement and motivation; a poorly prepared simulation, or one that encourages only reluctant or restricted participation, will lack assessment validity (Solomon, 2007).

Essays, and short-answer tests

Essays are commonly found in academic and professional courses, and for those curricula that are summatively assessed through essays (whether completed in examination conditions or over a longer period of time as project work), the use of essays as formative assessment, set by the teacher, provides useful practice and developmental feedback prior to the final examination. But they can be difficult for some. Students who are nervous or lack self-esteem, who have left school with unpleasant memories of written assignments, or who are returning to formal education after time away can find the process of writing an essay (as distinct from the topic being covered) difficult, which may affect reliability. Essay practice during term time can help here.

Setting short-answer tests can solve some of these problems. Rather than being faced by a single essay question, a series of short-answer questions provides a more structured framework for the student to follow. This can help build confidence in attempting written work and reduce the risk of misunderstanding the task, therefore increasing reliability. Careful choice of question can also be used to ensure coverage of the syllabus, which further aids validity. The drawback of short-answer exercises compared to an essay is in the level of analysis and detail; it is easier to encourage detailed, critical work in a longer essay-style format rather than in a short-answer assessment.

Multiple-choice questionnaires or quizzes

A multiple-choice questionnaire allows the teacher to cover a large body of knowledge or understanding quickly and thoroughly simply by setting at least one question for each topic covered in the curriculum. The questions can be structured in a number of ways (true or false, or giving four possible answers and asking the candidate to select the correct one). It is easy to pitch questionnaires at different levels simply by making the questions more demanding. They are easy and quick to mark, irrespective of the difficulty of the questions. Multiple-choice questionnaires can therefore be both valid and reliable. The disadvantages of multiple-choice questionnaires are the time they take to prepare and that it is easy to produce a questionnaire that is trivial and lacks rigour. If done properly, constructing the test and checking all the answers is a lengthy process. And the possibility of guessing answers reduces validity. For an informal formative assessment, a quiz is more straightforward to construct, although it may not be as reliable, particularly if students are grouped into teams.

Presentations

Asking students to prepare and deliver a short presentation can provide a valuable alternative to written work. As well as assessing the knowledge and understanding of the topic being covered, presentations also afford teachers the opportunity to assess a variety of functional skills (ICT, literacy, communication). For students who are reluctant or nervous writers, presentations offer a useful alternative format. Other students may be nervous about any form of public speaking, however, and this might impact on the reliability of the assessment. Another drawback to using presentations for assessment is the time involved: as well as the actual presentations, the amount of time needed for setting up, and for giving feedback, can be considerable. The potential for repetition is a more significant drawback; the prospect of sitting and listening to several presentations on the same subject matter can be daunting. To reduce the risk of boredom and repetition, therefore, presentations should be planned so that they cover a variety of relevant topics.

Observation

The simple act of watching a student or group of students at work is arguably one of the most effective forms of assessment in further education. Observations in workplaces, seminar rooms or workshops are commonly found across a number of different curriculum areas. If the observation is part of a summative assessment, the use of an observation pro forma where specific criteria or competencies are listed can ensure validity. However, in order to ensure reliability, it is vital that the observer is properly qualified in the subject matter that is being assessed through observation. In informal formative assessment contexts, observations can still be useful. Careful attention to students' tone of voice, posture, body language or action can be as fruitful a form of informal formative assessment as an impromptu question-and-answer session.

Giving feedback

Feedback is an essential component of assessment for learning, and can be understood as a conversation, spoken and/or written, between two people: the teacher or trainer and the student. During this conversation, the teacher has several questions that she or he will wish to have answered: How much has the student actually learned? What new skills have been acquired? What new knowledge has been grasped? The feedback dialogue has two main features, therefore: first, to tell the student that they have mastered a new skill to the required standard, or demonstrated knowledge and understanding to the required level; and second, to provide advice and support for those students who have not yet reached the required level of competence or who have not yet understood fully the body of knowledge being studied (Armitage and Renwick, 2008; Ecclestone et al., 2010; Tummons, 2011). If feedback is clear, specific, supportive, timely, understood and appropriate, then it should encourage learning, help students make sense of what they need to do next and motivate students to further engage with their programme of studies.

There are six key features of good feedback.

1. Feedback should be clear and unambiguous

The language that is used when giving feedback should be clear, concise and easy to follow, straightforward, and written in everyday language. If more specialised language is needed, then it is important for the teacher to ensure first that the student understands what the words used actually mean. Finally, it is important that the student understands what actions are needed to develop or improve their performance both in relation to future assignments and also (if required) if the current assignment has not been passed.

2. Feedback should be specific

Offering specific comments allows the teacher or trainer a good way to open the feedback conversation. Specific comments relating exactly to the task that the student has completed or accomplished are effective in reinforcing existing good progress and encouraging further achievement. Similarly, corrective feedback needs to be unambiguous. The student needs to know exactly in what way the task that they have completed is inadequate or incorrect. Here, reference to learning outcomes/objectives can be helpful (normally relating to summative assessment) in maintaining the specificity of the feedback. Good feedback should therefore refer explicitly to the criteria or learning outcomes that are at hand.

3. Feedback should be supportive, formative and developmental

Good feedback should allow the student to build on her or his past successes and at the same time move away from errors in understanding or mistakes in technical execution. Feedback should always include an element of feedforward and highlight, where appropriate, aspects of the completed task that relate to future assessment tasks within the programme of study.

4. Feedback should be timely

The exact timing of feedback will depend on several factors: the time it takes for the tutor to mark written work or organise practical demonstrations; the availability of tutor and student to meet; whether or not an assessment needs to be graded internally or externally; and the nature of the assessment itself (informal formative assessment of a class-based activity can be instantaneous). Allowing for differences as a consequence of the exact type of assessment in question, feedback that is as immediate as practical will be the most useful to the student. It is worth noting that colleges and awarding bodies set guidelines as to the time by which students can expect to receive feedback for summative assessments.

5. Feedback should be understood

Having read or listened to feedback, the student should be able to understand how they have performed in reference to the objectives/outcomes and/or criteria for the assessment and the course; he or she should be able to describe and then perform those steps necessary for further development either for the current assessment (if competence has yet to be achieved) or for the next assessment or course, and above all the student should be able to make sense of the assessment, and the feedback from it, as a learning episode within the course or programme of study. Teachers should use open-ended question-and-answer techniques if there is any doubt as to the student's understanding of any feedback that has been given.

6. Feedback should be delivered in an appropriate environment

In some assessment contexts, particular consideration should be given to the environment in which the feedback is given, allowing for the nature of the curriculum and the needs of the student. Giving marked work back to a group of students is of course appropriate, but if one of the students either needs or asks for more detailed support, a follow-up meeting on a one-to-one basis may be necessary. If one-to-one feedback is not possible (e.g. when giving feedback relating to a practical task while in the workshop), the teacher should be sensitive to volume and tone of voice and should, if required, find a quiet corner or space in the workshop away from the main business of the session.

Key theory

How tutors give feedback

In a study of over 250 different portfolios, Tom May explored the different characteristics of the written feedback provided by the assessors of a number of different work-based qualifications (May, 2013). He found that although feedback was invariably positive in tone and task-focused, relatively less time was spent evaluating the progress that students had made or the distance that they might need to travel to reach their next goal. Feedback practices remain, perhaps unsurprisingly, very different between assessors and between different curriculum areas.

Chapter summary

Assessment is arguably the single aspect of the role of the trainer or teacher that has the most direct impact on the future lives and careers of students. The consequences of the assessment decisions that we make last for lifetimes and shape future careers, opportunities for further study, employment patterns, even where people choose to live. As such, getting assessment right is a powerful professional obligation. It can be very difficult to establish a perfectly valid and/or reliable assessment, and mistakes can and do happen. But if we can make our assessments *tolerably* valid and reliable, then we are doing well. At the same time, it is still worth thinking about whether or not students are assessed too often, and whether we should, as teachers and trainers, think about raising our voices to argue for fewer assessments of higher quality, rather than a proliferation of assessments that are flawed in their design or execution.

References

Armitage, A. and Renwick, M. (2008) *Assessment in Further Education*. London: Continuum.

Colley, H. and Jarvis, J. (2007) Formality and informality in the summative assessment of motor vehicle apprentices: a case study. *Assessment in Education: Principles, Policy, and Practice*, 14(3): 295–314.

Ecclestone, K., Davies, J., Derrick, J. and Gawn, J. (2010) *Transforming Formative Assessment in Lifelong Learning*. Maidenhead: McGraw-Hill.

Edwards, R., Minty, S. and Miller, K. (2013) The literacy practices for assessment in the vocational curriculum: the case of hospitality. *Journal of Vocational Education and Training*, 65(2): 220–235.

Hamilton, M. (2009) Putting words in their mouths: the alignment of identities with system goals through the use of individual learning plans. *British Educational Research Journal*, 35(2): 221–242.

May, T. (2013) Identifying the characteristics of written formative feedback used by assessors in work-based qualifications. *Journal of Vocational Education and Training*, 65(1): 18–32.

Powell, S. and Tummons, J. (2011) *Inclusive Practice in the Lifelong Learning Sector*. Exeter: Learning Matters.

Solomon, N. (2007) Reality bites: bringing the 'real' world of work into educational classrooms. In M. Osborne, M. Houston and N. Toman (eds), *The Pedagogy of Lifelong Learning*. London: Routledge.

Tummons, J. (2011) *Assessing Learning in the Lifelong Learning Sector*, 3rd edn. Exeter: Learning Matters.

13
LIVING AND LEARNING

Jim Crawley

Key words – post-compulsory education and training; further and adult education; adult and continuing education; community; community-based learning; community research; informal learning; lifelong learning; network learning

Introduction

> ### Key questions
>
> What is 'living and learning'?

Like most of education, and particularly post-compulsory education and training, the area that we are calling 'living and learning' is diverse, changes people's lives, and is difficult to define and describe. Because of this, the approach of the chapter is selective, with an aim to provide a representative selection of ideas, examples and issues from and about 'living and learning' that will help familiarisation with this area as a part of PCET, and to appreciate the huge contribution it makes to the sector and the community as a whole.

The chapter opens with a definition of 'living and learning' and then continues in four sections. The first section considers the key concepts and ideas behind living and learning, and how it is located within the PCET context overall. The second section showcases examples of the ways living and learning takes place in communities and the resulting benefits. The third section considers how living and learning has fared and is faring in a time of austerity, and the chapter closes with some positive suggestions for how this crucial part of PCET can be sustained by using localised networks linked together by 'acts of connection'.

Defining 'community' and 'living and learning'

To define 'living and learning', we need to consider ideas about what constitutes a 'community', as this is crucial. Craig (2011) has provided a helpful definition, and he argues that there are three basic meanings of 'community':

1. *A geographical community.* This includes people living within a fairly well-defined physical space. The space could be, for example, a discrete housing development, a neighbourhood, a rural village or a refugee camp.

2. *A community of identity.* This community can exist within and between geographical communities, and a wide range of communities of identity with different needs and identities can exist side by side, and they can also overlap with each other. These identities can be cultural, political, gender-based, occupational, recreational, ideological or many others. A sports team, international friendship group, trade union or political party would be examples of a community of identity.

3. *An issues-based community.* This community focuses on particular issues such as improving housing conditions, improving road safety at school crossings or protecting aspects of the environment. The activity may involve campaigning around those issues. Greenpeace, a local parents group campaigning for better school funding and Amnesty International would all be issues-based communities.

Most communities will involve elements of one or more of these types of community and can involve all three. Understanding 'community' is important because it is at the heart of our definition of living and learning. Whether a more structured form of teaching and learning is involved, or the experience is completely led by the learner, learning always naturally occurs in all communities where people are living. Our definition below focuses this particular part of PCET on learning that does not often take place within an official educational establishment:

> *'Living and learning' is the individual or collaborative learning that takes place in a community rather than in an educational institution. It is often informal, is led mainly by individuals and communities themselves, and focuses on enhancing their everyday lives through learning individually and together.*

There are many locations and situations in which 'living and learning' occurs, and it is not reliant on being part of a specific sector of education. Post-compulsory education and training does, however, provide the most appropriate home as PCET has a proud tradition of adult education in the community, vocational training in the occupational areas of a community, and engaging with community development. Our definition links these traditions together.

Introducing living and learning

Key questions

What are the key principles and values of living and learning?

Learning in communities

Because of the scope of living and learning, there are many ideas and theories about the key principles and values involved. The list below summarises some of the features that can be identified as common across most situations and activities.

Learning starts with a small, local focus

The activity, whether involving an individual or a group of people, starts with a small, local focus. That locality can be the interests of the people involved, a need identified by an individual, or a geographical location that is close to those involved either physically or personally. The learning can grow from small and local to connect a broader community or grow into something larger, but it does tend to start small and local (Purcell and Beck, 2010).

Learning involves critical and self-reflection

Like many other ideas about learning, it is suggested that living and learning involves self-reflection, so that the individual can review their thoughts and actions, and then make changes to what they do or how they act to absorb and apply their learning from reflection. Critical reflection is more focused on identifying aspects of a community that can be improved, and critical reflection is the vehicle that can help think this action through (Purcell and Beck, 2010).

Learning involves plans and action for all the community (including hard-to-reach areas) by the community

As a process continuing from the previous principle, living and learning takes forward the ideas and learning from critical and self-reflection, develops action plans, then instigates actions that can take place in any part of the community, but which are generally aimed at improving the community for all (Purcell and Beck, 2010).

Learning builds social capital, skills and confidence in the community

'Social capital' is a now widely used term that Robert Putnam popularised in his book *Bowling Alone* in 2001, and is essentially a way of describing the social links between members of communities that build a community into a healthy and socialised whole. Social capital is often known as the 'glue' that holds communities together, and the growth in social capital can combine with learning new skills from living and learning so that participants gain confidence both individually and in their connections and collaborations with others (Popple, 2011; Putnam, 2001).

Learning can enhance well-being and provide a route towards transformation for individuals and communities

As the reflection, activity, social capital and confidence grows through living and learning, this can, and often does, contribute to individual, group and community well-being, and if this activity is sustained, can lead to further benefits for the individual, group and community (Duckworth and Smith, 2017; Popple, 2011).

Key questions

Where does living and learning fit in the overall landscape of PCET?

Diversity and range

Of all the fields in PCET, living and learning has the greatest diversity and range of learning opportunities, settings, learning sites, activities and communities involved. Learning could take place in a field near a primary school; with a group of Forest School volunteers; on a building site as apprentices learn bricklaying by working with a skilled tradesperson; volunteering at a local library; getting a football pitch ready before a match; taking part in a community reading group; and millions more. All ages could be involved, and the diversity of backgrounds, cultures and experiences can be limitless. In terms of resources, rooms and facilities from organisations such as schools, colleges and businesses, as well as village, church and community halls, may be used. Open spaces, houses, sports facilities, workplaces and mobile venues could all also play a part. Given that living and learning is so multifaceted and multidimensional, it is difficult to get an overall idea of the numbers involved. With some careful searching of relevant data, it is possible to get some strong indicators of scope and scale.

Numbers involved in living and learning

- There were 2.4 million adult (19+) learners participating in government-funded further education in 2016/17 (DfE, 2018a).

- It is estimated that in 2016/17, 11.9 million people formally volunteered once a month and 19.8 million formally volunteered once a year (NCVO, 2018).

- In 2016/17, there were almost 500,000 apprenticeship starts (DfE, 2018b).

There have been government surveys of adult learning since 1997, and the most recent Adult Education Survey (DfE, 2018a) contains data for 'informal learning'. The survey defines this as 'self-directed learning with the aim of improving knowledge of a subject' (DfE, 2018a, p5). The survey carried out in 2016 found that 'two-thirds of respondents (66%) engaged in informal learning in the last 12 months. A respondent's age or sex did not influence informal learning participation rates' (DfE, 2018a, p30). The survey sampled over 8,000 members of the community, and although the data are not related to actual numbers in the report, it is reasonable to conclude that millions are involved in informal learning.

These numbers relate to aspects of living and learning rather than its whole, but they do give a strong indication that the volume of members of the community engaged in living and learning is very significant, and indeed in the millions each year.

Key questions

What are the key benefits of living and learning?

The views of those involved in the Adult Learning Survey (DfE, 2018a) give an important indication of the benefits they believed they had gained from 'informal education'. They included 'better performance in their current job' and 'personal benefits (e.g. meeting other people, refreshing skills on general subjects etc.), and learning new tasks' (DfE, 2018a, p26). Much living and learning takes place through volunteering, and it has been estimated that the financial value to the nation of 'formal volunteering was estimated at £22.6bn in 2015' (NCVO, 2018). Government-sponsored research from 2012 investigated the well-being and financial value of adult learning, and found 'It would not be unreasonable to conclude that an adult learning course that improves life satisfaction has a value to those who receive it of somewhere between £754 and £947' (DBIS, 2012, p6).

The numbers and benefits of living and learning introduced in this section are, like this area of PCET, somewhat difficult to establish with clarity and precision. What does, however, strongly emerge is an area of education that is highly valuable in a number of significant ways, which involves huge numbers of people, but which many people would probably be unable to identify as part of the education sector as a whole. Living and learning can claim its place alongside the rest of PCET as often significant, in scale, scope and value, but equally often invisible to many in society.

Showcasing living and learning

Despite the recent history of austerity, and as the figures already cited make clear, much living and learning still takes place, and somehow even manages to thrive, in such an unhelpful context. This section offers three examples of living and learning, celebrates the resulting learning and achievements, and gives some insights into why and how they succeed. They also showcase the benefits that accrue to the participants and the communities involved.

Community-based learning: men's sheds in Australia

As the term suggests, 'community-based learning' is learning that takes place in the locality where the learners live and actively participate in that community, and allows them to have learning experiences, reflect on and consider/carry out change in their own lives and/or their community.

Ormsby et al. (2010) carried out a research project into the use of 'men's sheds' as a community-based learning activity and reviewed some of the research in the field. Research into the provision and support of 'men's sheds' as a space for members of the community to spend time and engage in individual and/or group activity found this to be 'culturally, socially and psychologically important' and to 'provide a sense of purpose and autonomy; link generations of men in the family; transcend age and class' and that it could 'become the primary source of activity for retired men' (p607). The small project that was established meant that the sheds 'operated one or two days a week offering predominantly woodwork activities producing children's toys and nesting boxes for native birds and animals'. They were 'operated by the local government organisation with a paid coordinator' who 'informed potential volunteers about the study and the opportunity to participate' (p608). Five participants were interviewed about their participation and its effects, and the themes that emerged were:

- the group as a 'company of fellas' focusing on how the group of older men formed up into a socially engaged 'company';

- the notion that 'everybody's got a story to tell' where the experiences and conversations between participants validated their accounts of their experiences and lives;

- a reassurance that they have 'still got some kick' or that they felt that they may be old, but this did not mean they could not still achieve;

- a 'feeling of accomplishment and satisfaction' in the work completed and the use to which it had been put;

- the process of the project helping in 'passing on your experiences' or the growth of confidence in reflecting on experiences with others;

- something less positive, where others could 'get on your goat', which is self-explanatory; and

- the valued idea that 'nobody's boss' or that the process was a shared and democratic experience.

(p609)

Overall, the results of this project, although involving a small number of participants, did reinforce other benefits that had been identified from previous research. There was evidence that the use of community-based learning through 'men's sheds' found community-based space for 'engaging and meaningful activities' could 'positively impact the health and well-being of older Australian men'. The activities involved helped to 'address numerous aspects of ageing and retirement such as the loss of daily meaningful routines, health issues, lack of physical and mental stimulation in retirement, and lack of new or continued learning opportunities'. There was also evidence that the availability of 'meaningful activities' and 'an environment or "men's space" where older men can simply meet and enjoy being in each other's company' brought further benefits (p609).

The study also connects to larger themes and ideas such as developing what the World Health Organization (2007) refers to as 'age-friendly cities', where physical environment features in cities facilitate active aging in socially inclusive ways (p5). This study is a powerful example of community-based learning.

Community research: South West Foundation's Community Researcher Programme

In 2007, South West Foundation, an independent charitable foundation, trained 200 community members from deprived communities across south-west England as community researchers, and these community researchers involved more than 4,000 people in community research projects. 'Community research' is another term that has a range of interpretations, but this version involved the foundation providing six days of training in the techniques, skills and approaches of carrying out research for local community groups and organisations. The training also included advice and guidance about how to select and carry out research into issues, facilities and challenges within their own communities, how to analyse and interpret the data, and make use of it in further community action. Community researchers then carried out research into projects of their own choosing and used the results to further their own goals in the community.

The results of the projects were wide-ranging, and included organising of community events; successful fundraising activities (one group raised £150,000 for a local skatepark); setting up children's clubs; meetings with community workers, agencies, funders and local councillors; community researchers becoming mentors for other groups; improving local play facilities; and a growth in community confidence. An older people's group in Devon researched the effect of withdrawing wardens from certain properties for older people and interviewed over 150 residents. The results demonstrated that the changes were actually working. A group of mainly young mums in North Somerset interviewed local community members about their priority concerns on one particular large housing estate. The findings were presented to a seminar of local councillors, housing associations, local community members and others, and the group were given free use of an empty shop to continue and reinforce their work.

An external evaluation of the project found that the community research had 'proved a powerful tool that has had lasting effects on both communities and individuals' (South West Foundation, 2014, p5). Benefits for individuals included increasing the skills and confidence of participants; enabling them to be more major contributors to their local communities; making use of the influencing skills gained through the sharing results from their research projects; and moving more confidently towards employment when they had been unemployed. Benefits for the wider community included the views and results of the research often being put into community action; the creation of more small community groups and community resources, including a community hub, skatepark and groups for older and younger people; improved relationships and interaction with local agencies and councils; and a general increase in community engagement.

Community research has proven to be a particularly effective form of living and learning, especially when the members of the community carry out all aspects of the research themselves.

Informal learning in the workplace

Manuti et al. (2015) suggest that informal learning in the workplace is integrated with daily routines as an 'inductive process of reflection and action' which can be influenced by chance', and is usually 'linked to learning of others' (p5).

The place of informal learning in living and learning is central, and the following example is not so much a detailed single example as a review of a range of informal learning in the workplace. This review was carried out for the then-named Department for Education and Employment (DfEE) in 1999. It showcases how informal learning in workplaces can help to develop individual workers and the overall workforce as a 'learning community'. The review draws some valuable conclusions, which are still relevant today despite the report being compiled in 1999. They include:

- Formal and informal learning are part of a continuum and work best in combination.

- Most informal learning in the workplace does not take place consciously.

- Successful informal learning develops greater worker engagement with their company and their colleagues.

- Informal learning can also result in bad habits and unsuccessful learning.

In DfEE (1999), several case study examples of varying sizes and types of business were included, and one was a small hairdressing company. This case study business was found to have carried out the following steps to support informal learning in their workplace:

- The company was shown to have a strong culture of learning and used informal learning well with a small workforce.

- Many staff were involved in teaching, learning and assessment activities.

- The company gave 'considerable time to talk to and explain the business to their staff in meetings and as part of ordinary work discussions'.

(p19)

Their combination of informal and formal workplace learning was highly successful, and was shown to be part of a process that contributed to business growth, employee satisfaction, engagement and well-being, and increased profitability. The business also grew into becoming involved in training and supporting other companies as well as their own employees.

Connections between aspects of living and learning

The examples showcased in this section address all of the key values and principles of living and learning, which are that learning starts with a small, local focus; involves self and critical reflection; involves plans and action for all the community (including hard-to-reach areas) by the community; builds social capital, skills and confidence in the community; and can enhance well-being and provide a route towards transformation for individuals and communities. Whether it takes place in the work-place, in the community, in an individual's home, in a shed, in a classroom, or in any other location, people and communities are connecting as an ongoing process through living and learning.

The challenges facing living and learning

As this chapter is being written, a new report from the United Nations (2018) has reviewed the UK's strategy and implementation of austerity measures, and concluded:

> Many aspects of this program are legitimate matters for political contestation, but it is the mentality that has informed many of the reforms that has brought the most misery and wrought the most harm to the fabric of British society.

(p3)

The whole of PCET has faced a challenging environment under the austerity measures, and this section of the chapter will consider some of those challenges and discuss some of the elements that help the work to survive.

Key questions

How has living and learning fared in a time of austerity?

Towards the start of this chapter, figures showing the very high numbers of people involved in living and learning were encouraging and helped to establish the depth and breadth of this part of PCET. Unfortunately, like all areas of the public sector, PCET has suffered under the recent austerity measures. In the areas we have identified as within living and learning, challenges have been particularly severe.

There have been cuts of up to 24 per cent in further education and adult skills, and the number of adults participating in adult learning is the lowest since figures were recorded by the Learning and Work Institute (2018). The Association of Colleges (AoC, 2015) calculated that over 190,000 adult learners would be lost to adult education in 2016 alone with cuts of that size.

Small voluntary and community sector groups, who also have a large and varied engagement with living and learning, were suffering early in the years of austerity, and research by South West Foundation (2011) found that:

> The future for community groups is looking very uncertain. 56% of the small community groups who took part in this research have less than 6 months' running costs in reserves. 49% are experiencing difficulties in raising fund for this year, 78% are having difficulties in raising funds for next year.
>
> 55% of small community groups currently get no developmental help and support from other agencies. 51% of those who do get support receive this help and support from their Council for Voluntary Services.
>
> 37% of small community groups that receive help get this from their local authority.
>
> Significant numbers of small community groups are closing or have already closed.
>
> (p3)

More recent research on trends on the voluntary and community sector in the north reinforce some of the pressures caused by austerity:

> Times are particularly hard for organisations based in poorer areas: they are twice as likely to be financially vulnerable than those in the richest areas. In the period 2014–2016, a quarter used reserves for running costs.
>
> More than 30% of organisations that rely heavily on public sector funding are struggling, compared with just 15% of those funded from private or voluntary sector sources.
>
> (IPPR, 2017, p12)

As we have already found in this chapter, data that specifically refer to all of what we are defining as living and learning are extremely difficult to find. It is, however, clear from the research cited above that this part of PCET has suffered considerably under austerity policies. For such a low-key area of PCET, it is somewhat surprising perhaps that it has not declined more than it might have done. The report cited above (IPPR, 2017) expressed some surprise that the essentially voluntary nature of community action allows it to still exist, and even thrive, under the harshest conditions. One of the key reasons for this is that much living and learning takes places 'below the radar'.

Key theory

'Below the radar'

The Third Sector Research Council has published a number of studies which have discussed and exemplified individuals, groups and activities that operate 'below the radar' (BTR) (McCabe, 2010).

(Continued)

(Continued)

This term, as the name suggests, describes how these individuals, groups and activities operate in a zone of activity that does not engage significantly with government, policy and funding, and which can operate without reliance on external funding. Much of the activity we have included within the realms of living and learning would take place below the radar. Those involved had a passion and determination that sustained their activity, and their operation below the radar meant they could pursue their own goals and agendas, not one set by others. There are of course disadvantages with being below the radar, including a lack of visibility and voice, but there is also a relative freedom, and the feeling that being BTR keeps the activity out of harm's way. Whereas a large, well-funded organisation may appear to attain more significance, the benefits of living and learning education for society, workplaces and community has a significance that is more readily sustainable.

Towards the future

Key questions

How can communities continue to live and learn?

At the time of writing, living and learning finds itself in a situation of considerable pressure and difficulty, but, as we have seen, it also possesses a great depth of commitment, reservoirs of participation and a history of resilience. This is partly because the learning involved is often self-initiated and self-motivated, and that appears to provide a key component of sustainability. Research has also shown that areas such as adult and community education, community-based education, informal learning in the workplace and community action are less in need of government funding to keep going than some others (even though they are often even more starved of resources), and that much of their activity is below the radar. These positive characteristics do not, however, insulate them completely from what at the moment looks like a very uncertain future. Funding for learning in PCET overall and resources and funding to provide development, support and outreach activities have all been savagely reduced. Social justice demands, however, that such an essential, beneficial and indeed relatively low-cost part of education deserves much more than bare survival. Living and learning deserves to be supported so it can thrive, maintain and strengthen its position as the heartbeat of community well-being.

We would argue that one answer might be that we should all be making continuing use of 'acts of connection' and campaigning and taking community action to support the establishment of groups of community members who can support taking this forward. We are suggesting these would be 'community area learning networks' (CALNs).

'Acts of connection' (Crawley, 2018) are a way of explaining how much of the activity we have described in this chapter takes place. Individuals, groups and communities come together, take part in learning, and establish connections with each other of various types as part of the process of living and learning. The connections can be personal, practical, occupational, individual and collaborative, and indeed a combination of all of these and more. At their best (not always), those connections build through engagement, critical reflection and individual or combined action into community learning and community action that can benefit the community of those who are connected, whether it is in the workplace, the home, an organisation or a locality. These 'acts of connection' are crucial to the development, reinforcement and healthy survival of living and learning.

Seeding and supporting those acts of connection in a learning context can happen through serendipity, but research has shown it can work better when supported through networks of people and also by appropriate use of technology (Veugelers and O'Hair, 2005). If there was a local community-based infrastructure with paid and volunteer staff who could help support living and learning across all the communities described at the start of this chapter, this could ensure the long-term future of living and learning. They would agree on a localised group of priorities and may have access to grant funding, training and support, but they would need to be independent organisations to ensure fairness and to protect any possible campaigning role. We are proposing that community area learning networks (CALNs) could carry out that role. They could be the means by which social and economic capital through living and learning could be encouraged to grow and be sustained. Examples of such network-supported activities do exist, and South West Foundation (2004) has researched and evaluated them.

Two examples to illustrate the model of community learning networks

South West Foundation's research on networks operating in the voluntary and community sector provide our two examples.

South West Seniors Network

They work with and support '28 older people's forums throughout the South West' that connect:

> 22,000 older people who can feed their views into the regional forum through their own local networks. From the information provided and from other networks at least 4,000 individuals have taken direct action in the networks and 1,000 organisations are members of the networks that are being supported, with many others being affected by their actions and activities.

> (South West Foundation, 2004, p4)

Cornwall Disability Research Network (CDRN)

The Cornwall Disability Research Network brought together academic researchers and social researchers into disability issues, and some of the members have personal experience of disability. Local disabled people with an interest in research into disability issues also now take part in this network. The network includes representatives from a number of universities, including the University of Strathclyde, Manchester University, Cornwall College Social Work Department, and the University of Plymouth Faculty of Health and Social Work.

With a small grant of £1,500, the network undertook a number of activities, including bringing researchers together, helping to overcome social exclusion by encouraging researchers to adopt a grassroots perspective based on consultation with people with disabilities – rather than taking a 'top-down' approach. Individual members with disabilities identified issues and flagged them up with researchers. As a result, their research is based on real problems, concerns and issues that directly affect people with disabilities. Through contact with others in a similar field, they gain peer recognition, credibility and respect for their work. The network has helped people with disabilities to connect with:

- county- and district-level public sector workers;

- learning disability services;

- academic researchers at universities in the South West and across the UK; and

- healthcare professionals.

(adapted from South West Foundation, 2004, p10)

The wider establishment and support of community learning networks could be transformational, even if it started with a small pilot project, and the future of living of learning could be assured. There is no doubt that living and learning will continue. Individuals and groups, organisations, employers, and communities will benefit and grow. Understanding and community cohesion will improve as long as living and learning continues. If only governments would take more account of this often invisible part of PCET, the future could be bright for living and learning.

Chapter summary

This chapter first introduces definitions of 'community' as geographical, identity-based or issues-based, or a combination of any and all from Craig (2011), and then 'living and learning' as an often informal process we engage in for ourselves and for the broader community, including the workplace, to enhance living in that community for all.

The first section explores the theoretical thinking from a range of perspectives that underpins the key principles and values of living and learning, including Duckworth and Smith (2017), Popple (2011), Purcell and Beck (2010) and Putnam (2001). These are summarised as understanding that learning starts with a small, local focus; involves critical and self-reflection; involves plans and action for all the community (including hard-to-reach areas) by the community; builds social capital, skills and confidence in the community; and can enhance well-being and provide a route towards transformation for individuals and communities. An indication of the range, scope, breadth and depth of living and learning is featured next, including figures that demonstrate it to be an area in which millions of UK citizens are involved in an ongoing basis, partly through volunteering, partly through more formal adult and continuing education, partly through their workplace, and in many other ways and locations or learning sites.

The second section of the chapter proceeds to showcase examples of living and learning from the areas of community-based learning, community research and informal learning. The examples range across 'men's sheds' in Australia, community research in south-west England and informal learning in the workplace across the UK. Some of the research and theories involved in these aspects of living and learning are also introduced, including DfE (2018a), DfEE (1999), Manuti et al. (2015), Ormsby et al. (2010) and South West Foundation (2014). Overall, the examples demonstrate in their breadth and range how the overarching principles and values of living and learning are manifested in practice, and reinforce the benefits of living and learning.

The third section explains how PCET as a sector has faced a particularly challenging environment under the austerity measures that have been in progress since 2008. Some of those challenges are reflected upon, alongside some of the characteristics of living and learning that help it to survive. The concept of operating 'below the radar' (BTR) from McCabe (2010) is introduced as one of the ways in which living and learning has a certain amount of in-built resilience and sustainability, and that the passion and motivation which helps it to take place in the first place can also help it to keep going.

The final section of the chapter looks to the future of living and learning, and reinforces the difficult situation that all of PCET is in, and the need to look forward to positive strategies for survival. The chapter closes with what is felt to be a two-part solution, which is to maintain, support and extend living and learning through 'acts of connection' (Crawley, 2018), and to support, develop and sustain living and learning through the establishment of community learning networks.

Living without learning would not really be living. Good luck with your own living and learning!

Further recommended reading

Craig, G., Mayo, M., Popple, K., Shaw, M. and Taylor, M. (eds) (2011) *The Community Development Reader: History, Themes and Issues.* Bristol: Policy Press.

This book has a wide range of chapters around the area of community development that will take the reader's understanding much further than the items used in this chapter, and is one of the best books in that field.

Eraut, M. (2004) Informal learning in the workplace. *Studies in Continuing Education,* 26(2): 247–273.

This is one of the most read articles in the field of informal learning at work.

Hawtin, M. and Percy-Smith, J. (2007) *Community Profiling: A Practical Guide – Auditing Social Needs.* Maidenhead: McGraw-Hill.

Takes a beginner through the thinking, stages and activities involved in 'community profiling', which has many similarities with community research.

Knowles, M.S., Holton III, E.F. and Swanson, R.A. (2012) *The Adult Learner.* London: Routledge.

Known as 'the classic text' on adult learning from Malcolm Knowles (now with additional writers since his death in 1997). This will take the reader's understanding of adult learning, and in particular the notion of 'andragogy', further and deeper.

Veugelers, W. and O'Hair, M. (2005) *Network Learning for Educational Change.* Maidenhead: Open University Press.

The full book takes the idea of network learning further than the item referenced in this chapter, in particular in the ways in which technology can support network learning.

References

AoC (2015) *The Effect of Proposed Cuts in Adult Education*. London: AoC.

Craig, G. (2011) Introduction. In G. Craig, M. Mayo, K. Popple, M. Shaw and M. Taylor (eds), *The Community Development Reader: History, Themes and Issues*. Bristol: Policy Press.

Craig, G., Mayo, M., Popple, K., Shaw, M. and Taylor, M. (eds) (2011) *The Community Development Reader: History, Themes and Issues*. Bristol: Policy Press.

Crawley, J. (2018) *Just Teach in FE: A People-Centred Approach*. London: Sage.

DBIS (2012) *Valuing Adult Learning: Comparing Wellbeing Valuation to Contingent Valuation*. London: HMSO.

DfE (2018a) *Adult Education Survey, 2018*. London: HMSO.

DfE (2018b) *Statistical First Release: Further Education and Skills 2018*. London: HMSO.

DfEE (1999) *Informal Learning in the Workplace*. London: HMSO.

Duckworth, V. and Smith, R. (2017) *Further Education in England: Transforming Lives and Communities – Interim Report*. London: Universities and Colleges Union.

IPPR (2017) *Third Sector Trends in the North of England: A Summary of Key Findings*. Manchester: IPPR North.

Learning and Work Institute (2018) *Rates of Adult Participation in Learning – 2018*. Leicester: Learning and Work Institute.

Manuti, A., Pastore, S., Scardigno, A.F., Giancaspro, M.L. and Morciano, D. (2015) Formal and informal learning in the workplace: a research review – formal and informal learning in the workplace. *International Journal of Training and Development*, 19: 1–17.

McCabe, A. (2010) *Below the Radar in a Big Society? Reflections on Community Engagement, Empowerment and Social Action in a Changing Policy Context. Working Paper 51*. Birmingham: Third Sector Research Centre, University of Birmingham.

NCVO (2018) *UK Civil Society Almanac: Volunteering Overview*. Available at: https://data.ncvo.org.uk/a/almanac18/volunteering-overview-2015-16/#Formal_volunteering accessed 7/11/18

Ormsby, J., Stanley, M. and Jaworski, K. (2010) Older men's participation in community-based men's sheds programmes: older men's participation. *Health & Social Care in the Community*, 18: 607–613.

Popple, K. (2011) Models of community work. In G. Craig, M. Mayo, K. Popple, M. Shaw and M. Taylor (eds), *The Community Development Reader: History, Themes and Issues*. Bristol: Policy Press.

Purcell, R. and Beck, D. (2010) *Popular Education Practice for Youth and Community Development Work*. London: Learning Matters.

Putnam, R.D. (2001) *Bowling Alone*. New York: Simon & Schuster.

South West Foundation (2004) *No Boundaries: A Study of Networks and Empowerment*. Camerton: South West Foundation.

South West Foundation (2011) *Crisis and Contradiction: Research into the Current Issues Facing Small Voluntary and Community Organisations*. Camerton: South West Foundation.

South West Foundation (2014) *Engaging Outcomes: An Evaluation Report on South West Foundation's Community Researcher Programme*. Camerton: South West Foundation.

United Nations (2018) *Statement on Visit to the United Kingdom, by Professor Philip Alston, United Nations Special Rapporteur on Extreme Poverty and Human Rights, London, 16 November 2018*. London: United Nations.

Veugelers, W. and O'Hair, M. (2005) *Network Learning for Educational Change*. Maidenhead: Open University Press.

World Health Organization (2007) *Global Age-Friendly Cities: A Guide*. Geneva: World Health Organization.

14
WORK AND LEARNING

Jonathan Tummons and Adeline Yuen Sze Goh

Key words – employability; New Vocationalism; work-based learning; work-related learning

Introduction

There is nothing new in the idea that being at work in some way involves more or less formal processes of learning. Indeed, today (in 2018), the UK government is in the process of restructuring technical qualifications, including new funding for apprenticeships. Aaron Bradbury and Vicky Wynne discuss apprenticeships in Chapter 24, and so we will not spend time discussing them here. Rather, our focus is on the broader processes of work as a practice that often and necessarily involves learning, and on the different kinds of qualifications apart from apprenticeships that students in further education colleges or private training providers might be working towards. At the same time, it is important to remember that lots of learning happens at work that is not in any way accredited or otherwise provided with formal credentials.

The variety in the qualifications available to young people and the organisations that deliver these qualifications is reflected in the different ways in which learning at or through work is understood by researchers, teachers, qualification bodies, and policymakers. There is work-based learning (WBL) and then there is work-related learning (WRL). There is also workplace learning, which is not quite the same as informal learning in the workplace. But if we avoid splitting too many hairs, we can find a broad consensus that focuses on learning and work in two main ways: learning that takes place through work, in the workplace itself; and learning that takes place through activities that are related to work and in an educational institution. For example, we might think about the different ways in which a hairdresser might be working towards her qualifications. She might be working at a salon, starting off by only being allowed to perform fairly minor tasks such as sweeping up, or shampooing clients' hair, or mixing colours, before moving onto more complex tasks such as dying or styling hair. Or she might be attending her local further education college, practising her skills in a salon-style environment that has been constructed within the college to simulate the real-world working environment. Either way, she is learning, and it is through and alongside work that the learning is being encouraged or facilitated.

In this chapter, therefore, we shall pick apart the relationship between work and learning and think about the different models of provision that are to be found within the PCET sector, as well as some of the different ways by which these models of provision have been researched, and what this all means for teachers and trainers in the sector as a whole.

Jonathan Tummons and Adeline Yuen Sze Goh

Key questions

How should we define work-based learning and work-related learning?

Identifying provision

There are many different types of work-based learning and/or work-related learning programmes that are offered in the PCET sector. These learning programmes might have different goals, ranging from upskilling for a specific occupational role, to providing generic employability skills for new entrants to a workforce. Some provide ways into employment, and others provide opportunities for progression. And they provide different benefits to the different stakeholders involved. Learning can take place in many different contexts, and there may not even be any formal teaching involved. In brief, the provision of work-based and work-related learning is complex and far from standardised.

Work-based learning: some models and definitions

We have already hinted at the fact that there are many ways through which different researchers and writers have provided definitions of work-based learning (we shall come back to work-related learning later in the chapter). At the same time, these different frameworks have much in common. The European Centre for the Development of Vocational Training is an organisation within the EU that evaluated research, training and policy relating to vocational education and training. In their report on work-based learning (CEDEFOP, 2015), they offered the following definition of WBL as:

1. Intended and structured training or learning.

2. Being of direct relevance to the current or future tasks expected of the learner.

3. Taking place in a workplace context, which means either in the workplace, in settings simulating the workplace or outside the workplace, but with specific learning tasks that must be directly applied in the workplace and reflected upon afterwards.

In proposing this model of WBL, the authors draw a clear distinction between WBL, on the one hand, and what they refer to as *work-relevant* training, on the other. From this perspective, it is the intention to provide learning that is directly relevant to the job being done, or to be done, by the learner through engagement with work, that defines WBL. And there is a tacit acknowledgement of the theoretical perspective that such learning might rest on, through reference to *reflection* on the tasks in question. For all of us working in PCET, reflection as an element of learning is nothing new: reflective practice is a central element of all of the professional qualifications that teachers and trainers work towards. We shall return to learning theory as it pertains to WBL later in the chapter.

Perhaps unsurprisingly, the CEDEFOP report begins by acknowledging that there are many different definitions of WBL. To illustrate this point, we can refer to a somewhat different approach to providing a framework for exploring work and learning that comes from the *lifelong learning* literature. From this perspective, Morgan-Klein and Osborne (2007) propose three different strands of work-based learning, consisting of:

1. *Learning for work*, consisting of all forms of vocational education and training, whether they are to be found in a college or private training provider, or whether delivered online for learners working at home, or even within schools.

2. *Learning at work*, consisting of training and development programmes that are delivered within organisational contexts, either by members of the organisation or by external trainers or consultants.

3. *Learning through work*, consisting of learning job-related knowledge and competence, acquired through the actual work of doing the job in question.

While these two models of WBL have much in common, there are differences in emphasis that are worth considering. Coming from a lifelong learning perspective, Morgan-Klein and Osborne foreground the many different contexts within which WBL might be found, rather than restricting it to the workplace or even to a work-related simulated environment, a context for WBL that the CEDEFOP report does not address. But it is in Morgan-Klein and Osborne's reference to the potential role for schools in the provision of learning for work that a more complex issue is to be found. FE colleges in the UK have long been used to welcoming 'school-aged' students through their doors, putting paid to the myth that colleges should only be used as 'dumping grounds' for school students who have become disaffected with mainstream education, and instead providing meaningful opportunities for vocational education and training (Harkin, 2006). Since Harkin's research was published, the age at which young people are statutorily required to remain in education or training has increased from 16 to 18. Alongside the ever-greater demands for courses and curricula that deliver 'employability', the sense that education and training have to be work-related, if not necessarily work-based, seems to be increasingly important for a variety of stakeholders – government ministers, funding agencies and employers.

Key questions

What are the key debates relating to the quality and utility of work-based learning and work-related learning?

Key theory

Employability

Employability is the term used to gather together and describe those skills that employers expect students to acquire while at college in order to prepare them for the world of work. The definition of 'skills' that is proposed by notions such as 'employability skills' is generic, seeing skills as something that can

(Continued)

(Continued)

be acquired in a variety of ways and applied to different employment or educational contexts. That is, employability skills are transferable. A typical list of the kinds of attributes that are defined as employability skills might include: creativity; autonomy; team working; communication skills; time management skills; and literacy and numeracy skills.

At first look, a list of skills such as these would seem to be uncontroversial. However, meaningful criticisms of the 'employability agenda' continue to be put forward. And even though employers consistently complain that too many college leavers lack the right employability skills, they continue to give more jobs to people with academic qualifications than vocational ones. A student having the skills, knowledge, attitudes and behaviours required to look for, gain and maintain employment in the labour market can be seen as 'employable'. In this sense, employability is positioned as an individual characteristic. The responsibility is on the individual to take responsibility for their education and training, and by extension for their economic and social well-being; it is not the direct responsibility of the state.

There are two problems for us to think about here. The first is the extent to which employability skills are indeed transferable. For many occupations, specific qualifications are obviously necessary. Becoming a nursery worker requires more than just a range of generic qualifications and good results in functional skills tests: it requires specific qualifications and experience. A student on a business studies course might consider a range of possible employment options on completion of their studies. But going to work for a credit card insurance company in a call centre will surely require quite different skills from going to work as an office junior for a high-street firm of solicitors, simply because they are two such different employment contexts. The second issue relates to the individual capacity of the student. Put simply, if a student successfully completes her programme of study – and as such can be said to be 'employable' – but fails to find employment, what happens next? Will she need to undergo more training to become 'more' employable? Will she need to accept entry-level employment and then commit to more on-the-job training in order to progress?

The PCET sector can be said to contribute to the employability agenda in two ways, therefore. First, the sector provides courses that allow employability skills to develop within the curriculum. This might be through embedding such skills within a broader curriculum, or through the provision of specific employability skills courses. FE colleges in particular can be effective in bringing the world of work 'into the classroom', through the provision of realistic working environments such as training salons and through the organisation of work placements and such like. Second, the sector provides specialist provision that purports to address the skills that young people need to find work. But significant concerns can be raised as to the quality of such provision and the extent to which the employability skills that they deliver are aligned to the world of work, as research indicates that specific 'employability' programmes invariably lead to unskilled or low-skilled work characterised by low pay, low status and low job security (Atkins, 2009).

We can now see how maintaining a clear dividing line between work-based learning and work-related learning is far from straightforward, not least because it is hard to ascertain exactly where one stops and the other starts, particularly when they can all be gathered together as elements of the 'employability agenda'. We can also now see some of the different ways through which the politics of WBL and WRL start to become visible, through considering the extent to which an individual student or employee is responsible for their own employability and therefore their own employment. We shall discuss the politics of WBL and WRL later. But first, we shall consider work-related training as a discrete pattern of provision.

Blurring boundaries: work-related learning and work-based learning

Work-related learning is the term used to describe broader processes that can be understood as consisting of three more specific elements (Huddleston and Oh, 2004):

1. Learning *about* work: that is, learning how public sector and private sector businesses actually operate, what they do, what kinds of jobs people do in such businesses, and so forth.

2. Learning *for* work: that is, developing employability skills (as discussed above) in order to help the transition from education and training to the world of work.

3. Learning *through* work: that is, using work activities (although not within the context of paid employment or a full-time apprenticeship) as a context for learning.

If the gap between WBL and WRL is difficult to identify when we consider the places within which learning happens or the age of the learners involved, it is more straightforward to identify in terms of accreditation and formality of provision and/or organisation. Work-based learning by definition requires the learner to be at work; it is through her position as a worker that the learner is able to engage – sometimes voluntarily, sometimes compulsorily – with learning within what has been termed a *workplace curriculum* (Billett, 2008), an idea that allows us to fix the position of the learning, and the scope or content of what is to be learned, very firmly within the workplace. Work-related learning, by contrast, is a concept that allows us to consider how mainstream college provision prepares people for work, allows people to gain and then enhance work-related skills, and even work towards occupationally linked qualifications, without actually having to be in paid employment. In a way, WRL provides a bridge between WBL, a specific, localised pattern of provision for education and training, and employability, a more generalised concept that applies across many areas of the PCET curriculum. Facilities to provide work-related learning and training are found within many FE colleges.

Hair and beauty salons

Many FE colleges have hair and beauty salons that are used by trainees. These are usually open to the public as well. It is important to note that they provide learning experiences that are not only related to the profession (i.e. hairdressing or beauty therapy), but are also related to the management and administration of a typical business in the sector. Using computer systems to book appointments, taking payments and reconciling a cash register are three examples of the kinds of transferable employment skills that can be practised.

Training restaurants and kitchens

Catering colleges often have restaurants that are open to the public as well as to staff and students, and that cater for large events such as Christmas dinners, as well as small private bookings. As with hair and beauty salons, there are also opportunities for learning more generic business skills.

Construction sites

Within the construction curriculum, it is common for students to find themselves acquiring new techniques and skills within simulated environments. Electrical installation students work within workshop bays that allow them to practise wiring up junction boxes. For trowel occupations, students build walls and arches in large open spaces. Joinery students build miniature pattern pieces. Some colleges go one step further and actually buy houses for students to rewire, plaster and decorate. The house becomes a teaching and learning space – arguably as integral a part of the college as the workshops.

Airline cabin crew training

A small number of colleges that offer training for cabin crew staff have gone to tremendous lengths to recreate a realistic working environment by purchasing decommissioned aeroplanes for trainees to work in. One of the authors of this chapter (Jonathan) worked at a college where the cabin crew course team had bought an old aeroplane fuselage. On one occasion, he expressed surprise to one of his PGCE students, who taught the cabin crew trainees, that such a large piece of equipment had been purchased. Her response, accompanied by a look of disbelief, was, 'How else do you think we can train the students properly? How can we prepare stewardesses and stewards for work if they've never been assessed in a plane, even if it's only on the ground?'

Opportunities for authentic learning

One of the key elements of any work-related learning programme is the idea that learners will be able to experience an authentic environment for learning through the provision of simulated activities and contexts such as those described above. Any form of provision within a college or other institution such as a private training provider would therefore need to establish such environments. Generating authentic provision might require particular kinds of equipment to reflect current industry practices, and particular locations and environments to reflect the world of work.

Authenticity is arguably the most important element of the work-related curriculum. Through the provision of a realistic working environment, perhaps within a college or otherwise through gaining access to other relevant sites (through work placements and so forth), it is argued that a suitably authentic pedagogic context can be provided within the WRL curriculum. One example of such provision is through *traineeships*. The traineeship programme is an education and training programme with work experience included, aimed at securing the best opportunity of progressing either to an apprenticeship or other sustainable work. They last between six weeks and six months, with the actual length of the planned traineeship reflecting the needs and trajectory of the learner. The work experience provided therefore offers exposure to a real workplace for learners who lack workplace skills, knowledge, attitudes, confidence and behaviour. The role of the employers themselves is therefore crucial to the success of the traineeship. Employers work with college providers to design the content of the work preparation training, incentivised by the fact that for traineeships, the employers are not required to pay young people for their work.

Traineeships represent a recent aspect of a longer-standing approach to the provision of education and training within the PCET sector, usually referred to as New Vocationalism, and we discuss this later on. But it is important to note that work-related learning need not be restricted to pedagogic, experiential activities such as those listed above. Another way of thinking about work-related learning is to consider learning not in relation to a specific trade or sector of industry or business, but in relation to the wider notion of work as an aspect of everyday life and experience. In this sense, work-related learning might include typical activities such as the following.

Work or enterprise projects embedded within a curriculum

It is common practice for learners on many different programmes (e.g. business studies, web design) to complete projects that are designed to imitate real-world issues and problems. The authenticity and value of such projects can be increased through establishing links with local businesses and employers who might help design the tasks, evaluate them (but not assess them – the assessment decision will always, necessarily, be made by a member of teaching staff), and even make use of the product or outcome in some way.

Mentoring and coaching

Many work-related curricula encourage opportunities for engagement with local, regional or even national businesses and employers through mentoring and coaching. This might involve activities such as helping young people prepare application forms and curricula vitae, or providing careers guidance and advice. Many organisations actively seek out opportunities for their employees to engage with colleges in this manner, either through formal mentoring and coaching arrangements or through one-off activities such as inviting guest speakers to visit students.

Visits to workplaces

In 2012, the coalition government abolished compulsory work experience during secondary school. Michael Gove, the then Secretary of State for Education, commissioned the Review of Vocational Education, conducted by Professor Alison Wolf of King's College London, known as the Wolf Report, in 2010. As such, the provision of other work-related experiences fell to the PCET sector. Such visits are seen as important even if they do not constitute a formal curriculum element.

It does not require much of a leap of imagination, or a substantial body of empirical research, to conclude that the 'real-life' aspects of learning through being an apprentice, or through continuing vocational training within the workplace, are in some way qualitatively different from the 'real-life' elements of a work-related programme. Nonetheless, the authenticity that both types of provision rest on is central, and forms a key element of the theoretical explanation for both WBL and WRL.

Theorising work-based learning and work-related learning

There are in fact several ways through which we might consider the theorisation of work-based and work-related learning. Some of these have already been introduced within this book. The theory of learning within *communities of practice* (discussed in Chapter 11) is just one example of a relatively recent reimagining of apprenticeship learning. By contrast, theories that are often placed within the adult education tradition, such as experiential learning, are also used to explore how people learn at work. And we have already seen from the CEDEFOP paper above that theories of reflection in and on action are also employed. Perhaps inevitably, mindful of the variety of theories of learning, teaching and instruction that are to be found in the literature, there are several ways to theorise learning at and through work. Some theories are more robust and more applicable than others, however, and so it is always a worthwhile exercise to consider different approaches and to evaluate those that offer the most insight.

Key questions

What are the different theories that we might use to explore work-based learning and work-related learning?

Revisiting learning theory

Throughout this book, the importance of using theory when appropriate and meaningful has been stressed: teaching is a profession, after all, and as such should rest on a profound body of professional knowledge, which will include theory. In Chapters 10 and 11, Janet Lord and Mike Saunders provided an overview of a range of theories of learning, drawing from both psychology and neuroscience (in Chapter 10) and sociology and social theory (in Chapter 11). Theories such as these, when used critically and appropriately, can therefore help to theorise the ways in which people learn at or through work.

There are a number of different theoretical approaches that can be usefully applied to considering learning in workplace or work-related contexts. As we have noted above, learning theories are discussed extensively in earlier chapters, and here we will only briefly discuss some of the commonly used approaches that relate closely to learning and work.

Communities of practice theory

Learning is a process that happens almost all of the time where we learn from observing others, doing work, reading instructions, or learning through experimenting with different options. In an apprenticeship model, WBL can be seen as participating in a community of practice, where learners work under a more experienced and skilled supervisor who helps them to understand and master their new occupation. In this process of mastering their trade, they will also learn to communicate in the jargon used in the particular occupation, acquiring the customs and habits that are only rarely formally taught in a college environment. However, communities of practice theory raises questions as to the extent to which these skills are transferable, if what is learned is situated. The considerable variety of experience between different workplaces means that any application of communities of practice theory would require fine-grained, site-specific research (Fuller et al., 2005).

Experiential learning theory

The role of experience and reflection on experience as a central aspect of learning is commonly found within theories of adult learning generally, but is best known through the work of David Kolb, who, drawing on the much earlier work of John Dewey, argued that knowledge is gained as a result of personal and environmental experiences. Kolb (1984) emphasised the importance of particular actions for experiential learning to occur, specifically that learners must: be actively involved in the learning experience (i.e. not be passive recipients); be able to reflect on the experience; be in possession of the capacity to reflect on the experience; and be able to use the new knowledge gained. It is a popular theory, but often used uncritically, and other writers, notably Peter Jarvis, have questioned the relationship between experience and knowledge (Jarvis, 2010).

Informal and incidental learning

Once again coming from a broader adult education tradition, theories of informal and incidental learning in workplaces were established primarily through the work of Victoria Marsick. She argued that for people at work, learning might be either informal – invariably based on experience but always planned for – or incidental – the unintentional consequence of a different activity (Marsick and Watkins, 1990). She placed a focus on the places within which people work, exploring the extent to which they might be conducive to learning, and arguing that for learning to happen, organisations needed to value the judgement and autonomy of their staff. The critique of such approaches rests on the extent to which organisations can be constructed or changed in order to afford such opportunities for learning, as well as on the validity of what people learn on an incidental basis.

Expansive and restrictive environments for learning

In their research on apprenticeships, Alison Fuller and Lorna Unwin focused on the nature of the environment within which people learn at and through work (Fuller and Unwin, 2003). Drawing on a social practice approach to learning (communities of practice, above, is one example; others are discussed in Chapter 11), they argued that workplaces as learning environments ranged from being expansive to being restrictive. Expansive environments allow new workers time and resources to get to know the job, afford workers opportunities to make meaningful decisions, and encourage wider application and distribution of skills. These environments are conducive to learning. Restrictive environments, by contrast, discourage working across teams or boundaries, focus on short-term targets only, and fail to engage workers in meaningful decision-making processes, limiting opportunities for learning and development (Tomlinson, 2013).

The politics of work and learning

It goes without saying that over time, wider political attitudes to the relationship between work and learning have changed. And while it is beyond the scope of this chapter to provide a detailed history of policies and statutes relating to work and learning – which would have to start, at least in England, during the time of Queen Elizabeth I – some more recent shifts in thinking are important to consider if we are to have a critical as well as practicable understanding of learning at and through work. The PCET sector as a whole, it has been persuasively argued, has long been particularly prone to governmental influence, not to say interference, in a way that schools and universities are not (Edward et al., 2007).

New Vocationalism

Historically, vocationalism referred to the need to ensure that sufficient people receive an education that is appropriately linked to the world of work, and that has been designed in such a way that the perceived needs of employers have been accounted for. At the heart of this vocationalism lay a particular model of employment that – put simply – saw further education colleges working relatively independently from each other, responding to local and regional employment and labour market pressures, where young people who attended college, undertook apprentices or participated in day-release training programmes were trained for roles in specific industries and trades.

The decline and political neglect of much of the traditional manufacturing sector in the 1970s and 1980s rendered this model of vocationalism redundant, leading to the emergence of New Vocationalism. Instead of providing a vocational education for people who would be working in particular industrial or manufacturing sectors, FE colleges instead had to respond to two new pressures. The first of these pressures was the need to provide a more 'general' vocational education to students following more ambiguous pathways into employment. In this model, students would be equipped with 'transferable', general skills that would prepare them for the workplace, rather than sector-specific or subject-based skills. The second pressure was the need to keep more people in education and training for longer in order to ease pressure on a labour market that was already struggling to cope with the number of people seeking to enter. Successive measures enacted by governments of all hues to increase participation rates and ages (rendering the term 'post-compulsory' education and training somewhat redundant when considering that young people now have to remain in some form of education and training up to age 18) required the expansion of the vocational curriculum to include both new courses that reflected the expanding service sectors, and providing new curricula that would be sufficiently attractive to sustain the engagement of more and more young people who were now being required, and variously pressurised or induced, into staying in education and training for longer, irrespective of the extent to which these curricula were aligned to the world of work more generally, or a specific occupation or trade more specifically.

From continuing education to human resources development

Terms such as continuing education, adult education and lifelong education – often used interchangeably – became prominent in the early part of the twentieth century, and for a long time focused on ideas concerning the wider ongoing education – as distinct from training – of adults. Engaging in continuing education was seen as an important aspect of citizenship (particularly, in the UK, after the end of the First World War), an essential element of the developmental needs of human beings. However, over time, a more functional and economic perspective emerged and became dominant, which reduced continuing education to more employment and business-focused needs. Continuing education that was not centred on the world of work became marginalised, described as *recreational learning*, and mostly ignored by policymakers. At the same time, education has, during the last 50 years or so, become increasingly positioned as being a key economic driver upon which the economies of nation states rely as manufacturing declines and so-called 'knowledge economies' emerge. For a country to prosper, economies must become more productive, and this process is seen as resting on the knowledge and skills that individual workers possess: their human capital.

Thus, the more human capital that each worker can accumulate, the more she or he can increase their value to the labour market, and their productivity within it. Alongside this, businesses and organizations started to establish human resources departments in order to develop or expand the skills of the workforce. Within this framework, it is the individual who becomes the focus. The concept of *meritocracy* augments the concept of human capital, and places the individual as being responsible for her or his own life chances, employment prospects and educational development. In this way, any individual can cross social barriers and through enhancing their skills and qualifications, achieve economic rewards that also are of benefit to the wider national economy.

Criticism of the concepts of human capital theory and meritocracy is trenchant, and revolves around the ways in which such an approach ignores social and structural factors. Significant bodies of research argue that access to education and training is not the same for everyone; instead, it depends on wider social, economic and geographic factors. At the same time, human capital theory assumes an unproblematic relationship between education/training and employment/economic growth that is arguably unfounded, and fails to specify how particular forms of educational provision might directly impact on economic output.

The emergence of credentialism

One of the more complex problems to arise as a consequence of New Vocationalism and the neoliberal climate of human resources development is the rapid growth of credentialism. Credentialism refers to the ever-expanding use of formal accredited qualifications across all areas of educational provision, including adult education, work-based and work-related learning, and apprenticeships, which is a consequence of the expansion of educational provision more broadly. Simply put, there are more courses and programmes of education and training than ever before, leading to the award of more qualifications and certificates than ever before. The emergence and subsequent dominance of competence-based training and education has led to a demand for the accreditation and certification of kinds of learning, training and experience that historically were not wrapped up within formal curricular or assessment structures.

At first look, this might seem to be an entirely beneficial process. Learners can gain qualifications for episodes of training and education that historically might have been invisible, and then use those qualifications as a transferable form of capital in order to change their employment status. Forms of predominantly trade- or craft-based training and education can be publicly accredited for the first time and, it is argued, provide legitimate learning opportunities for people for whom formal schooling and/ or the academic curriculum has not, for whatever reason, been beneficial or appropriate. Employers can make decisions based on robust credentials in relation to selecting or deploying their employees.

However, the proliferation of credentials has been criticised by those researchers who have argued that the ways in which policymakers have stressed the increased uptake of vocational programmes and awards in fact serve to restrict rather than widen opportunities for meaningful lifelong learning. This is because vocational and occupational qualifications are only ever targeted at a particular sector of the population – the 'working class' – who would be doing those kinds of courses anyway.

In this sense, the accreditation of previously informal patterns of workplace learning serves to entrench existing social and economic barriers within education systems more broadly. And a second critique revolves around the extent to which any competence-based qualification can satisfactorily capture the richness and specificity of what people learn within particular workplaces. From this perspective, any forms of learning – of workplace knowledge – are lost sight of if they are incapable of being simplified in the format required for a competence statement within a portfolio.

Chapter summary

In this chapter, we have explored a number of key issues:

- different ways of theorising work-based and work-related learning;
- current and recent political influences on the provision of work-based and work-related learning; and
- changing patterns of qualifications and credentials for learning through work.

It seems obvious to say that much learning takes place at work (here defined in terms of paid employment or voluntary work, or work experience gained during a placement in a recognised institutional setting). Work-based learning (WBL) is therefore here defined as learning that takes place at and through work, in either a formal or informal context. The formal provision of WBL is commonly linked to wider notions of employability and might relate either to specific occupational skills or competencies, or to generic or transferable skills that are perceived as being desirable for employees to possess or further develop. Informal WBL, by contrast, is simply a term used by writers and researchers to describe the incidental learning that takes place in the workplace, but which is not formally recognised or captured within a qualifications framework. Apprenticeships rest on notions of WBL, as do college and university courses that require students to undertake work placements. It is the authenticity of the workplace that gives value to this learning: WBL is required to be based in the real world of work, not in a simulated environment. Those curricula that aim to prepare students for the world of work, but which do not contain formal requirements for a placement, for day or block release or other similar access to the workplace, are referred to instead as work-related. In order to provide meaningful work experience to students, many further education colleges have established business-style environments within their institutions. However, notwithstanding the best efforts of colleges to create authentic working environments, college-based salons or training restaurants are self-evidently qualitatively different to their 'real-world' counterparts. As such, the extent to which such institutions offer work-based or work-related learning continues to be argued over.

References

Atkins, L. (2009) *Invisible Students, Impossible Dreams: Experiencing Vocational Education 14–19*. Stoke-on-Trent: Trentham Books.

Billett, S. (2008) Learning through work: exploring instances of relational interdependencies. *International Journal of Educational Research*, 47(3): 232–240.

CEDEFOP (2015) *Work-Based Learning in Continuing Vocational Education and Training: Policies and Practices in Europe*. CEDEFOP Research Paper No. 49. Luxembourg: Publications Office of the European Union.

Edward, S., Coffield, F., Steer, R. and Gregson, M. (2007) Endless change in the learning and skills sector: the impact on teaching staff. *Journal of Vocational Education and Training*, 57(2): 155–173.

Fuller, A. and Unwin, L. (2003) Learning as apprentices in the contemporary UK workplace: creating and managing expansive and restrictive participation. *Journal of Education and Work*, 16(4): 407–426.

Fuller, A., Hodkinson, H., Hodkinson, P. and Unwin, L. (2005) Learning as peripheral participation in communities of practice: a reassessment of key concepts in workplace learning. *British Educational Research Journal*, 31(1): 49–68.

Harkin, J. (2006) Treated like adults: 14–16-year-olds in further education. *Research in Post-Compulsory Education*, 11(3): 319–339.

Huddleston, P. and Oh, S. (2004) The magic roundabout: work-related learning within the 14–19 curriculum. *Oxford Review of Education*, 30(1): 83–103.

Jarvis, P. (2010) *Adult Education and Lifelong Learning: Theory and Practice*, 4th edn. London: Routledge.

Kolb, D. (1984) *Experiential Learning*. Englewood Cliffs, NJ: Prentice Hall.

Marsick, V. and Watkins, K. (eds) (1990) *Informal and Incidental Learning in the Workplace*. London: Routledge.

Morgan-Klein, B. and Osborne, M. (2007) *The Concepts and Practices of Lifelong Learning*. London: Routledge.

Schuller, T., Brassett-Grundy, A., Green, A., Hammond, C. and Preston, J. (2002) *Learning, Continuity and Change in Adult Life*. London: Institute of Education.

Tomlinson, M. (2013) *Education, Work, and Identity: Themes and Perspectives*. London: Bloomsbury.

15

KNOWLEDGE, SKILLS AND COMPETENCE IN VOCATIONAL LEARNING

Samantha Jones and Catherine Lloyd

Key words - knowledge; skills; competence; competency; vocational; standards; practice; context; setting

Introduction

In this chapter, we will explore the role of knowledge, skills and competence in vocational learning. We will begin by briefly considering what is meant by vocational learning, before presenting an overview of knowledge, skills and competency, and how they feature in policy, qualifications and syllabi. We consider factors that influence policy and development within vocational education and present three approaches to vocational education as described by Young (2004). This leads onto an exploration of the three terms in more depth, in each section linking the theories presented to professional practice. Beginning with knowledge, we explore the concept of vocational knowledge with reference to the work of Eraut (2000, 2004) before moving on to examine the influence on practice using the work of Loo (2018).

In the section on skills, we explore the work of Gamble (2002) and Sennett (2008) on the teaching of craft skills and relate this to vocational learning in practice settings. We then move on to consider competence using research carried out by Brockmann et al. (2008) on models of competence-based vocational education to inform our understanding.

This is followed by consideration of the transferability of knowledge, skills and competence between different contexts, an issue that is fundamental to vocational teaching.

Knowledge, skills and competence: policy, qualifications and syllabi

The range of courses and breadth of occupational areas covered by the sector is extensive. These include full-time, part-time and work-based routes to enable individuals to progress into employment or onto higher study. Underpinning this is a wide range of different qualification types and awarding bodies, some sector-specific, others providing qualifications across a number of areas. Each qualification will contain information on the content that should be delivered. This syllabus content indicates knowledge and skills that should be covered by an individual studying for the qualification in preparation for employment or further study. This may be set out in terms of learning outcomes, and covers what the individual should know (knowledge), what they should be able to do (skill) or how they should perform (competence) to achieve the qualification. The assessment criteria give guidance on what and how this learning should be assessed. In some cases, grading criteria links to how well assessment is performed; in others, the performance is judged as either pass or fail. Thus, qualifications act as the guidance for moving learners from one state of knowledge, skills or competence to another.

Although qualifications will have required outcomes, there is scope for the lecturer to interpret these and adapt the delivery to their setting. For example, it may be possible to select different optional units, write assessments and devise practical sessions. It is the lecturer's role to decide how the content will be taught and what in the syllabus to emphasise, and as such vocational lecturers do have some input into what is taught in their classroom.

Key questions

Who decides what knowledge, skills and competencies an individual needs to perform an occupation?

Michael Young (2004) describes three approaches to vocational education: the knowledge-based approach, the standards-based approach and the connective model. Each he sets in its historical context, understanding these will help to frame the issues raised within this chapter – how and why knowledge, skills and competence are taught as they are in further education.

Knowledge-based vocational education developed in the late nineteenth century at a time when scientific development and engineering led industrial development and the economy. These skills and their underpinning knowledge could not be learnt on the job, and contra to the way in which application of knowledge to the workplace is so central to vocational teaching today, at this point in time application to the workplace was often forbidden from teaching. As such, the curriculum grew to be separate from the context in which it was used, eventually causing criticism in the late 1970s to early 1980s. Much of this criticism centred around academic specialists setting the syllabus and examinations, as it was argued this was anachronistic and that these specialists had become too detached from the realities of the workplaces.

The answer to this criticism took the form of a standards-based curriculum. Driven by the employers who felt excluded from the knowledge-based approach, it began to exclude colleges and lecturers from vocational and academic backgrounds from shaping the qualifications. These standards-based qualifications concentrated on what people were able to do, shifting the focus away from (but not entirely excluding) what they needed to know. They offered learners opportunities to show competence in standards common across all subjects applied to their setting at five levels. This meant that a learner could start at level 1 and develop their competencies over a period of time, eventually progressing to a level 5 qualification. The competencies were judged against National Occupational Standards (NOS). These are the standards of performance individuals must achieve when carrying out functions in the workplace, aligned to specifications of the underpinning knowledge. Much of the success of the qualification rested on the engagement of employers to set standards and knowledge criteria that created variable quality in the qualifications. As a result, there are examples, such as accountancy, that had well-developed standards, with others, such as retail, being little more than a list of low-level tasks and knowledge requiring little thought or development.

The final approach Young (2004) discusses is the connective approach, which aims to bring together the previous two approaches, recognising how knowledge is used in the workplace. Technical Certificates are a good example of this. These qualifications tried to balance on-the-job training and the knowledge base. Although they sought to bring together skills and knowledge, they were often critiqued for failing to link the knowledge tested to the skills displayed. Hence, learners could be required to demonstrate changing a gearbox but only complete written tests on the correct camber for wheel alignment. Recent changes to apprenticeship provision, with the move to End Point Assessments, have sought to remedy this issue. On these qualifications, learners participate in professional discussion that requires them to explain the knowledge brought to bear on the specific skills they have displayed.

At the present time, government policy concentrates on employers, sector skills councils and awarding bodies to develop the curriculum. The focus of much vocational education is on employer-led reforms that aim to provide businesses with employees who are able to demonstrate the knowledge, skills and competencies they require. At the time of writing, the UK government has specified 15 new technical routes and is developing T-Level (technical-level) qualifications with extended work placements. Young (2004) and Young et al. (2014) argue that employer dominance may have unintended consequences, as a focus on the performance of a task, rather than the knowledge that underpins this performance, may be detrimental to workplace performance for the employer, and for the employee it may prevent them from accessing powerful knowledge. Powerful knowledge, Young argues, is that which can help a learner predict, explain or see alternatives, as without this kind of knowledge a learner cannot look beyond their present job, both in terms of improving it or improving their own future. This suggests that perhaps a balance needs to be sought between the needs of the workplace and the development of the individual.

Key questions

Who should educational knowledge benefit, the individual or society?

The chapter will now go on to explore each of these three key terms – knowledge, skills and competence – with the intention of linking each to professional practice.

Knowledge

In this section, we begin by considering what knowledge is before we discuss vocational knowledge and its characteristics. We will explore Eraut's (2000, 2004) work on types of tacit knowledge, linking this to classroom practice, before considering what knowledges are required for those who teach vocational education, by considering Loo's (2018) conceptual framework of what he calls occupational teaching.

What is knowledge?

Classically, knowledge is reliant on ideas of truth and justification; it is something that can be rationalised and often supported by evidence or argument. Elgin (2007) explains how 'knowledge differs from (mere) right opinion through having a tether to secure it or hold it fast' (p417), the tether being the rationalised evidence or argument. All of this, she argues, implies that knowledge is a fixed mark whose tethers and fixers do not change. There are elements of this kind of knowledge in most vocational curricula – concepts from maths and geography are found in surveying, statistical concepts are found in business studies – but we would start this section by arguing that this classical definition of knowledge is insufficient to encapsulate all of the knowledge types taught in vocational education. This is because some knowledge has fixers and tethers that do change (e.g. knowledge around marketing to individuals will have changed through the 2018 General Data Protection Regulation, and construction knowledge and practice would have recently changed in light of the Grenfell tragedy). It is also because some forms of knowledge are subjective (e.g. aesthetics in the arts) or physical (e.g. ball or tool control in sports and construction trades). These may have principles and guides, but these tend to be fluid, so this suggests that vocational knowledge may well be a complex entity.

What is vocational knowledge?

Winch (2010) separates out the concepts of subject knowledge and practical knowledge, and this is a good place to begin an exploration of what vocational knowledge is. It is knowing how to do something and knowing about the subject, but we have already suggested that this is not all that vocational knowledge is. Vocational knowledge does include large amounts of subject knowledge, often called propositional knowledge. In this respect, it shares commonalities with schools and universities. However, vocational knowledge contains more than this subject or propositional knowledge.

Looking at the below theory box, Michael Eraut argues that vocational knowledge also includes the concept of tacit knowledge. This knowledge is often the kind that we use to bring together knowing how to do something and knowing about a subject.

Key theory

Eraut (2000, 2004)

Michael Eraut discusses three types of tacit knowledge: tacit understanding of people and situations; routinised actions; and the tacit rules that underpin intuitive decision-making. These are influenced by the context and setting in which work occurs. Tacit knowledge is personal knowledge that develops as you do a job, as you begin to develop routines to help you work effectively in the workplace and make decisions quickly. This develops as you have exchanges with people and in situations in the workplace, and you begin to learn 'what works in this circumstance'. At this point, your tacit knowledge develops, often without you even realising it.

Tacit knowledge helps us use our theoretic knowledge in the workplace. Eraut describes the expert not as someone who knows a lot, but as the person who is able to quickly and effectively deploy theoretical or

(Continued)

(Continued)

propositional knowledge. This quick and effective use of this knowledge allows us to deal with situations at work where we need to work intuitively and helps us deal with circumstances that demand greater productivity. Basically, in stressful, fast-moving situations, or when greater demands are placed on us at work, those with greater tacit knowledge are better able to cope. However, as environments and cultures shift over time, tacit knowledge may lose its value if it does not keep up with these changes.

Tacit knowledge is loosely defined as things we know but can't explain to others. Eraut argues we can learn this knowledge explicitly, like learning how to change gears in a car, or through practice, experience or socialisation, like learning the ways to behave in a new organisation or learning how correctly kneaded bread should look and feel. He argues that tacit knowledge can be used in four contexts: understanding situations, decision-making, skilful action and monitoring.

Let us consider how tacit knowledge can be used in teaching. Understanding people and situations is a key knowledge of lecturers that is often overlooked, yet it underpins much of the communication decisions we make and how we classroom-manage. For example, how you may explain global supply chains would be different to level 2 and level 5 learners, not just because of the level, but you would take into account the different levels of life experience, work experience and confidence of these two groups. You may draw on your experience of when you have taught the subject before and lost the group with too high a level of explanation, or failed to communicate an important point effectively. You may consider how you were taught and use that as your stimulus. Deciding the approach to take can involve complex decision-making, and requires skilful action and also monitoring of the situation to ensure the success of the approach taken. Similarly, good classroom managers understand their students and subjects. This can be evidenced in planning sessions which don't create solutions that will elicit poor behaviour from students, such as long periods of waiting for others to finish, and within the sessions by ensuring tensions are not created within the classroom that may cause behavioural problems. Tacit knowledge is used to respond to the individual in front of you, often calling on your previous successes or disasters to inform decisions and monitor learners' responses to the situations. This may involve reviewing your previous and current performance in order to make a decision on how best to act with skill in the situation in which you find yourself. You may recognise in the learner an experience you have had, or a learner you have previously taught. So, in the teaching of a specific subject to a specific group of learners, in the planning of sessions and the performance within the session tacit knowledge is used to understand situations, make decisions, act skilfully and monitor.

Key questions

What knowledge is required for successful performance in your vocational area?

So far, we have considered how vocational knowledge can be different to classical 'truth'-bound forms of knowledge, exploring how it may be tacit and is created by experience and judgement. We have touched on how this can make vocational knowledge different to the knowledge commonly used in schools and universities, which tends to focus on propositional or subject knowledge.

Key theory

Loo (2018)

Loo has created a framework for what he calls occupations teaching. What is argued is that occupational teaching is a more complex process than is often understood, and that occupational lecturers are integrating their occupational and teaching pools of knowledge to create learning experiences that prepare individuals to join an occupation.

In Loo's model, decisions regarding the use of occupational knowledge and teaching knowledge run parallel to each other. When considering the occupational knowledge, the lecturer needs first to consider which element of the occupational knowledge to present to the cohort in front of them. They may have a detailed understanding of this knowledge and need to choose the right element of it to present to the class. Next, they will then consider how this knowledge is used with the occupation to make further decisions regarding how they will teach this subject to a class. Finally, they bring together the occupational knowledge and the know-how from work to create what Loo calls occupational content knowledge.

A similar parallel process happens for the teaching knowledge: a broad teaching or pedagogical approach is taken by drawing on teaching theory (e.g. a lecturer may chose a constructivist approach and aim to build on the previous lesson). This is then reconsidered in light of the learners or resources available to create what Loo calls applied pedagogical knowledge. At the end of this process, the occupational lecturer brings together the two parallel processes and integrates the applied occupational knowledge with the applied pedagogical knowledge to create the learning experience that reflects the needs of the workplace, the learners, the occupational and their teaching knowledge.

As an example, if a tutor is asked to teach strategy, they may explore their theoretical knowledge of that subject and start by selecting a simple tool such as SWOT (strengths, weaknesses, opportunities and threats) analysis. The lecturer may look to their teaching knowledge and decide on a constructivist approach as they feel this could build on previous knowledge the group has learnt. Next, they may think about the requirements of the class and of the awarding body and decide on a case study-based approach. Alongside this, they may think about how this is used with an occupation (e.g. procurement) and think about how this business function uses this to identify issues in supply chains. They will then go on to think about specific situations in which this knowledge is used. Finally, they will bring these knowledges together to create a case study that focuses on using SWOT to identify supply chain issues. This integrates the best way to teach the knowledge, but will also make the knowledge useful to the learner by allowing them to simulate an occupational relevant scenario. In this way, the lecturer can then highlight some of the work-related knowledges around the use of SWOT, perhaps looking at tools that will allow you to analyse features that the SWOT highlights, or how to categorise elements that don't seem to fit naturally into one specific box. Hence, Loo's model offers us an insight into how dual professionals use these different knowledges in practice.

In this section, we have explored the ways in which vocational knowledge can be categorised and how the knowledge bases in vocational education are far wider-ranging than is sometimes acknowledged. We have used examples to illustrate how the nature of the knowledge being taught may necessitate a different approach to teaching, and how this centres on the dual professionalism of the vocational lecturer.

Skills

In this section on skills, we will discuss the history of the term and its link to craft-based apprentice-ships and acquisition of skills for a particular role or purpose. Central to this is consideration of Sennett's (2008) work *The Craftsman* and Gamble's (2002) work on the teaching of craft skills. These approaches have been selected as they focus on the intangible nature of craft skills, which require very different methods of teaching, something we believe is an essential differentiator between skill and knowledge.

Sennett (2008) looks back into history and describes the handing down of knowledge from genera-tion to generation through apprenticeship; skills at this point were a source of economic power, so were carefully guarded by guilds. Within these guilds, apprentices would learn through imitation from a craftsman whose role was not only to train, but to set the standards that apprentices should reach. Training, in this context, was for the head as well as the hand, so skills could be practised to enable them to be used thoughtfully, and eventually the apprentice could work at a self-aware level and so could self-correct. Keeping standards high and places limited were vested interests for these guilds and the community that formed around them.

Often linked with practical occupations, however, many of these traditional crafts involved a tacit knowledge base that was highly contextualised, unwritten and often unspoken, and therefore difficult to observe. Gamble (2002) further elaborates on the idea of tacit forms of teaching. The first method, modelling and imitation, she argues, is essential as much of what is taught cannot be verbalised. The second, visualisation, is both a communication tool, allowing the designer to communicate to the craftsperson what they wish them to produce, and a production tool. During production, the crafts-person needs to be able to hold in their head the image of the ideal whole and how the elements they are producing will be part of a proportional whole. These skills, Sennett (2008) argues, are obtained through practice and problem-solving in practice settings.

Key questions

The term skill is used in many areas of vocational learning. What skills do you consider are needed to be successful in your own occupational area? Are these specific or general?

Key theory

Sennett (2008)

Sennett (2008) describes skill as a 'trained practice' (p37). He stresses the importance of practice and makes a link between higher-level skills and the ability to maintain more sustained periods of practice. Sennett does not agree that there is a transferability of skills. He maintains that skills are not a 'laundry list of procedures' (p107), but form a culture around the actions.

Sennett argues that the culture and skills are developed in the workshop. This is where the practice, the contact with tools, the verbal explanation, the problem-solving, habits and skills-based routines all take place.

Sennett offers a perhaps more complex view of skills than is used in present policy and syllabi. It involves tacit knowledge, knowledge that cannot be written down; for example, how it feels when an action is carried out correctly, passed down in key physical settings, by more experienced individuals, who pass down notions of standards, routine and correct practices.

Sennett's work draws a line from the medieval guild apprentices to the modern day. Many of the teaching methods and issues that were considered important then are still valuable to practice now. The centrality of practice in a workplace, or an environment that mirrors it, is important. The lecturer as the 'master craftsman', passing on good habits, routine, skills, standards and ways of being, is also central, but perhaps problematic for lecturers, assessors, awarding bodies and policymakers as they are things that are difficult to articulate onto a syllabus. There are lines here to be drawn to the designing of assessments that aim to mirror industry problems, and to the importance of correctly resourced teaching facilities. However, there is much debate over both, and perhaps this is not the point for us to join it.

Skills often gain complexity as a learner applies them to their workplace. In this example, we will discuss the delivery of first-aid training to outdoor education learners. In a basic level 3 first-aid course lasting six hours, the skills are modelled as Gamble and Sennett recommend and taught as a routine. This routine practised in a classroom environment becomes 'muscle memory', with the aim being that the skills are deployed competently if the learner finds themselves required to give basic first aid. However, in a more advanced 16-hour first-aid skills programme at level 3, the learners begin to apply these skills to the outdoor education environment. Here, the complexity of skills increases and learners are taught how to transfer and develop these routinised skills to dynamic environments (e.g. in wet, cold or restricted environments, or on slopes, at height or environments vulnerable to the weather), thus, as Gamble suggests, requiring the learner to visualise the whole situation and judge how to act skilfully. Here, the learners require a greater level of problem-solving to competently deploy these skills in challenging environments.

In this section, we have explored the background and context to the acquisition of skills for a particular trade or craft. Using Sennett, we have identified the importance of sustained practice in mastering skills under the supervision of a lecturer and how lecturers model practice and standards at ever-greater levels of complexity to develop the problem-solving skills required to act skilfully.

Competence

In this section, we will begin by considering definitions of competence and draw links between competence and performance in the workplace. We will present two models of competence-based vocational education and training described by Brockmann et al. (2008). This will be followed by consideration of how competence is perceived and assessed within vocational education and the debates surrounding this.

Key questions

What do you understand by the term competence? What role does it have to play in vocational learning?

The concept of competence has been the subject of much debate among researchers in this area and the term itself can be defined in a number of different ways depending on the context and approach taken. These numerous definitions have resulted in differences in how competence is approached, understood and assessed. There are also differences between competence and competencies and how these are understood. In general terms, competence can be seen as a development of the concept of skills, and relates to the notion of being competent when performing tasks or activities relevant to an occupation. It includes a broader focus on employability and employment, which it could be argued is missing from a purely skill- and task-based approach. Competency is associated with performance in the workplace, so is therefore dependant on the context in which the job role will take place. This links to the previous section on skills, where Sennett (2008) describes the process of learning from more experienced individuals in workplace settings.

At the start of this chapter, we explored Young's (2004) three approaches to vocational education and how these influenced curriculum development and delivery. Competence-based training, because of its links with employment, has been used as a means to address skills needs (e.g. through National Vocational Qualifications, discussed at the start of the chapter, and more recently through the new apprenticeship standards). These work-based learning qualifications focus on the skills developed while in the workplace and include a proportion of off-the-job training such as day release at a college. They provide opportunities for individuals to participate in training directly linked to employment. The aim of the curriculum is for the learner to develop and demonstrate competence through this combination of on- and off-the-job training.

There are different models of competence in vocational education and training as described by Brockmann et al. (2008).

Key theory

Brockmann et al. (2008)

Brockmann et al. have researched competence-based vocational education and training in a number of European countries. They identified two approaches: a skills-based model and a knowledge-based model. The skills-based model is practical in its approach, with the emphasis on learning skills in a workplace setting. This involves breaking down an occupation into a series of tasks that need to be undertaken, and assessment is made of the individual's performance in completion of these tasks. Competence is assessed through the individual's ability to demonstrate skills in completion of the tasks to a required standard. The knowledge-based model is broader and includes theoretical and practical knowledge and competencies alongside more general education aimed at providing individuals with the ability to problem-solve and deal with complex situations. Competence in this model is more general and viewed in terms of capacity rather than performance.

Brockmann et al. (2008) identify that traditionally, England has followed a skills-based model, focused on direct observations of performance of specific tasks. Competence is assessed through these observations and tutors will visit learners in the workplace to observe and monitor progress. This is considered a behaviourist approach (Hyland, 1997) as the focus is on the behaviours demonstrated by the individual that can be observed by the assessor. They then make a judgement on whether or not the individual's performance has met the required standards to be considered competent.

The knowledge-based model is broader and brings together both theoretical and practical aspects to develop individuals, promoting the development of problem-solving skills that will enable them to transfer their learning to different settings and contexts. There is also the inclusion of general education, and consideration is given to the development of characteristics to support an individual's progression in the workplace.

As the English system focuses on the skills-based approach, it is this model that shall be critiqued. As this approach focuses on individual tasks, its key criticism is that it fails to acknowledge how these tasks are interrelated and link together to perform the whole. It has also been suggested that a focus on performance of tasks is too narrow and can neglect the knowledge and understanding elements of the role. An example of this would be where an individual can perform the skills required to compete a task without fully accessing or understanding the knowledge base. There is also the risk that this approach focuses on the minimum level of performance an individual must display in order to be competent (Hyland, 1997). Skills-based models of competency are often seen in qualifications that tend to hinge around the creation of a portfolio to exemplify a candidate's ability to complete a task competently, with the focus on collection of evidence to demonstrate that standards have been met. Often accompanied by books that provide a bullet-pointed framework of what to do in order to complete the qualification, with some brief explanations of the underpinning knowledge, these qualifications require little evidencing of how well the underpinning knowledge is understood by the candidate, or how the candidate may have used the knowledge they have to problem-solve. All emphasis is on the portfolio exhibiting the end product as evidence of a suitable understanding of both practice and theory.

At the time of writing, steps have been taken to review and develop work-based training qualifications to include a more integrated method of assessment with the intention that it will enable the individual to demonstrate their ability, understanding and other skills such as problem-solving. This links to the connective approach discussed at the start of this chapter (Young, 2004).

To assess work-based qualifications, individuals must themselves provide evidence that they are occupationally competent in the subjects and areas they are assessing. Central to this is ensuring that the assessor remains up to date and familiar with developments and current practices in their area through undertaking continuing professional development. This, it can be argued, is a key part of being a dual professional, as discussed earlier in the chapter.

In this section, we have described how competency in further education is most often referred to in terms of work-based qualifications such as apprenticeships. We have looked at both skills and knowledge-based models of competency and discussed issues surrounding assessment of competence.

Transferability of knowledge, skills and competence

There is much discussion around the concept of transfer of knowledge, skills and competence from one setting to another (e.g. from college to the workplace or between different workplaces). While this is often discussed theoretically, the practical realities of the process are sometimes ignored. Eraut (2004) discusses the difficulty of transferring tacit knowledge into written or explicit forms, and explores the problems inherent in transferring explicit knowledge from a university to workplace practice. This certainly suggests that transferring skills, knowledge and competence may be more difficult than is recognised in post-compulsory education, with prevalent notions of 'key skills', 'thinking skills' and ideas that a checklist of good practice in teaching will ensure that good practice in a workshop will be transferable to good practice in work-based or formal classroom teaching.

These notions of transferability are often linked with skills in a more general sense rather than the identification of skills specific to a particular trade or occupation. Hence, as discussed above, we are often discussing thinking skills or problem-solving skills as if they are entities in their own right. However, in support of Billett (2004), Eraut (2004) and Rogoff and Gauvain (1984) also argue that the likelihood of transfer between different settings is unlikely. They explain that this is likely to be because different settings have different norms and conventions (e.g. the way you solve a problem in a fast-moving customer-facing environment may be very different to that in an engineering firm).

Chapter summary

In this chapter, we have explored vocational learning in terms of knowledge, skills and competence. We began by considering different approaches to vocational education as described by Young (2004) and different knowledge types (Eraut, 2000, 2004) before considering what this means for teaching practice using the work of Loo (2018). In the section on skills, we related the work of Gamble (2002) and Sennett (2008) to vocational learning in practice settings. We then moved on to consider competence-based vocational education using research carried out by Brockmann et al. (2008) to inform our understanding.

- Technical education links back to apprenticeships and practical ways of working.

- Vocational learning combines the knowledge, skills and competencies needed to perform a role.

- There are many different ways of classifying knowledge and these will affect the way the knowledge is taught.

- Skills are traditionally associated with hand skills and learning a trade or craft.

- Competence is commonly used in relation to performance in the workplace.

Recommended further reading

Rose, M. (2005) *The Mind at Work: Valuing the Intelligence of the American Worker*. Harmondsworth: Penguin.

References

Billett, S. (2004) Learning through work: workplace participatory practices. In A. Fuller, A. Munro and H. Rainbird (eds), *Workplace Learning in Context*. London: Routledge.

Brockmann, M., Clarke, L. and Winch, C. (2008) Knowledge, skills, competence: European divergences in vocational education and training (VET) – the English, German and Dutch cases. *Oxford Review of Education*, 34(5): 547–567.

Elgin, C.Z. (2007) Education and the advancement of understanding. In R. Curren (ed.), *Philosophy of Education*. Oxford: Blackwell.

Eraut, M. (2000) Non-formal learning and tacit knowledge in professional work. *British Journal of Educational Psychology*, 70(1): 113–136.

Eraut, M. (2004) Informal learning in the workplace. *Studies in Continuing Education*, 26(2): 247–273.

Gamble, J. (2002) *Retrieving the General from the Particular: The Structure of Craft Knowledge*. Available at: www.researchgate.net/profile/Jeanne_Gamble/publication/237834233_Retrieving_the_general_from_the_particular_The_structure_of_craft_knowledge/links/59d64d16458515db19c4f4ba/Retrieving-the-general-from-the-particular-The-structure-of-craft-knowledge.pdf

Hyland, T. (1997) Reconsidering competence. *Journal of Philosophy of Education*, 31(3): 491–503.

Loo, S. (2018) *Teachers and Teaching in Vocational and Professional Education*. London: Routledge.

Rogoff, B. and Gauvain, M. (1984) The cognitive consequences of specific experiences: weaving versus schooling among the Navajo. *Journal of Cross-Cultural Psychology*, 15(4): 453–475.

Sennett, R. (2008) *The Craftsman*. New Haven, CT: Yale University Press.

Winch, C. (2010) *Dimensions of Expertise: A Conceptual Exploration of Vocational Knowledge*. London: Bloomsbury.

Young, M. (2004) Conceptualising vocational knowledge: some theoretical considerations. In A. Fuller, A. Munro and H. Rainbird (eds), *Workplace Learning in Context*. London: Routledge.

Young, M., Lambert, D., Roberts, C. and Roberts, M. (2014) *Knowledge and the Future School Curriculum and Social Justice*. London: Bloomsbury Academic.

16
MAKING SENSE OF LIFELONG LEARNING

Sherene Meir and Carol Azumah Dennis

Key words – lifelong learning; learner motivation; widening participation; workplace learning; learning careers; credentialism; returning to study

Introduction

> ### Key questions
>
> Why in the latter part of the twentieth century did the idea of lifelong learning become so important to policymakers across the industrialised world?

Lifelong learning is not a new concept. In 1919, the final report of the Adult Education Committee of the Ministry of Reconstruction recommended that adult education 'is a permanent national necessity, an inseparable aspect of citizenship, and should be both universal and lifelong' (Field, 2000, p14). There was a strong liberal, non-vocational leaning in this early nineteenth-century understanding of adult education, which valued learning as an end in itself rather than as a means to some other end. In the 1960s, the United Nations Educational, Scientific and Cultural Organization (UNESCO) declared lifelong education as the principal concept for all its educational planning, policymaking and practice for the future. From its inception, the concept was ambiguous and no clearly defined notion of lifelong education prevailed (Wain, 2001). At the beginning of the 1990s, the Conservative government proposed turning Britain into a 'learning society'; by 2000, lifelong 'education' had become lifelong 'learning' and the radical undertones in its earliest usage gave way to increasingly economistic implications. The broad tenets of the learning society are contested, but can be broadly summarised as:

- The economic competitiveness of the nation is ultimately determined by the skills of its people.

- Globalisation and technology are akin to natural phenomena: uncontrollable with potentially devastating impact. The nation state's only rational response is to weather the storm by upskilling its workforce.

- A modernised education is responsive to the needs of employers or, as Blair once phrased it, 'Education is the best economic policy we have' (cited in DfEE, 1998).

- The responsibility for learning is passed on to the individual, who is charged with renewing their skills on a regular basis to ensure their continued employability.

Each of these propositions is highly problematic and has been subject to eviscerating critique (Ainley, 1998; Coffield, 1999; Hodgson, 2000). Underpinning each tenet is the assumption that education exists to service the economy, and that if individuals possess skills and attributes desirable to industry, this alone would unsettle what Finegold (1993) refers to as the 'low-skill equilibrium' – the long-term tendency for Britain to be a low-skill, low-wage economy. But this focus on education, ensuring that industry has access to a supply of highly skilled employees, belies the extent to which the inadequate demand for skills from British employers is partly what drives personal and public underinvestment in education and training (Keep, 2016).

Over the period of the last 100 years, therefore, we can see a significant shift in the ways in which lifelong learning has been constructed through policy, which in turn reflects shifting philosophies of lifelong learning, from the liberal tradition of the 1919 report, to the neo-liberal culture of the present. In this chapter, we explore these different philosophies of lifelong learning and consider what these mean for the ways in which we understand the trajectories of lifelong learners.

The nature of participation in education

Key questions

Do we now live in the learning society envisioned by policymakers?

The Adult Participation in Learning Survey, produced by what was the National Institute of Adult Continuing Education (NIACE), which became Learning & Work (L&W) in 2017, is the longest-running and most frequently occurring study of adult learning in the UK. The survey series began in 1996 and offers a unique view of the level of participation in learning by adults. The surveys are conducted annually among 5,000 research participants, all of whom are aged 17 and over. They are each asked about their experiences of learning, when they last took part in learning and how likely they are to take part in learning in the future. Overall, the survey concludes that participation in learning is unevenly distributed across society. L&W introduce their most recent data set with the observation that participation in 'learning is determined by social class, employment status and prior learning' (Learning & Work, n.d.). In 1998, around the time that the learning society become a policy focus rather than policy aspiration, the survey noted that males, younger people, people who were employed, those working in professional, managerial or other non-manual occupations, those who stayed in full-time education, or those who left school with better qualifications were the most likely to take part in learning (Beinart and Smith, 1998). Some five years later, in 2003, when New Labour's policy surrounding lifelong learning was at its most effervescent, the report cites 76 per cent of adults as participating in learning – a 2 per cent increase from the 1997 participation rate of 74 per cent.

Yet, while the actual number of participants in learning had improved substantially (the report opens by pointing out that national targets had been met; Fitzgerald et al., 2002), the profile of participation had not significantly altered. Overall, the report found the profile of who does and who does not participate in learning, based on social class, employment status and prior learning, remained consistent. The headline figure of 76 per cent participation is dramatically reduced with particular cohorts: people aged 70 and over (28 per cent), those with no qualifications (29 per cent) or with basic skills difficulties (52 per cent), and adults living in the most deprived areas (67 per cent). The major motivation cited by most adults for participation in learning was job-related.

Key theory

What is the relationship between lifelong learning and social class?

Exploring the relationship between social class and lifelong learning is important, both because participation data shows sustained disparities between individuals based on class - despite policies seeking to widen participation - and because class is significant to how individuals perceive and make choices about education.

Through his work, French sociologist, anthropologist, philosopher and public intellectual Pierre Bourdieu (1930-2002) sought to understand the dynamics of power in society, particularly the diverse and subtle ways in which social hierarchies based on class are reproduced across generations.

Bourdieu viewed the education system in industrialised societies as a mechanism through which class inequalities were legitimated. Success in education is facilitated by the possession of highly valued cultural attributes and a sense of belonging to a group of people for whom education is a norm. Those who do not possess these traits are almost always failed by the education system. However, success or failure in education is largely viewed as down to individual effort (or lack of). It is assumed that those who do well do so because they were intelligent enough or hard-working enough. Thus, educational credentials are able to reproduce and legitimate social inequalities. The relationship between the possession of desirable cultural attributes and educational success is ignored, and those who succeed are determined to have done so by dint of their own personal effort (Sullivan, 2002).

There are several 'thinking tools' associated with Bourdieu's work that enable sociologists to establish an empirical understanding of the relationship between education and social class, most notably habitus, field and cultural capital. It is Bourdieu's notion of habitus that is of greatest interest here. He explained habitus in terms of the ways in which a person's background influences the way they think, feel and behave. Habitus renders some practices (such as participating in formal learning) unthinkable if they fall beyond the cultural background of the individual. Habitus is both individual and collective. It is formed by a person's individual history, but largely influenced by family, class, race and gender. As a result of habitus, hierarchical social structures - which produced the habitus in the first place - are reproduced. An individual's current social situation becomes internalised, so that habitus becomes multilayered, synthesising the past with the present (Macqueen, 2017, p35). In Bourdieu's terms, 'Habitus is a kind of transforming machine that leads us to "reproduce" the social conditions of our own production' (Bourdieu, 1990, p87).

Bourdieu can be used to think about various aspects of lifelong learning and adult education, including:

- how class affects individuals' views about, and sense of belonging within, formal education;

- the repetition or reproduction of patterns of inequality within the education system; and

- the impact of habitus on how learners, their family and peers experience return to education.

Conceptions of learning and motivation to study

An early critique of lifelong learning policy was identified by Coffield (1998), who notes the strategic thrust of policy but also highlights an important absence:

> In all the plans to put learners first, to invest in learning, to widen participation, to set targets, to develop skills, to open up access, to raise standards, and to develop a national framework of qualifications, there is no mention of a theory (or theories) of learning to drive the whole project. It is as though there existed ... such widespread understanding of, and agreement about, the processes of learning ... that comment was thought superfluous.
>
> (p4)

Taking Coffield's (1998) critique as a starting point, this chapter explores conceptions of learning as pivotal to exploring lifelong learning. Particular conceptions enable the articulation of different and distinct motivations for returning to study. It is not our intention to offer a detailed analysis of different learning theories. Instead, we use these conceptualisations as a heuristic through which to explore the circumstances within which adults return to learning.

Conceptions of learning provide a language for learners to voice their motivations. The terms used in public discourse to frame what learning is and why it is a personal or public imperative influences how adults understand and speak about what they are doing and why. How learning is talked about in the public domain influences what and how adults understand and articulate their motivations. It is from this premise that we explore returning to studying through conceptualisations of learning. The discussion is based primarily on published literature. However, to illustrate our argument, we also draw on primary data generated through a series of peer discussions undertaken with adult students registered on an Access to Higher Education (AHE) health and social care programme in a further education college in the south-west of England.

The AHE research was undertaken by Meir in 2018. In total, 17 participants between the ages of 19 and 40 volunteered to take part in the research. All the students were approaching the end of their programme and the research facilitated their course and self-evaluation. While the primary research question for the research undertaken was 'How does returning to studying impact on adult learners' confidence?' at the same time discussions were broad and expansive, with a sub-research question of 'What motivates adults to return to study?' All participants were given pseudonyms to protect their identity. For the purposes of this chapter, the data were re-analysed using the four conceptions of learning discussed below as a lens.

Exploring and explaining lifelong learning

The line of thinking we now pursue is one that explores different notions of learning as embedded within lifelong learning, and we discuss these with the explicit intention of outlining what they imply for adults' motivations for returning to study.

Key questions

How are ideas about learning related to our ideas about teaching, being a student, being a non-traditional student and providing a good education?

Learning as acquisition

Arguably the most prevalent notion of learning implied by lifelong learning is that of 'learning as acquisition'. In this model, learning is conceived of as gaining basic units of a substance such as entity (e.g. concepts, qualifications, dispositions), which can be accumulated, cultivated and combined with other units to form richer, more complex structures. In metaphorical terms, the human mind is conceived as a container to be filled with desirable materials that become the property of the learner. Lifelong learning policy privileges the acquisition of concepts, qualifications or dispositions that enable individuals to take their place within the workforce.

When AHE students who took part in this study framed their motivation, they drew upon a view of learning as a thing they acquire to fulfil an external purpose. They frequently emphasised the product rather than the process of learning: a qualification and enhanced employment prospects. This would seem to echo Britton and Baxter's (1999) study of mature students, who associate this motivational narrative with 'credentialism'. Students view themselves as stuck in a rut, bored, underemployed – doing a job that neither stimulates nor challenges them – as Tracy exemplifies:

> The job I was doing before working for a property consultancy, which is so ... like ... office politics, stuck in a rut, people working there for 30 years, not really contributing to society.

> Tracy, AHE student

Having reached an impasse in their lives through lack of formal qualifications, education provides a means to an end – a credential that allows them to move forward towards a career.

It is not our intention to adjudicate between these different conceptions of learning. Each are accepted as providing valuable insight. However, an individualistic view of learning as acquiring knowledge or credentials for instrumental use may be contrasted with a less outcome-oriented view of learning.

Learning as a reflective process

This second conception of the learning implied by lifelong learning incorporates an understanding of learners' lived experiences. Learning as a reflective process reframes learning as an individual process of personal 'meaning-making' (Fenwick and Tennant, 2004, p60). Frequently cited as an example of this conception, Kolb (1984) views learning as a reflective process involving the learner making connections between a learning experience and previous learning. Mezirow (1997) also posits meaning-making as learning, suggesting that 'transformative learning' occurs when individuals alter their perspectives and are able to put new perspectives into action within their lives.

This process of meaning-making can and frequently does include the desire to make sense of who we are and how we fit into the world around us (Beck, 1992; Giddens, 1991). Contemporary society requires individuals to recreate a role and place for themselves as the rigidity of previously held social and cultural expectations no longer hold. The motivation to do something 'meaningful' for oneself is evident within many adult learners' narratives, perhaps underpinned by notions of what constitutes 'meaningful' choices within public discourse about learning. A shifting perspective of herself seems to partially inform Tracy's decision to pursue nursing:

> *I've always thought I would make a good nurse and ... then when my parents were ill and stuff and they passed away, I realised I probably would have the strength to look after people that were sick and not get too emotionally attached.*
>
> Tracy, AHE student

Studying is not just a means to a desired career here, but a way of showing herself to be a particular type of person with the inner resources she perceives as necessary to doing a particular job.

Britton and Baxter (1999) categorise the motivations of some of the learners within their study under the heading 'unfilled potential', which posits learning as a means of 'reclaiming' a self that has been hidden or a self that circumstance has not allowed to flourish. For learners whose motivation to learn is discussed as a process of personal meaning-making, there is often a specific transformative catalyst that sparks their return to education, making it seem possible or achievable, when previously it did not:

> *I never really thought I was clever enough to do something like this ...? I never, ever imagined myself going to university, that just weren't me ... so I just didn't do anything about it and then my sister did it and I thought ... if she can do it, so can I ...*
>
> Lizzie, AHE student

Osborne et al. (2004) and West (1995) elaborate upon this narrative as most prevalent among older adults, especially women, who experience life-changing events such as children leaving the home, bereavement or relationship break-ups. In one example, 'Janice' returns to study after going through a difficult time with one of her children and deciding it was time to 'Do something for yourself!' (Britton and Baxter, 1999, p184), while 'Brenda', in her early fifties, describes returning to study as a means of gaining her 'own little bit of identity' at a time when she is experiencing relationship problems. She hoped studying would allow her 'to rebuild the house a little bit – instead of it being on sand ... that would make me feel my own person, I would really discover who I am and not who other people want me to be' (West, 1995).

It is possible to identify a class-based exclusion here. Reay (2003) argues that narratives of self-transformation or personal fulfilment are inaccessible to working-class women, whose cultural background does not value self-centred individualism. However, Britton and Baxter (1999) frame self-fulfilment as universal, a 'recognisable cultural narrative of our times' (p186), readily available to adult learners explaining their experiences.

Learning as a practice-based community process

The difficulty with learning as a reflective process is that it is surprisingly insular. Reflecting carefully or critically on experience is not always possible. Indeed, as we have so far implied, what we imagine to be our experience is created through and by the discourses we inhabit (Garrick, 1999). To ask that a narrator reflect critically on their experience is akin to asking a fish to describe water.

Our third conceptualisation, learning as a practice-based community process, avoids some of these limitations by recognising learning as almost entirely situational. In the work of Lave and Wenger (1991), learning is conceptualised as thoroughly embedded within context. It is relational and social, rather than located within the head of a person in the form of cognition. Most often associated with apprenticeship learning in the workplace, Lave and Wenger (1991) reframe learning not as acquisition, but as participation. They focus on the workplace as a site for learning. It is social participation, rather than cognition or indeed critical reflection, that allows newcomers to learn from more accomplished and experienced practitioners, enabling them to move from peripheral to full participation within a community of practice.

In considering our overall theme of adult motivations for returning to study, considering learning as a practice-based community process implies a focus on workplace learning (even though workplace learning itself may be viewed more broadly as *learning in, through or for the workplace*). Arguably, there is some overlap here with learning as acquisition, since discussions about learning and the workplace quickly turn towards the economist antecedents of lifelong learning: the need to improve productivity and performance within a competitive global economy that requires highly skilled and appropriately qualified employees willing to learn and relearn continually.

But policy rhetoric about a knowledge economy must be countered by the dystopian reality of skill underutilisation (Keep, 2016). Braverman's deskilling thesis points to the importance for workers to be easily exchangeable and replaceable, leading to an impoverished workplace that restricts autonomy and deskills employees (Braverman, 1974). Alongside deskilling runs a polarisation thesis, with some jobs becoming more meaningful while others are increasingly monitored and controlled. This polarisation is sedimented in a 'chain of cumulative dis/advantage' (OECD, 2003). In a pattern that replicates patterns of participation elsewhere, those who are well qualified and relatively privileged are more likely to participate in and benefit from workplace learning, in contrast to those with fewer qualifications, less status and diminished opportunity (McPherson and Wang, 2014). Stimulating work stimulates learning and the willingness to participate in training (Silvennoinen and Nori, 2017).

In their study of more than 500 basic skills students in low-skilled and low-status employment, Evans and Waite (2010) identify several motivations for participating in workplace learning. Over half the cohort – as might have been expected – cited a generic desire to 'learn new skills'. This was closely followed by one-third wanting to 'improve work performance'. Other motivations featured include curiosity, wanting to make up for missed earlier educational opportunities, wanting help with specific job-related skills, the desire to help children with school work, wanting self-improvement, and personal development. To illustrate the contingent fluidity of learning motivations, Evans and Waite (2010) cite pre-participation outcomes desired from study in comparison to post-participation desirable outcomes of study. In other words, what people say they want from participation may change depending on when they are interviewed. In narrative terms, we live our lives looking forwards, prospectively, but understand, analyse and classify them, looking backwards, retrospectively.

This means that static ideal-type classifications are misleading as they are unable to incorporate the shape-shifting nature of experience. In later work, Evans et al. (2011) develop a metaphor – social ecology – to allow a theoretical framework sophisticated enough to grapple with workplace learning as embedded within a system of self-sustaining interdependent social relationships (p365). Understanding return to studying in, through or for the workplace using the social ecology metaphor allows us to understand the fluctuating connections between social institutions such as the labour market, workplace and community, and how they overlap with social roles such as employee, citizen and family member.

Key theory

Learning careers

As has been discussed, participation in lifelong learning is highly patterned. Exploring learning careers helps to understand these patterns in individuals over the life course and draws out some of the implications of different lifelong learning policies on individuals' choices over time.

The concept of a 'learning career' allows us to contextualise learning, 'acknowledging the social and cultural influences and their impact on individual identity' (Goodlad, 2007, p107). Learning episodes through the life course of an individual may be aggregated into typologies. Gorard et al.'s (1999) large-scale study of adults in a single community in South Wales identified 11 lifetime learning trajectories, each of which provide an insight into adult learners' decision to return or not return to study. Their research, which included both participant and non-participant trajectories, distilled 11 'lifetime learning trajectories' down to an aggregated fivefold typology: non-participant, transitional, delayed, lifetime and immature.

Their work identified some 40 independent variables that have a significant impact on participation, which were collapsed into five broad factors:

1. *Time.* When respondents were born determines the availability or non-availability of opportunities for learning and social expectations.

2. *Place.* Where respondents are born and brought up shapes their access to locally available learning opportunities. Those in economically disadvantaged areas have fewer opportunities for participation.

3. *Gender.* Men consistently reported higher levels of participation in formal learning than women. In this study, women were more likely to be transitional learners. More recent survey data suggest that women have significantly higher participation rates (Egglestone et al., 2018, p6).

4. *Family.* This remains the single most influential factor in determining participation. Parents' social class, educational experience and religion shape the material and cultural importance attached to education.

5. *Initial schooling.* This provides the necessary qualifications that make further or higher education a viable option or not.

Gorard et al.'s (1998) study concluded that structure rather than agency is most significant in determining participation in lifelong learning: 'those characteristics which are set very early in an individual's life, such as age, gender and family background, predict later "lifetime learning trajectories" with 75 per cent accuracy' (p9).

This study, and its implications, can be used to think about different aspects of lifelong learning, including:

- key structural barriers to participation such as place and family;

- how much 'choice' different individuals/social groups have over participating or not participating in lifelong learning; and

- how/whether initiatives to increase participation can account for the multiple factors that coalesce to determine participation.

Learning as an embodied interdependent process

This conceptualisation views what we learn, who we are as learners and our learning environment as interdependent; there is no separation between the person who learns and the context within which they learn (Fenwick and Tennant, 2004). The metaphor of a conversation may be helpful here. In the dynamics of a conversation, each contribution shapes the nature of the interaction. Participants, the relational space and the rules of engagement are changed, dislodged, distorted or confirmed by each utterance, which in turn impacts upon the original contributor. Consistent with the idea that person and context are an inseparable whole, Davis et al.'s (2000) work on complex adaptive systems shows that systems (not just the humans embedded within them) remember, forget, recognise, hypothesise, err and adapt (p66). Systems, not just people, learn.

There are several implications of this notion of learning for our overall theme of return to studying. It implies that participation in learning is more pervasive than it is within other typologies. Learning is a normal, natural (perhaps even inevitable) activity. Everything from courses to conversations might legitimately be defined as learning. Livingstone's (1999) study of adults in Canada documented the existence of what he referred to as a 'learning iceberg' (p2). The iceberg metaphor implies that there exist layers and levels of learning that persist beneath the surface of the learning that is often talked about and subject to policy intervention. The study highlights the existence of a rich abundance of usually invisible learning activity, concluding that adults spent some 15 hours per week on *informal* learning. This rich abundance occurred beyond the auspices of the curricula provided by educational institutions, and thus it remained hidden.

Realising the vision of lifelong learning

Key questions

What would make lifelong learning for all a fully realised vision?

Once viewed through the prism of informal learning, participation profiles are completely undermined. The vast majority of social groups – whether defined in terms of age, race, gender, class, nationality or ableism – showed remarkably similar distributions in the time spent devoted to learning projects. People participate in informal learning without necessarily recognising it as learning (Tough, 2002). It is something they do out of desire rather than instrumental necessity. More recent studies have also echoed this notion of learning as co-emergent, particularly its ecological premise. Hodgson and Spours (2013) explore participation in a way that is reminiscent of an ecosystem.

Hodgson and Spours' (2013) work focuses on the 'overlooked middle': young people who leave school as middle to low attainers. The theoretical model of participation they develop has three components, defined in terms of the interaction between overlapping levels. The individual, their learning identity, and the lifeworld of family and friends they inhabit is connected to international trends in globalisation, migration and the national economy via the more complex set of relationships that surround learners more immediately – such as their local college or workplace, and the varying professionals with whom they come into contact (Hodgson and Spours, 2015). They conclude their analysis by constructing what they refer to as ideal-type local learning ecologies (LLEs): 'low opportunity and progression equilibria' (LOPEs) and 'high opportunity and progression ecosystems' (HOPEs). The overall point being made here is that learning as an embodied co-emergent process implies participation as complex, involving more than individual disposition or decision-making and the structural determinates that surround them. The individual is part of a holistic dynamic system, able to change and mutually changed by politics, policy, economics, funding, demography, and social and educational factors.

It is notable that the most recent adult education participation figures released by the Department of Education show a steady decline in participation in government-funded further education between 2011 and 2018. There was a particularly steep fall in adult learners participating in English and maths courses, with 12 per cent fewer adults participating in 2018 than in 2017. The L&W (formally NIACE) survey indicates that a participation rate of 37 per cent (current or recent learning) is the lowest in 20 years of their survey being conducted. It represents a 4 per cent reduction since 2015 and a 9 per cent reduction since 2001 (Egglestone et al., 2018, p20). Austerity has driven dramatic reductions in the capacity of further education to offer learning opportunities.

Chapter summary

Lifelong learners have always been difficult to define as a single group: alongside the student attending a recreational pottery class, we might find the student who is attending a computer skills class in order to enhance their employability. Within a course brochure from the WEA, we might find history and literature courses listed alongside family learning courses to encourage young parents to read with their children. Lifelong learning has, throughout the previous century, encompassed employment-focused training, recreational learning, second-chance provision and access. More recently, lifelong learning policy has promoted a public narrative about learning that posits economic benefits as central, both for the individual, in terms of employability, and for the nation, in terms of competitiveness within a global economy. Participation data, however, demonstrate the failure of policy to significantly alter the profile of those adults involved in learning; social class, prior qualifications and type of employment (or lack of employment) have remained important to determining the likelihood of participation in education, and are structural determinants that shape an

(Continued)

(Continued)

individual's opportunity to return to studying. The decline in participation in government-funded learning alongside the withdrawal of funding from further, adult and workplace education provision, as well as the growth in precarious work and skills underutilisation, poses ongoing questions as to the extent to which motivation to return to study is a freely made choice or is determined by 'structural determinants' such as class, ethnicity, gender and location.

Although not amenable to policy intervention and barely recognised within studies on participation, informal learning may reinvigorate the radical 'universal and lifelong' vision of learning posited by the Adult Education Committee of the Ministry of Reconstruction in 1919. With dwindling opportunities for participation in further, adult or workplace learning, the numbers of adults participating and the place, purpose and profile of existing institutional learning is doubtful (Dennis, 2016; Hodgson, 2015; Keep, 2014). Paying greater attention to informal learning may be a catalyst for shifting narratives about who and what learning is for.

References

Ainley, P. (1998) Towards a learning or a certified society? Contradictions in the New Labour modernization of lifelong learning. *Journal of Education Policy*, 13(4): 559–573.

Beck, U. (1992) *Risk Society: Towards a New Modernity*. London: Sage.

Beinart, S. and Smith, P. (1998) *National Adult Learning Survey 1997*. London: DfEE.

Bourdieu, P. (1990) *The Logic of Practice*. Stanford, CA: Stanford University Press.

Braverman, H. (1974) *Labor and Monopoly Capital: The Degradation of Work in the Twentieth Century*. New York: Monthly Review Press.

Britton, C. and Baxter, A. (1999) Becoming a mature student: gendered narratives of the self. *Gender and Education*, 11(2): 179–193.

Coffield, F. (1998) A fresh approach to learning for the learning age: the contribution of research. *Higher Education Digest*, 31: 4–6.

Coffield, F. (1999) Breaking the consensus: lifelong learning as social control. *British Educational Research Journal*, 25(4): 479–499.

Davis, B., Sumara, D. and Luce-Kapler, R. (2000) *Engaging Minds Learning and Teaching in a Complex World Opening Words*. Mahwah, NJ: Lawrence Erlbaum Associates.

Dennis, C.A. (2016) Further education colleges and leadership: checking the ethical pulse. *London Review of Education*, 14(4): 116–130.

DfEE (1998) *The Learning Age: A Renaissance for a New Britain*. London: The Stationery Office.

Egglestone, C., Stevens, C., Jones, E. and Aldridge, F. (2018) *Adult Participation in Learning Survey 2017*. London: DfE.

Evans, K. and Waite, E. (2010) Adults learning in and through the workplace. In K. Ecclestone, G. Biesta and M. Hughes (eds), *Transitions and Learning through the Lifecourse*. London: Routledge.

Evans, K., Waite, E. and Kersh, N. (2011) Towards a social ecology of adult learning in and through the workplace. In M. Malloch, L. Cairns and B.N. O'Connor (eds), *The Sage Handbook of Workplace Learning*. London: Sage.

Fenwick, T. and Tennant, M. (2004) Understanding adult learners. In G. Foley (ed.), *Dimensions of Adult Learning*. Berkshire: McGraw-Hill.

Field, J. (2000) *Lifelong Learning and the New Educational Order*. London: Trentham Books.

Finegold, D. (1993) Breaking out of the low-skill equilibrium. *Education Economics*, 1(1): 77–83.

Fitzgerald, R., Taylor, R. and Lavalle, I. (2002) *National Adult Learning Survey (NALS) 2002*. London: National Centre for Social Research.

Garrick, J. (1999) The dominant discourses of learning at work. In D. Boud and J. Garrick (eds), *Understanding Learning at Work*. London: Routledge.

Giddens, A. (1991) *Modernity and Self-Identity: Self and Society in the Late Modern Age*. Cambridge: Polity Press.

Goodlad, C. (2007) The rise and rise of learning careers: a Foucauldian genealogy. *Research in Post-Compulsory Education*, 12(1): 107–120.

Gorard, S., Rees, G., Fevre, R. and Furlong, J. (1998) Learning trajectories: travelling towards a learning society? *International Journal of Lifelong Education*, 17(6): 400–410.

Gorard, S., Rees, G. and Fevre, R. (1999) *Learning Trajectories: Analysing the Determinants of Workplace Learning*. Paper presented at the ESRC Seminar Series Working to Learn, University of Surrey.

Hodgson, A. (2000) The challenge of widening participation in lifelong learning. In A. Hodgson (ed.), *Policies, Politics and the Future of Lifelong Learning*. London: Kogan Page.

Hodgson, A. (2015) *The Coming of Age for FE? Reflections on the Past and Future Role of Further Education Colleges in England*. London: Institute of Education.

Hodgson, A. and Spours, K. (2013) Tackling the crisis facing young people: building 'high opportunity progression eco-systems'. *Oxford Review of Education*, 39(2): 211–228.

Hodgson, A. and Spours, K. (2015) An ecological analysis of the dynamics of localities: a 14+ low opportunity progression equilibrium in action. *Journal of Education and Work*, 28(1): 24–43.

Keep, E. (2014) *What Does Skills Policy Look Like Now the Money Has Run Out?* London: Association of Colleges.

Keep, E. (2016) *Improving Skills Utilisation in the UK: Some Reflections on What, Who and How?* SKOPE Research Paper No. 124. Oxford: SKOPE.

Kolb, D. (1984) *Experiential Learning: Experience as the Source of Learning and Development*. Englewood Cliffs, NJ: Prentice Hall.

Lave, J. and Wenger, E. (1991) *Situated Learning: Legitimate Peripheral Participation*. Cambridge: Cambridge University Press.

Learning & Work (n.d.) *Participation Survey: NIACE*. Available at: www.niace.org.uk/our-work/promoting-learning-and-skills/participation-survey

Livingstone, D. (1999) *Exploring the Icebergs of Adult Learning: Findings of the First Canadian Survey of Informal Learning Practices*. Research Report. Ontario: University of Toronto.

Macqueen, S. (2017) *Narratives from Non-Traditional Students in Higher Education*. Unpublished PhD thesis, University of Queensland.

McPherson, R. and Wang, J. (2014) Low-income low-qualified employees' access to workplace learning. *Journal of Workplace Learning*, 26: 462–473.

Mezirow, J. (1997) Transformative learning: theory to practice. *New Directions for Adult and Continuing Education*, 74: 5–12.

OECD (2003) *OECD Employment Outlook towards More and Better Jobs*. Paris: OECD.

Osborne, M., Marks, A. and Turner, E. (2004) Becoming a mature student: how adult appplicants weigh the advantages and disadvantages of higher education. *Higher Education*, 48: 291–315.

Reay, D. (2003) A risky business? Mature working-class women students and access to higher education. *Gender and Education*, 15(3): 301–317.

Silvennoinen, H. and Nori, H. (2017) In the margins of training and learning. *Journal of Workplace Learning*, 29(3): 185–199.

Sullivan, A. (2002) Bourdieu and education: how useful is Bourdieu's theory for researchers? *The Netherlands' Journal of Social Sciences*, 38(2): 144–166.

Tough, A. (2002) *The Iceberg of Informal Adult Learning* (New Approaches to Lifelong Learning No. 49). Ontario: University of Toronto.

Wain, K. (2001) Lifelong learning: small adjustment or paradigm shift? In D. Aspin, J. Chapman, M. Hatton and Y. Sawano (eds), *International Handbook of Lifelong Learning*. Dordrecht: Springer.

West, L. (1995) Beyond fragments: adults, motivation and higher education. *Studies in the Education of Adults*, 27(2), 133–156.

17

OFFENDER LEARNING AND PRISON EDUCATION

Sharron Wilkinson

Key words – prison education; nested organisations; policy impact; complex adaptive systems; stakeholders

Introduction

The prison system in the UK has been developed as one solution to the issue of how society should deal with offenders, and part of this approach is to provide an education service that contributes towards the rehabilitation of offenders by helping them to gain qualifications that can lead to employment.

Adult offender learning in the English prison system is part of the further education (FE) sector and is delivered via the Offenders' Learning and Skills Service (OLASS). Teaching generally takes place in buildings with locked doors and barred windows that are surrounded by fences topped with razor wire and walls 20 feet high and 6 feet deep. What it is like to work in offender learning and the experiences of the prison education workforce are not widely known, as prison education is hidden from public view. This chapter aims to shed some light onto this part of the FE sector and the experiences of those who work in it. The chapter will begin by providing a brief outline of how the role and purpose of prison education has been determined by the role and purpose of the prisons, and then examine the present state of prison education in England. Using concepts drawn from complexity, organisational and management theories, the chapter will consider the role and purpose of prison education and its place within the English prison system. The chapter will conclude by comparing prison education with mainstream FE and asking the question: Is teaching in prison any different to teaching in mainstream further education?

A brief history of prison education

Key questions

How do social and political changes influence approaches to education?

Prison education has developed alongside the prison system over a period of almost 200 years, with the need for some form of education in prisons first being proposed by John Howard in 1777. The notion that religion and educational instruction could be used to reform prisoners was reaffirmed in the Gaols Act 1823, which heralded a reformatory phase in criminal justice and a change in attitude, from retribution through harsh punishments, to reform through work and education that would give prisoners the practical skills they would need to gain employment on their release. However, the rising crime rates in the mid-nineteenth century meant that this reformatory regime was soon replaced with a more retributive penal approach that focused on occupying prisoners in dull, monotonous labour such as oakum picking. Prison education in the form of religious instruction was provided by prison chaplains. The Gladstone Report in 1895 proposed that the purpose of imprisonment should be a combination of deterrence and reformation, and that the role of education was to provide prisoners with the basic skills in English and maths, so that on their release they would be able to undertake useful labour.

This regime continued into the twentieth century until the appointment in 1921 of a new Prison Commissioner, Sir Alexander Patterson, who proposed that education in prisons should be used to encourage creative expression through music, art, discussions and play readings, as well as lessons in basic skills. These new subjects were taught in adult education evening classes by volunteers such as university professors and head teachers. In 1947, the responsibility for prison education passed to the newly established local education authorities. This change did not have an impact on the curriculum; however, there was an impact on the status of prison educators as they were no longer to be volunteers, but paid, qualified teachers employed by the local authority. The aim was that the standards of prison education provision would be brought into line with those of national mainstream education. The Further and Higher Education Act 1992 differentiated between further education (FE) in colleges for 16–19-year-olds and recreational education for adults in adult education services. The outcome was that any policies related to professional standards and teacher training applied only to those prison educators who were employed by FE colleges, but not those employed in AE who were working in a system that was fragmented, localised and generally isolated from mainstream education until well into the twenty-first century.

Prison education in the twenty-first century

Key questions

What role, if any, does education have in the prison system?

In 2001, the government established the Offenders' Learning and Skills Unit (OLSU) and transferred the responsibility for prison education to the Department for Education and Skills (DfES), which worked in partnership with the Home Office to provide prison education services. The National Offender Management Service (NOMS), established in 2004, was responsible for the running of prison and probation services, rehabilitation services, and contract managing private sector prisons and services, including education. In order to provide a cost-effective and efficient system, competitive tendering for prison education through the Offenders' Learning and Skills Service (OLASS) was implemented in 2006. The prison education contracts were awarded to further education (FE) providers, which finally brought all prison education departments into the FE sector. One consequence of the new centralised system was that for the first time, the regulations and policy reforms that had previously only applied to those prison educators employed by the FE sector now applied to all prison educators.

In 2015, the new Conservative government's Secretary of State for Justice, Michael Gove, proposed an urgent review of the provision of prison education that would identify ways in which prisons could offer the right courses and qualifications to enable prisoners to secure jobs on release. The recommendations of the review *Unlocking Potential*, published in May 2016, were that prison education should include more personal and social development (PSD) courses and more arts, music and sports activities alongside the basics of maths and English (Ministry of Justice, 2016a). However, following the result of the EU referendum in June 2016, Liz Truss was appointed as the new Secretary of State for Justice and immediately instigated a review of the prison service. The report *Prison Safety and Reform*, published in November 2016, recommended that 'maths and English … need to be at the core of prison education' (Ministry of Justice, 2016b, p30), with the aim of preparing prisoners for employment on their release.

This focus on maths and English is also linked to the belief that a member of the prison population is more likely to be functionally illiterate than a member of the population at large, and this is generally supported by the available data. For example, Creese (2015) compared data on prisoners' literacy levels with the 2011 Skills for Life survey, and found that 'in the general population 85% have literacy skills at L1 or L2 whereas in prison this is only 50%' (p5). However, this is a skewed comparison as the gender balance in the general population is approximately 50 per cent male and 50 per cent female, whereas in the prison population the gender balance is approximately 95 per cent male and 5 per cent female.

The way that prison education was funded also changed, with the control of the education budget being given to prison governors who would be able to 'buy in' the education services that would meet the needs of the prison population while also fulfilling the requirements of local employers. In 2016, the control of OLASS was taken away from the Skills Funding Agency and given to the Ministry of Justice, whose *Education and Employment Strategy* for prisons in England and Wales emphasised that the role of prison education was to equip prisoners with the skills they required to enable them to gain employment on release (Ministry of Justice, 2018a). It can be seen, then, that the prison education curriculum was, and still is, determined by an employer-driven approach, and the focus on skills for employment has remained central to both prison education and penal policy.

Key theory

Complex adaptive systems

It is thought that the study of complex adaptive systems (CASs) was founded in the late 1980s by a group of American economists and physicists who were interested in studying complex systems and the individuals who were part of those systems (Anderson et al., 1988). More recently, CAS theory has been applied to systems outside the natural sciences. One example is the work of Plsek and Greenhalgh (2001), who defined a CAS as 'a collection of individuals with freedom to act in ways that

(Continued)

(Continued)

are not always totally predictable, and whose actions are interconnected so that one agent's actions changes the context for other agents' (p625). From this definition, they proposed a set of basic principles that could be used to understand the ways in which CASs work and their impact on individuals within the system. Two of these principles are:

1.   Individuals' actions are based on internalised rules that may not be shared, explicit or fixed, and they respond to the environment in different ways based on their own 'mental models' of the system, which depend upon their position within the system.

2.   Systems are embedded within other systems and co-evolve.

(Plsek and Greenhalgh, 2001, p626)

How does this link to practice?

1.   Prison officers, prison teachers and offenders may all have different mental models, and consequently different views of the role of the prison system and prison education.

2.   The prison system in England possesses some of the properties of a complex adaptive system in that it has evolved through changes in the social, political and economic environment that have influenced changing views on punishment and the purpose and role of prison in society. Consequently, the role and purpose of prison education has been dictated by the perceived role and purpose of prisons; this can be seen in the way that prison education has changed and adapted to the changes in the prison system, outlined in the history section above. These changes have dictated the practice of prison teaching and learning as they have determined what was taught, how it was taught, where it was taught, when it was taught and by whom.

What impact does it have on teaching?

This has implications for teaching practice and the offenders' learning experience as each group may possess different ideologies regarding the role and purpose of prison education. The prison officers' position in the system is one of authority, and their role is to maintain order; this is also part of the teachers' position, but their authority is secondary to that of the prison staff. Offenders also have their own views on education, which are shown in their attitudes and behaviour in the classroom. Tension between the different mental models can lead to conflict in relationships, disruptive behaviour, lack of support for teachers and education services, and an 'us and them' mentality. This can result in teachers spending more time dealing with behavioural and attitudinal issues than they do teaching.

The prison system in the twenty-first century

Key questions

How might prison teachers feel like 'outsiders' inside a closed system?

There are a total of 131 adult prisons in the UK: 106 in England, 6 in Wales, 4 in Northern Ireland and 15 in Scotland. This figure does not include the Youth Custody Service (15 establishments) or immigration and foreign national prisons (3 establishments). Of the 106 prisons in England, 94 are public sector and 12 are contracted, there are 10 women's prisons, and 13 are classified as long-term/high-security. There is also the Youth Custody Service, which has seven establishments in the Youth Custody Estate, five in the public sector and two contracted, as well as eight Secure Children's Homes. The education services for those held by the Youth Custody Service (10–17-year-olds) is contracted out to different providers but should match that which is provided for the same age group in mainstream education. In 2016, there were approximately 900 10–17-year-olds in custody receiving on average 17 hours a week of education (Ministry of Justice, 2016c). The public sector estate is divided into geographical groups, each managed by a Prison Group Director (see Table 17.1).

Table 17.1 Public sector prison estate

Public Sector Prisons North		Public Sector Prisons South	
Cumbria & Lancashire	5	Avon & South Dorset	4
East Midlands	5	Devon & North Dorset	4
Yorkshire	7	Bedfordshire, Cambridgeshire & Norfolk	5
Greater Manchester, Merseyside & Cheshire	5	Hertfordshire, Essex & Suffolk Group	5
West Midlands	7	South Central	4
Tees & Wear	4	Kent, Surrey & Sussex	6
North Midlands	4	London	6

Source: Ministry of Justice (2018b)

Prison education is part of the further education (FE) sector and is delivered via the Offenders' Learning and Skills Service (OLASS), which is managed by the Ministry of Justice. In 2018, the OLASS contracts for prison education were being delivered by four contractors, Weston College, Milton Keynes College, NOVUS (formerly The Manchester College) and People Plus (formerly A4E). The largest contract was held by NOVUS, who provide education services in over 60 establishments, ranging from HMP Northumberland in the Tees & Wear group to HMP Ford in the Kent, Surrey & Sussex group.

Different views of prison education

Key questions

What is the purpose and role of prison education?

A number of different writers (e.g. Costelloe and Warner, 2003; Simonot et al., 2008) have focused on identifying what they believe are the key issues in prison education. This approach has also been taken by pressure groups such as the Howard League for Penal Reform and the Prisoners' Education Trust, who survey prisoners' views and experiences of prison education. Other than through their representatives, the views of prison teachers are rarely heard. Two research studies that have tried to address this are Nahmad-Williams' *The Cinderella Service* (2011) and Wilkinson's *The Wicked Problem of Prison Education* (2017), which examined prison teachers' perceptions and experiences of prison education and asked what they believed was the purpose of prison education. Some of the views expressed by the teachers were:

- 'It's about growth and development.'

- 'To give them confidence and a better life on release.'

- 'Educating that person so that they can make different choices.'

- 'It should be used to support the offender irrespective of what background they come from.'

- 'It's about equality, not punishment.'

- 'It should not be about profits and targets.'

The comments above make no mention of literacy and numeracy skills or of the future employment prospects for prisoners, all of which are central to the government discourse on prison education that sees improving learning and skills as the solution to the problem of reoffending and ignores the fact that crime is a symptom of other more complex issues. These teachers believe that education should provide much more than competency in maths and English. For them, education should be an agent for change that enables learners to have a greater understanding of their own motivations and behaviours to support them in choosing not to reoffend. It is also about social justice and equality that values the prisoners as individuals who have a right to an education service that is not based on the one-size-fits-all profit-based approach that has been promoted by the OLASS contracts system.

Key theory

Stakeholder theory

Stakeholder theory has its roots in business, economics and management theories, but has been applied to other areas such as health (Green et al., 2018) and education (Janmaat et al., 2016). Friedman and Miles (2006, pp5-8) identified 55 definitions of the term 'stakeholder', but proposed that Freeman's (1984) definition, 'any group or individual who can affect or is affected by the achievement of the organization's objectives' (p46), is the one that is the most widely accepted. When considering stakeholders and prison education, this definition can be extended to include those who perceive that they can affect or are being affected by the achievement of the organisation's objectives, even if this is indirectly (i.e. it affects their moral values and beliefs). When considering organisations such as schools, hospitals and prisons, there is the belief that they ought to behave in an ethical way (i.e. for the good of society or for the good of certain stakeholders such as service users).

How does this link to practice?

What is deemed as ethical is not always agreed on or achieved as it is judged subjectively on what 'ought to' happen and how people should be treated. This subjective judgement becomes more complex when the role and purpose of the organisation is unclear or disputed and when stake-holders cannot or do not agree on the role and purpose of the organisation. There is also a moral dimension to stakeholder theory in that there is the assumption that all stakeholders' interests are valued when deciding how the organisation should be managed. In prison education, different stake-holders have different mental models of what prison education is or should be. Each stakeholder or stakeholder group will possess different views, priorities, values and frames of reference that deter-mine their views on the purpose and role of prison education. This in turn affects what is taught, when, how, why and to whom.

What impact does it have on teaching?

Prison education focuses on a narrow range of subjects and is driven by government policy that con-centrates on the basic skills and training that they believe will lead to employment for ex-offenders. Teaching is confined by the prison regime, which dictates the working day, and security protocols, which override anything else. As stakeholders, prison teachers have no control over these two factors and have to adapt their teaching to fit in with the restrictions that are placed upon them. For example, being able to access the internet in the classroom or taking students' work to mark at home, things that teachers in mainstream education may take for granted, are not available to prison teachers. Prisoners are also stakeholders and their views are rarely, if ever, taken into consid-eration. All prisoners are expected to obtain qualifications in literacy and numeracy, whether they wish to or not, and being coerced into attending an education class can cause them to feel resent-ment and anger, which is often directed at the teachers. As another group of stakeholders, the view of some prison staff is that education does not, or should not, have a role in the prison system. This may result in their attempts to undermine the teachers' authority or through their reluctance to pro-vide support for the teachers when they are dealing with aggressive or abusive prisoners.

Key questions

In an organisation, which stakeholder's views should be the most dominant?

How does policy impact on prison teachers and teaching?

The status of prison teachers means that they are governed by FE, prison education and penal poli-cies simultaneously. These policies determine the purpose of prison education, its content, mode of delivery, and the type and calibre of the people employed to deliver it. Being subject to these differ-ent sets of policies puts prison teachers in a position that is underpinned by the fact that although they work within a prison setting, they are not employed by the prison service. They are expected to deliver all of the policy requirements of their employers while being restricted by the policies and practices of the prison system. They are part of, but set apart from, the system, often geographically distant from the education provider and ideologically distant from the prison system. They have to work cooperatively with those who, to a large extent, determine their working conditions and environment, and the fact that prison education is delivered in the prison estate, but is not part of the prison service, presents a complex set of issues in an environment where security overrides any other consideration (Wilkinson, 2017).

When a new penal policy is implemented, it may have unforeseen consequences that impact beyond the immediate environment. For example, changes in sentencing policy between 2003 and 2015 led to a substantial increase in the prison population, which in turn placed a strain on the infrastructure and services, including education. Further education policy has focused on the needs of learners and employers, sometimes without considering the impact it may have on the teaching staff. For example, the government's Further Education Workforce Strategy (DBIS, 2014) detailed the reforms that were needed in the FE sector in order to raise the quality, effectiveness and efficiency of teaching staff. The plans that were proposed to achieve these outcomes assumed that they could be achieved by all teachers in FE, but no consideration had been given to the difficulties prison teachers might have in meeting them while working in a secure environment. Prison education policy recommendations can sometimes contradict each other. For example, the recommendations of the review *Unlocking Potential* (Ministry of Justice, 2016a) were that prison education should include more personal and social development (PSD) courses and more arts, music and sports activities alongside the basics of maths and English. However, following the result of the EU referendum in June 2016, Liz Truss, the new Secretary of State for Justice, instigated a review of the prison service. The report *Prison Safety and Reform*, published in November 2016, recommended that education in prisons should be focused on developing prisoners' maths and English skills with the aim of helping them find a job on release. The effectiveness of the education service was to be determined by measuring prisoners' achievement levels when first in custody and when released, and also the number of qualifications and accredited courses completed by prisoners.

Is teaching in prison different to teaching in mainstream FE?

The Foster Report proposed that the core purpose of FE is to deliver 'the skills the economy, businesses and individuals need' (Foster, 2005, p2) and the Ministry of Justice (2018a) proposed that prison education is 'to give individuals the skills they need to unlock their potential, gain employment and become assets to their communities' (p1). These are two propositions that differ very little in their focus. Therefore, to determine whether prison education in England is in any way different to mainstream further education, it may be useful to compare some key areas; these are set out in Tables 17.2 and 17.3. Table 17.2 uses data from the Ministry of Justice and the Association of Colleges. The statistics in Table 17.3 are based on limited data collected in 2015 as part of a government review of offender learning.

Table 17.2   Similarities and differences between prison education and FE in England in 2018

	Prison education	Mainstream further education
Number of establishments	106 prisons in England	207 colleges in England
Number of students	Potentially 80,000+ (total prison population) Number studying higher education courses is unknown	1.4 million adults study or train in colleges 151,000 study higher education courses

Funding	Ministry of Justice 100%	DfE 75%, HEFCE 2%, tuition fees 13%, other 10%
Management	Prison governor sets the strategy, commissions the providers and manages the delivery of education provision. Generally has no experience of working in educational settings.	College principal/CEO, who generally has experience of working in educational settings and/or business qualifications
Diversity	Estimated at 33% of students who have a self-reported learning difficulty and/or disability	17% of students have a learning difficulty and/or disability
Environment	Focus on security and containment	Focus on education and training
Curriculum	Maths, English, ICT and ESOL to level 2. Catering and hospitality, construction, planning and the built environment, and cleaning and facilities to level 2	Vocational qualifications and academic qualifications. A small number of colleges also award taught degrees up to level 7.

Sources: Association of Colleges (2018) and Ministry of Justice (2018a)

Table 17.3 Comparison of ETF data on staff profiles in public sector prison education and further education in England

	Public sector prison education	**Mainstream further education**
Number of staff employed	4,000 (estimated)	52,575
Age range	Under 40 26.4%	Under 40 33.6%
	Over 40 73.4%	Over 40 64.3%
Number of staff with a salary above £42,000	0.1%	2.3%
Staff turnover	11%	15%
Full-time contracts	55.7%	45.4%
Main subject taught	English, languages and communication 14.6%	English, languages and communication 10.4%
	ICT 7.9%	ICT 4.1%
	Mathematics 7.6%	Mathematics 1.8%
	Engineering 1.4%	Engineering 7.6%
	Humanities 1.1%	Humanities 4.8%

Source: Education and Training Foundation (2015)

Key questions

What are the challenges of teaching in prison?

Tables 17.2 and 17.3 provide only a partial picture of the contrast between prison education and mainstream FE colleges. Examining what key stakeholders think are the issues that are unique to prison education can provide us with a much broader view and more points of comparison.

Wilkinson's (2017) research on prison education investigated the views of different stakeholder groups; some of the key issues identified by prison teachers were:

- *Churn.* The movement of prisoners in, out and between prisons, which means that prisoners are removed from classes without informing the teacher or the prisoner.

- *The security-focused prison regime.* The prison regime and security protocols severely curtail what resources are permitted in a prison setting; they also restrict conversations with and about prisoners.

- *Negative attitudes towards education from prisoners.* This can be due to previous negative experiences of education, and some prisoners do not see the value of education, as when they are released they believe they can make more money committing crime than they can in regular employment.

- *Negative attitudes and lack of support from prison staff.* Officers, whose role it is to enforce discipline, fail to assist the teachers when they have problems with the prisoners' behaviour.

- *Results-based funding payment by qualification is restrictive.* Providers are not able to differentiate spending levels according to need; funders dictate how much can be spent per learner, and on what.

- *Outdated and difficult-to-access IT resources.* In 2015, some prisons were still using Windows 2003 software and floppy disks in IT classes to store students' work.

- *Behaviour management linked to mental health, drug and alcohol use.* Specifically, the rise in the use of new psychoactive substances, such as Spice, which is not detectable by drug tests.

- *The limited range of courses that are on offer.* The focus on literacy, numeracy and IT (i.e. employability skills and the exclusion of arts, humanities and personal development courses).

- *The lack of opportunity for students to progress beyond level 2.* As level 2 is the benchmark for employability, the government will not fund any courses above this level.

- *Feeling isolated/excluded from mainstream FE and from the prison.* There is a lack of opportunities to network with FE colleagues, and the teachers felt that there was a 'them and us' situation within the prison, with the education department being seen as an 'inconvenience' to the prison regime.

- *Prison education contract providers focusing on making a profit rather than educating the prisoners.* For example, in 2013/14, the contract value awarded to NOVUS to provide prison education services was worth £74,575,081 (Skills Funding Agency, 2015).

The research also highlighted issues identified by other stakeholders: government, policymakers, academics, pressure groups, prison teachers' representatives and the prisoners themselves. Some of the issues they identified were:

- the lack of incentives for prisoners to learn;

- overcrowding;

- the low priority afforded to education by the prison staff and governors;

- inadequate teaching standards in some prison education departments, as evidenced by Ofsted inspections;

- lack of job-specific training for educators;

- lack of job-specific qualifications for educators;

- intermittent and unpredictable attendance;

- roll-on roll-off classes;

- constraints on the movement of prisoners and teachers;

- difficulty in building relationships of trust in a secure environment where no personal anecdotes or details can be revealed, as this may lead to grooming and manipulation by prisoners;

- the lack of professional status for prison educators; and

- insecurity in employment terms and lack of parity with the FE sector.

All of these issues would seem to portray a very negative view of prison education, and this is not always the case, as although it can be very frustrating at times, there can also be some very positive aspects. The aim of this chapter was to provide the reader with an insight into offender learning and what it is like to teach in a prison setting. By comparing mainstream further education with prison education, it can be seen that there are some key differences, some of which are a consequence of the secure environment within which prison education takes place. There are also other factors that affect prison teachers, including their secondary status in the prison system.

Chapter summary

- Prison education has a long history that has been determined by changes in the penal system.

- The values and beliefs of people working in a complex system are influenced by their position in that system.

- Prison teachers are 'nested' within two complex parallel systems that can give rise to conflict and negatively affect their teaching.

- Different stakeholders have different views on the role and purpose of prison education.

- The core purpose of mainstream FE and prison education may be similar but the environment and the teaching experience are very different.

- There are a number of issues identified by key stakeholders that may be said to be unique to prison education.

Further recommended reading

Friedman, A.L. and Miles, S. (2006) *Stakeholders: Theory and Practice*. Oxford: Oxford University Press.

This book explores the concept of stakeholders and critiques the various stakeholder theories. It uses practical examples to investigate a wide range of stakeholders in national and international contexts.

Rogers, L. Simonot, M. and Nartey, A. (2014) *Prison Educators: Professionalism against the Odds*. London: UCU & IOE.

This is a report of a survey of prison teachers and their views on prison education that identifies the issues that they feel affect their teaching.

References

Anderson, P.W., Arrow, K.J. and Pines, D. (eds) (1988) *The Economy as an Evolving Complex System*. Redwood City, CA: Addison-Wesley.

Association of Colleges (2018) *College Key Facts 2017–18*. Available at: www.aoc.co.uk/sites/default/files/Key%20Facts%202017-18_1.pdf

Costelloe, A. and Warner, K. (2003) *Beyond 'Offending Behaviour': The Wider Perspectives of Adult Education and the European Prison Rules*. Paper presented to the 9th EPEA International Conference on Prison Education, Langesund, Norway.

Creese, B. (2015) *An Assessment of the English and Maths Skills Levels of Prisoners in England*. London: Centre for Education in the Criminal Justice System at UCL Institute of Education.

DBIS (2014) *Further Education Workforce Strategy: The Government's Strategy to Support Workforce Excellence in Further Education*. Available at: www.gov.uk/government/uploads/system/uploads/attachment_data/file/326000/bis-14-679-further-education-workforce-strategy-the-government-strategy-support-workforce-excellence-in-further-education.pdf

Education and Training Foundation (2015) *SIR Interim Dashboard-Offender Learning-2015*. Available at: www.excellencegateway.org.uk/content/etf2349

Foster, A. (2005) *Realising the Potential: A Review of the Future Role of Further Education Colleges*. London: DfES.

Freeman, R.E. (1984) *Strategic Management: A Stakeholder Approach*. Boston, MA: Pitman.

Friedman, A.L. and Miles, S. (2006) *Stakeholders: Theory and Practice*. Oxford: Oxford University Press.

Green, R.H., Evans, V., MacLeod, S. and Barratt, J. (2018) A qualitative study of the perspectives of key stakeholders on the delivery of clinical academic training in the East Midlands. *JRSM Open*. https://doi.org/10.1177/2054270417741843

Janmaat, G., McCowan, T. and Rao, N. (2016) Different stakeholders in education. *Compare: A Journal of Comparative and International Education*, 46(2): 169–171.

Lawler, E.J. (1992) Affective attachments to nested groups: a choice-process theory. *American Sociological Review*, 57(3): 327–339.

Ministry of Justice (2016a) *Unlocking Potential: A Review of Education in Prisons*. Available at: www.gov.uk/government/uploads/system/uploads/attachment_data/file/524013/education-review-report.pdf

Ministry of Justice (2016b) *The Prisons Safety and Reform White Paper*. Available at: www.gov.uk/government/uploads/system/uploads/attachment_data/file/565014/cm-9350-prison-safety-and-reform-_web_.pdf

Ministry of Justice (2016c) *Review of the Youth Justice System in England and Wales*. Available at: https://assets.publishing.service.gov.uk/government/uploads/system/uploads/attachment_data/file/577103/youth-justice-review-final-report.pdf

Ministry of Justice (2018a) *Education and Employment Strategy*. Available at: https://assets.publishing.service.gov.uk/government/uploads/system/uploads/attachment_data/file/710406/education-and-employment-strategy-2018.pdf

Ministry of Justice (2018b) *Map of Prison Estate (England & Wales)*. Available at: www.justice.gov.uk/downloads/contacts/hmps/prison-finder/prisons-map-18-v2.5.pdf

Nahmad-Williams, L. (2011) *The Cinderella Service: Teaching in Prisons and Young Offender Institutions in England and Wales*. Unpublished PhD Thesis, Department of Criminology, University of Leicester.

Plsek, P.E. and Greenhalgh, T. (2001) The challenge of complexity in health care. *BMJ*, 323:625. Available at: www.ncbi.nlm.nih.gov/pmc/articles/PMC1121189/pdf/625.pdf

Simonot, M., Jeanes, J., MacDonald, J., Nicholl, M. and Wilkinson, I. (2008) *Initial Teacher Training Project for Teachers and Instructors in Prison and Offender Education*. London: London Centre for Excellence in Teacher Training.

Skills Funding Agency (2015) *Statistical First Release Further Education and Skills: Learner Participation, Outcomes and Level of Highest Qualification Held (SFA/SFR28)*. Available at: www.gov.uk/government/uploads/system/uploads/attachment_data/file/552598/SFA_SFR_commentary_March_2015_FINAL_March_2015.pdf

Wilkinson, S.F. (2017) *The Wicked Problem of Prison Education: What Are the Perceptions of Two Key Stakeholder Groups on the Impact of Tame and Wicked Approaches to Prison Education?* Unpublished EdD thesis, Faculty of Education, University of Hull.

18
PARTICIPATION AND INCLUSIVITY IN ADULT LEARNING: INTERNATIONAL PERSPECTIVES

Rose Cook

Key words – adult learning; adult education; international comparison; lifelong learning

Introduction

> ### Key questions
>
> What are the key international policies on adult learning?
>
> How can we assess the state of adult learning globally?

Global discussions about adult learning have intensified in recent decades due to a number of inter-related processes. First, technological innovation and the move from manual to intellectual labour means that more complex skills are required to participate in the economy. Global markets for goods and services and a rise in international migration mean that adults may need to improve their skills in order to obtain employment within complex global workforces. These skills can be gained through adult learning, which can supplement compulsory education or work experience. Adult learning is also increasingly recognised as a way for societies to build social cohesion, boost well-being and encourage active citizenship (Schuller and Desjardins, 2007; Schuller et al., 2004).

There has been a proliferation of policy in the area of adult learning at the international level. For example, adult learning is central to UNESCO's Education 2030 Framework for Action, a vision for education agreed by policymakers from 160 countries in 2015 (UNESCO, 2015). UNESCO's adult learning strategy aims to increase levels of participation in adult learning internationally (UNESCO, 2009) and to improve the accessibility of adult learning among individuals who most need it, including disadvantaged groups. Lifelong learning is also included in the United Nations' Sustainable Development Goals. Sustainable Development Goal 4 is to 'ensure inclusive and equitable quality education and lifelong learning opportunities for all' (United Nations, 2015). Similarly, the EU's Lisbon Strategy, launched in 2000, included goals to increase the supply and uptake of adult learning, and to improve its quality. This was updated with the Europe 2020 agenda on education, which also stated the aim of boosting adult learning participation as a means to promote employability (Roth and Thum, 2010).

It is important to assess how different countries are performing in light of these internationally agreed-upon goals. What is the level of participation in adult learning, and is it inclusive to a range of different people in society? The first challenge in assessing participation and inclusivity of adult learning is creating an internationally comparable definition of adult learning. It is not always straightforward to identify what counts as adult learning because of varying education system structures, as well as different conceptions of adulthood, teaching and learning (Tight, 1996). For example, who counts as an adult learner? In some countries, an adult over the age of 25 participating in a course at a university would be termed an adult learner or 'non-traditional' student, as distinct from someone under 25 in their first period of study. However, in other countries, this adult would not be distinguished from any other higher education student. Adult learning is typically classified into 'formal' and 'non-formal' varieties, where formal refers to institutional courses of study leading to a recognised qualification, and non-formal refers to any activity that could be considered learning, including activities undertaken by an individual in their own home or at work. However, the boundaries between formal and non-formal adult learning are not always obvious (Desjardins, 2017), and it is difficult to measure and validate learning that does not take place in mainstream educational institutions (Colardyn and Bjornavold, 2004).

The ability to study adult education patterns internationally improved with the advent of the Programme for the International Assessment of Adult Competencies (PIAAC) in 2012. This study was primarily intended to assess adults' skills in literacy, numeracy and problem-solving, but also collected detailed data on the education and training activities adults had undertaken in the 12 months preceding the survey, with clear definitions of what constitutes formal and non-formal learning. Survey respondents also answered questions on their income, education, employment status and working life. Because the survey data are collected from individuals, contain detailed information on adult learning and are nationally representative, they can be used to assess both the level of participation and the inclusivity of participation at the national level in all the participating countries.

This chapter uses the international data from PIAAC to analyse: (a) levels of participation in adult learning (how many adults participate); and (b) its inclusivity (to what extent all individuals in society have a chance to participate in adult learning). The next section of the chapter introduces the PIAAC data in more detail, before presenting the empirical analysis of adult learning participation and inclusivity. Empirical findings are discussed alongside the theories that have been used to understand why participation rates vary across countries and across different groups in society. The chapter finishes with a discussion of the Nordic countries' distinctive approach to adult learning, followed by a conclusion, referring back to the key arguments about adult learning and providing an outlook for future international comparative research on adult learning.

Terms and definitions in international adult learning policy and research

This chapter uses the term 'adult learning' to refer to learning opportunities undertaken by students aged 16 years or over, including on-the-job training, adult higher education, labour market programmes, and learning for civic and leisure purposes. In the international context, a number of different terms are used to refer to adult learning. These are sometimes used interchangeably, but although they overlap, they also have distinct meanings:

- *Post-compulsory education and training (PCET).* The term typically used in England and Wales to refer to all educational activity that does not take place in schools and universities. This includes traditional learning opportunities (such as GCSEs and A levels) offered to adults, training leading to vocational qualifications, work-based learning opportunities, and community-based education programmes such as literacy and numeracy classes.

- *Lifelong learning.* This term gained currency in the 1960s and 1970s, and refers to the notion of education being accessible throughout life, rather than confined to childhood, adolescence or early adulthood. It is typically used to refer to this concept rather than to any specific educational provision (see Tight, 1996), but is also used as a catch-all term for all adult learning activities, including those taking place inside and outside formal educational settings.

- *Adult learning and education.* In 2015, UNESCO proposed a more inclusive term, 'adult learning and education' (ALE). ALE includes any programme or initiative that aims: (a) to equip adults with literacy and basic skills; (b) to provide continuing training and professional development; and/or (c) to promote active citizenship through what is variously known as community, popular or liberal education (UNESCO, 2016).

Participation in adult education: international comparisons

Data

To assess the level of participation in adult learning and its inclusivity internationally, this chapter uses data drawn from the PIAAC study. PIAAC is a large-scale international study coordinated by the Organisation for Economic Co-operation and Development (OECD), an intergovernmental organisation with 36 member countries, founded in 1961 to stimulate economic progress and world trade. PIAAC measures the proficiency of adults in 'three information-processing skills essential for full participation in the knowledge-based economies and societies of the 21st century' (OECD, 2013, p1): literacy, numeracy, and problem-solving in technology-rich environments. In addition, PIAAC collected data on respondents' basic demographic characteristics, educational attainment and participation, labour force status and employment, social outcomes, and the use of skills. This included comprehensive questions on whether individuals have participated in adult learning and what type of activities they have undertaken. Thus, since its release, PIAAC has become a major source of evidence on adult learning across OECD countries.

Sample

The analysis in this chapter includes data from 28 OECD countries (Austria, Belgium [Flanders], Canada, Chile, Cyprus, the Czech Republic, Denmark, Estonia, Finland, France, Germany, Greece, Ireland, Israel, Italy, Japan, the Netherlands, Norway, Poland, the Slovak Republic, Slovenia, South Korea, Spain, Sweden, Turkey, the UK [England and Northern Ireland] and the US). The sample for this chapter includes all adults aged 16–65, excluding those who could not complete the assessment due to disabilities, and adults currently in mainstream education (such as completing a university degree or still studying at school).

Variables

As part of the PIAAC background questionnaire, participants were asked about their involvement in different adult learning activities. The activities were grouped into two categories:

- *Formal adult learning.* Education undertaken to obtain a qualification. Defined as organised opportunities for learning for the needs of persons aged above compulsory schooling age who are not in the regular school or higher education system in their first of initial cycles of education.

- *Non-formal adult learning.* Covers a diverse range of activities, including on-the-job training, seminars and workshops, distance education, and other courses.

How to measure participation in adult learning?

There are different ways of measuring participation in adult learning. For example, one can assess the incidence (the proportion of all adults in a given country who participated in adult learning in a given time period), the time spent participating, or the prevalence (the participation rate multiplied by the average number of hours per participant) (Desjardins, 2017). The present analysis focuses on incidence – the proportion of adults who participated in adult learning in the 12 months prior to the PIAAC survey in 2012. It should be noted that this does not provide a perfect assessment of the extent and intensity of adult learning activity, since countries could have low numbers of people participating at a high rate, or large numbers of people participating at a low rate, neither of which is captured by incidence.

How to measure inclusivity of adult learning

There are many possible ways to assess the inclusivity of adult learning. This chapter focuses on identifying differences in participation related to educational qualifications, immigrant background, and gender, which have previously been identified as important characteristics in relation to adult learning (e.g. Boeren, 2017; Boeren and Holford, 2016; Boeren et al., 2010). A country's adult learning system is considered more inclusive if there are fewer differences between groups in participation levels. For example, where there is less of a difference in participation between those who are highly educated and those who have low levels of education, a country's adult learning system will be considered more inclusive.

Analysis results: participation in adult learning

Key questions

What proportion of adults participates in adult learning?

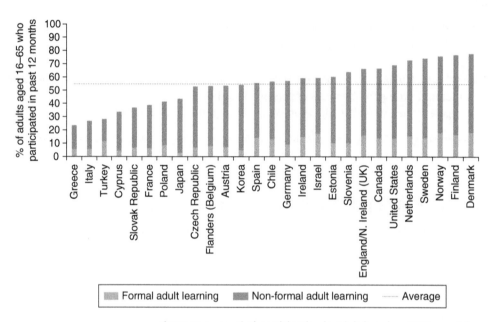

Figure 18.1 Level of participation in adult learning, OECD countries, 2012

Source: Author's analysis of data from PIAAC (OECD, 2013)

Notes: Base: adults aged 16–65 who are not studying in mainstream education. Weights applied.

There is wide variation across countries in levels of participation in adult learning and in the types of adults who participate (see Figure 18.1). The highest levels of participation, between 70 and 80 per cent, are found in the Nordic countries – Denmark, Finland, Norway and Sweden – as well as in the Netherlands. In contrast, the level of participation is between 20 and 30 per cent in countries such as Greece, Italy and Turkey. The Nordic countries therefore have participation rates up to 60 percentage points higher than the Southern European countries represented here (although Spain has a higher participation rate of 56 per cent). English-speaking countries such as the US, Canada, Ireland and the UK have rates of participation between 60 and 70 per cent, while East Asian, Eastern European (with the exception of Slovenia, whose participation rate is higher, at 64 per cent) and Central European countries tend to have participation rates of between 40 and 60 per cent.

Formal and non-formal participation

In all countries, levels of participation in non-formal learning are far higher than levels of participation in formal adult education. This reflects the broader range of activities designated 'non-formal learning' (including on-the-job training, seminars and workshops, and distance education). Participation in formal adult learning is generally lower in all countries but is comparatively high in the Nordic countries. It is comparatively very low (below 10 per cent) in Japan, South Korea, France and Cyprus. However, it should also be noted that some countries, although they have relatively low participation in adult learning overall, have relatively high participation in formal learning. For example, in Israel, 60 per cent of adults participated in adult learning (as compared to almost 80 per cent in Finland, Norway and Denmark), yet almost 20 per cent pursued formal learning, a similar level to those high-participation countries. The balance between formal and non-formal participation reflects the extent to which adult learning is integrated into the mainstream education system, including the openness of conventional learning opportunities to those who are older than the main target group (Desjardins, 2015). For example, if it is relatively easy for older adults to access higher education degrees, the level of participation in formal adult learning will be higher. In contrast, where the mainstream educational institutions are closed to adults, and adult-specific formal learning opportunities are not widespread, adult learning is more likely to take place in a non-formal capacity, if at all.

What drives participation?

Several factors have been noted in the research literature as barriers or facilitators to adult learning participation at the country level. Most important among these is arguably the level of state investment in adult learning. In the absence of state investment, provision is left to private or semi-private providers. This can be ineffective because there may be few incentives for private providers to provide quality learning opportunities, and potential participants may lack information on what is available and its potential rewards (Desjardins and Rubenson, 2013). The overall level of participation in adult learning appears to be somewhat related to a country's prosperity. For example, Desjardins (2015) observed a correlation between countries' gross domestic product (GDP, a measure of prosperity) and the level of participation in adult learning. We can see this from the fact that the relatively prosperous Nordic countries tend to have higher participation rates than the less prosperous economies of Southern Europe (see Figure 18.1). This may be explained by more prosperous countries having more funds to invest in providing and incentivising adult learning. However, the association between prosperity and adult learning participation is not perfect – some countries with similar levels of prosperity to the high-participation Nordic countries, such as Canada and the US, do not have similarly high levels of participation. It therefore seems that factors beyond economic development are relevant to explaining variations in adult learning participation across countries.

As well as the level of participation, the focus of adult learning can vary. For example, in some countries, adult learning is more allied to culture, identity and well-being, whereas in others adult learning is more strongly tied to employment. These policy foci result from a combination of history, culture and political realities. For example, the history of labour influences the development of educational institutions and skill formation systems over time (Thelen, 2004). Where skill-intensive industries have traditionally been dominant, adult learning opportunities are more closely tied to vocational skills, as is the case in Germany. The nature of the education system in a country may also influence people's motivation to undertake adult learning. For example, in countries such as Austria and Germany, young people can choose to undertake either academic or vocational second-ary education tracks. This means that people emerge from schooling with more specialised skills and knowledge, and may have less need to undertake job-related training later in adulthood (Brunello, 2001). These cross-national variations in the focus of adult learning mean that although participa-tion rates in formal and non-formal education are revealing, they tell us relatively little about the nature of the learning adults are undertaking in different countries.

Key theory

The Programme for the International Assessment of Adult Competencies

Boeren et al. (2010) suggest that participation in adult learning can be understood as a match between learners (the micro level), educational institutions (the meso level) and conditions at the broader country level (the macro level). They also draw attention to inequalities in participation and how this can affect the overall participation rate in a given country. They term this perspective a 'micro-meso-macro' perspective on adult learning. Boeren et al. (2010) draw on earlier work by Cross (1981), which specified the following barriers to adult learning participation:

- *Institutional.* Policies/practices that actively make it more difficult to participate in adult learn-ing, particularly for disadvantaged groups, e.g. a lack of provision or opportunity (at the right time or location), high user fees or entry qualifications.

- *Situational.* Associated with an individual's life stage/situation, e.g. family obligations, place of residence.

- *Dispositional.* Psychological barriers, e.g. perception of reward or usefulness, motivation, etc.

Cross's and Boeren et al.'s theories share a multidimensional understanding of what enables par-ticipation in adult learning. Other authors, such as Rubenson and Desjardins (2009), concur with this multidimensional perspective, suggesting that the decision to participate in adult learning is an interaction between the educational opportunities provided by the state (and/or private providers) and individuals. The relative weight of structural and individual factors for determin-ing adult learning participation is a matter of debate among scholars of adult education in an international context. However, these scholars all emphasise the power of national policies and culture in shaping the extent to which individuals can overcome common barriers to accessing adult learning opportunities.

According to the 'bounded agency' model, different levels interact to determine levels of participa-tion and inclusivity of adult learning systems. Therefore, participation rates at the country level are likely to reflect a complex combination of factors that vary across societies, including individ-ual motivations, situational barriers, institutional constraints and national policy. Therefore, when analysing adult learning internationally, it is important to assess both overall rates of participation *and* which groups of adults are more likely to participate. The interplay between micro, meso and macro factors in determining adult learning participation is summarised in Figure 18.2.

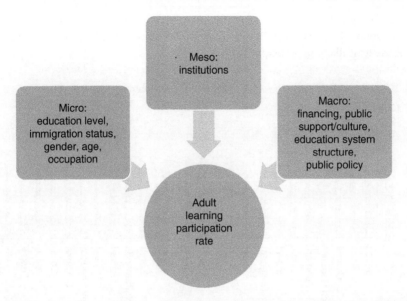

Figure 18.2   Micro-meso-macro determinants of adult learning participation

Analysis results: inclusivity of adult learning

Key questions

How inclusive is adult learning in terms of gender, education level and immigrant status?

Education level

In all countries, those who already have the highest levels of educational attainment are most likely to participate in adult learning (see Figure 18.3). In most countries, the majority of higher-educated adults have participated in non-formal adult learning. In Finland, this is as high as 81 per cent. In contrast, participation rates among low-educated adults tend to be lower. This is particularly the case in countries such as France, Greece, the Slovak Republic and Turkey, where the proportion of low-educated adults who have participated in non-formal learning activities is 10 per cent or below.

Participation in formal adult learning is lower across all education levels. However, we still see an 'educational gradient' in most countries, whereby the highest educated are the most likely to participate. In some countries, the educational gradient in participation is less pronounced – in Canada, Denmark, Estonia, the Netherlands and Norway, for example. In some countries, participation rates among low-educated adults are relatively high, at around 20 per cent; this is the case in Denmark and Norway, but also in Germany and Israel. In other countries, such as Belgium, Chile, Cyprus, Greece, the Slovak Republic and Slovenia, participation rates of low-educated adults are extremely low. In Japan and South Korea, participation rates in formal adult learning are very low across all education levels. This 'educational gradient' in adult learning access is often attributed to familiarity with the education system and access to jobs that have greater requirements for training (Boeren and Holford, 2016; Boudard, 2001). Overall, this suggests that those most in need of learning opportunities are often the least likely to participate.

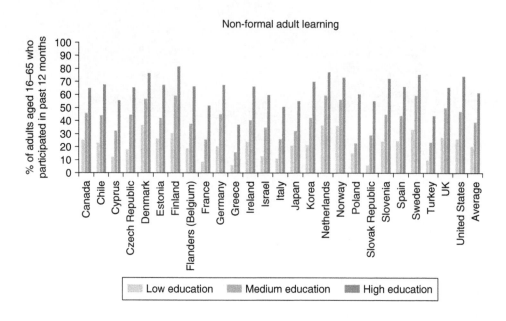

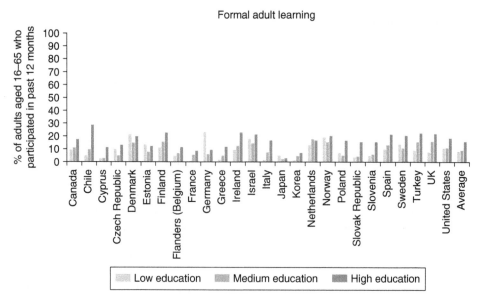

Figure 18.3   Education and participation in adult learning, OECD countries, 2012

Source: Author's analysis of data from PIAAC (OECD, 2013)

Note: Base: adults aged 16–65 who are not studying in mainstream education. Weights applied. Austria is excluded due to data on education level being unavailable. 'Low education' = less than upper secondary (ISCED 1, 2 and 3C short). 'Medium education' = upper secondary (ISCED 3A, 3B, 3C long and 4). 'High education' = tertiary education (ISCED 5A, 5B and 6). ISCED is the International Standard Classification for Educational Degrees (see UNESCO Institute for Statistics, 2012).

Immigration background

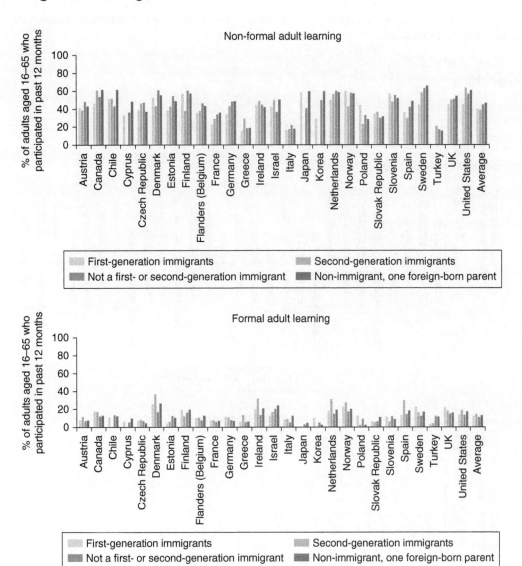

Figure 18.4   Immigration background and participation in adult learning, OECD countries, 2012

Source: Author's analysis of data from PIAAC (OECD, 2013)

Note: Base: adults aged 16–65 who are not studying in mainstream education. Weights applied.
Some immigrant groups are too small to analyse (e.g. second-generation immigrants in Cyprus).

The highest rates of participation in non-formal adult learning tend to be among non-immigrants or non-immigrants with one foreign-born parent (see Figure 18.4). However, in some countries, participation rates among first-generation immigrants are relatively high (e.g. Denmark, Finland, Japan, Norway and Slovenia). Rates of formal adult learning participation are generally relatively low among all groups; however, some countries appear to do better at facilitating participation among first- and second-generation immigrants. For example, in Denmark, 26 per cent and 37 per cent of first- and second-generation immigrants, respectively, participate in formal adult learning. Similar patterns are seen in Finland, Norway and Sweden. Participation is also relatively high for second-generation immigrants in Ireland and the Netherlands.

Gender

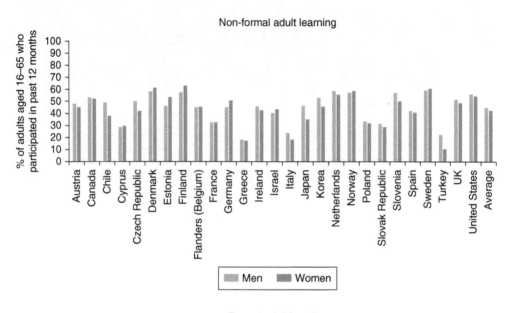

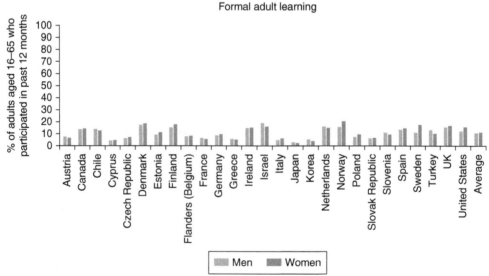

Figure 18.5   Gender and participation in adult learning, OECD countries, 2012

Source: Author's analysis of data from PIAAC (OECD, 2012)

Notes: Base: adults aged 16–65 who are not studying in mainstream education. Weights applied.

Gender differences in adult learning participation are not large (see Figure 18.5). However, in some countries, women are more likely than men to participate in formal adult learning (Italy, Norway, Poland, Sweden and the US). In Turkey, Japan and South Korea, women are less likely than men to participate in all forms of adult learning, and in some countries (Chile, the Czech Republic, Italy, Japan and Slovenia) women are less likely to participate in non-formal learning. These variations reflect prior findings, suggesting that there are differences in the types of learning men and women choose (Boeren and Holford, 2016).

The Nordic model of adult learning

Although education, immigration status and gender (as well as factors that have not been considered in this chapter, such as age and family background) are linked to participation in all countries, there is variation cross-nationally in the extent to which these factors constitute barriers to adult learning (see also Boeren and Holford, 2016; Desjardins, 2017). This suggests that educational institutions and countries' policies and culture (the macro level) play a role in encouraging or limiting participation both in general and among more disadvantaged groups.

Key questions

Why do Nordic countries have comparatively high levels of adult learning participation, and why are their systems more inclusive?

Nordic countries (Denmark, Finland, Norway and Sweden) generally have the highest levels of overall participation and the lowest levels of inequality in adult learning participation, in terms of enabling low-educated adults and those with immigrant backgrounds to overcome barriers to participation (see Figures 18.1 and 18.3–18.5). This section considers some of the reasons why that is the case. According to Rubenson (2006), the Nordic countries' approach to social welfare, the industrial relations typical in these countries, and the civil society and culture associated with adult learning can jointly account for their success in promoting adult learning.

Social welfare

Nordic countries share a common approach wherein the state, in comparison to corporations or the family, is the key provider of social welfare (Esping-Andersen, 1999). A key aspect of this model is the aim of limiting unemployment through active labour market policies. In contrast to passive labour market policies, which rely primarily on providing replacement income to those who are unemployed or unable to work, active labour market policies focus more strongly on labour market reintegration, including via the provision of training. The Nordic active labour market approach intends to improve employability, reduce the demand on welfare services, and increase the skills supply. It also aims to correct mismatches between the compulsory education, i.e. the fact that the training people receive through compulsory education does not necessarily prepare them for the realities of employment across their adult lives (Rubenson, 2006). This is one reason for relatively high adult learning participation among those who are low-educated and also among immigrants. In most Nordic countries, provision of formal adult learning (both job training and language classes) is key to facilitating immigrants' labour market participation and integration into society (see Clausen et al., 2009).

Industrial relations

Another reason for the high levels of participation in adult learning in Nordic is that these countries tend to have comparatively large numbers of workers enrolled in trade unions (Ebbinghaus et al., 2011). These unions have influence on employers and on national employment policy, and can advocate for their members to access adult learning opportunities. The rate of participation in adult learning is particularly high among blue-collar workers (who are often unionised) in Nordic countries, boosting overall participation rates and making adult learning more inclusive overall (Rubenson, 2006).

Civil society and culture

Adult learning provision in Nordic countries includes programmes provided by civil society organisations, known as 'popular' adult education. This variety of adult learning stems from late nineteenth- and early twentieth-century popular movements that spread their ideas through adult learning. This resulted in state-subsidised civil society institutions unique to Nordic countries such as 'folk high schools' and 'adult education associations'. The diversity of learning opportunities in Nordic countries contributes to a high level of visibility of adult learning and means that more people can participate in ways that suit them (Rubenson, 2006).

Public policy

Sociologists have long observed that educational institutions tend to reproduce inequalities, in that those who benefit the most from educational opportunities are those who are already more likely to succeed in life; moreover, institutions reward the qualities of privileged groups (e.g. Bourdieu and Passeron, 1977). In the area of adult education, this is illustrated by the fact that adults who are already more educated are more likely to access adult education than those who are lower-educated, who could stand to benefit more (see Figure 18.3). Aside from the history, culture and broader societal conditions that promote both the supply and demand of adult learning, state-level commitments to mitigating inequalities in society have boosted inclusivity of adult learning in Nordic societies (Korpi and Palme, 1998; Rubenson, 2006). Inclusivity-boosting policies typically involve targeting provision effectively to disadvantaged groups, thereby mitigating the inequality-reinforcing effect of adult learning. On the supply side, this includes providing subsidies to adult education providers. On the demand side, strategies to boost the demand for adult education include providing targeted information and financial incentives (such as vouchers and subsidies).

Demand for adult learning can also arise from the effects of other social policies. Given that time constraints are frequently cited as a barrier to participating in adult learning (e.g. Boeren et al., 2012), policies aimed at freeing up people's time can be effective levers to boost participation rates. For example, providing free childcare and leave from employment creates more time for people to participate in adult learning (Desjardins, 2017). Since Nordic countries tend to have well-developed childcare and parental leave policies, this stimulates demand for adult learning among those with caring responsibilities. Another policy specifically aimed at freeing up people's time to take part in adult learning activities is educational leave. For example, since 1999, all adults in Norway who have been working at the same employer for two years or more are entitled to take up to three years off to take up a course of study on a full-time or part-time basis (Norwegian Labour Inspection Authority, 2017).

Chapter summary

Despite a growing global focus on boosting participation and promoting inclusiveness in adult learning, there is wide variation across countries in the extent to which these goals have been achieved. This chapter has illustrated this using data from 28 OECD countries. The highest levels of participation, between 70 and 80 per cent, are found in Denmark, Finland, Norway and Sweden, as well as in the Netherlands. In contrast, the level of participation is between 20 and 30 per cent in countries such as Greece, Italy and Turkey. In all countries analysed, levels of participation in non-formal education are far higher than in formal adult education, suggesting that most adult learning is undertaken by individuals under their own initiative or for job-related reasons, as opposed to in formal educational institutions. This suggests that all countries could improve in their offer of formal learning opportunities for adults.

In all countries, highly educated adults are more likely to participate in adult learning. However, the participation of low-educated adults in formal learning opportunities is relatively high in the Nordic countries, as well as in Germany. There is no clear pattern across countries in terms of immigrant status and participation in non-formal learning, but the numbers of first- and second-generation immigrants participating in formal adult learning opportunities is relatively high in the Nordic countries. Gender differences in adult learning participation are not large. In some countries, women are more likely than men to participate in formal adult learning (Italy, Norway, Poland, Sweden and the US). In Turkey, Japan, and South Korea, by contrast, women are less likely than men to participate in all forms of adult learning, and in some countries (Chile, the Czech Republic, Italy, Japan and Slovenia) women are also less likely to participate in non-formal learning.

Participation and inclusivity are intrinsically linked. Where more diverse groups of adults can participate in adult learning, the overall participation rate is higher. The variation in overall participation rates and inequalities in adult learning participation across OECD countries suggests that although barriers to participation are relatively universal, these can be mitigated to some extent by conditions within individual countries that promote or dissuade people from participating in adult learning opportunities, thereby boosting the overall participation rate. This provides validation of the micro-meso-macro theoretical framework of adult learning participation, which suggests a dynamic interplay between societal conditions, institutions and individual characteristics. Although this chapter has not empirically analysed what determines rates of participation and inclusivity of adult learning, it has highlighted factors suggested by the previous literature, including approaches to social welfare, industrial relations, civil society and public policy. This suggests that to achieve the globally agreed-upon goals of promoting adult learning participation and inclusivity, proactive approaches are needed, beyond resources and investment, or relying on individuals to self-select into adult learning opportunities.

(Continued)

(Continued)

Much of the international research on adult learning has focused on the success of the Nordic countries in promoting adult learning, providing revealing insights into their comparative success. However, more research is needed on how barriers to adult learning can be overcome where boosting participation remains a big challenge (e.g. in Southern Europe). Moreover, countries such as the Netherlands and Germany are successful in promoting some aspects of adult learning without the Nordic approach. It should be noted that the Nordic approach to adult learning originates from a combination of adequate and well-directed resources, a distinctive cultural legacy of adult learning, and the Nordic approach to social welfare. These countries' focus on inclusivity of adult learning for less educated and immigrant populations in turn boosts overall participation levels. This approach may be difficult for other countries to emulate directly, in light of demographic and political differences. It therefore appears that although boosting participation in adult learning and promoting its inclusivity are universally supported goals, the achievement of these goals is both enabled and constrained by countries' diverse history, culture and public policies.

Further recommended reading

Boeren, E. (2016) *Lifelong Learning Participation in a Changing Policy Context: An Interdisciplinary Theory.* London: Palgrave Macmillan.
Desjardins, R. (2017) *Political Economy of Adult Learning Systems: Comparative Study of Strategies, Policies and Constraints.* London: Bloomsbury Academic.

References

Boeren, E. (2017) Understanding adult lifelong learning participation as a layered problem. *Studies in Continuing Education*, 39(2): 161–175.
Boeren, E. and Holford, J. (2016) Vocationalism varies (a lot): a 12-country multivariate analysis of participation in formal adult learning. *Adult Education Quarterly*, 66(2): 120–142.
Boeren, E., Nicaise, I. and Baert, H. (2010) Theoretical models of participation in adult education: the need for an integrated model. *International Journal of Lifelong Education*, 29(1): 45–61.
Boeren, E., Holford, J., Nicaise, I. and Baert, H. (2012) Why do adults learn? Developing a motivational typology across 12 European countries. *Globalisation, Societies and Education*, 10(2): 247–269.
Boudard, E. (2001) *Literacy Proficiency, Earnings, and Recurrent Training: A Ten Country Comparative Study.* Doctoral dissertation, Institute of International Education, Stockholm University.
Bourdieu, P. and Passeron, J.-C. (1977) *Reproduction in Education, Society, and Culture.* Beverly Hills, CA: Sage.
Brunello, G. (2001) *On the Complementarity between Education and Training in Europe.* IZA Discussion Paper Series, No. 309. Bonn: Institute for the Study of Labor (IZA).
Clausen, J., Heinesen, E., Hummelgaard, H., Husted, L. and Rosholm, M. (2009) The effect of integration policies on the time until regular employment of newly arrived immigrants: evidence from Denmark. *Labour Economics*, 16(4): 409–417.
Colardyn, D. and Bjornavold, J. (2004) Validation of formal, non-formal and informal learning: policy and practices in EU member states. *European Journal of Education*, 39(1): 69–89.

Cross, K.P. (1981) *Adults as Learners: Increasing Participation and Facilitating Learning*. San Francisco, CA: Jossey-Bass.

Desjardins, R. (2015) *Participation in Adult Education Opportunities: Evidence from PIAAC and Policy Trends in Selected Countries*. Background paper for the Education for All Global Monitoring Report 2015.

Desjardins, R. (2017) *Political Economy of Adult Learning Systems: Comparative Study of Strategies, Policies and Constraints*. London: Bloomsbury Academic.

Desjardins, R. and Rubenson, K. (2013) Participation patterns in adult education: the role of institutions and public policy frameworks in resolving coordination problems. *European Journal of Education*, 48(2): 262–280.

Ebbinghaus, B., Göbel, C. and Koos, S. (2011) Social capital, 'Ghent' and workplace contexts matter: comparing union membership in Europe. *European Journal of Industrial Relations*, 17(2): 107–124.

Esping-Andersen, G. (1999) *Social Foundations of Postindustrial Economies*. Oxford: Oxford University Press.

Korpi, W. and Palme, J. (1998) The paradox of redistribution and strategies of equality: welfare state institutions, inequality, and poverty in the Western countries. *American Sociological Review*, 63(5): 661–687.

Norwegian Labour Inspection Authority (2017) *Working Environment Act*. Available at: www.arbeidstilsynet. no/contentassets/e54635c3d2e5415785a4f23f5b852849/working-environment-act-october-web-2017.pdf

OECD (2013) *OECD Skills Outlook 2013: First Results from the Survey of Adult Skills*. Available at: www.oecd. org/skills/piaac/Skills%20volume%201%20(eng)--full%20v12--eBook%20(04%2011%202013).pdf

Roth, F. and Thum, A.E. (2010) *The Key Role of Education in the Europe 2020 Strategy*. CEPS Working Document No. 338. Brussels: Centre for European Policy Studies.

Rubenson, K. (2006) The Nordic model of lifelong learning. *Compare*, 36(3): 327–341.

Rubenson, K. and Desjardins, R. (2009) The impact of welfare state regimes on barriers to participation in adult education: a bounded agency model. *Adult Education Quarterly*, 59(3): 187–207.

Schuller, T. and Desjardins, R. (2007) *Understanding the Social Outcomes of Learning*. Paris: OECD.

Schuller, T., Preston, J., Hammond, C., Brassett-Grundy, A. and Bynner, J. (2004) *The Benefits of Learning: The Impact of Education on Health, Family Life and Social Capital*. London: Routledge.

Thelen, K. (2004) *How Institutions Evolve: The Political Economy of Skills in Germany, Britain, the United States, and Japan*. Cambridge: Cambridge University Press.

Tight, M. (1996) *Key Concepts in Adult Education and Training*. London: Routledge.

UNESCO (2009) *Global Report on Adult Education and Learning*. Paris: UNESCO.

UNESCO (2015) *Education 2030: Incheon Declaration and Framework for Action for the Implementation of Sustainable Development Goal 4*. Paris: UNESCO.

UNESCO (2016) *Recommendation on Adult Learning and Education 2015*. Available at: https://unesdoc. unesco.org/ark:/48223/pf0000245179

UNESCO Institute for Statistics (2012) *The International Standard Classification of Education 2011*. Available at: http://uis.unesco.org/en/topic/international-standard-classification-education-isced

United Nations (2015) *Transforming Our World: The 2030 Agenda for Sustainable Development*. Available at: https://sustainabledevelopment.un.org/post2015/transformingourworld/publication

19

POST-COMPULSORY EDUCATION AND TRAINING IN AOTEAROA NEW ZEALAND

Annelies Kamp

Key words - New Zealand; Treaty of Waitangi; cultural responsiveness; qualifications frameworks; kaupapa Māori; talanoa

Introducing Aotearoa

> ### Key questions
>
> Is post-compulsory education influenced by where you are in the world?

Aotearoa New Zealand (Aotearoa) is a bicultural South Pacific nation with a population of nearly 4.8 million people. The country is characterised by economic and political stability: in 2016, the defining characteristics of Aotearoa that were ranked highest by New Zealanders were 'freedom, rights and peace' and 'environment' (mean rating 9.1), followed by 'the people in New Zealand' (mean rating 8.5) (Stats NZ, 2016). While Aotearoa has long prided itself on egalitarian commitments in social policy that were enshrined in the first half of the twentieth century, there is increasing recognition that policy directions in the latter years of that century changed that egalitarian status; by the twenty-first century, Aotearoa was reported to be the OECD nation most affected by the impact of growing inequality (OECD, 2014). According to the OECD, inequality affects growth by undermining education opportunities for some children, lowering social mobility and 'hampering' skills development.

While it is acknowledged that Aotearoa has a developing cultural pluralism (Kelsey, 1999), it is officially a bicultural nation comprised of the signatories to the *Tiriti o Waitangi* (Treaty of Waitangi): *tangata whenua* (people of the land) and *tauiwi* (non-Māori). The treaty, signed in 1840 between representatives of the British Crown and more than 500 Māori chiefs, resulted in the declaration of British sovereignty over Aotearoa. More than 175 years on from its signature, the treaty remains a vital document in Aotearoa; treaty settlements related to breaches of the agreement continue to be negotiated between the state and Māori, and in social policy arenas, including education, commitments to the treaty are fundamental to the way that Aotearoa conceptualises policy, undertakes implementation, and measures achievement and excellence. Aotearoa is further characterised by its position as a Polynesian nation; cultural concerns are also foregrounded for the large population of Pasifika peoples who call Aotearoa – and Auckland City in particular – home (Stats NZ, 2013).

The Tertiary Education Strategy 2014–19 is explicit in its responsibilities in light of the treaty:

> In recognising the role of Māori as tangata whenua and Crown partners under the Treaty of Waitangi, TEOs (Tertiary Education Organisations) must enable Māori to achieve education success as Māori, including by protecting Māori language and culture, and to prepare for labour market success. Tertiary education also contributes to Māori cultural outcomes – such as greater knowledge and use of Māori language and tikanga Māori, and development of mātauranga Māori. TEOs have a responsibility to contribute to the survival and wellbeing of Māori as a people.
>
> (New Zealand Government, 2014, p7)

According to Macfarlane (2013), over recent decades a 'quiet revolution' has seen culturally responsive epistemologies and methodologies assume a presence in tertiary institutions in Aotearoa; the 'call to respond to the disparity that exists between cultures with respect to academic achievement is one that is now heard and acknowledged widely by a large majority of educators' (p1). In practice, this refers to a commitment to equity in achievement for Māori, *as* Māori, in ways that sustain identity and culture. For educators, it lays down challenge to Western expectations of the form that post-compulsory education and training 'should' take. This chapter seeks to illuminate the cultural dynamics that surround post-compulsory education and training in Aotearoa, offering insights from this context to teaching and learning in other education and training contexts.

The cultural, economic and social role of PCET in twenty-first-century Aotearoa

Key questions

Does PCET shift over time and space?

System and structure

In Aotearoa in the twenty-first century, post-compulsory education and training is largely synonymous with 'tertiary' education; 'tertiary education' is the dominant terminology. Young people who remain in secondary school beyond the compulsory age (currently from 6 to 16 years of age) are, however, included in tertiary participation figures, where they are enrolled within a dedicated secondary tertiary programme (the government also uses the term 'further education' at times, in reference to post-16 provision). An influential aspect of the context in Aotearoa is the full integration of post-compulsory education and training into one system, in the context of an economy that has, since the 1980s, been governed with a neo-liberal ethos (Findsen, 2012b; Leach, 2014; Roberts, 2009; Shore, 2010; Zepke, 2009). Thus, to a greater or lesser degree, successive governments have favoured decreased central control of educational provision and increased reliance on market competition, arguably to drive both quality and value for money. In 2017, approximately 400,000 students were enrolled in tertiary education, including foundation education, community education, vocational education and higher education. This provision is delivered by around 1,000 providers, including universities, institutes of technology and polytechnics, private training establishments, and *wānanga* (recognised tertiary institutions providing a range of qualifications based on Māori principles and values), in addition to a limited number of community education providers (Shephard, 2017) (see Figure 19.1).

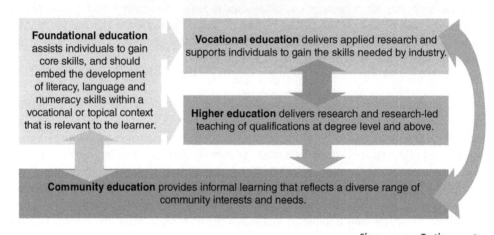

Figure 19.1   Tertiary sector map
Source: New Zealand Government (2014, p22), Creative Commons Attribution 4.0 International Licence

Participation in tertiary education is, as is the case elsewhere, influenced by economic shifts. Each economic recession in Aotearoa has been associated with increases in retention in the senior secondary school and, either directly or indirectly, in participation in higher levels of tertiary education (Smart, 2009). Increased retention in secondary school, for whatever reason, results in increasing enrolment in higher courses through the impact of higher opportunity for attainment of entrance qualifications. Changes in government policy have also had an impact in increasing engagement in tertiary education. The introduction of Aotearoa's three-level senior school qualification in 2002 – the National Certificate of Educational Achievement (NCEA) – was associated with an increase in the number of learners attaining the qualification given its modularised approach to learning and the shift away from normative high-stakes summative examinations. A further influential factor has been government funding policies, both the imposition at times of funding caps for some programmes of study and, in 1992, the introduction of student loans to move the cost of tertiary education provision from the state to the individual. This shift to 'user pays' was in keeping with neo-liberal leanings of respective governments. Loans for fees and living costs were progressively made interest-free. In 2018, the incoming Labour-led coalition government commenced a progressive introduction of fees-free tertiary education for New Zealanders who had not previously studied at tertiary level (**www.feesfree.govt.nz**); by November 2018, 41,800 learners were receiving fees-free tertiary education (Hon. Hipkins, 2018).

At the 'heart' of both secondary and tertiary education in Aotearoa is the New Zealand Qualifications Framework (NZQF) that was implemented in 1991 (**www.nzqa.govt.nz**). At implementation, the

10-level NZQF was argued to be the most comprehensive standards-based qualification system in the world (Philips, 2003), moving beyond vocational education to include school and higher education. Economic downturn and higher unemployment in the 1980s contributed to the implementation of the NZQF: economic restructuring at the time was premised on radical arguments for a less regulated economy that would improve efficiency and promote enterprise. A unitary framework for qualifications was seen as essential to this in promoting a seamless education system (Allias, 2010). The NZQF would eventually be broadened: the NCEA as the school-based initial qualification at levels 1–3 would move to a structure of 'achievement standards' – an adaptation of the 'unit standard' of the NZQF – and while universities would eventually adopt a separate statutory quality assurance body (Universities New Zealand), higher education qualifications appear on the NZQF at levels 7–10 and have moved to a learning-outcomes based approach.

The NZQF is based on a number of principles that are pivotal to the efficacy of education and training in the context of Aotearoa. First, the NZQF is *needs-based*: qualifications are valued on the basis of their relationship to the skill needs of stakeholders. Where appropriate, there is explicit acknowledgement of the cultural and social aspirations of Māori, Pasifika or other communities. For example, providers are supported to develop dedicated qualifications, and to deliver and assess unit standards, that sustain Māori culture, such as Unit Standard 23006, 'Demonstrate knowledge of how a carver shows meaning in their carvings'. The second principle is *focused on outcomes*: clearly specified outcomes ensure each qualification is transparent in its purpose, its comparability and its portability. Outcomes not only make explicit what a graduate can 'do, be and know', but also the pathways they can follow beyond their current study. The third principle is *flexibility*. In Aotearoa, qualifications can be achieved in a range of contexts, including workplaces. This allows learners to achieve in ways that suit their education, work or cultural needs and aspirations. Recognition of prior learning (RPL) – the term used by the New Zealand Qualifications Authority (NZQA) to identify the potential to recognise skills and knowledge gained through work, independent study, informal learning or life experience – is facilitated, as is credit transfer (CRT), which allows recognition of credit gained in former, formal learning. Finally, principles of *trust and accountability* allow for the co-development of qualifications involving a range of stakeholders.

Alongside these principles, the importance of *lifelong learning* is acknowledged. The stated intention to value learning gained in both formal and informal learning, at different stages of life and in a 'range of places and ways', including on-job, online, by distance and in formal learning environments. In short, 'the NZQF does not put limitations on how or where people can learn' (NZQA, 2016, p3).

Reform, review and renewal

The development of New Zealand's fully integrated tertiary education system and transformational NZQF (Raffe, 2014) were a response to government perceptions of a fragmented qualification system, of lower than desirable participation, and the need for increased skills and higher employment figures (Crawford, 2016). With the election of a centre-left Labour-led government in 1999, a number of reforms in tertiary education were initiated. The new government shifted the focus away from a purely competitive model of supply to one where the tertiary education system would be connected as a system (Slater, 2009). This resulted in the first Tertiary Education Strategy (Ministry of Education, 2002). The strategy articulated the vision for all post-compulsory education, including the more informal adult and community education sector (Leach, 2014), to form a single, coordinated 'tertiary' education system under one administrative structure, the Tertiary Education Commission (TEC).

This structure has persisted. The most recent Tertiary Education Strategy 2014–19 (New Zealand Government, 2014) is centred on six priorities: delivering skills for industry, getting at-risk young people into a career, boosting achievement of Māori and Pasifika, improving adult literacy and numeracy, strengthening research-based institutions, and growing international linkages. In 2017, the Productivity Commission – an independent Crown Agency – undertook a review of tertiary education (New Zealand Productivity Commission, 2017). In response, the government has flagged four areas for attention moving forward:

1. Creating a more student-centred system in which informed, engaged students can access opportunities best suited to them.

2. Meeting the needs of industry and employers through relevant, responsive and supportive teaching environments with high-quality teaching.

3. Improving performance across the system to deliver better outcomes from current programmes.

4. Enabling and encouraging innovative new models and providers so there is greater experimentation with approaches and more competition, including from new providers.

(New Zealand Government, 2017)

There are eight publicly funded universities (including a university of technology, previously the largest polytechnic), 20 polytechnics or institutes of technology, three *wānanga*, and several hundred private training establishments, which include trades training, language institutes, religious-based training organisations and a variety of vocational colleges. Competence-based apprenticeship has remained a key component of the industry training subsystem; however, fewer than 10 per cent of young people progress to apprenticeships, and these remain highly gendered (Nairn et al., 2007; Piercy et al., 2006). Schools are also active in the post-compulsory landscape through offering 'aligned' courses for learners who wish to integrate some higher education or vocational learning into their senior school programme for NCEA.

The entire education system in Aotearoa, including tertiary education, is currently under review by Jacinda Ardern's Labour-led coalition government, as detailed in the Education Work Programme (Hon. Hipkins, 2017). The 'main components' of this extensive plan of work comprise 10 areas: early learning strategy; school governance; future-focused education workforce; learning support; school property; a 'programme of change' for vocational education, including industry training providers; research; NCEA review; lifting achievement of Māori students; and lifting achievement of Pasifika students. The outcomes of this system review, and the questions posed by Shephard (2017), will become evident in the coming months.

Moving beyond cultural responsiveness in PCET

Key questions

What difference does a worldview make to teaching and learning?

Post-compulsory education and training: a Māori worldview

As Māori have recognised education as being increasingly essential to economic inclusion in the context of late modernity, participation in tertiary education has increased. However, increased participation did not in and of itself necessitate changes to structures of tertiary education that would enable Māori to succeed *as* Māori (Ministry of Education, 2003) (see Figure 19.2). The principle of *tino rangatiratanga* (self-determination) is evident in the emergence of institutions that cater for Māori learning needs – *wānanga* – as part of the tertiary education system in Aotearoa (Findsen, 2012a). Wānanga are 'characterised by teaching and research that maintains, advances, and disseminates knowledge and develops intellectual independence, and assists the application of knowledge regarding āhuatanga Māori (Māori tradition) according to tikanga Māori (Māori custom)' (**www.nzqa.govt.nz**).

Close focus

In keeping with the obligations of the *Tiriti o Waitangi*, tertiary education in Aotearoa aspires to respond to the particular rights of Māori. The Māori Tertiary Education Framework (Ministry of Education, 2003) outlined the first collective Māori agreement on a strategic direction for tertiary education. It includes five guiding principles for a 'healthy system': *whakanui* (to celebrate inclusiveness); *toi te mana* (empowerment); *ngā kawenga* (responsibility); *ahu kāwanatanga* (partnership); and *tino rangatiratanga* (self-determination).

Whakanui relates to the acknowledgement and accommodation of Māori realities; in this, Māori contributions and innovations are 'included and respected as a natural part of the system'. *Toi te mana* means Māori are to be empowered to influence the tertiary system, at all levels. The third principle of *ngā kawenga* requires that the tertiary system be accountable to Māori and reflective of Māori goals and aspirations for advancement. In *ahu kāwanatanga*, the fourth principle, the reference is to achieving shared visions in partnership and building that shared vision on shared responsibility, contribution and accountability for all Māori. Finally, *tino rangatiratanga* is concerned with supporting self-determination for Māori, enabling provision by Māori and preserving Māori ownership in tertiary education (Ministry of Education, 2003, p15).

These principles articulate into seven priority areas for tertiary education: lifelong learning pathways; kaupapa Māori provision; learning environments; advancement of *whānau, hapū* and *iwi* (family, subtribes and tribes); Māori-centred knowledge creation; Māori leadership; and Māori as sustainable wealth creators. The nature of the principles and priority areas reflect the holistic nature of the Māori worldview.

The Māori Tertiary Education Framework is presented as a *niho taniwha* (tooth of the *taniwha* - a water monster of Māori legend) structure with *Te Ao Māori* (the Māori world) at the apex. *Niho taniwha* as a traditional pattern emphasises accountability to every dimension, responsiveness to Māori values and development, equity and balance, desire to participate in the tertiary system, the cutting edge that tertiary qualifications offer *iwi* development, and the *kōkiri* - a traditional fighting formation that spearheads the forward thrust of Māori (Ministry of Education, 2003, p13).

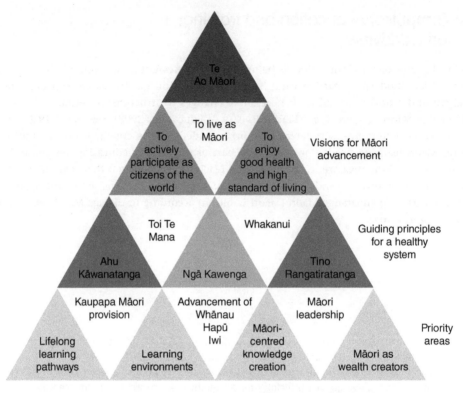

Figure 19.2 Māori Tertiary Education Framework

Source: New Zealand Government (2003, p13), Creative Commons Attribution 4.0 International Licence

Post-compulsory education and training: a Pasifika worldview

'Pasifika peoples' is a term taken up by government in New Zealand to depict those people who identify – either through migration or ancestry – with the Pacific Islands. It is a term that elides the ethnic and cultural diversity of Pacific Islands peoples in Aotearoa, including but not limited to Fijian, Samoan, Tongan, Tokelauan, Niuean and Cook Islander. This is a youthful population: 46.1 per cent were less than 20 years old at the 2013 census, compared with 27.4 per cent for the population of Aotearoa. Pasifika are the fourth largest major ethnic group in Aotearoa, behind European, Māori and Asian ethnic groups. Almost two-thirds of the Pasifika population (62.3 per cent) were born in New Zealand and 92.9 per cent of the population live in the North Island, the great majority in Auckland City. Only 7.1 per cent of Pasifika people live in the South Island (Stats NZ, 2013). In 2013, 7.4 per cent of the population of Aotearoa identified as Pasifika.

The poor performance of Pasifika students relative to *palagi* (European) students has been a source of concern for decades (Taleni et al., 2018). One in five Pasifika students leave compulsory education without any qualification, while another one in five will leave with NCEA level 1. Thirty-six per cent of Pasifika school leavers in 2013 gained the equivalent to NCEA level 3, 14.2 percentage points below that of non-Pasifika students (Ministry of Education, 2013). Pasifika completion rates in tertiary education have increased from 55 per cent in 2006 to 75 per cent in 2015. However, this remains well below the 85 per cent completion rate for non-Māori and non-Pasifika (Tertiary Education Commission, 2017).

In their Pasifika Education Plan 2013–2017, the Ministry of Education established a vision for Pasifika students: 'five out of five Pasifika learners participating, engaging and achieving in education, secure in their identities, languages and cultures and contributing fully to Aotearoa New Zealand's social, cultural and economic wellbeing' (Ministry of Education, n.d.).

In pursuit of this vision, the Pasifika Education Plan outlines three goals for tertiary education. First, Pasifika students participate and achieve at all levels at least on a par with other learners in tertiary education; second, tertiary education will use research and evidence effectively to achieve the goals of the Pasifika Education Plan; and third, Pasifika people will form a highly skilled workforce that fully contributes to New Zealand's economy and society. The Pasifika Education Plan – now extended until the end of 2019 – has as its target that Pasifika students will participate and achieve at all levels at least on a par with other students in tertiary education. The goals were further distilled to a number of focus areas for tertiary education organisations.

Focus area 1 concerned the use of information to increase transitions into higher levels of education and employment. The need to target transition information and support to Pasifika learners and their parents, family and community 'using the voices that speak to them' was acknowledged. Here, actions have included, first, community-focused public awareness campaigns and, second, partnerships between Achievement in Multicultural High Schools (AIMHI) in Auckland and tertiary education organisations (AIMHI secondary schools were established in the 1990s as part of a developmental project working with eight schools with high enrolments of Pasifika and Māori learners). The third action focused on the effectiveness of careers advice for Pasifika students. In focus area 2, the actions of tertiary education organisations were scoped. Here, the aim was to support these organisations to strengthen their focus on improving participation and achievement for Pasifika learners. References to best practice and continuous improvement in regard to what works for Pasifika are noted in two actions. The first was that those providers with the largest local Pasifika populations (mainly in Auckland and Wellington) would be required to have organisational-wide strategic and operational plans to improve participation and achievement rates for Pasifika students, for which they would be held accountable. The second action was to identify and scale up evidence-based initiatives that work for Pasifika. These initiatives would be judged on the basis of the Tertiary Education Commission Māori and Pasifika Investment Plan Assessment Framework (Tertiary Education Commission, 2018). Focus area 3 concerns community and the contribution of the broader community (families, churches, employers and government) to improve the system for Pasifika. The focus here is collaboration and co-creation of localised solutions for Pasifika. Three actions were, first, the development and delivery of a community-focused collective plan; second, the use of community information channels so Pasifika learners, families and communities could access the right information at the right time; and third, the use of established initiatives such as Māori and Pasifika trades training consortia to engage with community.

The commitment for Māori and Pasifika students to not only experience equity in academic achievement, but to do so first and foremost as Māori and Pasifika, has particular implications for how tertiary education providers engage with teaching and learning. These implications have been captured in the concept of a culturally responsive pedagogy of relations (Bishop and Glynn, 1999). For Māori, this is manifest in theories of kaupapa Māori (Smith, 2003) and related principles of self-determination, cultural aspiration, culturally preferred pedagogy, socio-economic mediation, extended family structure and collective philosophy. Kaupapa Māori, for McMurchy-Pilkington (2001), is 'critical theory at a localised level' (p73). Yet kaupapa Māori 'does not put aside Pākehā knowledge or culture; rather it extracts the excellence from both worlds' (Ross, 2008, p5). In this, tertiary education in Aotearoa brings together, and benefits from, the best of Māori and Pākehā worldviews.

Ako and Talanoa as pedagogies for Aotearoa and elsewhere

In traditional Māori society, knowledge was to benefit the collective; thus, it was inclusive, cooperative, reciprocal and obligatory (Lee, 2005). Maged et al. (2017) researched the nature of teaching and learning relationships in *wānanga*. Within *wānanga*, teaching and learning is premised on *whanaungatanga*, relationships that are reciprocal, building through shared experiences and working together, which generates a sense of belonging. It includes *ako* – teachers and learners both initiate learning, and each learns from the other, and learners exercise self-determination in respect of the learning process, and become co-inquirers with their educators and their peers (Bishop and Glynn, 1999). Particularly in *wānanga* – but also in other educational and social policy contexts in Aotearoa – the spirituality inherent in *Te Ao Māori* is made manifest in the material world through *tikanga*, such as the use of *karakia* (prayers), *waiata* (songs) and *pōwhiri* (formal welcome). In Aotearoa, the NZQF includes *mātauranga* Māori qualifications: qualifications developed from a Māori perspective in consultation with *whānau*, *hapū* and *iwi*, with support and expertise of Māori Governance and Working Groups.

In their study of best practice for Māori and Pasifika learners in private training establishments, Marshall et al. (2008) found similar themes. Their research identified three key components to creating a holistic approach to learning in Aotearoa: first, adopting the surrogate *whānau* concept; second, creating a sense of belonging; and third, creating a sense of greater humanity and inclusivity for all cultures. This triad is often acknowledged as preferred for Māori and Pasifika learners (Cram and Pipi, 2001). The surrogate *whānau* concept includes manifesting the role of an otherwise absent family unit: taking on the guidance role usually provided by family; building and reinforcing trust; developing familial and friendship-based relationships with learners; and ensuring the organisation as a whole functions as a recognised family unit. The second component – creating a sense of belonging – is engendered in part by the surrogate *whānau* concept. Belonging enables learners to develop and sustain community links. The creation of belonging was dependent on the 'quality and vision' in the organisation, and connected to a sense of commitment of all to kaupapa Māori. The third component of the best practice approach argued for in the research – a greater sense of humanity – is achieved through all learners and staff being supported in strengthening their own cultural and personal identity and being respective of the cultural and personal identity of others. In this, the organisation was able to provide an environment that was more holistic and supportive than any individual could generate alone (Marshall et al., 2008).

Peer support has also been used as an effective mechanism to contribute to a sense of belonging for Māori and Pasifika students who are studying by distance. The Open Polytechnic – one of the largest providers of tertiary education to Māori and Pasifika students in Aotearoa – has undertaken research on mechanisms to support first-year Māori and Pasifika students, including peer support that aligns with the Māori understandings of *tuākana-tēina* (the relationship between an older person and a younger person). A programme of culturally relevant peer support was implemented with 150 first-year Māori and Pasifika students, with the aim of welcoming students to their new learning community and supporting them in gaining whatever help they needed to succeed. Proactive contact with students allowed support to be channelled at those times that have been identified as critical for student progress (Simpson, 2000).

Key questions

How might insights from Aotearoa New Zealand influence the approach to teaching and learning in tertiary education in other contexts?

In Aotearoa, our commitments to the treaty oblige teachers, professionals, education leaders and contributing partners in post-compulsory education to ensure Māori can succeed *as* Māori, including protection of Māori language and culture; tertiary education organisations have a responsibility to contribute to the survival and well-being of Māori as a people. This responsibility presents both challenges and opportunities for tertiary providers. Our Tertiary Education Strategies have been underpinned by governments' responsibilities under the treaty. However, *all* learners benefit from high-quality, relevant information, support and advice while they are still in compulsory schooling and considering their future learning options, just as they benefit from a sense of belonging consistent with their sense of identity, when they engage. All *whānau* (family) benefit from being informed about and able to engage in conversations about post-compulsory education, its processes and its benefits. Research, particularly research by Māori and Pasifika, focused on what works from the standpoints of their unique cultural strengths, and contributes to their communities of concern, giving insights into how teachers can build their capacity to work with other groups of learners who are culturally, linguistically, physically or socially diverse. The insights from the collective knowledge creation in *mātauranga* Māori offer potential in a complex world where we are encouraged to collaborate. This is not a case of replacing existing structures and pedagogies that are working well for many students; it is about enriching them through weaving together the best of both Māori and Western worldviews.

At the more advanced levels of tertiary education, the development of *wānanga* in Aotearoa has offered immense insight into the potential of post-compulsory education to respond to overcoming disparities in the levels of academic achievement in a given society. What are the implications of these insights for post-compulsory educators beyond Aotearoa? Prochnow and Macfarlane (2008, cited in Macfarlane, 2013, p4) adapted the work of Cartledge and Kourea (2008) to present a sequence of introspective questions that educators, including tertiary educators, can use to uncover biases that may negatively influence their practice:

1. Does the ethnicity of the students in my class influence my perspectives/biases in terms of how I respond to and manage their learning? If so, how?

2. What is the correlation (negative/positive) between my behavioural interactions with students and their ethnicity?

3. How are my responses being perceived by the students?

4. How are my responses being perceived by the students' peers?

5. Is the learning of my students improving? How do I know that? If not, why not?

6. How equitable and culturally appropriate are my class/lecture management strategies?

7. How do I know?

8. Do my class/lecture management strategies facilitate long-term change(s) or do they merely cater for the here and now?

9. How do I identify cultural influences on, and explanations for, various learning styles and behavioural nuances?

10. How do I currently respond to/address positive and long-term learning and behavioural change in my students? Do I influence and empower their prosocial skills?

11. What class/pedagogical management skills do I need to develop? Do I effectively manage these in the present environment of diversity?

12. How can I improve my management/instructional skills so that I am not resorting to teaching ideology/processes that proceed solely from a Western scientific space?

Chapter summary

- Aotearoa has a unitary post-compulsory education and training system with a comprehensive qualifications framework at its heart. The system is oriented to economic outcomes; however, this is mediated to some extent by the obligation of governments to provide a system that works for Māori *as* Māori.

- In Aotearoa, a commitment to biculturalism and the rights of *tangata whenua* embedded in the treaty does not diminish in a context of growing multiculturalism among *tauiwi*.

- While Aotearoa ranks well in international comparisons, the post-compulsory system has not served Māori and Pasifika peoples as well as it services non-Māori and non-Pasifika peoples. Tertiary education organisations are held accountable for achieving equity.

- Kaupapa Māori is an approach to teaching and learning that brings the richness of *Te Ao Māori* and other cultures alongside Western worldviews in ways that can enrich learning for all. There is no one right way to implement kaupapa Māori: it begins in building relationships based in authentic partnership and a commitment to self-determination.

Glossary

ako: to learn and to teach; indicative of the reciprocal nature of the pedagogic relationship

Aotearoa: New Zealand

āhuatanga Māori: Māori tradition

ahu kāwanatanga: partnership

hapū: sub-tribe

iwi: tribe

karakia: prayers

mātauranga Māori: Māori knowledge

NCEA: New Zealand Certificate in Educational Achievement

ngā kawenga: obligation and responsibility

NZQF: New Zealand Qualifications Framework

pākehā: New Zealander of European descent

palagi: a non-Samoan person

pōwhiri: a formal welcome from the *tangata whenua*

talanoa: a conversation; an exchange of ideas and thoughts

tangata whenua: people of the land; the local tribe

tauiwi: non-Māori; people coming from afar

Te Ao Māori: the Māori world

TEO: Tertiary Education Organisation

tikanga: Māori custom

tino rangatiratanga: self-determination

Tiriti o Waitangi: Treaty of Waitangi

toi te mana: empowerment

tuākana-tēina: a teaching and learning peer relationship between an older person and a younger person

waiata: song

wānanga: tertiary institution that caters specifically for Māori learning needs

whakanui: to celebrate inclusiveness

whānau: family

whanaungatanga: a relationship based on shared experiences that provides a sense of belonging

Further recommended reading

Bishop, R. and Glynn, T (1999) *Culture Counts: Changing Power Relations in Education*. Auckland: Dunmore Press.

This book traces the development of cultural dominance and subordination in Aotearoa, before introducing the kaupapa Māori response. It promotes self-determination as guaranteed in the Treaty of Waitangi as a metaphor for power-sharing and has as its goal the advancement of educational outcomes and life opportunities for Māori children and those from other cultures.

Tobias, R.M. (1999) Lifelong learning under a comprehensive national qualifications framework: rhetoric and reality. *International Journal of Lifelong Education*, 18(2): 110–118.

This paper explores critical questions about changes in aspirations for lifelong learning in post-compulsory education and training in the context of the establishment of the qualifications framework.

Crawford, R. (2016) *History of Tertiary Education Reforms in New Zealand*. New Zealand Productivity Commission, Te Kōmihana Whai Hua o Aotearoa.

This history reviews policy reform over the past three decades.

References

Allias, S. (2010) *The Implementation and Impact of National Qualifications Frameworks: Report of a Study in 16 Countries*. Geneva: International Labour Organization.

Bishop, R. and Glynn, T. (1999) *Culture Counts: Changing Power Relations in Education*. Auckland: Dunmore Press.

Cartledge, G. and Kourea, L. (2008) Culturally responsive classrooms for culturally diverse students with and at risk for disabilities. *Exceptional Children*, 74(3): 351–371.

Cram, F. and Pipi, K. (2001) *Determinants of Māori Provider Success: Provider Interviews Summary Report*. Auckland: Māori Research Development.

Crawford, R. (2016) *History of Tertiary Education Reforms in New Zealand*. New Zealand Productivity Commission, Te Kōmihana Whai Hua o Aotearoa.

Findsen, B. (2012a) Engagement of older adults in higher education: international perspectives from New Zealand and Scotland. *The Adult Learner Journal*, 13–26.

Findsen, B. (2012b) Where have all the flowers gone? The wilting of university adult and community education in Aotearoa New Zealand. *ACCESS: Critical Perspectives on Communication, Cultural & Policy Studies*, 31(1): 89–95.

Hon. Hipkins, C. (2017) *Education Portfolio Work Programme*. NZ Ministry of Education: Wellington.

Hon. Hipkins, C. (2018) *Update on the First Seven Months of the Fees Free Policy*. Available at: www.beehive.govt.nz/release/update-first-seven-months-fees-free-policy

Kelsey, J. (1999) *Life in the Economic Test-Tube: New Zealand 'Experiment' a Colossal Failure*. Available at: www.converge.org.nz/pma/apfail.htm

Leach, L. (2014) Adult and community education policy in Aotearoa New Zealand 2000–2014: neoliberal influences? *International Journal of Lifelong Education*, 33(6): 705–720.

Lee, J. (2005) *Māori Cultural Regeneration: Purakau as Pedagogy*. Paper presented at the Centre for Research in Lifelong Learning International Conference, Stirling, Scotland.

Macfarlane, A. (2013) *Huakina mai: Doorways toward Culturally Responsive Education*. Wellington: Ako Aotearoa.

Maged, S., Rosales-Anderson, N. and Manuel, W. (2017) The spiritual footsteps of teaching and learning. *New Zealand Journal of Educational Studies*, 52: 271–284.

Marshall, J., Baldwin, K. and Peach, R. (2008) *Te Rau Awhina: The Guiding Leaf. Good Practice Examples of Māori and Pasifika Private Training Establishments Research & Knowledge*. Wellington: New Zealand Qualifications Authority.

McMurchy-Pilkington, C. (2001) Māori education: rejection, resistance, renaissance. In V. Carpenter, H. Dixon, E. Rata and C. Rawlinson (eds), *Theory in Practice for Educators*. Auckland: Dunmore Press.

Ministry of Education (2002) *Tertiary Education Strategy 2002–2007*. Available at: www.education.govt.nz/assets/Documents/Ministry/Information-releases/R-Education-Portfolio-Work-Programme-Purpose-Objectives-and-Overview.pdf

Ministry of Education (2003) *Māori Tertiary Development Framework*. Wellington: New Zealand Government.

Ministry of Education (2013) *Pasifika Education Plan: Monitoring Report 2013*. Available at: www.educationcounts.govt.nz/publications/series/22967/pasifika-education-plan-monitoring-report-2013

Ministry of Education (n.d.) *Pasifika Education Plan 2013–2017*. Wellington: New Zealand Government.

Nairn, K., Higgins, J. and Ormond, A. (2007) Post-school horizons: New Zealand's neo-liberal generation in transition. *International Studies in Sociology of Education*, 17(4): 349–366.

New Zealand Government (2014) *Tertiary Education Strategy 2014–2019*. Wellington: New Zealand Government.

New Zealand Government (2017) *Delivering a Strong and Effective Tertiary Education System for New Zealanders*. Wellington: New Zealand Government.

New Zealand Productivity Commission (2017) *New Models of Tertiary Education*. Wellington: New Zealand Productivity Commission | Te Komihana Whai Hua o Aotearoa.

NZQA (2016) *The New Zealand Qualifications Framework*. Wellington: New Zealand Government.

OECD (2014) *Inequality Hurts Economic Growth, Finds OECD Research*. Available at: www.oecd.org/newsroom/inequality-hurts-economic-growth.htm

Philips, D. (2003) Lessons from New Zealand's National Qualifications Framework. *Journal of Education and Work*, 16(3): 289–304.

Piercy, G., Murray, N. and Abernethy, G. (2006) Women's participation in education and training in New Zealand: is the 'learn while you earn' option accessible to all? *Journal of Vocational Education & Training*, 58(4): 515–529.

Raffe, D. (2014) Explaining national differences in education-work transitions. *European Societies*, 16(2): 175–193.

Roberts, P. (2009) A new patriotism? Neoliberalism, citizenship and tertiary education in New Zealand. *Educational Philosophy & Theory*, 41(4): 410–423.

Ross, C. (2008) *Culturally Relevant Peer Support for Māori and Pasifika Student Engagement, Retention and Success*. Wellington: Open Polytechnic.

Shephard, K. (2017) Discovering tertiary education through others' eyes and words: exploring submissions to New Zealand's review of its tertiary education sector. *Journal of Higher Education Policy & Management*, 39(1): 4–19.

Shore, C. (2010) The reform of New Zealand's university system: 'after neoliberalism'. *Learning & Teaching*, 3(1): 1–31.

Simpson, O. (2000) *Supporting Students in Open and Distance Learning*. London: Kogan Page.

Slater, G. (2009) The development of adult and community education policy in New Zealand: insights from Popper. *Journal of Education Policy*, 24(6): 697–716.

Smart, W. (2009) *Ebbs and Flows: Participation in Post-Compulsory Education over the Economic Cycle*. Tertiary Sector Performance Analysis and Reporting, Strategy and System Performance. Wellington: Ministry of Education.

Smith, G.H. (2003) *Kaupapa Māori Theory: Theorizing Indigenous Transformation of Education and Schooling*. Paper presented at the NZARE/AARE Conference, Hyatt Hotel, Auckland.

Stats NZ (2013) *2013 Census Quick Stats: About a Place*. Available at: http://archive.stats.govt.nz/Census/2013-census/profile-and-summary-reports/quickstats-about-a-place.aspx?request_value=13067&tabname=Culturaldiversity

Stats NZ (2016) *Wellbeing Characteristics 2016: Important Characteristics When Defining New Zealand.* Available at: www.stats.govt.nz/topics/society

Taleni, T., Macfarlane, S., Macfarlane, A. and Fletcher, J. (2018) Tofa liuliu ma le tofa saili a ta'ita'i Pasefika: listening to the voices of Pasifika community leaders. *New Zealand Journal of Educational Studies*, 53(2): 177–192.

Tertiary Education Commission (2017) *Pasifika Operational Strategy 2017–2020.* Wellington: Tertiary Education Commission.

Tertiary Education Commission (2018) *Investment Plan Assessment Framework.* Wellington: Tertiary Education Commission.

Zepke, N. (2009) A future for adult lifelong education in Aotearoa New Zealand: neoliberal or cosmopolitan? *International Journal of Lifelong Education*, 28(6): 751–761.

20
COUNTRY PROFILE: FINLAND

Jane Pither and Natalie Morris

Key words – trust; teacher autonomy; long-term education planning; PISA; assessment; inclusivity

Introduction

This chapter provides an overview of the Finnish further and adult education (FAE) system. It aims to draw out some of the key points about Finnish FAE that are different from English FAE.

Finnish education became visible outside Finland in the early part of the twenty-first century when the Organisation for Economic Co-operation and Development's Programme for International Student Assessment (PISA) results (e.g. OECD, 2010) were published and Finland was at the top of the league table. The UK did not feature in the top 10. It became clear that Finland has a distinctive approach to education.

This derives from the overarching ethos of Finnish education, which, according to Sahlberg (2015), is not to come top of league tables (even though they routinely do), but '[to create] a socially fair and inclusive education system that provides everyone with the opportunity to fulfil their intentions and dreams through education' (p62). Prominent on the Ministry of Education and Culture (*Opetus -ja kulttuuriministeriö*) website is the statement that the system is designed to offer 'equal opportunities for education for all' (OKM, 2018). This has been a key driver for Finland throughout the development of its education policies, in line with its establishment of a modern welfare state.

In Finland, education across all levels is free at point of access (with the exception of early childhood education before the age of 6 and some adult education). Unlike the rigidly prescriptive approach of English Early Years education, Finnish preschool is pedagogically planned, supporting the individual child's development, and follows a National Core Curriculum for Early Childhood Education and Care (OPH, 2018a).

Compulsory education starts at the age of 7 and finishes at the age of 16. Formal basic education takes place within a comprehensive school (*peruskoulu*) system. After this, students can choose between a general upper secondary school (*lukio*), leading to a national matriculation certificate after three years, or a vocational upper secondary school (*ammatillinen oppilaitos*), achieving a competence-based upper secondary qualification after three years. Qualifications from both pathways allow progression to higher education. This access is an important element in the design of the vocational education system in Finland.

Despite recent slippage in international league tables, the Finns have not changed their fundamental educational purpose (based on equal opportunities for all) nor some of their more significant policies; for example:

- starting formal education later;

- focusing on individual development;

- holding national testing only at the age of 18–19; and

- valuing the professionalism of teachers.

How does Finland help its pupils and students to engage in education and to achieve consistently high standards? To understand this, we need to explore the ethos of education within this remarkable country.

Finland – the country

Key questions

What is distinctive about Finland?

Location and language

Finland is in Northern Europe, bordered by Norway, Sweden and Russia. Part of it lies within the Arctic Circle and its southern shores are broadly in the same latitude as the Shetland Islands. The country is largely rural, with a total population of about 5.6 million, over 1 million of whom live in the Helsinki (the capital) conurbation.

Finland has two official languages, Finnish and Swedish. Finnish is not related to Scandinavian languages such as Danish and Swedish, but is derived from Finno-Ugric languages far to the east, having common roots with Hungarian. Swedish-speaking Finns can participate in education from preschool to university in their first language. English is also widely spoken and is offered in most schools from the third grade (age 9).

History

For much of modern times, Finland belonged to Sweden but became a Grand Duchy of Russia in 1809. In common with many other countries during the nineteenth century, a nationalist movement led to the achievement of independence from Russia in 1917. Notably, women gained the vote in 1906, and in 1907 Finland elected 19 women Members of Parliament. This number has been rising steadily since then.

Finland is therefore a young country and has been independent since 1917, although during the Second World War it fought the Winter War with Russia (1939–1940) and engaged in a military coalition with Germany, but subsequently fought against them in 1944–1945. As a result, its borders were redefined in favour of Russia at the end of the war. However, it was never occupied, and subsequently Finland has been respected for its neutrality. Finland joined the European Union (EU) in 1995 and its currency is the euro. Finland does not have a monarch, but elects a president every five years.

Education

While Finland is smaller than some other OECD countries, the numbers in education aren't small. Table 20.1 shows a broad comparison with England. Although the levels of education do not match exactly and the demographic profile may be slightly different, it is clear that the percentage of the population engaged in combined vocational and adult education in Finland (15.63 per cent of the total population) is far higher than in England (5.93 per cent of the total population). The overall percentage of the population engaged in education in Finland is also noticeably higher.

Table 20.1   Numbers of students in education in Finland and England

	Finland (2017)		England (2016/17)	
	Numbers (thousands)	Percentage of total population	Numbers (thousands)	Percentage of total population
Comprehensive education	544 (from age 7 to 16)	9.87	8,669 (from age 5 to 18)	15.69
Upper secondary education	137	2.49	-	-
Vocational education	215	3.89	3,282	5.93
Adult education	647	11.74		
Higher education	303	5.49	1,892	3.42
Total in education	1,846	33.48	13,843	25.04
Total population	5,513	100	55,268	100

Sources: Department for Education (2017), Government UK (2017), Higher Education Statistics Agency (2018), Office for National Statistics (2017) and Statistics Finland (2018a, 2018b)

Finland's further and adult education policy

Key questions

How does Finland's further and adult education policy differ from England's?

History of FAE policy

FAE policies are designed to encourage the development of skills in a knowledge-based economy. This has been a relatively new approach, as industrialisation only took hold in Finland after the Second World War, requiring the development of different skills. Prior to that, Finland's economy had largely been agrarian. More recently, in order to increase the reach of vocational education routes, the links between vocational upper schools and universities have been strengthened. The overarching aims are to ensure that students are ready for working life, but also to foster lifelong learning and the development of further skills in the workplace (Sahlberg, 2015).

Planning

Finland's further and adult education (FAE) is fully integrated into its overall education system, unlike the English system. This system (as described in the first section) is relatively new, universal education having been legally established after the Second World War, with a comprehensive school arrangement being introduced in 1970.

Unlike England, the Ministry plans the national education structures and strategy through a series of five-year plans, building in a more measured approach to reform. This is translated into a high-level curriculum plan by the Finnish National Agency for Education (*Opetus hallitus*) (OPH, 2018b). Provider structures and pedagogic approaches are then determined through consultation at the local level. Municipalities are encouraged to consider local conditions, such as the economy and culture, when creating curriculum content.

Funding of education

Vocational upper secondary education is free, although students pay for textbooks and materials. Meals are free and travel costs are reimbursed. After initial VET courses, students may be charged a fee for further or specialist vocational training. Some adult education is self-funded or provided by employers (e.g. apprenticeship training and staff development).

Although funding has become tighter over the last 10 years (since the recession in 2008), Finland still offers free education for young people and unemployed adults and subsidises other adult education. Some funding is allocated centrally from the national budget, whereas other funding is contributed by the municipalities. Finland has also attracted European funding to support some of its initiatives. There is a greater overall public investment in education in Finland (5.6 per cent of GDP in 2015) than in England (4.2 per cent). However, there is more private investment in education in England (1.9 per cent of GDP in 2015) than in Finland (0.1 per cent) (OECD, 2018). This clearly relates to the contrasting views of education in the two countries. The Finnish state aims to provide a fair education system as an entitlement of an inclusive society (OKM, 2018), whereas in England education is increasingly viewed as a commodity within a market state.

Initial vocational education and training (IVET)

Initial vocational education is delivered in schools at upper secondary level (16–19-year-olds) running in parallel with general upper secondary education. Students apply to enter the vocational upper secondary schools after basic education, or may remain in basic education for an extra year to ensure they are ready for this next step.

Approximately 42 per cent of young people followed this IVET pathway in 2016; this has increased from 36 per cent in 2001. Overall, 95.2 per cent of young people entered upper secondary education in 2016 (OPH, 2018b). However, although many successfully complete their education, Finland has also had concerns about both the levels of youth unemployment and the levels of those not engaged in education, employment or training (NEETs). A Youth Guarantee (*nuoristakuu*) was introduced in 2014 to offer every unemployed young person under 30 work or education and training within three months of becoming unemployed (Youth Guarantee, 2018). Initial information suggests that the level of NEETs is slowly falling and youth unemployment is beginning to decline (Eurostats, 2018).

Adult education

The Finnish policy on adult education began with the objectives of improving the literacy of the general population, providing access to qualifications and also supporting non-accredited and leisure-based learning. Adult education is offered in upper secondary schools for adults wishing to sit the matriculation exam or a vocational certificate, as well as in specific adult vocational educational centres. Adults are also encouraged to continue formal education at the universities and universities of applied science. There are also courses for unemployed adults, which are publicly funded, and courses based in the workplace, where some are subsidised and some are paid for by the employer.

Lifelong learning is encouraged and promoted in Finland. There are many opportunities across the country for both job-related and informal learning. Finland has a high percentage of adults who access learning (both formal and informal) on an annual basis (27.4 per cent in 2017), according to Eurostats (2018). This is significantly above the UK percentage of 14.3 per cent and the EU average of 10.9 per cent for the same period.

Special educational needs and disabilities

Finnish policy is that students with special educational needs and disabilities (SEND) are routinely taught in mainstream schools as part of a preventative approach to SEN. This leads to a relatively high number of students receiving support at primary-age stages, but fewer students needing support in the later stages of their education, including vocational education (Perry and Wilson, 2015). This is a key part of the inclusive ethos of Finnish education, and is based on the principle that many of us will need additional support to reach our goals at some point in our lives (Sahlberg, 2015).

Structure of Finnish further and adult education (FAE)

Key questions

How do Finnish structures for FAE compare with English structures?

Finnish vocational upper secondary schools (*ammatillinen oppilaitos*) are run, in the main, by the regional municipal authorities. On receipt of a licence from the Ministry, municipalities (local authorities) interpret the national policies and educational objectives set by the Ministry and the Finnish National Agency for Education to decide on funding allocations and curriculum requirements within their municipalities. The individual providers then make their own administrative arrangements to provide educational services and teachers determine the pedagogies that will be used. There are currently 96 vocational upper secondary schools, offering provision to some 179,000 students as of 2017, both IVET students and adult learners (Statistics Finland, 2017).

Of these schools, some work collaboratively with other education partners, often combining a vocational upper secondary school and an adult vocational and workplace learning centre, and, in the case of the Kuopio municipality, a folk high school (Pohjois Savon Opisto) (Finnish Folkschool Association, 2018) with a UAS campus. Some specialise in particular subjects (e.g. culinary, tourism and business, or welfare and culture). Most serve between 1,000 and 5,000 16–19-year-olds and adults. Most vocational schools have a managing committee and are led by a principal who has both teaching and higher academic qualifications, as well as a qualification in educational administration.

Adult vocational education centres (*ammatillinen aikuiskoulutuskeskus*) are smaller organisations and may be run alongside vocational colleges. They are financed by the municipality, although employers may pay for some training. In 2017, there were 20, accommodating 27,600 students (Statistics Finland, 2017). Liberal adult education takes place through a range of providers and formats – for example, summer universities (*kesäyliopisto*) and adult education centres (*kansalaisopisto*) – engaging an overall 553,000 students in 2017 (Statistics Finland, 2017).

Universities of applied science offer vocational degrees at various levels. Such courses are free, although continuing education courses (offered by all universities) may be fee-paying.

The variety of providers and offers contributes to high levels of adult education engagement in Finland, supporting the Finnish value of inclusion and the Finnish belief that social as well as economic benefits arise from lifelong learning.

Case study

Oulu Vocational College

The Oulu Vocational College (*Oulun seudun ammattiopisto*, OSAO) (one of the largest colleges in Finland) is run by the Oulu Region Joint Authority for Education (*Oulun seudun koulutuskuntayhtymä*) to 'provide education services rooted in practical work life, anticipating the challenges of the future'. The authority's general assembly runs the college through a board, to whom the college director/principal reports. The college is divided into eight business units, in different parts of the region, with a joint services section. There are approximately 10,000 students and the college employs about 900 staff (65 per cent of whom are teachers). In 2018, over 2,500 students graduated from OSAO, 87 of them having passed the matriculation examination alongside their vocational programme.

A wide range of programmes is offered, but 46 per cent of students study technology and transport with a further 18 per cent undertaking social services, health and sport courses. Six per cent of students study natural resources and the environment. The college offers apprenticeships, labour relations training and management training, in addition to both IVET and further and specialist vocational qualifications as well as short courses. As well as emphasising the partnerships between local employers and the college for workplace learning, as well as staff development and premises hire, OSAO facilitates its students learning in other parts of Europe.

OSAO Edu Ltd provides visits and training packages for international professionals who are interested in vocational education and training. Themes include operational culture, school management, learning environments, entrepreneurship, and learning methods and teaching. Student groups are also encouraged to experience cultural exchanges in northern Finland, as well as to learn more about vocational education or to study English language.

The college also showcases its position in the community by offering services to the community such as housebuilding, car repairs and dressmaking.

Source: Produced with kind assistance from Oulu Vocational College (2018)

Finnish students

Key questions

How does the Finnish student experience differ from an English one?

A breakdown of the number of hours spent on each subject in comprehensive schools can be found in Figure 20.1. One of the features of the Finnish allocation of school hours is the allocation of time to subjects that may be considered 'softer' by the English education system, such as art and design. Thirty-three per cent of teaching time is dedicated to subjects such as physical education, arts, crafts, music, social studies and religious studies; another 28 per cent of teaching hours are allocated to science and maths, leaving 33 per cent for languages (both foreign and domestic) and 6 per cent for optional subjects. By contrast, England does not dictate the number of hours each subject must be taught, but does dictate the subjects that are compulsory at each curriculum stage. For example, English, maths, physical education, computing and science are mandatory throughout compulsory education, but most other subjects stop being compulsory at age 14, allowing students to make GCSE subject choices. Some subjects are only compulsory later on, such as languages (ages 7–14) and citizenship (ages 11–16) (Department for Education, 2014).

The Finnish government guidelines provide a broad base of education before students enter upper secondary education. The post-16 curriculum has been recently refined to ensure a more successful transition from lower secondary school. Students are guided towards future study and encouraged to focus study effort towards their aims. Methods of teaching have been harmonised from lower to upper secondary school to focus on student-centred learning (Sahlberg, 2015).

What do they do next?

As outlined earlier, at the age of 16, Finnish students can choose to continue into post-compulsory education, via either an academic or vocational pathway. Both of these options provide qualifications and allow students to move into tertiary (undergraduate) education. There are 14 'research-based' universities (*yliopisto*) in Finland, including the University of Helsinki, a Times

100 university, and 25 universities of applied science (UASs) or polytechnics (*ammattikorkeakoulu*) (OKM, 2018). There are clear pathways from vocational upper secondary school into both university sectors and opportunities to transfer between the sectors. Doctoral research is only carried out in the research universities.

The UASs were established during the 1990s to provide vocational higher education, and have succeeded in expanding vocational opportunities at bachelor's and master's levels to the extent that many who would not previously have gained access to higher education became beneficiaries of it (Jorgensen, 2018; OKM, 2018). In 2017, 20,266 students enrolled at the universities, while 37,573 enrolled at the UASs (Education Statistics Finland, 2018).

Careers guidance

Careers guidance counsellors often have teaching qualifications, with an additional qualification in guidance and up to master's-level qualification in counselling (Kavlak, 2018). Careers guidance and counselling is available throughout the education system in Finland. In VET, the support focuses on the students drawing up their own plans and reviewing their own progress towards learning goals. About 60 hours of guidance and counselling are provided at this stage, coordinated by guidance counsellors (CIMO, 2014).

NEETs

While careers services make a significant difference to the outcomes for students in Finland (Kavlak, 2018), there are still students that become classed as NEET (not in education, employment or training). In 2017, 15–24-year-old NEETs in Finland were recorded as 9.4 per cent of the age group, compared with 10.3 per cent across the UK (Eurostats, 2018) and about 18.7% across Europe (Eurofound, 2017). Both sets of data have shown a decline in recent years. In both the UK and Finland, about 50 per cent of those classified as NEET are deemed to be unemployed, with the other 50 per cent deemed to be inactive in the labour and education markets.

Finnish teachers

Key questions

What role do teachers play in higher educational outcomes in Finland?

There are five types of teacher in Finland:

- *Kindergarten teachers*: licensed to teach preschool children and kindergarten children.

- *Primary school teachers*: normally assigned to one grade (school year) between grades 1 and 6, and teach a range of subjects.

- *Subject teachers*: teach specific subjects (but often more than one) in the upper grades of basic education (grades 7–9) in upper secondary school and in vocational schools.

- *Special education teachers*: either work with individuals or small intervention groups in mainstream schools.

- *Vocational teachers*: teach in upper secondary and vocational schools.

(Perry and Wilson, 2015; Sahlberg, 2015)

Finnish teachers are required to undertake training to master's level before they can teach (with the exception of vocational teachers, who must undertake three years of classroom teaching before they can complete a vocational teacher education programme). They are held in very high regard among the population. This originates from the change from Russian oversight to Finnish independence in 1917. State schools were greatly expanded at this time, partly to increase the sense of Finnishness among the population. Schools, and therefore teachers, were tasked with spreading this message, and as a result Finnish teachers are regarded as the transmitters of Finnish identity. While this may be the backdrop for the way Finnish teachers are viewed by their society, this is reinforced by the high level of training that teachers undertake, leading to a perceived level of professionalism unrivalled by most countries (Sahlberg, 2015).

Only 13 institutions across Finland have teacher education departments. This small number means that a high level of quality assurance and consistency across teacher education curricula can be achieved. Once teachers are qualified, there is no quality assurance system in place; they are trusted as professionals to carry out their jobs. This is an alien concept in England, but one that continues to produce excellent results for Finnish students.

Programmes and forms of continuing professional development (CPD) are agreed at employer (usually municipality) level and municipalities are required to fund at least three days of CPD per year for all teachers. Additionally, Finnish teachers are expected to carry out 35 hours of self-directed learning each year. This learning is not monitored or tracked by any external system. Instead, teachers are allowed to decide their own learning needs and how they wish to address them. Local autonomy is a strength of the Finnish system as it allows schools and teachers to respond to their own needs. In comparison, the English system places far more emphasis on a centralised, standardised approach. Sometimes Finnish schools want a more centralised support network, and some networks do exist to support schools with CPD needs.

Case study

Innokas: Finland's first ICT network for teacher CPD

Innokas is a network that promotes innovation education and technology in education in Finland. It was founded approximately 10 years ago in one school, in Espoo. The city decided that they wanted to provide in-service training for teachers and created learning centres for schools. Within one of these schools, Innokas was tasked with running the first Innovation and Technology Education Centre (ITEC).

(Continued)

(Continued)

The role of the ITEC was to provide training to in-service teachers training within Espoo. This quickly spread and a network was built from the original. Now based in the Faculty of Education Science at the University of Helsinki, Innokas has regional teams in 10 different areas of Finland: Espoo, Turku, Tampere, Jyväskylä, Kontiolahti, Kuopio, Lappeenranta, Larsmo, Oulu and Rovaniemi. Innokas is now able to offer a more extensive level of support, and the Innokas network 'organises professional development programs, research, events, and consultation for teachers' (**www.innokas.fi/en/**).

A key achievement of the Innokas network is the creation of a network of teacher education departments between several cities. Previously, each city department would carry out their own training, but the Innokas network has brought these cities together to share best practice and ideas, and standardise the approaches taken by each local participant in the use of innovation and technology in education. It is used to provide advice for teaching and learning, as well as technology products that schools can use to meet their own needs. There is a strong emphasis on partnership that now extends to youth services, libraries, municipalities and companies.

As well as in-service training for new teachers, Innokas is able to provide workshops for existing staff, ensuring that teachers are able to use the latest pedagogies with students. The majority of projects are funded by the Finnish government, but schools and companies can also buy training sessions from Innokas.

Innokas also carries out international research, working with countries such as China and the US. The aim of the Global Innokas network activity is to extend the development of the innovative school and the sharing of knowledge across national borders. Following the Finnish Innokas network model, the Global Innokas network builds on the principles of grass-roots collaboration between participating schools and networks and the versatile use of technology.

Autonomy and consistency in teaching

Students, parents and schools trust their teachers and allow them a high level of autonomy. Finnish teachers are held accountable to themselves and to their students, not to any external bodies (Paronen and Lappi, 2018). This intrinsic motivation might be attributed to the careful selection process of trainee teachers, or it may be due to the high levels of respect shown to teachers.

On a visit to Finnish schools in 2018, Finnish teachers described locking their classroom once the students had entered as this was 'their classroom'. This concept is an unusual one to English teachers, but one that seems to be working for Finnish teachers and students. What is particularly surprising, considering the level of autonomy Finnish teachers are afforded, is the level of consistency observed within Finnish schools. Consistency across schools and teachers within the country has equated to high consistency in PISA scores, even though the scores have dipped more recently. Updating previously successful systems to ensure they will continue to deliver education in the Finnish tradition is now a challenge for teachers, municipalities and the government (Sahlberg, 2015).

Interestingly, Finnish vocational teachers taught fewer hours (688 per year) than the English average (817 per year) at upper secondary level in 2015 (OECD, 2018, Table D4.1) and their pay was well above that of their English counterparts: $56,220 per annum in Finland, $45,343 per annum in England (OECD, 2018, Table D3).

Curriculum and assessment

Key questions

Can less assessment lead to more learning?

Assessment for learning outcomes

Finland does not have a national education inspection system. Instead, quality assurance is carried out through self-evaluation of provision by teachers and their institutions. However, there is a national evaluation of learning outcomes, carried out on a thematic basis by the Finnish Education Evaluation Centre (*Kansallinen Koulutuksen Arviointikeskus*, KARVI). This Centre evaluates all education, from early years to higher education, unlike the English systems. These evaluations are used for improvement by the institutions and nationally for finding out how the national objectives have been reached. There is no ranking of institutions (Finnish Education Evaluation Centre, 2018).

The principle of trust between local authority and education providers in Finland leaves the responsibility for the assessment of learning in the hands of the providers: 'The essential principles of system evaluation are linked to transparency and trust, and an interaction between the evaluators and those evaluated' (Räisänen and Räkköläinen, 2014, p109).

In the classroom, Finnish teachers are responsible for determining the frequency, timing and subject of assessments for their pupils themselves. Despite this level of autonomy, a high level of standardisation in assessment is found across Finland. It has been found that Finnish teachers rely heavily on the use of high-quality textbooks (Norris et al., 1996), which could go some way in explaining the high levels of consistency in teaching, learning and assessment across Finland. Textbooks were formerly approved by the Finnish National Board of Education and, while they no longer do this, the text books published are co-created with highly experienced teachers, are research-based, and are published by a small number of publishing houses (Crehan, 2016). This is analogous with the teacher education process in Finland: low numbers of very high-quality resources with a high level of quality assurance.

Just like the providers' self-assessment, student assessment in Finland is designed to provide meaningful feedback in order to improve learning outcomes. Formative assessment is found to produce significant learning gains (Black et al., 2003), whereas high-stakes external testing can have the opposite effect and can hinder the learning process. In addition to teacher-led formative assessment, students are encouraged to peer and self-assess regularly. Standardised testing only happens up to twice during the students' school careers; all students receive a final assessment of secondary education, carried out by the teacher using samples of work from a two-year period. Students that wish to continue education will sit a matriculation exam, administered at the end of upper secondary school. This is the only externally set, high-stakes assessment taken by students in Finland. Information from student assessment is not shared outside the school.

Assessment in IVET follows a similar pattern to other school-based assessment, but also involves competence assessments and skills demonstrations.

Apprenticeships

Apprenticeship programmes are financially supported by both the state, which pays for training in an upper secondary school or adult vocational education centre, and the employer, who pays wages to the apprentice during the period of the apprenticeship contract (the costs of workplace training are reimbursed to the employer, however). Apprenticeships are generally undertaken by adults and, although growing in popularity more recently, are not on a large scale in Finland. In line with the overall policy of flexibility for students and equity between vocational and academic courses, an apprenticeship qualification can provide access to a degree course.

In 2017, 50,539 Finns were following an apprenticeship route, of which 55.5 per cent were female (Education Statistics Finland, 2018), which represents 0.9 per cent of the total population. By contrast, 1.6 per cent of the population was following an apprenticeship route in England in 2016, with 912,200 participating (House of Commons, 2018).

Role of employers

The challenge for vocational education and training, as in most countries, is to ensure that the school-based curriculum delivers what employers require. Finland has addressed this through a policy of strong cooperation between employers, unions, teachers, administrators and communities, developed over the last 50 years, although it is true to say the balance and strength of the partnerships has changed over this time (Olsen et al., 2018, p141). This operates at national and local (municipality) levels. The most recent consultations between these partnerships have led to increasing the amount of workplace learning included in the VET curriculum and allowing skills to be assessed through demonstrations of competence, to ensure that VET continues to meet the needs of the workplace (Sahlberg, 2015).

Future trends

Key questions

How is Finnish FAE policy changing?

As with other parts of their education system, the Finnish government reviews FAE systems and policies on a five-year cycle in a structured way, unlike England. After consultation and debate, from 2015 to 2017, the latest reforms were introduced in 2018. The Ministry for Education and Culture's own diagram (see Figure 20.1) summarises the intended operation, designed to reform the whole system in a single set of changes.

The aim of this FAE reform is to streamline this part of the education system. In line with previous reforms, the number of VET qualifications is reduced (originally 351, currently 164). However, students and employers will still understand the qualifications because the changes involve bringing subjects together. In order to reduce bureaucracy and make things simpler for providers, there will be a single set of qualifications for both young people and adults. The final reform has been to ensure portability

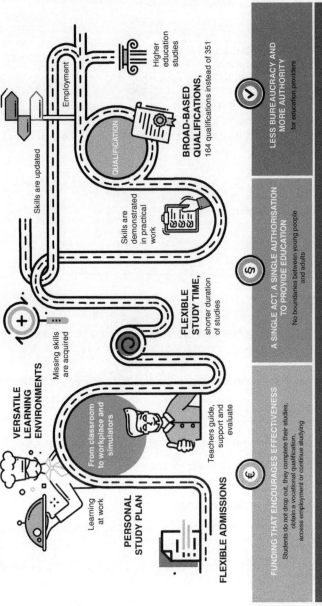

NEW VOCATIONAL EDUCATION AND TRAINING as of 1 January 2018

Working life is undergoing changes. New occupations keep on emerging and old ones disappear. Technology advances. Revenue models are renewed. Students' needs are becoming more and more individualistic. Skills need to be updated throughout careers.

VERSATILE LEARNING ENVIRONMENTS

Missing skills are acquired

From classroom to workplace and simulators

Learning at work

PERSONAL STUDY PLAN

FLEXIBLE ADMISSIONS

Teachers guide, support and evaluate

Skills are updated

Skills are demonstrated in practical work

Employment

Higher education studies

QUALIFICATION

FLEXIBLE STUDY TIME, shorter duration of studies

BROAD-BASED QUALIFICATIONS, 164 qualifications instead of 351

FUNDING THAT ENCOURAGES EFFECTIVENESS

Students do not drop out, they complete their studies, obtain a vocational qualification, access employment or continue studying

A SINGLE ACT, A SINGLE AUTHORISATION TO PROVIDE EDUCATION

No boundaries between young people and adults

LESS BUREAUCRACY AND MORE AUTHORITY

for education providers

#AMISREFORMI

OPETUS- JA KULTTUURIMINISTERIÖ
UNDERVISNINGS- OCH KULTURMINISTERIET

Figure 20.1   Reform of vocational education

Source: Reproduced by kind permission of the Ministry of Education and Culture, Finland (OKM, 2018)

of qualifications to harmonise the Finnish VET system with the European Qualification Framework and the European Credit System for VET (OKM, 2018b). This is unlikely to take effect in England. However, as in England, it is expected there will be fewer providers following this reform.

Although necessitated by funding shortages, these revisions were drawn up to preserve the underpinning themes of Finnish education:

- flexibility;

- catering for individual students' needs;

- providing access either to work or to higher education; and

- reinforcing the important role of teachers.

Finally, the Ministry has continued to stress that there continues to be a clear and important professional role for teachers:

- in curriculum planning;

- in school-level student assessment; and

- in fostering learning.

Chapter summary

Although this chapter provides only a brief overview of Finnish FAE, some key features have been brought out:

- Finnish education system developed alongside social and economic development in the twentieth century.

- High levels of participation in FAE.

- Full integration of vocational education with other parts of the national system.

- Clear links between planning and design of the education system and the Finnish ethos for education.

- Central planning and local decision-making.

- Opportunities for learning at different stages of life and in different ways, with a broad range of providers.

- Recognition of the importance of good and evolving relationships with employers to ensure the relevance of vocational training.

- Ongoing concerns about NEETs.

- Teachers play an important part in FAE.

- Little external testing of students.

- No inspection system, but a developmental self-evaluation of providers.

- Challenges of maintaining free education with declining budgets.

These play contributory parts in what Finland considers important in its inclusive education policy – equity and parity of esteem.

Further recommended reading

Desjardins, R. (2017) *Political Economy of Adult Learning Systems*. London: Bloomsbury Academic.

Jorgensen, C.H., Olsen, O.J. and Thunqvist, D.P. (eds) (2018) *Vocational Education in the Nordic Countries: Learning from Diversity*. London: Routledge.

Meinander, H. (2011). *A History of Finland*. London: C. Hurst & Co.

Michelsen, S. and Stenström, M.-L. (eds) (2018) *Vocational Education in the Nordic Countries: The Historical Evolution*. London: Routledge.

OPH (2017) *Finnish Education in a Nutshell*. Available at: www.oph.fi/download/171176_finnish_education_in_a_nutshell.pdf

References

Black, P., Harrison, C., Lee, C., Marshall, B. and Wiliam, D. (2003) *Assessment for Learning: Putting It into Practice*. Maidenhead: Open University Press.

CIMO (2014) *Lifelong Guidance in Finland*. Available at: www.cimo.fi/instancedata/prime_product_julkaisu/cimo/embeds/cimowwwstructure/25493_Lifelong_guidance_in_Finland.pdf

Crehan, L. (2016) *Clever Lands: The Secrets behind the Success of the World's Education Superpowers*. London: Unbound.

Department for Education (2014) *National Curriculum in England: Framework for Key Stages 1 to 4*. Available at: www.gov.uk/government/publications/national-curriculum-in-england-framework-for-key-stages1-to-4/the-national-curriculum-in-england-framework-for-key-stages-1-to-4

Department for Education (2017) *Education and Training Statistics for the United Kingdom 2017*. Available at: https://assets.publishing.service.gov.uk/government/uploads/system/uploads/attachment_data/file/657821/SFR64_2017_Text.pdf

Education Statistics Finland (2018) *Applicants Admitted, Students and Completers in Vocational Education and Training – Apprenticeships*. Available at: https://vipunen.fi/en-gb/_layouts/15/xlviewer.aspx?id=/en-gb/Reports/Ammatillinen%20koulutus%20-%20analyysi_EN.xlsb

Eurofound (2017) *European Semester Thematic Factsheet: Youth Employment – 2017*. Available at: https://ec.europa.eu/info/sites/info/files/file_import/european-semester_thematic-factsheet_youth_employment_en.pdf

Eurostats (2018) *Population and Social Conditions Tables (Education and Training)*. Available at: https://ec.europa.eu/eurostat/data/database

Finnish Education Evaluation Centre (2018) *Finnish Education Evaluation Centre*. Available at: https://karvi.fi/en/

Finnish Folkschool Association (2018) *Pohjois Savon Opisto*. Available at: www.kansanopistot.fi/?sivu=kartta&opisto=165

Government UK (2017) *Schools, Pupils and Their Characteristics: January 2017 Table 2a*. Available at: www.gov.uk/government/statistics/schools-pupils-and-their-characteristics-january-2017

Higher Education Statistics Agency (2018) *HE Student Enrolments by Level of Study (England) 2016/17*. Available at: www.hesa.ac.uk/news/11-01-2018/sfr247-higher-education-student-statistics/numbers

House of Commons (2018) *Apprenticeship Statistics: England*. Available at: https://researchbriefings.parliament.uk/ResearchBriefing/Summary/SN06113#fullreport

Jorgensen, C.H., Olsen, O.J. and Thunqvist, D.P. (eds) (2018) *Vocational Education in the Nordic Countries: Learning from Diversity*. London: Routledge.

Kavlak, Y. (2018) *Perceptions and Experiences of Finnish Upper-Secondary School Students Regarding Guidance and Counselling Services*. Available at: https://jyx.jyu.fi/handle/123456789/58776?show=full

Norris, N., Asplund, R., MacDonald, B., Schostak, J. and Zamorski, B. (1996) *An Independent Evaluation of Comprehensive Curriculum Reform in Finland*. Helsinki: National Board of Education.

OECD (2010) *PISA 2009 Results: Learning Trends – Vol V*. Available at: www.oecd-ilibrary.org/education/pisa-2009-results-learning-trends_9789264091580-en

OECD (2018) *Education at a Glance 2018*. Available at: www.oecd-ilibrary.org/docserver/eag-2018-en.pdf?expires=1539682491&id=id&accname=guest&checksum=2319ED7A989AC7671E878B453C87F3BC

Office for National Statistics (2017) *UK Population 2017*. Available at: www.ons.gov.uk/peoplepopulationandcommunity/populationandmigration/populationestimates/bulletins/annualmidyearpopulationestimates/mid2017

OKM (2018) *Reform of Vocational Upper Secondary Education*. Available at: https://minedu.fi/en/reform-of-vocational-upper-secondary-education

Olsen, O.J., Thunqvist, D.P. and Hallqvist, A. (2018) Building and construction: a critical case for the future of vocational education. In C.H. Jorgensen, O.J. Olsen and D.P. Thunqvist (eds), *Vocational Education in the Nordic Countries: Learning from Diversity*. London: Routledge.

OPH (2012) *Distribution of Lesson Hours in Basic Education*. Available at: www.oph.fi/download/179422_distribution_of_lesson_hours_in_basic_education_2012.pdf

OPH (2018a) *Early Childhood Education and Care*. Available at: www.oph.fi/english/education_system/early_childhood_education

OPH (2018b) *Education in Finland*. Available at: www.oph.fi/download/175015_education_in_Finland.pdf

Oulu Vocational College (2018) *Oulu Vocational College*. Available at: www.osao.fi/en/front-page.html

Paronen, P. and Lappi, O. (2018) *Finnish Teachers and Principals in Figures*. Available at: www.oph.fi/download/189802_finnish_teachers_and_principals_in_figures.pdf

Perry, C. and Wilson, J. (2015) *Special Educational Needs in Finland*. Available at: www.niassembly.gov.uk/globalassets/documents/raise/publications/2015/education/9015.pdf

Räisänen, A. and Räkköläinen, M. (2014) Assessment of learning outcomes in Finnish vocational education and training. *Assessment in Education: Principles, Policy & Practice*, 21(1): 109–124.

Sahlberg, P. (2015) *Finnish Lessons 2.0: What Can the World Learn from Educational Change in Finland?* New York: Teachers College, Columbia University.

Statistics Finland (2017) *Educational Institutions of the School System and Number of Students by Type of Educational Institution in 2017*. Available at: www.tilastokeskus.fi/til/kjarj_2017_2018-02-13_tie_001_en.html

Statistics Finland (2018a) *Population by Sex in 1750 to 2017*. Available at: http://pxnet2.stat.fi/PXWeb/sq/707cc7a0-58f1-4de0-85f6-16db59076dea

Statistics Finland (2018b) *Number of New Students in Vocational Training*. Available at: www.tilastokeskus.fi/til/aop/2017/aop_2017_2018-09-27_tie_001_en.html

Youth Guarantee (2018) *Nuorisotakuu*. Available at: https://nuorisotakuu.fi/en/frontpage

21

MENTAL HEALTH AND WELL-BEING IN THE POST-COMPULSORY SECTOR

Nichola Kentzer, Jane Dudeney and Janet Lord

Key words - mental health; well-being; institute role; strategy; emotional labour; therapeutic turn

Introduction

Mental health and well-being has become a key policy priority in the United Kingdom (UK). Recent concerning statistics that 50 per cent of mental health problems are established by the age of 17 years and 75 per cent are established by the age of 24 years (Mental Health Taskforce, 2016) place the education sectors, including further and adult education (FAE), firmly on the front line of this growing issue. Indeed, in 2015, the National Union of Students (NUS) highlighted a 70 per cent increase in the rates of depression and anxiety among teenagers both in higher and further education. Sadly, it is not only the student body that is affected by poor mental health. In 2017, the *Mental Health at Work* report highlighted that 60 per cent of employees had experienced mental health issues due to work, or where work was a related factor, underlining the vulnerability of staff (Business in the Community, 2017).

Drawing on a range of literature, this chapter takes the view that well-being for students and staff in the FAE sector is of key importance and recognises the valuable role that it can play in addressing the mental health of young people and adults. Although it is encouraging that 92 per cent of colleges have structures in place to support the mental health and well-being of staff and 81 per cent have a focus on student mental well-being embedded into tutorial work (AoC, 2017a), significantly more can be done. This chapter approaches this important topic area by offering case studies, reflective questions and exercises on how to improve mental health and well-being, and suggests a number of tools that may be useful in facilitating well-being outcomes for both students and staff. Throughout, staff and student well-being will be seen as symbiotic and an equal focus will be put on both.

Nichola Kentzer et al.

Mental health and well-being: a contemporary issue in education

Key questions

Why should mental health and well-being be a key issue for FAE?

The FAE sector cannot ignore the scale of the mental health issues faced by the population (see Figure 21.1) due to its diversity and reach (Foster, 2005). The sector caters for students that schools and higher education (HE) 'cannot or will not serve' (Hodgson et al., 2015, p1) and those that could be more vulnerable, having experienced difficulties at school (Warwick et al., 2008). Moreover, FAE

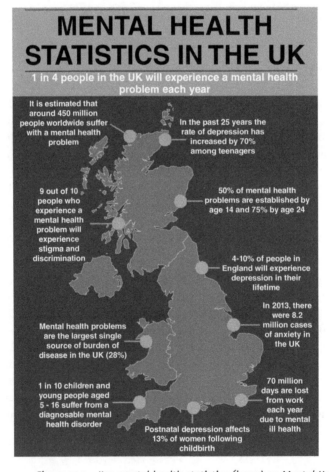

Figure 21.1   Key mental health statistics (based on Mental Health Taskforce, 2016)

Source: BelievePerform (2018)

makes a substantial commitment to students with additional needs (Perry and Davies, 2015). Whereas this might indicate a potential for an increase in resources to support learners in FAE, funding for 16–18-year-olds in general further education has in fact been cut more sharply since 2009 than is the case with funding for schools, preschool or higher education (Belfield et al., 2018). Perhaps, then, it is not surprising that staff in the FAE sector report experiencing stress (Kinman and Wray, 2013).

Despite these challenges in FAE, the sector has a 'huge potential' (Foster, 2005, p58), and research indicates that FAE can be used as an intervention for individuals with long-term mental health conditions (Morrison and Clift, 2006), hence why the sector should have mental health and well-being as a key agenda.

The importance of mental health and well-being awareness

Mental health is also referred to as 'emotional health' or 'well-being' (Mental Health Foundation, 2018), and 'just like physical health: everybody has it and we need to take care of it' (MIND, 2018). Individuals with positive mental health are associated with being able to make the most of their potential, through being able to think, feel and react in the ways that they need and want to live their lives. They can generally cope with life stressors and engage fully with family, workplace, community and friends. Conversely, poor mental health is associated with individuals who might find the ways that they are thinking, feeling and reacting becoming difficult, or even impossible to cope with. This can often be compounded by a fear of disclosure due to speaking out.

Campaigns such as Time to Change, run by MIND and Rethink Mental Illness, and the recent Mental Health Awareness Week driven by the Mental Health Foundation in May 2018, are playing a significant role in us having a better understanding of the issues, including stigma, surrounding mental health. It is hoped that with increased awareness, more people will be encouraged to seek help and not to struggle in silence. It is important, however, that raising awareness is only the start of the process, and that meaningful action follows.

Key theory

The impact of poor mental health on students and staff in FAE

A recent survey of 105 colleges and sixth form colleges reported that:

* 100% reported having students diagnosed with depression;

* 99% diagnosed with severe anxiety;

* 97% with bipolar disorder; and

* 90% with psychosis.

(AoC, 2017a)

The figures here highlight the scale of the issue. However, there are other factors that can impact both students with mental health concerns and the FAE sector that are not captured by the AoC figures. For example, the average maximum waiting time for a first appointment with childhood and adolescent mental health services (CAMHS) is six months, with nearly 10 months until the start of treatment. Of added concern, CAMHS are turning away almost one-quarter (23 per cent) of young people referred to them from treatment by GPs, teachers, concerned parents and others (Frith, 2016). Furthermore, during these delays in receiving appropriate treatment and support, three out of four parents say that their children's mental health deteriorated while waiting for NHS support, worsened when a child was moving from child to adult services (YoungMinds, 2018).

It is highly likely, therefore, that students who are attending courses in FAE might not have any awareness of their mental health needs, how any such needs might be diagnosed, or how they might be appropriately supported by external services. In addition to the associated 'symptoms' of the common mental health conditions that can significantly impact on lives, poor mental health is linked, unsurprisingly, to an increased risk of disruption to education (NHS, 2015). Indeed, the consequences of mental health problems in childhood and adolescence have been associated with poor educational attainment and poorer longer-term employment prospects (Goodman et al., 2011). Where a provision of mental health support services was in place, college staff noted that this had contributed to student retention, attainment and achievement (Warwick et al., 2008), highlighting the need for the FAE sector to act.

The impact of poor mental health of FAE staff is also an issue. One key characteristic of the sector is absenteeism. Evidence suggests that 12.7 per cent of all absence days (ill health) in the UK can be attributed to mental health conditions (ONS, 2018). Research by MIND (2013) highlighted that more than one in five employees agreed that they called in sick to avoid work when asked how workplace stress had affected them, 14 per cent had resigned, and 42 per cent had considered resigning when asked how workplace stress had affected them. This is of concern to the FAE sector as Kinman and Wray (2013) reported that just over 78 per cent of staff in FE and just over 70 per cent of staff in adult education agreed, or strongly agreed, that they found their job stressful, in a survey of over 7,000 staff. Further, staff that continue to work with poor mental health can have reduced productivity at work (presenteeism). This not only has the potential for substantial costs to employers (McDaid et al., 2011), but has an impact on the student population and on the wider staff team.

The role of the further and adult education sector regarding mental health and well-being

Key questions

What can the FAE sector do to promote positive mental health and well-being?

Although there are existing mental health support services for both adults and young people, the workplace, for staff, is 'an appropriate environment to educate individuals about, and raise awareness of, mental health problems' (Harnois and Gabriel, 2002, p3). For students, their place of study offers the potential to foster the development of resilience and provide opportunities for the delivery of interventions aimed at improving mental health (Murphy and Fonargy, 2012). We will consider how the FAE sector and individual institutes can play a role in promoting positive mental health and well-being in both staff and students.

Examining initiatives at the FAE sector and institutional level for supporting the mental health of students and staff

James (2003) published a report on healthy colleges to establish whether existing standards at the time, such as the Healthy Schools standard initiated by the World Health Organization (WHO, 1993), could be used in the further education sector. While this was based on health as a whole, rather than a focus on mental health, there are a number of points that can be drawn from the discussion. One model considered in the report was the early work by O'Donnell and Gray (1993), based on an Action Research project in Birmingham, that identified key factors for success in achieving a health-promoting college. Here, we can adapt these to direct the focus onto mental health and well-being promotion:

- *Appoint mental health coordinators* – with sufficient time and status.

- *Support from senior management* – making 'mental health and well-being' a key agenda point for decision-making, securing funding and giving work credibility.

- *Cross-college support* – empower the staff and students to establish a whole-college initiative.

- *Access external support* – including the creation of a network with other mental health coordinators in colleges and appropriate professional mental health services (e.g. CAMHS).

(adapted from James, 2003)

Further considering the role of the institution, James (2003) discusses how a health-promoting college could develop a framework to work from that considers the institution, environment, curriculum and relationships. The template presented in James' paper draws further on work by O'Donnell and Gray, and has been adapted here in Table 21.1 to demonstrate how mental health and well-being could be promoted.

Table 21.1   A template of 'health promotion' for a FAE institute

	Institution	Environment	Curriculum	Staff-student relationship
Health-risk behaviour	Mental health awareness, and information on available support mechanisms in induction programmes for staff and students	Provide information on the importance of awareness, and developing resilience	Provide sessions to raise awareness, promote well-being, and develop resilience and other appropriate coping mechanisms	Ensure that mental health and well-being is featured in events and health campaigns
Educational/ rational	Induction programme for staff and students to cover developing personal skills, including time management	Identify parts of the environment that may contribute to negative experiences	Explore causes and manifestations of poor mental health, promote well-being and positive mental health	Promote extracurricular programmes in mental health and well-being

(Continued)

Table 21.1 *(Continued)*

	Institution	Environment	Curriculum	Staff-student relationship
Self-empowerment	Encourage self-help groups	Encourage college members to contribute to maintaining a high-quality physical environment	Develop the skills of resilience, stress management and prevention	Encourage staff and students to expect and give respect and considerations from/to each other
Action for change	Establish a regular practice of reviewing workloads and mental health charter/support structure for staff and students	Prioritise and schedule a programme to upgrade the physical environment	Encourage students to plan and participate in programmes on positive mental health and well-being	Review communication channels between staff and students, develop strategies to increase communication

Source: Adapted from James (2003)

More recently, in June 2017, the Association of Colleges produced a resource pack for colleges to support student and staff mental health and well-being (AoC, 2017b). To examine the detail in the document is beyond the scope of this chapter, but we would recommend that institutions review the document (see the list of useful resources at the end of the chapter) and complete the self-assessment activity presented to examine current provision of mental health and well-being support for students and staff. This baseline will allow a strategy and action plan to be developed from senior management examining eight key areas: ethos and environment; curriculum; student voice; staff development and support; targeted support; parents and carers; external partnerships; and audit and monitoring.

Exemplar models of practices for institutes

Although there is legislation for workplaces and educational establishments to have provisions for physical first aid, there is currently no legislation that states the same for mental health. However, colleges do have a legal duty under the Equality Act 2010 to provide reasonable adjustments for students with disabilities, which includes people with mental illnesses such as schizophrenia, bipolar disorder and depression.

At present, the government are in their second year of commitment to train one member of staff in all state secondary schools in England in mental health first aid. This is not the case for FE colleges, who, unless regional funding is on offer, are expected to fund their own training or source training from other organisations (AoC Create or St John's Ambulance). Indeed, while it is encouraging that 46 per cent of colleges have been able to carry out mental health awareness for all staff and 77 per cent of colleges have staff trained in mental health first aid (AoC, 2017a), this should be a sector-wide priority. Research has shown that the earlier intervention takes place, the more likely it is that people will recover faster and have better outcomes for their health (Department of Health, 2014). Therefore, this would be a worthy investment for colleges to make and would hopefully improve the outcomes for anyone who needs support.

Case study

Policies for promoting positive mental health and well-being in colleges

Following a recent merger for the Bedford College Group, all college policies were examined to ensure that best practice from both colleges would be taken forward across all the sites. One of the key policies that was updated was the Fitness to Study policy. This replaced what may have previously been a disciplinary process for students not attending or falling behind on the course owing to mental health issues.

The Fitness to Study policy laid out some supportive strategies that could be put in place and allowed an opportunity for meetings to take place where realistic targets could be agreed upon that would hopefully support the student to achieve. If they couldn't meet these targets, there were three stages of the Fitness to Study model (replacing the three stages of the disciplinary model), and eventually a decision could be made that college was not the right place for the student at this time, and they would be withdrawn from the course. Unlike a disciplinary exclusion, though, this withdrawal was seen as non-critical and would not affect the student reapplying for the next academic year. Rather, the withdrawal would only be recommended if the student had fallen so far behind that it would be detrimental to their mental health to expect them to meet unrealistic expectations of passing, or if there were genuine concerns for the safety of the student themselves or others if they were to continue attending.

Reflecting on this case study, are you aware of the mental health and well-being policy used within your own institute? Who is the mental health and well-being lead/coordinator in your institute? Is there a published list of those staff trained in mental health first aid?

Staff and student mental health and well-being: the role of staff and students

Key questions

What can be done at the chalkface to promote positive mental health and well-being?

Unlike schools, FE colleges do not have personal, social and health education (PSHE) as a compulsory subject, making it harder to embed the topic of mental health and well-being. However, dedicated personal tutor (among other names) teams can act in a pastoral capacity to support students on their courses. Mental health and well-being could be included in the group tutorials that are delivered on a range of topics around personal development and employability.

Identifying role models for positive mental health and well-being within any curriculum design could be beneficial, as it is important for young people to understand that mental health problems can affect anyone at any time. Guest speakers from CAMHS, for example, could add to the delivery.

Approaches and strategies for staff and students

Free services within the community may be used for those seeking guidance or training in this area, such as services provided by local charities who are concerned with mental health. Institutes could prioritise funding for training in mental health first aid, allowing for in-house training (according to MHFA guidance) for key staff members.

While current research on mindfulness in teenagers and young people is less extensive, well-conducted mindfulness interventions have demonstrated that they can improve the well-being of those within this age range and can help to reduce anxiety and stress (Miners, 2008). A pilot study by Broderick and Metz (2011) called 'Learning to BREATHE' was carried out in America with 120 students with an average age of 17.4 years, which looked at a mindfulness curriculum created for a classroom setting. The qualitative feedback from this study suggested that although only in the preliminary stages, mindfulness could potentially provide a method for helping to enhance young people's emotion regulation and well-being. The participants reported increased feelings of calmness and highlighted that the intervention helped them to let go of distressing thoughts so that they could better manage their stress (Broderick and Metz, 2011).

Mental health and well-being at the heart of delivery and staff/student communities

We have discussed including mental health and well-being within the curriculum and drawing on the services of key staff, such as personal tutors, to lead support. However, these mechanisms are typically, in a college, only available during term time. This might be of concern when further education students have been known to seek help outside of traditional office hours, particularly during the evenings, nights and weekends (Gatti et al., 2016).

As such, the use of technology as an alternative support mechanism for mental health issues has been explored. Broglia et al. (2018), examining HE, FE and sixth form centres, found particular interest in email counselling, e-therapy, online communities and mobile phone apps. The authors note the cost implications of using such resources where email counselling, videoconferencing and well-being apps provide a cheaper alternative. A note of caution when using the mobile apps, however, is that not all have been developed with input from a healthcare professional (Sedrati et al., 2016). Despite this, the sector should look to alternatives for the support of staff and students, particularly where budgets are already stretched (Belfield et al., 2018).

Emotional labour

Key questions

What is emotional labour and how does it relate to further and adult education?

The term emotional labour originates in sociologist Arlie Hochschild's 1983 book *The Managed Heart*.

Emotional labour is about managing your feelings and emotions so as to fit with organisational policies and norms: a coffee barista always smiling, a funeral director looking solemn, and a PE teacher behaving energetically. These kinds of actions are called emotional labour because emotion management skills have become a saleable commodity, sold for a wage, and are used to produce organisational profits (Hochschild, 1979, 1983). Usually, the idea of emotional labour is seen negatively, but it is important to recognise that it can have positive connotations too; employees may enjoy performing emotional labour. Zapf and Holz (2006) suggest that what may cause stress is not expressing emotion per se, but the dissonance caused when the emotions that are required to be expressed are not actually felt. Emotional labour may also be defined as the labour involved in dealing with other people's feelings, a core component of which is the regulation of emotions (James, 1989, p15).

Does emotional labour happen in educational institutions? We will look at some of the research on this below, but it's worth looking at Cobble's (1999) ideas about education – that teachers are 'knowledge workers engaged in mental labour, but [they] are also service workers engaged in nurturing' (p23).

Teaching may be associated with both negative and positive emotional labour. On the one hand, having to be a 'caring teacher' may force teaching staff into a position where they feel they have to show themselves as caring, whereas in fact they are feeling grumpy, irritated or fed up. In other words, there is an emotional dissonance where what they feel or want to feel does not match the emotions they are displaying (Shuler and Sypher, 2000); behaving in this way may lead to such consequences as stress (Zapf and Holz, 2006). On the other hand, there might be positive aspects of the emotional labour that teaching demands; some teachers can and do enjoy their emotional work, even though they work in a profession that is seen as difficult and demanding (Isenbarger and Zembylas, 2006).

Emotional labour in education

Emotional labour requires individuals to induce or suppress feeling in order to sustain the outward countenance that produces the proper state of mind in others – in the case of teaching, the sense of being taught by an empathic and caring professional, as FE teacher trainees in a study by Avis and Bathmaker (2004) suggested. In this study, Avis and Bathmaker considered the usefulness of the notion of emotional labour in helping to make sense of FE teacher trainee experiences. They draw attention to the commodification of labour, threats to identity and the psychic costs involved in teaching. In other important work relating to FE, Robson and Bailey (2009) discuss the labour of learning support workers as well as teachers, considering how both teachers and learning support workers carry out emotional labour. They suggest that a reconceptualisation of the roles of these education professionals could be fruitful – a reconceptualisation where the FE teacher's experience and expertise lies in understanding how other people learn, and with a related key role to plan teaching and learning activities. This planning would include the contributions of learning support workers to meet the identified needs of the students – and not just of one or two particular students, as often happens. This is a model where teachers and support workers work flexibly and collaboratively in supporting their students' needs. Robson and Bailey suggest that such restructuring might help avoid many of the tensions and difficulties that are sometimes evident in the interacting roles of teachers and learning support workers in relation to emotional labour.

Part of the process that Hochschild describes concerns the commodification of emotional labour (i.e. the idea that emotional labour becomes like any other commodity to be sold on the labour market). The commodification process may result in an inauthentic sense of self, which can lead to alienation – feelings of dehumanisation and disenchantment that may result from not being able to distinguish real feelings, as well as from the loss of sincerity, genuineness and authenticity.

It is important to recognise that much of the work that has explored emotional labour has concentrated upon service workers, such as flight attendants and call centre workers (e.g. Mulholland, 2002; Taylor and Tyler, 2000), and that work that focuses on employees in these sectors often concentrates on the costs to the self of engaging in these forms of work. In teaching, the caring and other positive emotions that are often involved can also become a source of emotional strain, anxiety, anger and/or disappointment (e.g. Nias, 1993). These emotions become emotional labour when teachers try to control or change these negative emotions, and only to express more socially acceptable emotions – in college, these might be positivity, empathy, caring, and so on. In other words, emotional labour is what teachers perform when they engage in caring relationships, but they have to induce, neutralise or inhibit their emotions. Many accounts focus on emotional labour as exploitative, and therefore ignore its rewarding dimensions. However, Heather Price's (2001) work on teachers illustrates the satisfaction that can derive from such work, as does Bolton's (2001) work on nursing.

Is emotional labour gendered?

When thinking about emotional labour, a natural assumption might be that it is gendered. But what is the evidence? If we consider emotional labour as when individuals feel that they have to take care of others at work, then it is the case in many professions that women are assumed to be better than men at this sort of work (e.g. Cottingham et al., 2015), perhaps due to the perception that they have 'feminine' personality traits such as empathy and caring. As such, they are more often asked to mentor other staff or to do pastoral work. This is work that may well be unrecognised and unpaid (Duckworth et al., 2016). However, typical measures of success in educational organisations are examination results or retention figures (Department for Education, 2018) rather than success in a mentoring role, and so women doing these roles and engaging in emotional labour are less likely to be 'successful'. An interesting paper by Guy and Newman (2004) asks, 'What is it about women's jobs that causes them to pay less?' The authors suggest that it is emotional labour that provides the explanation. Emotional tasks such as caring and empathising 'are required components of many women's jobs. Excluded from job descriptions and performance evaluations, the work is invisible and uncompensated' (p289).

Sachs and Blackmore (1998) consider the situation particularly in teaching. They suggest that in schools (and there is no reason to suspect that the situation is any different in further and adult education), women are subject to complex emotional demands that come at them from all sides – from parents, peers and students, for instance. The emotions of women in such jobs are often 'regulated by emotional rules that are implicit within the organisational ethos of the education system' (Sachs and Blackmore, 1998, p14). The demands of the situations in which women work, and the emotional rules that determine their responses in work situations, are key to what women actually do, and to how their agency – or lack of it – plays out in the workplace.

Chapter summary

- Research and national statistics, involving staff and students, highlight the importance of mental health and well-being being a key focus for the FAE sector.

- The FAE sector has an important role to play in supporting the needs of all learners, as well as staff that are employed in the sector.

- Educational institutes provide a platform for increasing mental health and well-being awareness and for signposting to appropriate external support services.

- Educational institutes can become mental health-promoting colleges providing focused policy, environment, curriculum and trained staff.

- There are a significant number of free resources available for staff and students in colleges to access.

- Emotional labour, with links to the role of teaching, can be both a positive and a negative concept. It is important to self-audit and have an awareness of the potential implications.

Further recommended reading

AoC (2017) *Supporting Student Mental Health and Wellbeing in Colleges: A Resource Pack*. June 2017. London: Association of Colleges.

This document looks in more detail at the mental health and well-being self-assessment approach for institutes and is a useful starting point for action plan development.

Martin, C.R., Fleming, M.P. and Smith, H. (eds) (2016) *Mental Health and Wellbeing in the Learning and Teaching Environment*. London: Swan & Horn.

This book looks in more detail at the complexities of mental health in the context of the teaching and learning environment. It explores different approaches to bring improvements to schools and colleges helping to foster healthy environments.

Useful resources

www.mentalhealthatwork.org.uk – a gateway to documents, guides, tips, videos, courses, podcasts, templates and information from organisations across the UK.
www.mind.org.uk – online resources for employers, staff and students.
www.youngminds.org.uk – useful resources for schools and parents
www.aoc.co.uk/mentalhealthresourcepack – the AoC website holds materials to support colleges.
www.minfulnessinschools.org – school-based mindfulness activities.

References

AoC (2017a) *AoC Survey on Students with Mental Health Conditions in Further Education*. January 2017. London: Association of Colleges.
AoC (2017b) *Supporting Student Mental Health and Wellbeing in Colleges: A Resource Pack*. June 2017. London: Association of Colleges.
Avis, J. and Bathmaker, A.-M. (2004) The politics of care: emotional labour and trainee further education lecturers. *Journal of Vocational Education and Training*, 56(1): 5–20.

Belfield, C., Farquharson, C. and Sibieta, L. (2018) *2018 Annual Report on Education Spending in England.* Available at: www.ifs.org.uk/publications/13306

BelievePerform (2018) *Mental Health Statistics in the UK Infographic.* Available at: https://believeperform. com/product/mental-health-statistics-in-the-uk

Bolton, S.C. (2001) Who cares? Offering emotion work as a 'gift' in the nursing labour process. *The Journal of Advanced Nursing*, 32(3): 580–586.

Broderick, P.C. and Metz, S. (2011) Learning to BREATHE: a pilot trial of a mindfulness curriculum for adolescents. *Advances in School Mental Health Promotion*, 2(1): 35–46.

Broglia, E., Millings, A. and Barkham, M. (2018) Challenges to addressing student mental health in embedded counselling services: a survey of UK higher and further education institutions. *British Journal of Guidance and Counselling*, 46(4): 441–455.

Business in the Community (2017) *Mental Health at Work.* London: Business in the Community.

Cobble, D.S. (1999) History, women's work, and the new unionism. *The NEA Higher Educational Journal*, 15(2): 19–24.

Cottingham, M.D., Erickson, R.J. and Diefendorff, J.M. (2015) Examining men's status shield and status bonus: how gender frames the emotional labor and job satisfaction of nurses. *Sex Roles*, 72(7–8): 377–389.

Department for Education (2018) *School Performance Tables: How We Report the Data.* Available at: www. gov.uk/government/publications/school-performance-tables-how-we-report-the-data/

Department of Health (2014) *Achieving Better Access to Mental Health Services by 2020.* Available at: https:// assets.publishing.service.gov.uk/government/uploads/system/uploads/attachment_data/file/361648/ mental-health-access.pdf

Duckworth, V., Lord, J., Dunne, L., Atkins, L. and Watmore, S. (2016) Creating feminised critical spaces and co-caring communities of practice outside patriarchal managerial landscapes. *Gender and Education*, 28: 903–917.

Foster, A. (2005) *Realising the Potential: A Review of the Role of Further Education Colleges.* Annesley: DfES.

Frith, E. (2016) *CentreForum Commission on Children and Young People's Mental Health: State of the Nation.* London: CentreForum.

Gatti, F.M., Brivio, E. and Calciano, S. (2016) 'Hello! I know you help people here, right?' A qualitative study of young people's acted motivations in text-based counselling. *Children and Youth Services Review*, 71: 27–35.

Goodman, A., Joyce, R. and Smith, J.P. (2011) The long shadow cast by childhood physical and mental health problems on adult life. *Proceedings of the National Academy of Sciences of the United States of America*, 108(15): 6032–6037.

Guy, M.E. and Newman, M.A. (2004) Women's jobs, men's jobs: sex segregation and emotional labor. *Public Administration Review*, 64(3): 289–298.

Harnois, G. and Gabriel, P. (2002) *Mental Health and Work: Impact, Issues and Good Practices.* Available at: www.who.int/mental_health/media/en/712.pdf

Hochschild, A. (1979) Emotion work, feeling rules, and social structure. *American Journal of Sociology*, 85(3): 551–575.

Hochschild, A. (1983) *The Managed Heart: Commercialization of Human Feeling.* Berkeley, CA: University of California Press.

Hodgson, A., Bailey, B. and Lucus, N. (2015) What is FE? In A. Hodgson (ed.), *The Coming of Age for FE? Reflections on the Past and Future Role of Further Education Colleges in England.* London: Institute of Education Press.

Isenbarger, L. and Zembylas, M. (2006) The emotional labour of caring in teaching. *Teaching and Teacher Education*, 22: 120–134.

James, K. (2003) *A Health Promoting College for 16–19 Year Old Learners.* Leicester: NIACE, Department of Health.

James, N. (1989) Emotional labour: skill and work in the social regulation of feelings. *The Sociological Review*, 37(1): 15–42.

Kinman, G. and Wray, S. (2013) *Higher Stress: A Survey of Stress and Well-Being among Staff in Higher Education.* London: University and College Union.

McDaid, D., King, D. and Parsonage, M. (2011) Workplace screening for depression and anxiety disorders. In M. Knapp, D. McDaid and M. Parsonage (eds), *Mental Health Promotion and Mental Illness Prevention: The Economic Case.* London: Department of Health.

Mental Health Foundation (2018) *About Mental Health.* Available at: www.mentalhealth.org.uk/your-mental-health/about-mental-health

Mental Health Taskforce (2016) *The Five Year Forward View for Mental Health.* London: National Health Service.

MIND (2013) *Taking Care of Your Staff.* Available at: www.mind.org.uk/workplace/mental-health-at-work/taking-care-of-your-staff

MIND (2018) *Understanding Mental Health Problems.* Available at: www.mind.org.uk/media/34696343/understanding-mental-health-problems-2018-web-pdf.pdf

Miners, R. (2008) Collected and Connected: Mindfulness and the early Adolescent. Dissertations Abstracts International: Section B. *The Sciences and Engineering*, 68: 9.

Morrison, I. and Clift, S.M. (2006) Mental health promotion through supported further education: the value of Antonovsky's salutogenic model of health. *Health Education*, 106(5): 365–380.

Mulholland, K. (2002) Gender, emotional labour and teamworking in a call centre. *Personnel Review*, 31(3): 283–303.

Murphy, M. and Fonargy, P. (2012) *Mental Health Problems in Children and Young People.* Available at: https://assets.publishing.service.gov.uk/governement/uploads/system/uploads/attachment_data/file/252660/33571_2901304_CMO_chapter_10.pdf

NHS (2015) *Future in Mind: Promoting, Protecting and Improving Our Children and Young People's Mental Health and Wellbeing.* London: Department for Health.

Nias, J. (1993) Changing times, changing identities: grieving for a lost self. In R.G. Burgess (ed.), *Educational Research and Evaluation: For Policy and Practice?* London: Falmer Press.

O'Donnell, T. and Gray, G. (1993) *The Health Promoting College.* London: Health Education Authority.

ONS (2018) *Sickness Absence in the UK Labour Market.* Available at: www.ons.gov.uk/employment andlabourmarket/peopleinwork/employmentande,ployeetypes/datasets/sicknessabsenceinthe labourmarket

Perry, A. and Davies, P. (2015) Students count. In A. Hodgson (ed.), *The Coming of Age for FE? Reflections on the Past and Future Role of Further Education Colleges in England.* London: Institute of Education Press.

Price, H. (2001) Emotional labour in the classroom: a psychoanalytic perspective. *Journal of Social Work Practice*, 15(2): 161–180.

Robson, J. and Bailey, B. (2009) 'Bowing from the heart': an investigation into discourses of professionalism and the work of caring for students in further education. *British Educational Research Journal*, 35(1): 99–117.

Sachs, J. and Blackmore, J. (1998) You never show you can't cope: women in school leadership roles managing their emotions. *Gender and Education*, 10(3): 265–279.

Sedrati, H., Nejjari, C., Chaqsare, S. and Ghazal, H. (2016) Mental and physical mobile health apps: review. *Procedia Computer Science*, 100: 900–906.

Shuler, S. and Sypher, B.D. (2000) Seeking emotional labor: when managing the heart enhances the work experience. *Management Communication Quarterly*, 14(1): 50–89.

Taylor, S. and Tyler, M. (2000) Emotional labour and sexual difference in the airline industry. *Work, Employment and Society*, 14(1): 77–95.

Warwick, I., Maxwell, C., Statham, J., Aggleton, P. and Simon, A. (2008) Supporting mental health and emotional wellbeing among younger students in further education. *Journal of Further and Higher Education*, 32: 1–13.

WHO (1993) *Mental Health Programmes in Schools*. Geneva: WHO.

YoungMinds (2018) *A New Era for Young People's Mental Health*. Available at: https://youndminds.org.uk/media/2620/a-new-era-for-young-peoples-mental-health.pdf

Zapf, D. and Holz, M. (2006) On the positive and negative effects of emotion work in organizations. *European Journal of Work and Organizational Psychology*, 15(1): 1–28.

22

COLLEGE-BASED HIGHER EDUCATION

Kate Lavender

Key words – widening participation; Foundation degrees; work-based learning; graduate attributes; research and scholarly activity; marketisation; social mobility

Introduction

This chapter will explore the complex nature of college-based HE. It will begin by exploring key features of college-based HE provision and the qualifications it offers. It will then consider teaching and assessment in college-based HE and how this is influenced by aspects of the curriculum. The chapter will then move on to thinking about the broad range of activities that are undertaken to support the development of curriculum, teaching and learning, and subject specialism through research and scholarly activity in this context. The important issue of who participates in college-based HE will then be explored, which will lead to a discussion of the question: What can college-based HE offer that universities cannot?

Colleges and HE provision

Colleges have long been involved in the delivery of higher education provision; however, the way that this work has been referred to has been subject to change over a number of years. College-based HE has previously been referred to as college HE, HE in FE, higher vocational education (HIVE) and higher VET. These different terms account for the variety of higher education provision delivered in FE colleges, including the expansion of franchised provision with universities since incorporation. Prior to this, college-based HE provision took the form of short-cycle one-year Higher National Certificates (HNCs) and two-year Higher National Diplomas (HNDs), as well as a portfolio of higher professional qualifications such as those accredited by the Chartered Institute of Personnel and Development (CIPD) and the Association of Accounting Technicians (AAT), at level 4 and above.

When defining college-based HE, this chapter takes the position of Greenwood (2010), who suggests that college-based HE:

refers to all those activities that relate to the management, development, delivery and assessment of higher education qualifications and programmes taught in further education colleges ... HE qualifications and programmes refer to those that are at level 4 and above in the framework for higher education qualifications.

(p1)

Key features of college-based HE provision

Key questions

How do colleges respond to the work-based emphasis of many college-based HE courses?

What is 'higher' about college-based HE?

What are graduate attributes?

This section takes a look at the broad variety of HE work delivered in FE colleges, highlighting the emphasis on work-based, vocational and professional HE provision. It explores curriculum development in college-based HE, including the development of 'research-based' curricula. This leads to a discussion of employability and graduate attributes in college-based HE.

FE colleges have been delivering different forms of higher education for some time; however, this provision has expanded and diversified over recent years. As previously discussed, college-based HE provision originally took the form of short-cycle one-year Higher National Certificates (HNCs) and two-year Higher National Diplomas (HNDs); however, new two-year level 5 Foundation degrees were introduced to the college-based HE curriculum offer in 2000 to provide new and accessible routes to Higher Education. The qualifications were considered a key factor in widening participation in English HE, as well as contributing to local economies and a higher-qualified workforce. One key aspect of the Foundation degree curriculum was that it offered higher-level vocational and work-based qualifications. With this in mind, Foundation degrees were developed in consultation with employers to ensure a highly relevant work-based HE. To ensure the quality of such awards, the degrees were also developed and validated in partnerships with universities. This blend of academic and work-based or vocational provision makes Foundation degrees delivered in colleges distinctive; however, it is not without its challenges in practice.

Ensuring high-quality opportunities for work-based learning is one of those challenges. While one of the underpinning assumptions in the development of Foundation degrees and other forms of college-based HE was that they would provide routes to HE for those already in employment, they continue to attract students not in the field of work. The challenge to provide a work-based curriculum has been noted in research, with a range of work-based or work-related activities identified as part of the college-based HE offer. Reeve et al. (2007), in their comparative study of the work-based elements of HND/C provision in Scotland and Foundation degree provision in England, found that interpretations of what constitutes work-based learning were varied. Activities identified included: the use of placements; the establishment of virtual work-based learning environments; the use of industry specialists and employers to set briefs and projects to be completed in the college environment; and the simulation of workplace environments in the college. These examples demonstrate the variability of understandings of work-based learning in these HE contexts. Little and Brennan (1996) describe work-based learning as learning for work, at work and through work, which can be formal or informal and is gained through the experience of undertaking work tasks. Elements of this definition can be seen in the above examples in the way work-based learning is embedded into the curriculum.

The curriculum in college-based HE, as well as satisfying a work-based emphasis, is also required to be increasingly 'research-based' to satisfy the academic rigour of an HE programme. As with work-based learning, research-based learning is also open to multiple interpretations and uses depending on the context and discipline. Jenkins and Healey (2009), in their work on 'developing research-based curricula in college-based HE', identify four ways in which research is embedded in the college-based HE curriculum:

1. *Research-tutored* – engaging with discussions about research.

2. *Research-led* – learning about current research in the subject area.

3. *Research-oriented* – developing research skills for enquiry.

4. *Research-based* – undertaking research.

The extent to which research is embedded into the curriculum in these ways will vary depending on the subject area and levels; for example, research-based (undertaking research) is more likely to be a feature of level 5 and 6 provision, whereas discussions and learning about current research may be a feature of level 4 provision.

As all college-based HE is developed in partnership with universities and other validating bodies, the curriculum also has to satisfy the requirements of those partners at the relevant academic levels. Universities awarding the degrees have their own ethos and understanding of what attributes a graduate of their university ought to possess. Employability and graduate attributes have become increasingly important to universities and colleges in distinguishing themselves in the higher education market. Employability can be understood as 'a set of achievements – skills, understandings and personal attributes – that makes graduates more likely to gain employment and be successful in their chosen occupations, which benefits themselves, the workforce, the community and the economy' (Yorke, 2008, p11).

However, it must be noted that the types of activities associated with enhancing employability in HE are often associated with younger, full-time students with little or no experience of the labour market (Lavender, 2016). Many students studying in college-based HE are part-time, mature and employed; therefore, employability is likely to mean something different, particularly as a key feature of many college-based HE courses is work-based learning. In my 2016 PhD study of mature students studying in college-based HE, I found that for mature, part-time and employed students, employability may be associated with developing more traditional attributes of HE study through the development of academic and cultural capital (Lavender, 2016).

Key theory

Academic and cultural capital

Academic capital as a concept refers to the way in which a person can use qualifications or other educational experiences in becoming more mobile. There is some debate to the definition of Bourdieu's concept of academic capital, although one way in which Bourdieu operationalises the concept is by length of time spent in education (Bourdieu, 1984) or perceived quality of that education - i.e. attending a prestigious school or university (Bourdieu, 1988). According to Bourdieu (1984), academic capital can also be seen as converted from other forms of capital, such as cultural capital.

Similarly, others have conceptualised academic capital as based on institutionalised types of cultural capital important in the field of higher education (Naidoo, 2004). Therefore, the concept of academic capital does not just refer to the exchange value of one's qualifications, but includes dispositions and competencies seen as 'academic' or distinctive to the field of higher education participants.

These dispositions and competencies could be considered graduate attributes, and include confidence, authority, critical thinking, and research and enquiry skills. The inclusion of college-based HE qualifications within the overall field of higher education is why Leahy (2012) argues that the capital accrued by those studying HE in colleges can be equivalent to those studying in universities.

Teaching and assessment

Key questions

What is independent learning?

What are some of the tensions of supporting learning in college-based HE?

The previous section highlighted some of the key features of the college-based HE curriculum, including employer responsive work-based and the maintenance of the academic rigour of higher qualifications through research-based curricula, and the embeddedness of graduate attributes. This section will explore how lecturers have responded to these demands in their teaching and assessment. Current research that highlights distinctive pedagogies to support the diverse student body is drawn upon, and some of the tensions that arise are explored.

It is difficult to pin down what is distinctive about college-based HE pedagogies, as context, such as learning environment, and subject-specific requirements will affect how teaching and learning is enacted. However, there are some common pedagogical features of college-based HE and HE more generally that can be used to understand college-based HE practices. Some of the aims of higher education are to promote independent learning and foster critical thinking.

Gow and Kember (1990) describe independent learning as an increased capacity to learn, increased analytical skills and an ability to draw independent conclusions. One of the problems with this definition is that it seems to focus on the outcome rather than the process of independent learning. Race (2000), on the other hand, emphasises the process of 'becoming' in independent learning, and the empowerment of individuals to learn themselves. Similarly, developing critical thinking skills in students often requires a reorientation of their approaches to learning and understanding of knowledge acquisition and development.

In order to understand how to develop independent learning and critical thinking in students of college-based HE, we need to think more broadly about how students approach their learning. One theory that can help us to do this is Marton and Säljö's (1976) work on deep, surface and strategic approaches to learning.

Key theory

Deep and surface approaches to learning

Marton and Säljö (1976) developed the concepts of deep and surface approaches to learning when trying to understand how their students approach academic tasks, and what influenced these approaches.

Deep learning is associated with orientations to learning that are rooted in understanding the meaning of texts and ideas in order to learn them. Surface approaches were associated with orientations that are rooted in memorising discrete units of texts and ideas to be recalled later.

It should be highlighted that these categorisations are approaches students may adopt towards their learning, and not a description of the student or their capacity to learn. Students may move between approaches, depending on a number of factors related to their environment, including how they understand the purpose of assessment tasks, and the practical nature of learning (i.e. how much time they may have to dedicate to the task). This is what Marton and Säljö (1976), and more recently Entwistle (1998), have referred to as 'strategic' approaches to learning. These approaches have been used widely in HE pedagogic discourse, but less so in a college-based HE context. To demonstrate, below is a case study of how these concepts have been used to develop teaching practice in this context.

Case study

Student engagement with research: action research

In an action research project by Lavender and Lockwood (2017), deep, surface and strategic approaches to learning were used as concepts to understand how their students engaged with their undergraduate dissertations on their level 6 BA (Hons) (top-up) in Early Years. The team had identified varying levels of engagement with, and understanding of, the value and use of students' undergraduate research. Additionally, as students had all progressed from a Foundation degree in Early Years, they wanted to make sure that the students' research had occupational value. Therefore, the team wanted to understand what sorts of factors affected varying levels of engagement with

(Continued)

(Continued)

research throughout the dissertation module. They had hypothesised that the work-based focus of the students' prior Foundation degree study may affect how the students engaged with more traditional academic tasks, such as primary research. Therefore, we aimed to use pedagogic strategies that emphasised the importance of their research to the workplace, and invited industry experts to provide additional support in implementing research outcomes.

These concepts were important for us as they helped us to understand the engagement of our students with research and knowledge more generally. For example, those students who generally see knowledge as absolute often had a very fixed and routine view of what their research should be about and how they should report it. Their work was often descriptive and process-driven, and this was evident in their engagement with their research – or lack of it. These students produced work that lacked any engagement with the research process, by submitting a 'long essay' for their dissertation. Their approaches could be described as 'surface'.

Another group of students had more flexible approaches to their research, and acknowledged that knowledge was produced from multiple perspectives. However, they often wanted to know the 'right way' to do their research and saw the process as black and white; this was frustrating to them as research is messy and 'grey'. The motivation for these students appeared to be to understand how to do their research in such a way that they would get good grades, or even just pass the module. However, they were unable to see that there is no one right way to do or report their research. These students could be considered to demonstrate a 'strategic approach to learning' with their research.

The final two students were described as demonstrating deep approaches to learning and the research process. They had a knowledge-transforming approach to their work. They saw knowledge as provisional and used their research to provide evidence for reasoned interpretation. Their motivations were to understand how the impact of their research could be a benefit in their settings, and therefore developed a critical understanding of the research process.

These concepts helped us to think about how assessment tasks and activities in the classroom can be affected by our students' understanding of the task. We were able to unpick aspects of our teaching strategies that would help develop a deeper orientation to learning, and support individuals with the time and space to think in this way.

If deeper approaches to learning are associated with higher levels of independence and critical thinking among students, then what are the ways in which lecturers in college-based HE can encourage this? Ramsden (2003) suggests that deep approaches to learning can be fostered through developing teaching and assessment methods that promote active engagement with activities; that emphasise subject matter and the meaning behind it; by being clear about assessment expectations and relevance to the subject matter; by providing opportunities to contribute to the choice in the method and content of study; and by promoting an interest in the background knowledge of the subject matter or the discipline as a whole.

This section has highlighted the importance of understanding the nature and experiences of students when developing pedagogical strategies for teaching and learning in college-based HE. Often the way that these understandings are achieved by college-based HE lecturers is through specific forms of research and scholarly activity focused on developing pedagogy and practice, and on industry and subject enhancement.

Research and scholarly activity

Key questions

What forms do research and scholarly activity take in college-based HE?

What are the potential barriers to undertaking research and scholarly activity for college-based HE lecturers?

This section will discuss the broad ways in which research and scholarly activities are interpreted and carried out in the context of college-based HE. It will draw upon current research to understand the complex activities that are undertaken as scholarly activity in this context, which deviates from traditional notions of HE research.

Academic research in its broadest sense can be understood as work that generates new knowledge in a subject area. Traditionally, this work has been carried out in universities, and has provided theoretical insights that can support practice. However, more recently, research is being carried out by those who are the users of the types of insights that may be generated through research activity, such as teachers, nurses and practitioners. In the context of college-based HE, the engagement with research and scholarly activity by lecturers has been seen to contribute to a 'culture of HE-ness' (Feather, 2016). That is, that engagement in research and scholarly activity distinguishes college-based HE and those who teach it from other forms of vocational provision. However, in a higher education sector that is increasingly diverse, so are the forms of research and scholarly activity undertaken within it.

Research and scholarly activity can be understood as separate terms. Research is defined as 'a process of systematic investigation, carefully planned, thought through and executed, in order to find out the answers to particular research questions' (Tummons et al., 2013, p82). This definition is more akin to the traditional notions of university research, where the intention is to generate new and original knowledge, which may be published in journal articles. Scholarship, or scholarly activity, on the other hand, can be defined as 'a process of systematic reading, evaluation and discussion that allows the lecturer to establish a thorough, critical and up-to-date understanding on their specialism' (Tummons et al., 2013, p83). Scholarly activity, then, can be considered as a sustained engagement with new knowledge and developments in a specialism. These definitions are centred in lecturers' understanding and contribution to a specific subject or discipline; however, in institutions (both universities and colleges) with a greater focus on teaching and the improvement of practice, a third type of scholarship can be seen – pedagogic research. Researching one's own practice typically takes the form of 'action research' and aims to improve teaching practice in a particular context. The types of research and scholarly activity found in colleges are often a mixture of these, with colleges and lecturers developing their own distinctive definitions of research and scholarship with their own norms and cultures to suit their provision (Parry and Thompson, 2002).

Some of these activities include:

- *Higher degrees.* Lecturers teaching up to level 6 in college-based HE are often qualified to at least one level above the level they teach. Furthermore, partner universities may require college-based staff to be qualified to master's level, which involves an element of research in the form of the dissertation. Increasingly, lecturers are choosing to undertake further higher degrees such as PhDs in their subject area, or a professional doctorate in education.

- *HE/FE partnerships.* University partnerships, mentioned throughout this chapter, also hold opportunities for collaborative work in the form of research funding, networks with external examiners, and co-authorship of written work.

- *Training and CPD.* Colleges may offer HE-specific CPD to develop research cultures and give time to what is described as scholarship, earlier in this section.

- *Research networks.* College-based HE lecturers have more recently taken ownership of the research and scholarly activity as part of their work by developing regional research hubs, research meets, and events to celebrate the scholarly work of colleges.

While the development of research and scholarly activity has seen a celebration of the distinctive work of college-based HE lecturers, there remain barriers for lecturers in HE in the FE context, as documented in the work of Feather (2014, 2017).

The reality of undertaking research and scholarly activity is that it requires time, a luxury many lecturers in college-based HE do not have. Increased workloads, contact time with students and other civic duties related to teaching are considered higher in priority, or more immediately urgent. Access to funding and finding teaching cover to engage in research can also be problematic for lecturers in a culture that does not always support the types of research activities with which college-based HE lecturers may wish to engage (Feather, 2017). Increased institutional and personal pressures on college-based HE lecturers means that engagement with research and scholarly activity often relies on individual interest and goodwill. Furthermore, many lecturers, who have come through vocational routes themselves, do not always consider research and scholarly activity to be part of their practice as interpreters of knowledge (Feather, 2014) – 'these lecturers' strengths have typically lain in the ability to teach a broad range of cognate subjects to a variety of students at a number of levels' (HEQC, 1993, pp19–20).

While interest in engaging with research and scholarly activity has appeared to increase, very few lecturers are engaged in research in its traditional form. This is not a problem as, previously noted, college-based HE is different, its practices are shaped by institutional and cultural norms, and the type of scholarship undertaken is too.

Constructing the HE in FE learner

Key questions

What are the factors affecting participation in college-based HE?

How might students' backgrounds and experiences contribute to success in college-based HE?

Previous sections of this chapter have highlighted some of the distinct characteristics of college-based HE. The distinctiveness of this provision can also be seen in the construction of the college-based HE student. For example:

> *Higher Education offered in Colleges of Further Education is achieving increased recognition as a growing and responsive part of the wider higher education landscape. Colleges offer value for money HE courses which are available locally and respond to the needs of employers. They attract students who might otherwise be unable to study for higher level qualifications to progress not only in their studies but also in their careers.*
>
> (Widdowson, 2017)

As discussed earlier in the chapter, the provision of higher education in colleges offers much in terms of widening participation and access to students who would not have participated in university higher education. In 2016, there were 153,000 students studying HE in colleges. This represents just under 10 per cent of all HE students. The Education and Training Foundation found that in 2016, 51 per cent of students were full-time, 44 per cent were part-time and 5 per cent studied in the workplace. Furthermore, 70 per cent of college-based HE students were aged 21 or over, with 50 per cent over the age of 25 (ETF, 2016). This is in contrast to the majority of full-time undergraduates in university HE who are 18 and have progressed from school or college. College-based HE students do not only differ in age and mode of study, but in background.

College-based HE students are more likely to come from non-traditional backgrounds; this can be measured by POLAR category (come from areas that have low participation to HE), deprivation indices or qualifications on entry. College-based students are more likely to be studying in applied and vocational areas than science and humanities, and to be studying sub-degree-level HE qualifications such as Higher National Diplomas or Foundation degrees (ETF, 2016).

Given the profile of students participating in college-based HE, there is a clear classed element to participation in college-based HE. Individuals of lower socio-economic status are disproportionately represented in this context. There are a number of explanations for this. The first is that students from working-class backgrounds are more likely to be the first in their family to enter HE. This means they are less likely to have the cultural capital to navigate the terrain of higher education, and may choose what is familiar and local (Burton et al., 2011). Further education colleges are strongly located within local communities; members of communities are likely to know people who have attended the local college and who have recommended the provision.

Being the first in the family to participate in HE may also mean that students are unfamiliar with what to expect, and what is expected of them. Many students base their decision on an environment that seems more supportive and less alienating (Leathwood and O'Connell, 2003). In turn, this suggests that students already have some perceptions of HE practices before they enrol, and seek to minimise the risk of failure by choosing institutions that they feel will support them to overcome their perceived individual barriers.

There is also a gendered element to participation in college-based HE, particularly in regard to mature and part-time students. For many mature students, and particularly women, studying is not their only responsibility and it is not the main priority in their lives. Family and work commitments mean that students have less time to travel for their studies (Burton et al., 2011). Geographical location may be the primary factor in the choice of HE institution for these students.

With its emphasis on vocational as well as academic education, college-based HE could be considered as catering for students who consider themselves more 'practical', those who have been out of education and in work for some time, and those that have had negative experiences of education. Adults in further education are sometimes referred to as 'second-chance' learners, those who left formal schooling with 'untapped' or 'wasted' potential (Waller, 2004).

While these barriers are very real for some, what is often neglected is the way in which family, work commitments and the social class background of students can contribute to student success in HE. Skills that are developed during adults' lives can often be transferred to academia: organisation, prioritisation, patience and determination can all contribute to success; similarly, skills gained through experience of employment can also be transferred. A lack of confidence stemming from previous educational experiences or a significant gap in formal education is often perceived as an initial constraint on success. However, what is often overlooked is that some students may be more secure and confident in their choice and reasoning for studying a particular vocation/subject and have high levels of motivation to succeed.

The following case study demonstrates how some of these explanations for participation in college-based HE play out in the lives of students.

Case study

Narratives of widening participation

Daniel first came to the college at the age of 16 from school – he said he had been told by teachers at the school that he was not academic and would do better for himself if he became qualified in a trade. Daniel described himself as not being very good at reading or writing at school, so much so that he was not allowed to sit his GCSE English exam. Daniel had considered higher education when he was younger. He explained how he was interested in art, design and architecture, but committing to two or three years was too risky. He said that if he was not good enough or did not like it, then he would have failed and would leave without any recognition – and with a debt. As the college was his local provider of further education, it seemed like the logical place for him to become qualified. He had a choice between plumbing and electrical courses, so after finding a job as an electrical apprentice for a one-man company, he worked there for three years while studying to become qualified. Once qualified, Daniel began working for himself and frequently came back to the college to update skills and to complete courses that would enable him to progress in his business. He progressed through levels 2 and 3 at the college and then took further electrical short courses on and off, frequenting the college for a number of years. He had been looking around for higher courses that would interest him in the local area. The only one that seemed suitable to Daniel was at a college in a city nearby. However, Daniel had explained that, as he was self-employed, he would lose money on travelling and having to take a day off work to go. The process was to apply through UCAS too, and he 'wasn't quite sure where he stood with that'. While he was looking, he was contacted by his previous lecturer about a new opportunity; he went to speak to the course leader and decided that it sounded like something he might be interested in. His reservations about applications and location were not an issue at the local college, so he signed up to the new HNC in construction management.

Daniel's story demonstrates some of the difficulties faced by students in their choice of participation in higher education. He was diverted at school down a vocational pathway, despite his interests in pursuing a degree. His own understanding of the risks of higher education and his belief in his ability to succeed led him to further education. The familiarity and geographical location of the college played an important role in his return to college-based HE. Finally, his understanding of formal admissions procedures through UCAS seemed alienating, whereas the local college did not recruit students in this way.

What can college-based HE offer that universities cannot?

Key questions

What contribution does college-based HE make to the lives of students?

Much of this chapter has explored the distinctiveness of college-based HE, through the curriculum, teaching and learning, research and scholarly activity, and the students. However, this distinct type of higher education is positioned within a broader HE landscape that is subject to the same market forces as universities. College-based HE sits within the same regulatory framework as university HE, and works within the same policy context. The most recent and significant effects of policy have been the rise in tuition fees in 2012. This change in policy has opened up a discourse and culture of students as consumers. Colleges have positioned themselves within this market as providing a lower-cost university HE alternative (Henderson, 2018). The rhetoric is such that 'students will direct where money goes through their choice of course and institution' (Browne, 2010, p27). However, as we have seen earlier in this chapter, students' decisions about where to study are not solely based on cost.

The marketisation of HE also rests on the assumptions that HE is a level playing field; HE is a stratified system (Gallacher, 2006) and students who attend different institutions are likely to see differential outcomes. An analysis of HEFCE data by Avis and Orr (2016) found that 'graduates from FE colleges in 2010–11 employed full-time in professional occupations was 8%, compared with that of graduates from HEIs, which was 23%' (p58), and graduates from FE colleges were 4–6 per cent more likely to be unemployed than their HEI counterparts. Salaries of college-based HE graduates were also found to be 16 per cent lower than their HEI counterparts. These data show that while FE colleges provide access to HE for those that may not have participated (Bathmaker, 2016), they do not contribute to social mobility. Perhaps, then, the distinctiveness of college-based HE and its value is located in a commitment to improving the quality of individual lives.

In my 2016 study of mature student participation in college-based HE, I found that students benefited from increased confidence, autonomy, and a more critical understanding of their subject, work and society. These benefits are often a result of the commitment and expertise of lecturers in college-based HE, supportive pedagogic features of FE, and small class sizes with the space to carry out this work, which makes it distinctive (Gale et al., 2011; Lea and Simmons, 2012). This is echoed by Parry et al. (2012), who argue that the learning culture in colleges is distinctive from that in HEIs. It is this distinctive contribution college-based HE and those who teach in it make to individuals' lives that should be recognised and celebrated.

This chapter has made arguments to support the distinct contribution college-based HE makes to the lives of learners and the wider sector. These include a supportive learning environment, professionally and contextually relevant curriculum, geographically accessible locations, and lower fees. It has also highlighted the contribution that providing spaces for HE in these contexts makes to the development of critical and autonomous graduates. These contributions are made in an increasingly challenging policy and funding climate, and we cannot ignore the lack of evidence to support arguments that college-based HE supports social mobility or challenges rising levels of inequality in society. However, we can become more aware of the beneficial effects college-based HE has on individuals and their communities.

Chapter summary

- College-based HE offers a range of higher education provision, focusing on a blend of work-based or vocational learning and academic learning.

- Teaching and learning in college-based HE is varied, using pedagogical strategies seen in both HE and FE, and is responsive to work-based and academic requirements of college-based HE provision.

- Research and scholarly activity take a variety of forms within college-based HE, with lecturers increasingly defining the terms themselves.

- Students in college-based HE are likely to be mature, part-time, local, in employment, and studying vocational and sub-degree qualifications. Social class, age and gender may influence participation in college-based HE.

- While college-based HE may not contribute to social mobility and addressing societal inequalities, it can, and does, change students' lives.

Further recommended reading

For more detail about the historical developments of HNC, HND and Foundation degrees, see: Gallacher, J. (2006) Blurring the boundaries or creating diversity? The contribution of the further education colleges to higher education in Scotland. *Journal of Further and Higher Education*, 30(1): 43–58.

For practical guidance about the development of modules and courses in college-based HE, see: Tummons, J., Orr, K. and Atkins, L. (2013) *Teaching Higher Education Courses in Further Education Colleges*. Exeter: Learning Matters.

References

Avis, J. and Orr, K. (2016) HE in FE: vocationalism, class and social justice. *Research in Post-Compulsory Education*, 21(1–2): 49–65.
Bathmaker, A.-M. (2016) Higher education in further education: the challenges of providing a distinctive contribution that contributes to widening participation. *Research in Post-Compulsory Education*, 21(1–2): 20–32.

Bourdieu, P. (1984) *Distinction: A Social Critique of the Judgment of Taste*, trans. R. Nice. London: Routledge.

Bourdieu, P. (1988) *Homo Academicus*. Stanford, CA: Stanford University Press.

Browne, J. (2010) *Securing a Sustainable Future for Higher Education: An Independent Review of Higher Education Funding and Student Finance*. London: UK Government.

Burton, K., Lloyd, M.G. and Griffiths, C. (2011) Barriers to learning for mature students studying HE in an FE college. *Journal of Further and Higher Education*, 35(1): 25–36.

Entwistle, N.J. (1998) Approaches to learning and forms of understanding. In B. Dart and G. Boulton-Lewis (eds), *Teaching and Learning in Higher Education: From Theory to Practice*. Melbourne: Australian Council for Educational Research.

ETF (2016) *The Local Impact of College-Based Higher Education*. London: ETF.

Feather, D. (2014) Research to improve specialist knowledge: an HE in FE perspective. *Research in Post-Compulsory Education*, 19(3): 310–322.

Feather, D. (2016) Organisational culture of further education colleges delivering higher education business programmes: developing a culture of 'HEness' – what next? *Research in Post-Compulsory Education*, 21(1–2): 98–115.

Feather, D. (2017) Time! What's that? You're joking, I don't have any! *Journal of Further and Higher Education*, 41(5): 706–716.

Gale, K., Turner, R. and McKenzie, L. (2011) Communities of praxis? Scholarship and practice styles of the HE in FE professional. *Journal of Vocational Education and Training*, 63(2): 159–169.

Gallacher, J. (2006) Blurring the boundaries or creating diversity? The contribution of the further education colleges to higher education in Scotland. *Journal of Further and Higher Education*, 30(1), 43–58.

Gow, L. and Kember, D. (1990) Does higher education promote independent learning? *Higher Education*, 19(3): 307–322.

Greenwood, M. (2010) *Higher Education in Further Education Colleges*. Available at: www.heacademy.ac.uk/assets/documents/heinfe/higher_education_in_further_education__colleges_synthesis_Mar_10.pdf

Henderson, H. (2018) 'Supportive', 'real', and 'low-cost': implicit comparisons and universal assumptions in the construction of the prospective college-based HE student. *Journal of Further and Higher Education*, 42(8): 1105–1117.

HEQC (1993) *Some Aspects of Higher Education Programmes in Further Education Institutions*. London: Higher Education Quality Council.

Jenkins, A. and Healey, M. (2009) Developing the student as a researcher through the curriculum. *Innovations in Practice*, 2(1): 3–15.

Lavender, K. (2016) *Mature Students, Resistance and Higher Vocational Education: A Multiple Case Study*. PhD Thesis, University of Huddersfield.

Lavender, K. and Lockwood, J. (2017) *Understanding Student Engagement in the Research Process through the Use of a Collaborative Approach to Supervision Pedagogy: The Case of College-Based HE*. ETF Report, September 2017.

Lea, J. and Simmons, J. (2012) Higher education in further education: capturing and promoting HEness. *Research in Post-Compulsory Education*, 17(2): 179–193.

Leahy, S.M. (2012) The barbarians at the gate: playing the higher education game – observations from the periphery of the field. *Journal of Further and Higher Education*, 36(2): 169–185.

Leathwood, C. and O'Connell, P. (2003) 'It's a struggle': the construction of the 'new student' in higher education. *Journal of Education Policy*, 18(6): 597–615.

Little, B. and Brennan, J. (1996) *A Review of Work Based Learning in Higher Education*. London: DfEE.

Marton, F. and Säljö, R. (1976) On qualitative differences in learning: I – outcome and process. *British Journal of Educational Psychology*, 46(1): 4–11.

Naidoo, R. (2004) Fields and institutional strategy: Bourdieu on the relationship between higher education, inequality and society. *British Journal of Sociology of Education*, 25(4): 457–471.

Parry, G. and Thompson, A. (2002) *Closer by Degrees: The Past, Present and Future of Higher Education in Further Education Colleges*. London: Learning and Skills Development Agency.

Parry, G., Callender, C., Temple, P. and Scott, P. (2012) *Understanding Higher Education in Further Education Colleges*. London: BIS Research Paper No. 69.

Race, P. (2000) *500 Tips on Group Learning*. London: Kogan Page.

Ramsden, P. (2003) *Learning to Teach in Higher Education*. London: Routledge.

Reeve, F., Gallacher, J. and Ingram, R. (2007) A comparative study of work-based learning within Higher Nationals in Scotland and Foundation degrees in England: contrast, complexity, continuity. *Journal of Education and Work*, 20(4): 305–318.

Tummons, J., Orr, K. and Atkins, L. (2013) *Teaching Higher Education Courses in Further Education Colleges*. Exeter: Learning Matters.

Waller, R. (2004) 'I really hated school, and couldn't wait to get out!' Reflections on 'a wasted opportunity' amongst access to HE students. *Journal of Access Policy and Practice*, 2(1): 24–43.

Widdowson, J. (2017) *A Message from Our Chair*. Available at: www.mixedeconomygroup.co.uk

Yorke, M. (2008) *Employability and Higher Education: What It Is – What It Is Not*, 2nd edn. York: Higher Education Academy.

23

INFORMATION AND COMMUNICATION TECHNOLOGY IN THE POST-COMPULSORY SECTOR

Roy Halpin and Cheryl Reynolds

Key words – ICT; ILT; TEL; digital skills; digital literacy

Introduction

This chapter introduces information and communication technology as a contested notion that triggers polarised responses from education professionals. We discuss some of the key issues of implementing technology and how these might be overcome, before going on to highlight some of the myths and fads that surround technology in education. We finish on a positive note, arguing that our responses to educational technology are approaching a crossroads, with more mature, critically evaluative discussions about its pedagogical implications and more critically aware perceptions of what educational technology is and ought to be.

What it is, what it's not and why/where it makes sense to use ICT

Defining technology-enhanced learning

Providing a definition of educational technology (EdTech) is challenging because of its diversity and because of the rate at which it continues to evolve, both in terms of what is available and in terms of how, where, when and why it is deployed. One approach to this challenge is to attempt to list the different types of educational technology, focusing on those that are most novel and pervasive at the time of writing. There are, however, some important disadvantages to this kind of definition. First, it oversimplifies our conception of technology as merely a set of tools that we pick up and lay aside, remaining unaffected ourselves, a conception that we go on to challenge in our discussion below.

Second, such definitions rapidly become obsolete as technology evolves. Third, despite attempts to generalise, such lists tend to endorse particular platforms, devices and software 'solutions', drawing academic texts into a partial and complicit relationship with the EdTech industry. This is particularly problematic in the field of teacher education, because it influences the choices of a generation of trainee teachers as they enter a highly pressured and contested profession.

Instead, therefore, we have assumed a broader and more critical approach. Rather than merely enumerating a list of tools, we want to acknowledge how technologies act back upon us, altering what we say and do and how we relate to one another, to our employers, to our students and to our work as educators. Broadly influenced by Marshall McLuhan's (1994) maxim that 'we become what we behold ... we shape our tools and afterwards our tools shape us' (pxxi), we acknowledge that:

> Technology does not exist in a vacuum but is socially constructed, uneven, contested, contradictory, participatory and deeply entwined with everyday life. It is intensely political. It is defined by complex interactions between social actors and their context in its broadest sense: at the micro level of individuals and in classrooms; at the meso level of the institutions and regions within which they are based and at the macro level of global economies and nation states.
>
> (Reynolds, 2018, p39)

Seeing educational technology in this wider context is particularly important because we live in highly monetised and competitive times. We argue, therefore, that educators should turn away from the constant quest for the ideal set of 'tools', adopting instead a critical and critically aware disposition towards technologies that we adopt whenever we are presented with a new classroom 'solution' or online learning platform. This kind of disposition asks not just what the solution can do at the technical level, but also what effects it might have on participants, intended and unintended, constructive and destructive; not just what is to be gained, but what is to be lost, perhaps irrevocably, in the shift to a new approach; who stands to profit and whether their motives are congruent with the educational good or run counter to it. This is not to deny the many and varied benefits of educational technology, merely to acknowledge that the shift into using more technology in teaching and learning is not a neutral one and has potential both for good and ill, and that 'educational technology needs to be understood as a profoundly political affair – a site of constant conflict and a struggle between different interests and groups' (Selwyn, 2016, p94).

What works: where and when and why?

'What works?' (UK Government, 2013) is a common, current question within education and other areas of the public sector. In common with the medical profession, education is increasingly encouraged to be evidence- rather than eminence-led; endorsement by influential bodies or individuals is not enough to justify the use of technology in teaching and learning. Instead, it is argued, we need proof of impact. Nonetheless, educators and institutions have continued to be seduced by unproven technologies with monotonous regularity. More recently, however, a definite move towards the use of evidence-informed approaches has become evident.

In theory, finding robust evidence for what works in classrooms and other teaching spaces ought to be straightforward. However, there are a number of factors clouding our view, not least the language of positivity that surrounds the field – learning technologies, adaptive learning, personalised learning, interactive and engaging learning – all with the promise of making things better and easier for students and teachers. Perhaps not surprisingly, this positive narrative hails especially from those vested interests with something to sell, whether that be a commercial product or the promise of, for example, improved examination results or better ratings with external viewers and inspectors. Fewer discussions centre on the problematic consequences of technologies that are situated within social and cultural contexts. In other words, the 'usefulness' of any technology is totally enmeshed in the local situation and the technology is in constant dialogue with the social situation that surrounds it. Little wonder that in complex and highly pressured environments, things do not always end well. Digital tools regularly receive bad press due to factors often not related to the technology itself, such as a lack of investment in equipment and staff development, institutional culture and practices, and a lack of fully integrated, well-thought-through digital pedagogy.

Key questions

Why hasn't technology transformed education?

Cutting-edge technologies are expensive, unruly and time-consuming – not an appealing mix for either teachers or students. Once technologies become more accepted and available generally, then they begin to filter into and eventually penetrate pedagogy. Examples might include laptops and tablets finally becoming cheap enough and robust enough to be everyday classroom tools; widespread availability of Wi-Fi networks so that mobile working is a viable option; and applications such as virtual learning environments (VLEs) evolving into reliable and intuitive products that connect to other applications, often in the cloud, and therefore becoming more genuinely productive tools. Once these things are in place, and there is increased use and familiarity, then they begin to gain acceptance within the education arena. To some, this may seem as though education is always behind the curve. To others, this will look like a case of healthy scepticism, a 'prove it and I'll use it' approach in the face of an overwhelming number of options and opinions in a time- and cash-limited environment.

Where is the EdTech? The need for investment

The IT revolution, as far as general teaching, learning and assessment is concerned, is just around the corner … as it has been for nearly half a century. While almost every activity in our daily lives has been impacted by IT, teaching and learning, classrooms and workshops frequently remain obstinately non-digital. Education institutions themselves could no longer function effectively without significant IT resources, and the back-office logistical operation of most organisations is entirely reliant on robust and efficient systems. While the noise in the media is all about 'disruption' and the many and various ways that technology will change education irrevocably, the real focus and significant changes have occurred more in the back office than in the classroom.

Some of the key issues and barriers to successful implementation of technology within everyday pedagogy are: the lack of investment in staff development and equipment; institutional culture and practice that sees digital as an afterthought; and the subsequent lack of planned digital pedagogy.

Investment in staff development

Implementing new ideas takes time – for successful implementation, there needs to be real confidence in a number of factors: confidence by tutors using the kit for themselves (*Am I confident using this in front of a group?*); confidence in the infrastructure (*Will it work when I need it?*); and confidence that development time isn't time wasted (*Is this a fad? Will it really make a difference?*). To this end, the adoption of straightforward classroom projection and simple links to internet pages makes sense, whereas adopting technologies that require a greater investment of time is likely to be problematic. Coe (2013) argues convincingly that for continuing professional development to lead to real change, it needs to be at least 15 contact hours, preferably 50, and sustained over two terms. In other words, practitioners need time and support to embed, practise and gain confidence in using new technologies. How often is this reality in busy educational institutions?

Investment in equipment

The recent digital framework report from the Joint Information Systems Commission (Beetham et al., 2018) highlights poor and patchy access to modern equipment as a fundamental issue in further education. Many computers and peripherals are approaching five years old and are effectively obsolete, resulting in a real issue that equipment will simply not be fast or reliable enough to be of any use. Computers that take 10 minutes to join networks and become usable from a cold start are not infrequent, and this is time that tutors do not have and students do not have patience for. The need for investment in IT infrastructure and the computers that are used by staff and students is significant and often inadequate. That this level of investment has an impact upon budgets is without doubt, but as with much back-office material and process, it might not attract significant investment funding while everything, on the surface, seems to be functioning well. When infrastructure fails and whole networks shut down, action is quickly, if expensively, taken to avoid catastrophe. However, when individual staff or student computers slow down to the point of being unusable, they are generally left to gather dust, while teaching and learning moves back a step to a pre-digital age. It is in this context that the discussion around schools, colleges and small training providers investing in gadgets such as virtual reality, active teaching rooms and other toys from the shiny shop seems so bizarre. If money were available, then it would need to be spent on fundamental infrastructure first.

Institutional culture, practice and planned pedagogy

Alongside structural and investment decisions by senior management, the culture of an institution really does come from the top. Effective, positive change in the ways that digital tools are used can be driven from the head of the institution via clear strategy and policy. This can aid considerably in removing the issue of reinvention (see below), giving individuals and teams specific focus on elements of digital pedagogy. As with the staff development mentioned earlier, none of this is quick or cheap. Culture change takes leadership and time.

Within many large educational organisations, good examples exist of robust and capable digital systems for activities such as enrolment, tracking and attendance, tutorial and pastoral care, funding and finance decisions, and exams. Use of these systems doubtless gives the organisation a better chance to run their affairs appropriately, understanding the local environment and addressing student issues quickly and in real time. In many cases, this has been due to fundamental business needs (e.g. having reliable networks that are resistant to hacking by students or external forces) or due to the need to stay up to date with student tracking data, and thus the ability to return these data to funding agencies. These are seen as critical systems that the institution relies on to function and to create the audit trails that justify their funding.

Without doubt, in many institutions, technology for teaching and learning comes a poor second to such concerns, arguably due to the lack of a proven need. If the technology is not present, then students still get taught. In this context, EdTech can be framed as an expensive luxury in times of budgetary constraint. Few institutions have a *planned pedagogy* with digital strategy at its heart. Of course, this is all rather polemic, and there are examples of institutions where digital pedagogy is hard-wired, but these remain few and far between in all sectors of formal education.

Key theory

Modelling

Modelling of practice is something that teachers do every day with their students, especially in vocational subjects. Much of this is concerned with modelling, for example, appropriate teaching and learning behaviours; social or safety rules in the classroom, salon or workshop; or in the use of equipment to perform a specific task. It is this latter example of modelling and the use of ICT by teachers that is seen to be extremely varied and definitely problematic.

Poor modelling of ICT practice by teachers and by teacher educators may be due to, among other things, issues of confidence, planning or resourcing, resulting in the potential pedagogical advantages of the use of IT being lost – time is lost, distraction levels are high, and outcomes are not enhanced, and may even be detrimentally affected.

That this is repeated at all levels in the system does seem to be an issue. High-quality modelling of IT use by teacher educators is very varied, modelling by trainee and experienced tutors to students likewise.

One result is that it is often perceived to be easier and more effective to *not* use digital technologies with students. There exists a well-documented phenomenon of 'reality shock' or 'transition shock' (Korthagen et al., 2006; Tondeur et al., 2017) that new teachers feel as they move between training and employment. Due to the pressures and unfamiliarity of much of the role, new teachers may tend towards more traditional (i.e. the ones they themselves received) approaches and experience a 'washing out' effect of useful background theory. If the modelling of ideas and techniques, including the use of IT, has not been consolidated into new teachers' practice, then it stands to reason that it might get forgotten in the rough and tumble of daily teaching and learning.

Reinventing the IT wheel

A lack of strategic direction and clarity of purpose has often hampered the use of ICT within the post-compulsory sector, much as it has done in schools. This is not to say that there hasn't been some fabulous use of digital technologies in a wide range of disciplines, but the overall picture remains very mixed. With few members of staff specifically trained in project management, in the use of newer technologies or in digital pedagogy, the result has often been one of continual reinvention, endless numbers of small-scale projects that are locally quite successful, or not, dependent upon the availability and enthusiasm of individual teachers or technologists. Often, as a teacher moves on, the learning, the driver and the usefulness of a specific technology or strategy is lost. Enthusiastic early adopters and digital advocates are to be welcomed, but for implementation in the longer-term and a reduction in the stop-start new initiative cycle and its associated recurrent workload issues, there needs to be strategic direction and clear leadership at a senior level.

Sharing of resources and repurposing is not something teachers are always good at. Even within the same team, teachers have their own resources and ideas, and a lack of collegiality may mean that teachers are replicating the planning and resourcing of sessions. This has definitely been the case for straightforward materials such as worksheets and slides, and is potentially even more problematic with bespoke learning objects that need dedicated IT support to create and modify.

There are moves to counteract some of these issues, often in school settings where a standardised set of resources is used, tailored in a minor way by the individual teacher for delivery. While there may be some concerns over the creation, ownership and sharing of the materials, and also an argument that teachers are becoming boxed-in deliverers rather than active pedagogues, these challenges are misplaced. Digital technology, when used carefully, can be a powerful enabler in allowing for quick and easy updates to session materials, overall ease of storage, communications and sharing of ideas. Surely, allowing teachers to concentrate on delivering brilliant teaching and learning is a better use of time and brainpower than endlessly reinventing the same ideas and materials for lessons.

In summary:

1. Clear leadership is required. Institutional and team strategies need to be in place.

2. Digital advocates are to be welcomed. Allow space and time to play.

3. Stop endlessly writing and planning sessions. Share ideas and resources widely. Community and collegiate approaches to development need to be encouraged.

4. Use technology where it is potentially beneficial. Don't squeeze it in just because you can.

Key theory

Connected learning

Much of the potential for EdTech development centres upon students' own learning spaces rather than that of large academic institutions. In a significant change in recent decades, students often have greater access to, and use of, technology than their teachers or their college. The key to this change is the relatively low cost of laptops and smartphones and the widespread availability of Wi-Fi and social media.

Having one's own device or the ability to emulate a personal device via a web browser enables students to create their own digital desktop anywhere. These *personal learning networks* allow students to use technology as an adaptive tool and to be more in control of their own study – in time, space and place. They are combining social media and communications technology with the power of search engines; they are asking questions, finding solutions, writing ideas, and storing this information quickly and accessibly. Crucially, they are networking and creating dynamic communities. Arguably, they are recreating a simplified and functional version of the traditional college VLE, but in a way that suits the mobile way that they work (and at a fraction of the cost).

Myths and fads

This section will focus on some of the nonsense and blind alleyways into which the sector is too easily led. Educational myths and fads are an all too common issue across all sectors of education, and the post-compulsory sector is not immune to this. Sometimes it is a case of old or just plain 'wrong' theory that has been discredited; often it is the endless reworking and republishing of ideas so that the model or framework teachers get to work with has little resemblance to the original research. Unfortunately, colleagues in positions of influence such as consultants, managers or teacher educators are often the source of some of this junk theory. The reality is that many teachers across all sectors are subject to constant micromanagement, scrutiny and ever-increasing workloads. When faced with a seemingly useful idea or a shiny new IT widget, they often do not have the professional capacity to give it the pedagogical scrutiny it truly deserves. Vast sums of money have been spent on IT equipment over the years, from videoconferencing to interactive whiteboards to personalised learning systems. This isn't to say that these things cannot be useful, just that they often are not, because they are *technologically* rather than *pedagogically determined*. The sales force rather than the teachers are leading the conversation.

Folk devils and moral panics

Exploring the myths that surround educational technology is particularly important because of the amount of money to be made through mythologising its impact. In 2016, global education expenditure was estimated at over $5 trillion. As distribution and platforms scale internationally, the market is projected to grow at 17.0 per cent per annum (EdTechXGlobal, 2016). This is an already significant market with huge potential for growth, a highly lucrative industry operating within a fiercely contested and marketised system. The frequent claims that educational technology will transform or revolutionise learning should therefore be viewed with suspicion. Blaming technology for a host of educational ills should be treated with similar scepticism. Both of these polarised positions represent the kind of 'technological determinism' (Miller, 2003, p45) that ignores social factors and sees us as wholly subject to the effects of technology, both for good or ill. Little wonder, then, that myths abound.

Note, for example, the marketing hype in these ambitious claims from a range of educational technology providers:

- offers robust solutions to power school operations, drive student growth and unify the classroom experience;

- teaches students how government works by having them experience it directly;

- improves access to quality education for everyone; and

- gives complete control over your digital classroom.

Claims such as these that promise both ease and impact are seductive in a context where 'teachers' labour is characterised by underemployment and over-qualification, precariousness and the prevalence of "rotten jobs." In this context educational workers are subject to high levels of surveillance, rooted in regimes of performativity and institutional risk aversion' (Avis and Reynolds, 2017). The 'terrors of performativity' (Ball, 2003), aggravated by a long squeeze on funding in further education (Lucas and Crowther, 2016), make classroom practitioners, education leaders and researchers of educational technology particularly vulnerable to manipulation in ways that might affect their purchasing choices, their practices, and the impartiality and quality of their research. For these reasons, we argue for a move away from a purely instrumental and technicist engagement with EdTech and for a more critically aware, reflexive and questioning outlook. This is difficult when much of the research into the effects of technology in education remains 'disappointingly a-political and a-social, finding little common ground with critical educational studies and/or the sociology of education' (Selwyn, 2016, p156). However, there have been some notable recent attempts to debunk many of these myths, perhaps stemming from the 'What works?' movement and, ironically, from the opportunities for teachers to engage in critically evaluative discussion networks through social media.

The flawed concepts of digital natives and digital immigrants

The idea that there is a divide between those born into the internet generation and those born previously, and that this might in some way bestow an enhanced digital ability on younger people, is an appealing notion often quoted in the media. The original work by Prensky (2001a, 2001b) of digital immigrants and digital natives, while having merit, has been accepted to be too simplistic (Kirschner and De Bruyckere, 2017); there is essentially no difference in innate digital ability between the generations – it is essentially to do with usage and familiarity. Students use technology for their own purposes and familiarity comes with use. They do not have some special gift for the use of tech, just a dexterity and ability that comes from ownership of phones and tablets, and daily, if not hourly, use of common apps such as Facebook, WhatsApp and Instagram (at the time of writing, in 2019). Their learning of these technologies often occurs in their own space, so that all we see is their prowess, not their mistakes. As soon as we ask students to engage with less familiar software such as a VLE or productivity tool, they are often less enamoured and certainly less confident. The technologies to which we introduce students might be entirely appropriate for the job required but are not 'their' usual systems. In addition, these packages are often less intuitive to use than some common apps, sometimes due to the age of the software or the relative lack of money (e.g. compared to Facebook) that has been invested in their design. Often professional level software by definition has to be complex, and this can be off-putting for 'natives' who find that their IT skills and confidence might be lacking after all.

My space or their space: students don't think that digital is cool – they don't really want you on their patch

Another myth, and a potentially nightmarish place for teachers to go, is the idea that because young people use digital technology all of the time, and therefore because it is in some way accepted ('cool'?), then we can enhance our teaching and the engagement of students in their learning by joining them using 'their' technologies.

Two issues are inherent in this idea. First, as mentioned above, is the reality that not all students have the skills, confidence or readily available technology to join in. We make assumptions about their digital capabilities at our peril. Second, there is a significant issue of intrusion into students' personal space and the overlapping of personal and professional lives for both students and staff. As well as the difficulties that may be thrown up from data protection, safeguarding or legislative perspectives, there is also the sense that students are having conversations in their own space and time, and they often want to keep separate (as staff do) the systems they use for work or study and those for social space. Having distinctly separate online identities aids this overall feeling of separation. While it might be useful to infiltrate their systems and their communication channels to drop in a message about homework, their reaction to this intrusion might be more one of alienation rather than accommodation. Joining students in their digital social space rather than inviting them into our professional learning space is fraught with difficulties.

The distraction effect

The modern world bombards us with information that is constantly vying for our attention. By introducing digital technologies into our teaching and learning spaces, how can we be sure that the benefits to be gained are not outweighed by the issues, most crucially that of distraction? Distraction seems to come in two guises: inappropriate focus and split attention (multitasking).

Inappropriate focus within a session often occurs because the task or activity takes on greater importance in students' thinking than the content itself. A useful non-IT example might be to recall some science lessons remembered from school. For many people, these memories will involve explosions, flashes, smells and smoke. The activity, the visual, olfactory and aural experience, is the remembered element, not the science behind all that noise and distraction. In many adverts for teacher recruitment, science teachers are always blowing things up. If this is what we remember, then the point of the session is lost. When using ICT in teaching and learning, the often remembered element might be the quiz, the whizz-bang software or the colourful clip art or images. Maybe they will remember the time when the technology failed and students' attention therefore wandered off to other things. If technology becomes the thing, or the session becomes an exercise in using, for example, social media, then this is the element that students will remember, not the key outcomes actually planned for.

Split attention occurs when different media are competing for our attention. Despite claims that multitasking is possible, it is very difficult to do well. Driving a vehicle and texting are incompatible. Listening to a lecture and tweeting in real time is difficult to do well, and key threads in the conversation are easily missed. While it is possible to improve levels of concentration, the best solution is to reduce the external environmental loading. For our students, this will mean training to use devices appropriately and professionally, and removing as much as possible distractions such as social media and music (Sweller et al., 2011).

ICT as a disruptive force – not always

Digital disruption, the idea that new technologies will fundamentally change the way that we work and how systems function, is clearly an important aspect of our lives. However, assuming that disruption is always the case, or always necessary, seems to be missing the point. Messages in the media and from politicians that disruption *will* be beneficial are misguided as, once again, these messages are pushed out by individuals and by an industry that does not generally care for or understand the daily process of teaching and learning. The industry exists to make a profit, and it is wise to remember this. As soon as we start to use the language of business rather than education, then we clearly have a significant problem. If, however, digital technology is seen as an enhancement rather than a competitor to non-digital environments, then we might be getting somewhere.

Twenty-first-century skills: same ideas, just different technology

Alongside the idea of disruption by digital technology comes the notion that we need a new set of *twenty-first-century skills* that are fundamentally different to those of previous generations. Superficially, this idea has merit, but really it is just about developing appropriate skills for the technology of the age. Learning how to use IT and becoming confident in applying this to novel situations is really no different from learning how to drive or to operate complex machinery. It is unknown technology at the outset, and familiarity – deliberate practice – with the technology makes the difference. As described earlier, no one has an innate ability with new technology, but familiarity and practice lead to confidence and competence.

The seeds of change

The digital revolution has taken place in institutional management and back-office systems, but in terms of teaching and learning it is still (just) around the corner. Lack of investment in equipment, staff development and strategy has been problematic. However, there are signs of change on the horizon.

One distinct development has been the greater collaboration between individuals in different institutions globally that has been facilitated by social media and other digital networks. Writing about your work and ideas has never been easier, and immediate broadcasting and collaboration is possible via open-access media such as blog sites and Twitter. This has enabled voices and ideas to emerge that would never have been possible within more traditional institutional hierarchies.

Another element is the maturation of the research fields and frameworks that are focused upon this area. Readily available outputs might include the JISC Digital Capabilities Framework (JISC, 2018), the EU Digital Competencies Framework (Van den Brande, 2016) and the most recent derivative for further education, the ETF Digital Skills Competency Framework (ETF, 2018). As the fundamental research progresses, and as ideas such as those listed here become more widely known, discussed, refined and embedded, then they begin to reset the baseline of what is possible and what might be expected. There is a danger that these new frameworks become the next tick-box requirement, though they do also, arguably, give ammunition to front-line staff, via increased confidence and awareness, to push back against inappropriate technologies and distractive ideas.

The evidence suggests that finally, although nowhere near comprehensively, there is a change in thinking within some institutions. Success comes from a sense of purpose, a rationale, a thought-through strategy for the implementation of specific technologies *as part of a wider planned pedagogy* rather than as a senior leadership whim or technologically determined 'must-have'.

Chapter summary

- Defining EdTech is difficult. We have traditionally tended to focus on the tools rather than on their usefulness in the teaching, learning and assessment process.

- What works – where, when and why? This is specific to each individual situation, but there may be a gathering consensus that much of the technology available is more problematic than useful.

- Significant investment in professional development is required if new technologies are to be successfully integrated.

- Old, obsolete technology is worse than useless. It is a direct impediment to effective teaching and learning.

- Successful use of technology is more often seen in the logistics surrounding teaching and learning rather than in the classes themselves.

- Beware of the industry and the evangelists. Is it a fad or genuinely useful? A distraction or a potentially valuable tool?

Further recommended reading

Price, D. (2013) *Open: How We'll Work, Live and Learn in the Future*. London: Crux Publishing.

An interesting account of how the use of open data and digital systems is already changing the way that we live, work and learn.

Selwyn, N. (2016) *Is Technology Good for Education?* Cambridge: Polity Press.

Selwyn, N. (2017) *Education and Technology: Key Issues and Debates*, 2nd edn. London: Bloomsbury Academic.

Very accessible and digestible texts on some of the big questions surrounding technology in education.

References

Avis, J. and Reynolds, C. (2017) The digitalization of work and social justice: reflections on the labour process of English further education teachers. In C. Harteis (ed.), *The Impact of Digitalization in the Workplace: An Educational View*. Dordrecht: Springer.

Ball, S. (2003) The teacher's soul and the terrors of performativity. *Journal of Education Policy*, 18(2): 215–228.

Beetham, H., Newman, T. and Knight, S. (2018) *Digital Experience Insights Survey*. Available at: http://repository.jisc.ac.uk/6967/1/Digital_experience_insights_survey_2018.pdf

Coe, R. (2013) *Improving Education: A Triumph of Hope over Experience*. Available at: www.cem.org/attachments/publications/ImprovingEducation2013.pdf

EdTechXGlobal (2016) *Global Report Predicts EdTech Spend to Reach $252bn by 2020*. Available at: www.prnewswire.com/news-releases/global-reportpredicts-edtech-spend-to-reach-252bn-by-2020-580765301.html

ETF (2018) *Digital Skills Competency Framework*. Available at: www.et-foundation.co.uk/supporting/support-practitioners/edtech-support/digital-skills-competency-framework/

JISC (2018) *What Is Digital Capability?* Available at: https://digitalcapability.jisc.ac.uk/what-is-digital-capability/

Kirschner, P.A. and De Bruyckere, P. (2017) The myths of the digital native and the multitasker. *Teaching and Teacher Education*, 67: 135–142.

Korthagen, F., Loughran, J. and Russell, T. (2006) Developing fundamental principles for teacher education programs and practices. *Teaching and Teacher Education*, 22(8): 1020–1041.

Lucas, N. and Crowther, N. (2016) The logic of the incorporation of further education colleges in England 1993–2015: towards an understanding of marketisation, change and instability. *Journal of Education Policy*, 31(5): 583–597.

McLuhan, M. (1994) *Understanding Media: The Extensions of Man*. Cambridge, MA: MIT Press.

Miller, T. (2003) *Television: Critical Concepts in Media and Cultural Studies Volume II*. London: Routledge.

Prensky, M. (2001a) Digital natives, digital immigrants part 1. *On the Horizon*, 9(5): 1–6.

Prensky, M. (2001b) Digital natives, digital immigrants part 2: do they really think differently? *On the Horizon*, 9(6): 1–6.

Reynolds, C. (2018) *Digital Hiatus: Symbolic Violence in an Online Social Learning Network for Master's Level Students at a UK University*. Available at: http://eprints.hud.ac.uk/id/eprint/34603/1/Cheryl%20Reynolds%20FINAL%20THESIS.PDF

Selwyn, N. (2016) *Is Technology Good for Education?* Cambridge: Polity Press.

Sweller, J., Ayres, P. and Kalyuga, S. (2011) *Cognitive Load Theory*. New York: Springer.

Tondeur, J., Pareja Roblin, N., van Braak, J., Voogt, J. and Prestridge, S. (2017) Preparing beginning teachers for technology integration in education: ready for take-off? *Technology, Pedagogy and Education*, 26(2), 157–121.

UK Government (2013) *What Works Network*. Available at: www.gov.uk/guidance/what-works-network

Van den Brande, L. (2016) *The European Digital Competence Framework for Citizens*. Available at: www.dx.doi.org/10.13140/RG.2.1.4687.1281

24

APPRENTICESHIPS

Aaron Bradbury and Vicky Wynne

Key words – practice pedagogy; industry training; on-the-job training; vocational training; professional development; technical skills; apprenticeship pedagogy; vocational practice placement

Introduction

Apprentice: An individual who receives apprenticeship training to prepare them for a specific occupation or profession and, where applicable, End Point Assessment through an apprenticeship framework or standard.

Apprenticeship: A job with an accompanying skills development programme, which includes the training and, where required, End Point Assessment.

Apprenticeships are currently defined as providing practical training in a job alongside study, and while apprenticeships have traditionally been regarded as the vocational route to stable employment and skills, it is realistic to suggest that apprenticeships are currently going through one of their most challenging periods. Apprenticeships are an evolving model of learning and a vibrant model of education through vocational learning, through the landscape of intermediate to higher-level degree apprenticeships and the progression opportunities that they provide; and while apprenticeships have sometimes suffered from a poor reputation, they are now becoming an increasingly popular option for all ages, including existing employed staff as an opportunity for continuing professional development (CPD) or 'upskilling'.

The main difference between an apprenticeship and classroom-based vocational education is that in an apprenticeship, the 'learning' format involves most of the time being spent in work-based roles and some 'teaching'-based education (this can be both inside and outside of the organisation). In theory, apprenticeships should offer an excellent environment to gain employability skills to prepare the learner for a specific occupation or profession. These skills can range from team working, communication and specific occupational skills acquired while on the job. There is also the theoretical context that comes alongside the employability skills – therefore, skills-based learning with theoretical concepts being adapted and understood. For young people who have left compulsory education, apprenticeships allow a transition from school-based learning to something akin to the world of work. Apprenticeships allow employers to match the needs of the business to the needs that the apprentice will need for the job. The knowledge economy is seeing demand for higher-level skills, and in today's competitive labour market, having both the skills and experience is now seen as a vital component within employment.

History of apprenticeships and the lessons we learn today

This chapter explores the underpinning history, theory and composition of apprenticeships within the UK, with a detailed discussion around the landscape of higher-level apprenticeships, which also falls within the FE inspectorate and standards; the mode of learning that takes place which will emphasise new ways of how apprenticeships are being developed within the undergraduate market; and how learners have expectations of such new innovative ways of learning in a growing labour-demand market. Throughout the discussion, it is acknowledged there has been an emerging concern from academics, politicians and some employers around the robustness of apprenticeships and degree apprenticeships in their current iteration, compared to a traditional vocational or degree programme within a university or college. The chapter outlines an acceptance of changing policy, accepting the fact that this is a mode of learning within many modes of learning within the vocational arena. There will be clarification of the need for a range of opportunities for all learners to be able to complete a vocational intermediate or higher qualification (Fuller and Unwin, 2011; Guile and Young, 1998).

The re-emergence of apprenticeships has raised questions concerning many aspects of higher-level skills and vocational education, and therefore this has been managed with the introduction of higher/ degree apprenticeships and work experience being integrated into traditional HE courses, ensuring more employment-based programmes putting skills and knowledge at the forefront of learning. It is important to remember that the role of employers in apprenticeship learning cannot be under-estimated. Employers, typically represented within sector skills councils, have the responsibility of identifying industry needs, developing appropriately robust standards (a set of occupational competencies that cover knowledge, skills and behaviours), which includes an appropriate level of assessment to meet those needs, selecting and employing suitable apprentices, and engaging with a training provider to ensure these robustly developed standards are delivered. Sometimes a training provider can also be the employer.

This training/learning, employer/learning provider, and apprentice relationship needs to be ongoing, with the needs of the apprentice at the centre (see Figure 24.1).

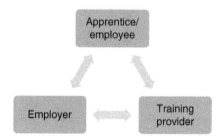

Figure 24.1   The triadic relationship between the apprentice, employer and training provider

While the role of employers in apprenticeships was identified earlier, they also hold the responsibility for the ongoing development of the apprentice; this comes with the caveat that employers must also ensure there is a genuine job available with a contract of employment long enough for an apprentice to complete their apprenticeship. Employers must pay an apprentice's wages and the role must help them gain the knowledge, skills and behaviours they need to achieve the apprenticeship, thus emphasising while employers have always played a role in apprenticeship development, employers have assumed an increased lead in developing the future workforce.

There are concerns that were raised by Chankseliani and Relly (2015), who demonstrated the low level of apprenticeship uptake. Some have questioned the ability of employers to be able to fulfil their duties as stakeholders in the development of higher degree programmes.

Over recent years, there has been an increase in public resources devoted to improving young people's awareness of apprenticeships. Yet while many teenage applications have steadily increased, many teenage start-ups at level 2 and 3 apprenticeships have flatlined. Recent government data have shown that only 26 per cent of apprenticeships actually come straight from school or college (DfE, 2017). Apprenticeships are seen to be a vehicle for driving social mobility, enabling young people to gain work-related skills for their future. They allow learners to think about their futures without compromising their financial commitment for many years to come. Therefore, for apprenticeships to be successful, this percentage must be improved. Previous UK governments have seen apprenticeships as a vehicle for getting more school and college leavers to earn and learn, which in turn allows for an increase in national productivity while learners gain valuable sector-specific skills in a real working environment.

While employers appear committed to increasing the opportunities around employment skills and training, there are many administration tasks that are included with this. Consequently, those that are designing apprenticeships need to ensure that there is parity in the experience that is comparable to the learning experience in other organisations. Carter (2010) and King et al. (2016) validated the need for a more flexible approach within the design of all programmes. However, to bring into the mix an apprenticeship model, which is scrutinised by government, plagued with quangos and which is a new experience for universities to take on board, raises complications. It is this experience that has guided us to where we are today. As part of the research discussed by Bravenboer (2016), it has been suggested that a partnerships approach is necessary for the apprenticeship model to work.

Key questions

How is the academic sector expected to develop and deliver a learning model so completely different from a traditional university model of learning yet still of a comparative robustness?

The evolution of apprenticeships

A brief history of apprenticeships

Apprenticeships in Britain started during the Middle Ages and were closely related to the medieval craft guilds; apprenticeships evolved by way of a contractual agreement between the master and servant initially in a few trades. Apprenticeships were 'sealed' through indentures (the precursors of today's contracts), which were legally binding documents.

The following two centuries saw a significant expansion in apprenticeships, which also prompted a gradual improvement of legislation.

The Health and Morals of Apprentices Act 1802 laid out additional conditions, including no more than 12 hours per day on the job, and the apprentice should be taught arithmetic, reading and writing (the precursors of today's functional skills). Apprenticeships remained popular with many occupations that involved practical elements of skills that were embedded towards the end of the nineteenth century.

However, by the 1960s, it was being argued that apprenticeships had not kept up with the ever-accelerating pace of industrial, technological and scientific advances of the time; that the apprenticeship 'time served' aspect was redundant, not focused on outcomes, and did not recognise fully how people acquired skills at different rates; and too often the important issue of standards (behaviours) were overlooked.

Apprenticeships are now recognised as a model of education that prepares the learner for an occupation. Such models are largely enhanced through workplace experiences. Apprentices are employed and distinctly positioned as learners and positioned as novice practitioners (Chan, 2013; Deissinger and Hellwig, 2005). However, for a long time the majority of occupational preparation has arisen mainly through learners' active and interdependent engagement in such occupational tasks, not always through being taught and not through models of education. That said, Billett (2014) states that educational institutions are a hybrid to bring both the occupational tasks and the learning together to establish an apprenticeship that we see today. While apprenticeships are viewed as educational models, they need to be equally understood as a mode of learning.

Key questions

How does an apprenticeship differ from other teaching models?

What is an apprenticeship today?

The modern apprenticeship evolving into the reformed apprenticeship

Apprenticeships are now available to anyone over the age of 16 living in England who is not in full-time education and is eligible to work in the UK. The current generation of modern apprenticeships are vastly different and significantly improved from the traditional versions, and with rising university fees and the scrapping of maintenance grants, apprenticeships present a very attractive alternative to HE for young people. Supporting this significantly improved model of an apprenticeship, it has been observed that the profile of the apprentice has also changed. There are now a higher proportion of apprenticeship uptakes in the 25+ group, but as stated there are more employed members of staff accessing the apprenticeship training rather than using apprenticeships as a 16+ mode of learning (IFF Research, 2017). In England, at present, there are three levels of apprenticeship:

- intermediate;
- advanced; and
- higher/degree.

The majority of apprenticeship starts have been held within a small number of companies; this has been recognised by the government in its current overhaul of the system, and so-called 'trailblazer' employers have been selected to participate in the design of what are called 'reformed apprenticeships'. The companies represent the following sectors: aerospace, automotive, digital industries, electrotechnical, energy, financial services, food and drink, and life and industrial sciences.

An apprenticeship is seen as having a 'real' job; an apprenticeship should be about entry to *a recognised occupation*, involve a substantial programme of *on and off-the-job training*, and under all circumstances the apprentice should be employed from day one. Apprenticeships are *employer-led*; employers set the standards, create the demand for apprentices to meet their skills needs, fund the apprenticeship, and are responsible for employing and training the apprentice. An apprentice is expected to work alongside experienced staff in the work setting to be able to gain specific job-related skills and behaviours, earn a wage, and be given time for study that is related to the role. This is currently referred to as '20 per cent off the job', the equivalent to one day per week, and is likely to include (but not exclusively) formal training by an organisation approved to deliver apprenticeship training, delivered either in or out of the setting (RoATP, 2016).

Apprenticeships lead to industry-developed and -recognised standards or qualifications, and most apprenticeships require an external assessment at the end of the programme (referred to as the End Point Assessment, EPA) to assess the apprentice's ability and competence within the job role. The decision to put an apprentice forward for EPA is made collectively with the apprentice, employer and training provider, thus demonstrating the strength of this triadic relationship.

While the role of the employer has been clearly demonstrated, the *needs of the apprentice* are equally important: to achieve competence in a skilled occupation, which is transferable and secures long-term earnings potential, greater security and the capability to progress in the workplace, but the contemporary apprenticeship is built on a set of standards, and the qualification provides public certification that the standard has been met. However, there are a number of apprenticeship standards that do not have a qualification embedded into them, which has caused uncertainty in the sectors where qualifications have always been seen as the gold standard, questioning the validity of such programmes.

The Richard Review of Apprenticeships (Richard, 2012) prompted the development of 'reformed apprenticeships', which were launched in 2013. Within this reformed model, employers would receive a high degree of freedom to develop high-quality apprenticeships that best meet the needs of specific occupations, with sufficient content and transferability to justify public investment.

- *System*. Relates to the national policy framework for apprenticeships, and is the remit of government funding agencies and national provider and employer stakeholder organisations.

- *Sector*. Operates through employer-led partnerships, professional bodies and sector skills councils who set occupational and accreditation requirements.

- *Standard*. Relates to the development and review of individual apprenticeship standards for specific occupations.

In 2018, the Department for Education reported on the progress of the Apprenticeships Reform Programme. The discussion included implementing apprenticeship reforms to continue to improve the quality of apprenticeships for all and the need to provide those skills that employers need, all to be delivered through a plan for 3 million high-quality new apprenticeships. Importantly, it was stated that all apprenticeships should be delivered through paid employment, lasting for a minimum duration of 12 months and involving sustained training and clear skills gain with at least 20 per cent off-the-job training.

The report went on to identify that apprenticeship reforms have increased the number of learning hours per learner, with apprentices expected to receive an average of 670 hours throughout their apprenticeship. The reforms also introduced the apprenticeship levy, requiring all employers with an annual pay bill of £3 million or more to invest 0.5 per cent of their pay bill in apprenticeship training.

Key questions

Do you agree or disagree that some elements of apprenticeships could be done just as well in class? If so, what would that be?

Key theory

From formal education to informal learning

According to Billett (2014), learning is not solely a property of formal education, but in fact is also informal, deeply embedded within other social activities, including work. This article describes the challenges of informal learning in knowledge-intensive industries, highlighting the important role of personal learning networks.

According to Bravenboer (2016), the idea of professional competence and challenges fragmented approaches to academic qualification and professional recognition. It is argued that academic programmes that are integrated with the requirements for professional recognition can resolve the potentially unhelpful differentiation between 'theory' and 'practice' and between 'knowledge' and 'competence'.

Intermediate apprenticeships

Further education and training providers have been at the forefront of providing apprenticeships at both the intermediate level and now more recently higher levels. It is with this in mind that questions the need to utilise the expertise and rigour within the further education and training forum. There is an opportunity for apprentices to begin their journey in further education at the intermediate apprenticeship level (2) and gain much-needed guidance and expertise from the well-informed and knowledgeable sector. This is appropriate to someone new to his or her role or without a formal qualification in the sector. Embedded within an intermediate level 2 apprenticeship standard is the requirement to achieve level 1 functional skills in English and maths. This allows for the 16-plus learner to gain a qualification in a set career, but also gain invaluable skills within English and maths, which is equivalent to GCSE grade 4, a national requirement now within many sectors, including, education, childcare, health and business.

This in return provides the employer with a safe and knowledgeable employee who can provide and record a high standard of practice. This approach requires a partnership to form and develop between the education/learning provider, learner and employer.

The higher apprenticeship

Higher apprenticeships are new phenomena that offer a different route to traditional university study and provide an opportunity to gain level 4 qualifications or above. Most apprentices gain an NVQ level 4, an HND or a Foundation degree; a level 6 higher apprenticeship is the vocational equivalent to a university degree; and some offer the opportunity to progress to level 7 (which is postgraduate degree level). Higher apprenticeships can take from one to five years to complete, and involve part-time study at a college, university or training provider, and are currently available in the following areas: business and IT; construction; creative, media and the arts; customer service and retail; energy; engineering and electrical; finance; health and care; hospitality and travel; manufacturing, processing and logistics; public services; and vehicles and transport.

Degree apprenticeships

Degree apprenticeships are designed by industry to bring together the very best in higher and vocational education. Apprentices achieve a full bachelor's or master's degree as a core component of the apprenticeship. A degree apprenticeship will test academic learning as well as wider skills and ability to do a job. Assessment will be either by using a fully integrated degree co-designed by employers and higher education institutions, or using a degree with a separate assessment of professional competence. The government is committed to expanding the number, range and quality of apprenticeships that offer training to degree level, and many more are currently being developed.

Apprenticeship degrees were highlighted within the Review of Vocational Education (Wolf, 2011), and constitute a recent development in vocational learning within the higher education sector, including HE in FE. They combine university study and workplace learning to enable apprentices to gain a full bachelor's or master's degree. The review conducted by Wolf (2011) gave clear recommendations for the future in regard to vocational apprenticeships, and reiterated changes that were needed within universities in regard to helping combat the national skills shortages in the UK.

The new focus on designing courses (both apprenticeship and non-apprenticeship), in partnership with industry, will pay dividends (Stockwell, cited in Morgan, 2017). They provide an opportunity for universities to diversify their offer and develop alternatives to traditional full-time on-campus study (Universities UK, 2016); however, they come with their challenges: ensuring they fit with the strategic development of the university, academic buy-in, and employer engagement, to name a few.

Table 24.1 demonstrates how the different levels are mapped against other programmes.

Table 24.1 Equivalency of qualifications

Name	Level	Equivalent education level
Intermediate	2	5 GCSE passes at grade A*-C or 9-4
Advanced	3	2 A-level passes/level 3 diploma/International Baccalaureate
Higher	4, 5, 6 and 7	Foundation degree and above
Degree	6 and 7	Bachelor's or master's degree

Source: https://assets.publishing.service.gov.uk/government/uploads/system/uploads/attachment_data/file/699397/Guide-to-Apprenticeships_090418.pdf

Apprenticeship development in England

In recent times, there has been a policy drive to increase the number of people undertaking apprenticeships in England, resulting in a rapidly developing range of both academic and vocational apprenticeships from level 2 to level 7.

One of the commitments made by the Conservative government in 2015 was to increase the number of apprentices to 3 million by 2020. However, although apprenticeship policy has been directed towards young people, the majority of the growth of provision has in fact been for workers currently employed over the age of 25. With increases in retirement age leading to an ageing workforce, are apprenticeships taking over the functions previously enacted by upskilling and retraining? As apprenticeships are not reaching their intended market or targets for uptake among under-25s, are they nevertheless demonstrating success in other areas?

Currently, apprenticeships are growing in terms of supporting current business outcomes, but an important area that they also support is opening many doors to widening participation for many learners seeking both employment and qualifications; specifically, the evolution of apprenticeships provides fantastic opportunities to develop career pathways within the health and social care sector (Bradbury and Murdoch, 2018).

The levy

The apprenticeship levy that was introduced in 2017 aimed to incentivise large firms, corporations and businesses to take on apprentices – a compulsory tax on employers to help fund the development and delivery of apprenticeships, with the aim of improving the quality and quantity of those available. Levy payers are employers with a pay bill of more than £3 million. They are required to pay the levy whether they employ an apprentice or not. Non-levy payers have a pay bill under £3 million, and will contribute 5 per cent towards the cost of the required apprenticeship, and the government will pay the remaining 95 per cent. Poor understanding or over-complication (Richmond, 2018) of the levy may have contributed to the slower update of apprenticeships than the government had anticipated.

Widening participation

There is a growing movement to increase and encourage the diversity of students accessing higher education. These drives to widen participation have many motivational factors, which include economic, institutional and social justice concerns.

Apprenticeships have evolved over the past five years and have become the government focus. However, employers remain concerned that many employees/learners are not ready for the world of work, and thus further training is needed for a highly skilled workforce. The launch of degree apprenticeships could increase participation in higher education from under-represented groups. Devlin and McKay (2017) discuss that this will give increasing opportunities into employment from socio-economic groups who may not have had the chance to go to university due to work commitments or cost. However, it is important to highlight that there is no widening participation agenda embedded within employer-led programmes or associated policies.

According to Universities UK (2016), degree apprenticeships may help widening participation by offering opportunities to non-traditional students. The integration of academic study with work-based training/learning means that students who like vocational methods of linking theory and practice may want to choose this route instead of going to university. From the same source, higher and degree apprenticeships could also support practitioners' progress into management and leadership roles, which in turn allows for progression in terms of financial stability and qualifications. There is a perception that students from less privileged backgrounds may be put off studying for a traditional full-time degree, for reasons that include cost and debt, and see employment as a more attractive option, and therefore this could be a way of attracting such students into HE (Vigurs et al., 2016).

Tackling social, cultural and economic barriers is evident within many policies, research papers and funding initiatives to enable individuals to reach their full potential. Examples include the development of initiatives such as Aim Higher, funded by the Office for Students, and the Department for Education's promotion of collaboration between schools, colleges and universities.

There are many positive reasons for offering apprenticeships and doing so through a degree or higher-level apprenticeship. For example, Antcliff et al. (2016) argued that employers engaging with higher-level apprenticeships were able to see them as good value and highlighted the positive contribution that apprentices make to outcomes. Antcliff et al. (2016) remind us that apprenticeships must be led by employers so that they are able to demonstrate the need for a skills industry. On the other hand, some academics may note that degree programmes already work this way, moving on to explore that universities are already pioneering work-based learning. It will take time to see the extent to which degree apprenticeship programmes will work in the way that the current government intends, and whether they are in fact going to be able to reconcile the academic context with the skills needed.

Funding and implications for other academic and vocational programmes

Funding for apprenticeships is drawn down from the Education and Skills Funding Agency (ESFA), who continue to define an apprenticeship as a job with an accompanying skills development programme. The job must have a productive purpose and should provide the apprentice with the opportunity to gain the knowledge, skills and behaviours needed to achieve the apprenticeship.

The apprenticeship strategy has a wide and inclusive remit, and as such should encompass workers who may have previously been excluded from vocational education; the apprenticeship strategy identifies that working fewer than 30 hours a week or being on a zero-hours contract must not be a barrier to successfully completing an apprenticeship. We then have to question the extent to which the opening of the floodgates to the take-up of apprenticeships (in a market where levy payers want to 'spend their money') will result in large numbers of apprentices being on programmes for long periods with little incentive to achieve and complete within the specified time as they continue to work in a zero-hours economy. In what ways will this improve the profile of apprenticeships?

It has to be acknowledged that the apprenticeship strategy has a serious commitment to developing the workforce, particularly with reference to individuals who may not previously have accessed or had the opportunity to access formal qualifications. Nonetheless it can be argued that, almost due to its urge to be inclusive, it has the potential to exclude some learners.

Further deterrents or barriers are presented by the inability of training providers to request additional funding in order to access training which may be offered at a cost above the funding band that the employer has paid directly to the main provider where this is part of the agreed apprenticeship, even if this would prove advantageous to both the employer and apprentice. This poses particular issues in the health and social care sector (one of the identified growth areas), where apprentices may be 'employed' in England but 'work' in Wales as geographical boundaries are variously defined.

While positively acknowledging the part that apprenticeships play in the widening participation agenda, and therefore contributing to closing the gap between rich and poor, it is disappointing to note that travel costs for apprentices are not met under any circumstances. This may result in apprentices undertaking programmes where the 'educational' input is offered on site (or very close to) as opposed to the most appropriate educational institute, and presents yet another barrier by disabling the students in their progression by not allowing them the opportunity to experience the college/university environment.

Chapter summary

If we had a crystal ball, we would be able to say what the future holds in terms of apprenticeships and work-based learning. As we do not, this chapter tells a story from where we were to where we are. The chapter allows us to think about how far we have come and track back on the mistakes that were made, allowing for critical thinking. Can these mistakes be avoided going forward, and can change be implemented with employers and practitioners in mind?

We have considered the impact that apprenticeships can have within employment-based routes for university-level qualifications. While research projects and published literature relating to degree apprenticeships are still relatively few in number, more are beginning to emerge.

The chapter has outlined a clear vision that apprenticeships are a new and evolving model of work-based learning.

The discussion looks at widening participation in the sense of access for all through different models. It is therefore important that we envisage widening participation for all, and not for the most disadvantaged. Could widening participation be seen through the eyes of practitioners who may not get these opportunities due to family commitments, work, or restrictions within their current roles?

The chapter proposes an evolving discussion, one that allows you to see where we are going in an ever-changing landscape of work-based learning and gaining opportunities for all.

References

Antcliff, V., Baines, S. and Gorb, E. (2016) Developing your own graduate employees: employer perspectives on the value of a degree apprenticeship. *Higher Education, Skills and Work-Based Learning*, 6(4): 378–383.

Billett, S. (2014) Mimesis: learning through everyday activities and interactions at work. *Human Resource Development Review*, 13(4): 462–482.

Bradbury, A. and Murdoch, J. (2018) *Above and Beyond: Widening Participation for Apprenticeship Learners within Health and Social Care*. FE News.

Bravenboer, D. (2016) Why co-design and delivery is 'a no brainer' for higher and degree apprenticeship policy. *Higher Education, Skills and Work-Based Learning*, 6(4): 384–400.

Carter, J. (2010) *Progression from Vocational and Applied Learning to Higher Education in England*. Report Prepared for the Rt Hon David Lammy MP, Minister of State for Higher Education. Final Report, November 2009. University Vocational Awards Council.

Chan, S. (2013) Learning through apprenticeship: belonging to a workplace, becoming and being. *Vocations and Learning*, 6: 367–383.

Chankseliani, M. and Relly, S.J. (2015) From the provider-led to an employer-led system: implications of apprenticeship reform on the private training market. *Journal of Vocational Education and Training*, 67(4): 515–528.

Deissinger, T. and Hellwig, S. (2005) Apprenticeships in Germany: modernising the dual system. *Education and Training*, 47(4/5): 312–324.

DfE (2016) *Progress Report on the Apprenticeships Reform Programme*. London: HMI Stationary Office.

Devlin, M. and McKay, J. (2017) *Facilitating Success for Students from Low Socioeconomic Status Backgrounds at Regional Universities*. Victoria: Federation University Australia.

Fuller, A. and Unwin, L. (2011) The content of apprenticeships. In T. Dolphin and T. Lanning (eds), *Rethinking Apprenticeships*. London: Institute for Public Policy Research.

Guile, D. and Young, M. (1998) Apprenticeship as a conceptual basis for a social theory of learning. *Journal of Vocational Education & Training*, 50(2): 173–193.

IFF Research (2017) *Apprenticeships Evaluation 2017*. London: DfE.

King, M., Waters, J., Widdowson, M. and Saraswat, A. (2016) Higher technical skills: learning from the experiences of English FE colleges and Australian technical and further education institutes. *Higher Education, Skills and Work-Based Learning*, 6(4): 329–344.

Morgan, J. (2017) Pearson: UK 'boutique university' to mesh with company strategy. *Times Higher Education*, 5 January 2017.

Richard, D. (2012) *The Richard Review of Apprenticeships*. London: School for Startups.

RoATP (2016) *Register of Apprenticeship Training Providers*. Available at: www.gov.uk/guidance/register-of-apprenticeship-training-providers

Richmond, T. (2018) *The Great Training Robbery: Assessing the First Year of the Apprenticeship Levy*. London: Reform Education.

Universities UK (2016) *The Future Growth of Degree Apprenticeships*. London: Universities UK.

Vigurs, K., Jones, S. and Harris, D. (2016) *Higher Fees, Higher Debts: Greater Expectations of Graduate Futures? A Research-Informed Comic*. London: SRHE.

Wolf, A. (2011) *Review of Vocational Education: The Wolf Report*. Available at: www.gov.uk/government/publications/review-of-vocational-education-the-wolf-report

25

PROFESSIONAL DEVELOPMENT IN FURTHER AND ADULT EDUCATION

Samantha Jones

Key words – staff development; professional development; improvement; transfer of knowledge and skills; context; practice; experimentation and collaboration

Introduction

In 2013, I was working as the advanced practitioner in the business department of a large general FE college. My institution covered many aspects of further and adult education (FAE), including adult education, higher education, further education, basic skills, sixth form, community-based, and special educational needs provision. I was just about to start my master's degree, and I was frustrated with the provision of professional development I saw in my college and other FAE organisations.

This chapter aims to take you on the journey that I went on. First, it will follow my reflections on my own experiences of CPD in the sector. Second, it will take you through what is already written about professional development in general and further education. Third, it will explore my research as a practitioner, spending three years undertaking research into professional development in my own college, what I learnt and what I feel it means for practice. Fourth, it will offer an alternative model to the whole organisation of professional development that is so common in the sector and analyse both models. This will bring me to the final section of the chapter, where I will suggest some guiding principles for continuing professional development in further and adult education.

Professional development in practice

Before I can explore what has been written about professional development in further and adult education, I should share my experience of 18 years of professional development. My initial observation is that poor-quality professional development, at least within the FAE organisations I have worked in, has some consistent features. First, it is almost always chosen by others and presented in the style of a menu; from this menu, I have had everything from full, limited and sometimes no choice about what I have taken part in. Second, 'my' professional development choices tend to reflect other people's priorities rather than my development needs. Recently, my time has been taken up with e-learning on the General Data Protection Regulation, but I also think back to attending compulsory organisation-wide training on differentiation when I was more than 10 years into my career and receiving good feedback from observers on this aspect of my teaching. Third, the CPD is delivered as a one-off session with no follow-up and little thought about how I might transfer the ideas or techniques presented at these events to my practice or classroom. Overall, I have sat in classrooms, conference halls and behind my desk, and been presented with hints, tips, or simply told how to update the skills and knowledge that someone else thinks are important to me, with insufficient thought given to how relevant the session is to my development or how I might express my learning in terms of improved teaching performance.

But that's the worst of my experiences, and I have been lucky enough to have experienced some excellent professional development. I have two examples here: both met my needs and priorities, considered how I might actually use the training in my practice, and, in the second example, I had a choice in attending. My first example followed the failure of an Ofsted inspection by the FAE organisation I was working in at the start of my career. It decided to arrange for Geoff Petty to deliver training, and this for me was great. He explained so much I didn't understand or know, and gave practical help and suggestions to use the concepts he'd taught in my classroom. This training was timely: I was a new tutor and had much to learn. But more than this, the session was well conceptualised. He looked beyond what he was teaching to how we might *use* this knowledge. The second example was a few years after this point, when I was fortunate to be invited to participate in Subject Learning Coach (SLC) training. This was a training programme that ran over nine months; it was part of the Success for All agenda of the New Labour government and run through the DfES Standards Unit. Sadly, both the body and the training were early victims of austerity cuts. The SLC programme aimed to model new approaches to develop the teaching of those tutors working in subject areas that traditionally struggled in Ofsted inspections. Through a series of lectures, activities and action learning sets that involved assessing the success of the supported experimentation in my classroom, they developed both my understanding of teaching *and* my practice. The peer coaching model and skills I'd been taught within the sessions allowed me to copy this formula within the business department I was working in at the time. It was conceptualised well; I developed and developed others. Thought had been given to how I would transfer my knowledge to my classroom and to others. This, for me, was both transformative to my teaching and empowering as I felt I understood and 'owned' my teaching practice. It has also influenced much of my subsequent career; my focus is on the support and development of others, including my work in teacher education, my work as a practitioner-researcher, and writing this chapter – a further attempt to pass on good ideas and practice!

To start to work towards this aim, I would like to move away from my own experiences to explore what is written in the academic literature concerning professional development.

Professional development in theory

Key questions

To what extent are FAE tutors 'dual professionals'?

Dual professionals

Although there is not a large amount written about the professional development of staff in FAE, there seems to be one idea that appears regularly. This is the idea of the 'dual professional' (Robson, 1998): the idea that practitioners in FAE have two elements of their practice that they must update, their teaching knowledge and their professional knowledge. I see it all the time in excellent teaching practice, from the motor vehicle trainer who creates additional units to reflect changes in the industry that the syllabus hasn't caught up with yet, to the surveying tutor who takes cohorts to manufacturers to keep up to date with new and expensive technology, ensuring that learners can apply these to both their assessments and industry practice. Good FAE practitioners need to be good teachers and know their subject well, and as practice in both areas changes over time, we need opportunities to stay up to date in our dual practices.

The challenge of balancing developing subject and teaching knowledge

This can be a challenging position to maintain in the sector. When I started teaching, I came straight from industry, and while my knowledge in this area was fresh and current, my teaching was less developed! Being a subject specialist was definitely my priority at this point in my career. There was an unspoken rule in my department that I was very attached to: that being knowledgeable in your specialist subject area was enough. While I still advocate the centrality of subject knowledge, I have subsequently seen the implications of simply 'knowing' a subject.

As I began to hone my own practice, very often reflecting on a lesson I felt had gone badly, or on the occasions I realised what I thought I had taught wasn't what my group had understood, I began to realise that 'knowing' a subject is not the same as being able to teach it. As I began to support other teachers, especially new teachers, I saw tutors who had great levels of knowledge or skills themselves yet couldn't break it down and represent it to the groups they were teaching. It was almost like the knowledge and skills were trapped within them. The more I taught, observed and spoke to other tutors, the more I came to see the complexity that was involved in taking the knowledge that you have from your own studies and the experience you have from employment or volunteering, breaking

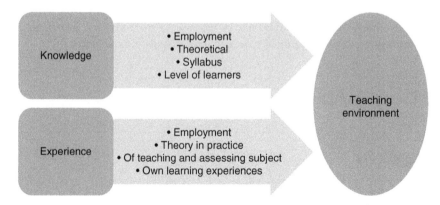

Figure 25.1   Teaching as an integration of different pools of knowledge and experience: the dual professional

them down, and then combining them in order to teach the syllabus in a way that is engaging and ensures that the learners develop the skills and knowledge to pass their assessment (see Figure 25.1). I began to see the importance of knowing how to teach your subject, as well as knowing the subject itself, and the importance of considering ourselves dual professionals.

I am suggesting in Figure 25.1 that as dual professionals, we bring together different knowledges and experiences related to both being a teacher and about our subject specialism. This is why I argue we need to develop ourselves as teachers as well as subject specialists. The next section aims to further explore the importance of the knowledge and experiences of an individual as it explores the idea of context.

The importance of context

If we intend to bring together the different knowledges and experiences of tutors, it follows that we need to consider the contexts of these tutors. Where they work, who and what they teach, and what their background may be will all be important factors to consider. These factors may impact both their motivation to learn and their ability to translate learning into practice. So, here, an example may be useful. When I was new to teaching, the training I have described in the introductory section from Geoff Petty was contextually relevant to me. Geoff also came from a sixth form background, so understood the learners and challenges I was facing; he taught theories and methods of structuring sessions and checking learning, which really helped me at a point in my career when I was developing my basic competencies. He also took into account that as an FAE tutor, I was likely to be time-poor, and created resources that were easy for me to adopt in the classroom; in fact, I still use his 25 ways of teaching without talking, which are still free to download.

Looking at the research box below, Petty's seemingly simple method of teaching theory and providing generic resources to be adapted in the classroom meets, for me as a new teacher, all three of the requirements of planned CPD described by Bound (2011).

Key theory

Bound (2011)

Bound explores the professional learning of vocational tutors. This study explored construction tutors embedding new forms of ICT that encouraged higher-level thinking into their teaching. While many of the tutors identified this as a learning need, some felt they were already expert in the use of ICT, and as a result considered that for them, the training was of less use. The study revealed that the changes to classroom practice after the training had been given was less than had been hoped. This was in part as the teaching in the department had traditionally been very instructional and low-level. This meant that all the resources used for teaching facilitated this low-level, instructional approach. The study found that adopting a new approach when all the existing resources are set up to facilitate different styles of teaching is problematic. Further constraints came from the organisational context; the tutors often wanted to use the approach but did not have time to develop new e-learning resources.

(Continued)

(Continued)

From this work, Bound summarised three factors that need to be considered when planning professional learning for vocational tutors:

1. the learning needs of the tutors themselves;

2. consideration of existing teaching practice may blend with the new; and

3. ways in which conditions around a tutor facilitate or constrain them.

Where context is not considered, it can prevent engagement with the learning and make the transfer of learning to the tutor's classroom more difficult or even unachievable.

Whose professional development is it?

Key questions

What would you consider to be the key factors that need to be considered when planning an episode of professional development that will meet your needs and context?

Who 'owns' our professional development?

Key theory

Orr (2009)

Orr (2009) explored the limitations and benefits of the now revoked 2008 regulations that all FE staff should complete 30 hours of professional development. While identifying that much of what took place in colleges was still staff development with a focus on counting hours rather than impact and the development of the tutor, he went on to conclude that the 'situation can only be ameliorated when those working and studying in colleges have more control over setting their own collective priorities, including CPD, in a rational rather than a performative manner' (Orr, 2009, p9) – i.e. when staff are included in discussions about what teaching, learning and development are, or should be.

As a general rule, the literature around professional development and my own experiences suggests that many FAE organisations are ignoring the complexity of FAE tutors and their teaching. Hence, many staff experience the 'differentiation whether you need it or not' and 'questioning technique for everyone' style of staff development. I think this is what Orr (2009) meant: development is more than counting the numbers of hours, or that all tutors are seen to be trained in whatever their organisation's top priority is that year. If management make the decisions, then they 'own' the development and are likely to ignore the context and needs of individuals. In this case, can it be called 'professional' development, as surely a professional would be part of the decision-making process?

Key questions

Why doesn't FAE concentrate its development on its core business, education and training?

As Orr (2009) records, in the past there have been initiatives, such as the requirement of the now defunct Institute for Learning, forerunner of the Society for Education and Training, to hand the responsibility for professional development to the tutors themselves. Such initiatives have failed, often as a result of FAE organisations not enabling tutors to identify and address their own priorities. Instead, they have maintained the primacy of the HR, professional development or quality departments as the decision-makers as they pursue their more immediate organisational or Ofsted priorities. So, despite the calls for tutors to choose and control their own professional development, they were still often faced with a 'menu' of sessions, or with compulsory sessions. One significant downside of focusing on the organisation rather than the individuals is that the context which seems to be so important to engagement and learning is lost. Another is that it may produce tutors who are able to track their learners and understand management information systems and the principles of good customer service, but they are less likely to be effective in the core business of educating.

What does the literature say 'works' in professional development?

This leads us to the question 'What does work?' Here, I am glad to say, there seems to be clear evidence of what the building blocks of good professional development are. Exploring the literature around 'what works', four issues are common across the reading:

1. context;

2. time and sustained practice;

3. collaboration; and

4. active learning.

Context

Already explored in the chapter, it is clear that a consideration of context is required to ensure that CPD is both relevant to the needs of tutors, and that the learning can be translated to practice.

Time and sustained practice

Garet et al. (2001), Kelly (2013) and Villegas-Reimers (2003) suggest that CPD needs to be a sustained process, and that teachers need sufficient time to engage with, reflect on and implement changes to their practice. 'One-off' training sessions with little or no follow-up or evaluation are limited in their capacity. The transfer of knowledge from the place where you learnt it, in your staff development, to another setting, such as your classroom, is a difficult task. Both Billett (2004) and Lave (1991) argue that knowledge and skills don't move well between different contexts such as this, so time and practice are required to support this process.

Collaboration

The third variable found within the 'what works' literature is collaboration. Cordingley (2015), Grangeat and Gray (2007), Powell et al. (2003), Putnam and Borko (2000), Wlodkowski (2003) and Young and Guile (1997) all recommend peer support for effective development. Collaborating with others who understand your subject allows you to contextualise the learning, thus making it more relevant for the 'teaching' of your learners.

Active learning

Active learning and experimentation gives teachers opportunities for hands-on learning in a coherent and content-specific manner. The need for this is supported within the literature by Cordingley (2015), Garet et al. (2001), Powell et al. (2003), Putnam and Borko (2000), Villegas-Reimers (2003) and Wlodkowski (2003). Both collaboration and active learning can help to create context by working and experimenting with others with whom you share priorities or elements of practice.

So, where does this literature leave us? It describes the need for context in a very fragmented sector where tutors often have a duality in the development of their practice. It sets out four clear recommendations for designing 'good' professional development.

So, how can we balance the needs of tutors and management? I would argue they both need to be addressed, but that this should involve clearly delineated time, space and money for each. Development that meets the organisation's priorities and is mandated by them should not be classified as professional development; it should be called staff development. Only the development chosen by the professional themselves aimed at their individual development priorities, I would argue, should be called professional development.

An alternative 'professional-led' model

Key questions

What would change in the sector if we stopped developing staff?

I am proposing a model of professional development based on tutors' choice. I have used this model in two research interventions, both at FEA institutions in the east of England.

The model I have used within both organisations is simple. I sit down with individual or small groups of teachers and discuss with them the principles of good professional development, much as

I have in this chapter. Then we begin to discuss what development they feel would benefit themselves and their learners, and how they might wish to access this learning in a manner that's meaningful and useful to them.

Case study

Benjamin's story

I'll use Benjamin as an example. Benjamin was a carpentry technician who wished to develop his knowledge of joinery. He wanted to do so for two reasons. First, he needed to be qualified in both carpentry and joinery to become a lecturer, a career move he was keen to take. Second, he often felt that his present knowledge and skills were insufficient to be able to help the classes he supported; as such, he sometimes lacked confidence in himself. Benjamin had previously tried to get this qualification on his own, working in the workshop when no one was using it, but had been unsuccessful. During our first meeting, we realised Benjamin needed a mentor to help him develop the knowledge and competency to pass the qualification, and a tutor to motivate him and keep him on track. What was proposed was that Benjamin would set himself targets with his tutor, staged throughout the year to complete the four elements of the qualification, and between these would work with his mentor. From the start, and without being prompted, Benjamin has addressed the four aspects that the theory suggests would be critical to a useful episode of professional development. He has given himself time for sustained practice by allowing a year to pass the qualification. By choosing something useful to him, and deciding on someone he respected to work with him as a subject-specific mentor, he has built in context and collaboration. Finally, by creating pockets of time within which to address the four elements of the qualification, he has given time for active experimentation; he has time to think, plan and make the items he needed to create to pass the qualification.

So, what did having all these elements in his intervention mean for Benjamin? How did it benefit him?

The collaboration provided Benjamin with a supportive environment to learn with, and through, his mentor. Benjamin found the technical drawings for a bespoke cabinet, which was part of his final assessment, really challenging, and put off starting it until his mentor was able to support him. At the end of his course, Benjamin recalled how working collaboratively and actively helped him learn: 'We all figure out how to do it [manufacture the bespoke cabinet] together'. More than this, this learning episode had an impact on Benjamin's own teaching practice as he described helping a learner who couldn't work out how to translate a drawing into a product: 'I have learnt how to break down technical drawings [on the course] ... and I can show him my work and explain how it was done. I couldn't have done that before the course'. What I would like to argue here is that learning with and through colleagues has not only been effective for Benjamin, but it has developed his knowledge *and* his teaching practice. Here, he is using the same teaching and learning technique that he found useful in his learning to help students in his classroom. This seems to be a useful tool to Benjamin in transferring what has been learnt on his course to his workshop practice.

The time, sustained practice and active experimentation also proved useful to Benjamin's learning. This allowed Benjamin the time and opportunity to remake the stairs he needed to produce. He took two attempts to complete them because he wanted 'to get it right'. The stairs that Benjamin made were on display in his workshop and were an outward show of his being a joiner, so Benjamin remade them to 'be the best I can be'. At the end of the course, he reflected:

> Doing the course, I made a lot of mistakes; I feel less worried now about making mistakes. If I go to help [a learner] and am not entirely sure what to do, I will work it through with them. I am not bothered about getting it wrong. You learn carpentry by making mistakes.

Here, I would argue that giving Benjamin time and space to experiment, practise and reflect has allowed him both to create a better end product and to develop confidence in his own professionalism. Again, this translates into his workshop, as he can point to the stairs and share the story of his own trial and error, and also to his teaching techniques, as he understands the value of learning from mistakes and adopts this philosophy into his practice.

Key questions

Is there a link between how you learn knowledge and skills and how you then teach this knowledge to others?

So, from this snapshot of Benjamin's experience I would invite you to think about how working with others who share his dual professionalism seems to have pushed Benjamin to display similar levels of professionalism himself, and the effect this has had on his approach towards his own learners. It is important to notice, first, how the methods of learning used in his own professional development – mentoring and problem-solving – have transferred across to his teaching practice; and second, that he has learnt more than just the skills of reading drawings and creating objects. He also seems to have developed an increased pride in the skills and objects he has developed. Bringing both of these developments together, as illustrated in Figure 25.2, Benjamin becomes not only a better carpenter, but a better *teacher* of carpentry.

Typical activities used in the 'professional led' model

- *Professional choice.* Participants have a large amount of input and choice into what they learn and how they learn it. The most regular choices have been working with others to improve specific areas of practice, knowledge or qualifications, although very specialist staff have chosen to update alone on expert systems and programmes.

- *Focus on subject specialism.* Context is key; tutors are choosing vocational or other updating tied to their context. Examples include Benjamin's qualification, and tutors' observations of colleagues from different organisations teaching the same provision and of learning new technology to keep up to date with practice in their industry.

- *Focus on transfer of knowledge.* The time, collaboration, active learning and sustained practice all help a tutor move what they are learning from concepts that may help them into new practice that transforms their teaching.

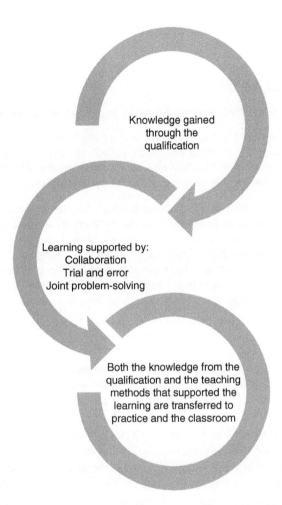

Knowledge gained
through the
qualification

Learning supported by:
Collaboration
Trial and error
Joint problem-solving

Both the knowledge from the
qualification and the teaching
methods that supported the
learning are transferred to
practice and the classroom

Figure 25.2   Model of Benjamin's learning

The future of professional development: a focus on vocational or subject-specific skills

This chapter has explored what theory suggests may lead to effective CPD, and how this theory not only supports my own research findings, but how my research may add to the creation of effective professional development. While I can't claim that my research findings reflect the whole sector (I worked with a small sample of tutors), the similarities between my findings and those of other researchers do lend a level of validity to my work.

It is important to ensure that CPD includes opportunities for the ongoing effective development of pedagogic practice. As explored by Gary Husband, the teaching and learning techniques covered during initial professional training are sometimes insufficient.

Key theory

Gary Husband (2015, 2018)

This work focused on the CPD experiences of 18 tutors at colleges in Scotland and Wales.

Husband points to a perceived lack of vocational skills updating and recommends that there should be an increased focus on the practical and vocational content of initial teacher training. Outside teacher training, he recommends that 'high-quality, valid and targeted CPD' (Husband, 2015, p227) should be developed to meet the needs expressed by the tutors he interviewed.

His work suggests that even in the induction and teacher education phase of development, support to enact what has been learnt on courses such as the PGCE or DET is required to make the learning effective. The work also expresses concerns that the experience that tutors have in their teacher training period may affect the choices they make for their professional development. For example, those who felt their training had been too theoretical may look for practical ways of transferring this knowledge to their classrooms in their initial development opportunities after completing their teaching qualification. He suggests that initial teacher training and professional development should be seen as a continuum.

In order to ensure context and collaboration wherever professional development does take place, be it initial or continuing, there needs to be a greater focus on the idea of the dual professional. In addition, I would like to suggest that greater consideration is given to updating the pedagogical skills of tutors with those who are willing and able to share practice. Moreover, greater consideration needs to be given to how these skills are developed: professional learning needs to be sustained over a period of time, and across different organisational contexts: classrooms, workshops or employers' premises. Full consideration of this issue is important as the methods that are used to learn are those that are most likely to find their way into this learning space. Finally, I would agree with Husband's (2018) call for structural changes to the organisation of professional development across the sector as a whole.

Chapter summary

In this chapter, I have explored current patterns of continuing professional development provision within the PCET sector, as well as some of the different ways by which these can be seen to be impacting on the professional practice of tutors. In summary, I would like to advocate the case for a 'cradle to grave' plan for tutors' professional development, in which they are the central participants. I would advocate that the distinct nature of FAE teaching is celebrated through an emphasis on the subject that the tutor is teaching and the best ways of delivering the skills, knowledge and behaviours required for *that particular subject*. As such I am advocating that tutors are viewed as dual professionals, and that the development of subject-specific pedagogies be seen as a central element of this.

Recommended further reading

Loo, S. (2017) *Teachers and Teaching in Vocational and Professional Education*. London: Routledge.
This book has been recommended as the thinking in it has heavily influenced Figure 25.1.

References

Billett, S. (2004) Learning through work: workplace participatory practices. In H. Rainbird, A. Fuller and A. Munroe (eds), *Workplace Learning in Context*. London: Routledge.

Bound, H. (2011) Vocational education and training teacher professional development: tensions and context. *Studies in Continuing Education*, 33(2): 107–119.

Cordingley, P. (2015) The contribution of research to teachers' professional learning and development. *Oxford Review of Education*, 41(2): 234–252.

Garet, M.S., Porter, A.C., Desimone, L., Birman, B. and Yoon, K.S. (2001) What makes professional development effective? Results from a national sample of teachers. *American Education Research Journal*, 38(4): 915–945.

Grangeat, M. and Gray, P. (2007) Factors influencing teachers' professional competence development. *Journal of Education and Training*, 59(4): 485–501.

Husband, G. (2015) The impact of lecturers' initial teacher training on continuing professional development needs for teaching and learning in post-compulsory education. *Research in Post-Compulsory Education*, 20(2): 227–244.

Husband, G. (2018) The professional learning of further education lecturers: effects of initial lecturer education programmes on continuing professional learning in Scotland and Wales. *Research in Post-Compulsory Education*, 23(2): 159–180.

Kelly, J. (2013) *2011–12 IfL Review of CPD: Making Professional Learning Work*. London: Institute for Learning.

Kennedy, A. (2005) Models of continuing professional development: a framework for analysis. *Journal of In-Service Education*, 31(2): 235–250.

Lave, J. (1991) Situating learning in communities of practice. In L.B. Resnick, J.M. Levine and S.D. Teasley (eds), *Perspectives on Socially Shared Cognition*. Washington, DC: American Psychological Association.

Orr, K. (2009) Performativity and professional development: the gap between policy and practice in the English further education sector. *Research in Post-Compulsory Education*, 14(4): 479–489.

Powell, E., Terrell, T., Furey, S. and Scott-Evans, A. (2003) Teachers' perceptions of the impact of CPD: an institutional case study. *Journal of In-Service Education*, 29(3): 389–404.

Putnam, R.T. and Borko, H. (2000) What do new views of knowledge and thinking have to say about research on teacher learning? *Educational Researcher*, 29(1): 4–15.

Robson, J. (1998) A profession in crisis: status, culture and identity in the further education college. *Journal of Vocational Education and Training*, 50(4): 585–607.

Villegas-Reimers, E. (2003) *Teacher Professional Development: An International Review of the Literature*. Paris: UNESCO.

Wlodkowski, R.J. (2003) Fostering motivation in professional development programs. *New Directions for Adult and Continuing Education*, 98: 39–48.

Young, M. and Guile, D. (1997) New possibilities for the professionalization of UK VET professionals. *Journal of European Industrial Training*, 21(6/7): 203–212.

26

THE COST OF EVERYTHING AND THE VALUE OF NOTHING: WHAT'S NEXT FOR THE FE SECTOR?

Gary Husband and Lou Mycroft

Key words – transformation; empowerment; policy actors; pedagogy; teacher education; professional development; petrification; good help; diffraction; anti-heroic leadership

Introduction

In this chapter, we sketch out the here and now and suggest possible futures for post-compulsory education and training (PCET) while exploring our confliction with the label itself. We then offer a number of different trajectories of thought and warning against inertia. The chapter will end with our vision of how a healthy, empowering 'FE' can be achieved.

To FE or not? A note from the authors

During the process of writing this chapter, we kept snagging on the acronym PCET. As a term generally used to describe post-school non-university education, it lacks logic and consistency: one of us is based in Scotland and one in England, after all. But it was more than that. The critical question is: Who defines what is compulsory? The answer encapsulated all that we are going to write about here: 'PCET' has education's problems inscribed in its DNA. As our writing tied itself into a Gordian knot, we were compelled to address this tension.

The education that takes place for people when they leave school, whether freely chosen or mandated, yet occurs outside of a university's higher education programme, is called many things by many people, sometimes mindlessly and other times intentionally, for ideological purposes. Our purpose here was to avoid introducing yet another term to the mix, so we have chosen to use the relatively least unburdened, in our view. We will refer throughout this chapter to FE, or further education.

Challenging assumptions

Key questions

How does the language we use about FE shape the way we think?

Identity and definition have dominated the discourse of FE over the last 20 years. Much has been made of the 'Cinderella sector' lost in its self-proclaimed crisis of definition, weighed down by an inability to coalesce, to form a consistent and ripple-free identity across all its manifestations (Daley et al., 2015). The notion that FE has been experiencing an extended identity crisis has been the subject of literature over two decades (e.g. see Elliot, 1996; Simmons, 2010), and those internalised messages play out in tensions and paradoxes: the 'wicked problems' faced by the sector, which endless rounds of thinking attempt to solve (Peters, 2017). To complicate matters of identity further, FE is all too often defined in economic rather than educational terms, leading to tense 'living contradictions' in working practice for all those involved (Illsley and Waller, 2017): the mission statement versus the bottom line.

We are interested in challenging the notion that FE lacks a comprehensible identity. Our work affords us the privilege of speaking with those working in FE, across its diverse subjects, vocations and curricula, and we observe no lack of purpose in pedagogical encounters. Could it be that FE actually *does* know itself, or at least it could do if it began to define its own fate? We argue that FE has a definition no more difficult to grasp than that of any other education sector (Husband, 2018). What it does lack is an audible and coherent voice.

For too long, we in FE have failed to challenge the ideology of successive governments: that education is primarily a means to a country's economic growth. Of course, Paulo Freire famously advocated engaging with the dominant discourse, but as Mayo (2009) explores, thanks to the inane 'public pedagogy' of mainstream news media, engagement is there but criticality is lacking. FE parrots the lexicon of advanced capitalism in pursuit of survival and falls into the trap of pigeonholing, culturally inhibiting and limiting itself (Simmons, 2010). The act of creating an identity limited to skills and economic development ensures FE remains within those constraints, as policy-focused funding creates a pervasive view of what is important. If FE is defined by a single purpose of providing human capital for a growth economy, that is all that it is allowed to be.

In the current UK (and wider) political climate, a landscape referred to by Avis (2018) as 'the fourth industrial revolution', the language of 'progress' has shifted any discussion away from value and towards cost and worth. Contemporary political debates are fought on economic terms: trade deals, currency value, cost of manufacture, the expense of migrating populations, and the cumulative perceived strain on the finances of the fifth largest economy in the world. This pervasive ideology of value in terms of 'economics only' filters through all avenues of public life and becomes internalised in synonyms for FE such as 'the skills system' (NUS, 2017). Where we once held a socially cohesive view of community and afforded a welfare state, we now think in terms of national cost and not national value. Where we once valued education as a universal right, it is now in the bailiwick of employers – the net producers of economic worth – with little funding or attention given to programmes of study that do not directly lead to 'employability' (e.g. see Crisp and Powell, 2016). Preparing people for work and an economically productive life has always been one element of learning; now it is the sole driving focus of measure, playing out in every aspect of FE, from 'revolving door' recruitment policies (Atkins, 2009) to a perfectionist culture of individual competence monitoring (Boreham, 2010). Organisations grab hold of the latest jargon, believing they need it to escape negative scrutiny – and unwittingly reinforce its hold on collective thinking.

FE's complexity is that it contains multiple identities within one collectively defined sector, dominated by the interests of its strongest and most articulate voice: general further education colleges, powerfully organised as the Association of Colleges (AoC). Other FE contexts are defined by what they are not; for example, 'non-traditional' is an unhelpful term for prison education, which is actually older (more 'traditional') than college-based FE (Coates, 2016).

The common assumption that further education is everything not done by universities or schools is inaccurate; the 'post-compulsory' learning trajectories of individuals are not always straightforward. FE has unhelpfully internalised some disempowering messages: the Cinderella in the head (Mycroft, forthcoming). The Sapir–Whorf hypothesis that the language we use shapes the way we think, and vice versa (Boroditsky, 2010), may have been popularised into sound bites (McWhorter, 2014), but their notion of 'linguistic relativity' offers a helpful critique of how political and ideological levers leak into the ecosystems of education and other social policy, influencing structures and practice. FE has a confused and contradictory lexicon, paradoxically combining the use of impenetrable jargon with ill-defined terms clinging on from a different world, leading to an inability to articulate its purpose with any clarity. This liminality leads to a culture of 'groupthink' where the absurd becomes normal and pedagogy – the theory and practice of teaching that should be at the heart of any discourse – is reduced to a set of capitalised policy sound bites: resilience, growth mindset, well-being, attainment gap. A rethink – or reimagining – of FE and its discourses is well overdue.

Instead of worrying about how to define what FE is and does, let's consider how we achieve what society needs from the sector, drawing on FE's multiple identities and cultures to support the notion of education for all. In this respect, the identity and purpose of FE are inextricably linked and quite clear: *further education should promote and support transitions of individuals through learning.* That is all the definition that is required in order to understand the ethos of the sector.

Vocabulary is key. Defining the FE sector by what it 'delivers' pushes us towards a mindset of outputs, attainment and economic viability. The lexicon of capitalism is an ill fit for what education can potentially achieve, and shapes not only how we think and view others, but also the organisational structures that constrain us. Within organisations, inequality is rife: in top-heavy structures stacked high with 'bullshit jobs' (Graeber, 2018) and in the precarity of some contracts versus the pension-protected security of others. Leadership and 'line management' become entangled, and line management, with its human resources weaponry, plays it safe. Risk aversion is everywhere, in thrall to the perfectionist demands of Ofsted (O'Leary, 2016). As O'Leary argues, all this 'management' constrains the agency of the teaching profession. It is therefore worth taking a fresh look at four of the terms we take for granted.

What do we call FE?

The term 'post-compulsory' signals conflicting things in different parts of the UK – the 'school' leaving age of 18 in England does not apply in Scotland, for example, meaning that the term has a different meaning north and south of the border. Further education's 'training and skills' suffix was an ideological move, signalling a shift to the employability agenda (McMurray, 2019) around the same time that 'teaching, learning and assessment' shifted emphasis from what the teacher did to what the student learned (that could be measured and monitored) (Coffield, 2014). Slippery terms are unhelpful and do nothing to enable effective discourse, particularly across contexts, disciplines and other silos. As we have explored above, it is difficult enough to get hold of an agreed definition of 'further education/FE', which is all we choose to grapple with here.

'Non-traditional' contexts

Within or outside of FE, an assumption exists that general further education colleges are the *sine qua non* manifestation of FE, and other sites – community education, private training and work-based learning, sixth forms (lumped in with schools), third sector provision, the growing educational portfolio in the criminal justice system – are additional. Again, we see the powerful relationship between language and structures of power, with the Association of Colleges having more significant clout than other sector bodies (in England), thus amplifying the voice of the most powerful partner. Understandable and worked hard for, yet this begs the question of how to assure that level of representation for all.

Lifelong learning

As things stand, both in England and Scotland, FE sits in the midst of an uncreative tension between being the saviour of the post-Brexit economy, on the one hand, and (the traditional narrative of) 'saving' lost souls, on the other. The turn-of-the-century adult education lexicon, which culminated in the short-lived repositioning of FE/adult education as 'lifelong learning' (Blunkett, 1990) survives in the form of Festival of Learning award winners and the like. FE writes the tragic life story genre brilliantly; what it lacks is a language to articulate those pedagogies that contribute to the transformation of the few.

(My) learners

When did students get to be called 'learners' in FE parlance? The concept of lifelong learning may be at the heart of this, but it is hard to pin down. It seems likely that 'learner' arose during a 1990s shift away from 'chalk-and-talk' teaching to the group-based learning that was popular around that time. Ironic, then, that in FE, the term 'learner' has come to be shaded with an othering tone – 'them', not us, or, as Kevin Orr (2018) put it, 'other people's children'. It is hard to resist an analysis that the overweening structural inequalities of FE find their human outlet in unequal relationships between groups of people.

These definitions are important in that they are derived from the ever-changing policy context that in itself is embedded in an economy-driven narrative of social policy. As FE becomes ever-more tied into the language and outputs of capitalism, employers seem to be asking for something quite different to the prevailing 'everyone gets there in the end' competence-based approach: contemporary research converges on 'deeper' skills and behaviours, such as autonomy, digital agility, teamwork and problem-solving (Pellegrino and Hilton, 2012; see also much more, of varying quality, since). Reddy (Daley et al., 2017) and others (e.g. see Dromey et al., 2017) have demonstrated that even when aligning funding to the fulfilment of the economic mission, FE still doesn't get it right: the varying quality apprenticeships of recent years are not always fit for purpose, sending plumbers, for example, out into industry with outdated skills and little business acumen. Young people in England, compelled to stay in education to avoid being defined as 'NEET' (a label that frequently causes the family income to be reduced) are forced to endure a revolving door (Atkins, 2009) of motor vehicle technology/plumbing (for boys) and hairdressing/health and social care (for girls), courses that rarely lead to gainful employment as they lack the required practical real working environment experience in sufficient level and depth. There is no formal gender pipeline, just unconscious stereotyping, often by all parties. Having been comprehensively failed by the school system, expectations that FE may also fix inadequacies in maths and English are correspondingly low (Anderson and Peart, 2016).

The conduits of policy influence are not accidental; to make its case to the Treasury, the Department for Education has to: (1) clearly understand what FE is capable of; and (2) take on board timely and persuasive briefings from the sector. As we have seen, the internalised nonsense around a confused identity ensures that we are collectively inarticulate (sterling recent efforts by the Association of Colleges being too little, too late). No pipeline means no visibility within a government department that does not itself sustain FE narratives from within its ranks of sixth form to university civil servants – and only hears the 'tragic life story' message from the outside. Until it can self-define and articulate a powerful message around pedagogy and practice, FE is missing the chance to be at the vanguard of new modes and patterns of work.

The transformation mirage

Key questions

Who, if anyone, needs to be transformed - and how?

Acknowledging that transformational experiences are mercurial and personal, it is important to set out our definition in order to explore what we describe as the transformational mirage. Aoki (cited in Pinar and Irwin, 2004) defines transformation in education as authentic learning, intervention and empowerment. These three factors, which enable distinct and profound change in an individual's perspective or circumstance, are a useful place from which to explore what is meant by transformation through education. We should be clear from the outset that we are not suggesting education isn't or cannot be transformational; on the contrary, where learners are able to fulfil their own purpose for learning – be that career or personal achievement – the impact is potentially life-changing. As teacher educators ourselves, we are humbled on a regular basis by students who harness the transformational fire of their own experience to ignite transformation in others. These stories are described glowingly by advocates as 'inspirational', and the 'passion' of adult educators to 'make a difference' is taken for granted in our profession. Our argument is that much of this is accidental – opportunities seized rather than practice grounded in transformative philosophies – and that the myth of the 'transformational teacher' is both patronising and contextually unachievable (e.g. see Ecclestone and Hayes, 2009). All too often these moving stories occur in spite of the education system, and not because of it. A clear and precise delineation between the *system* and *educators* is intentional here; however, it is important to acknowledge that educators are within and part of the system, and the problem of bifurcation is not as simple as we have implied. Despite this, it seems that some people are able to harness learning situations, make new sense of the world, and interpret their histories and agency in a new light, even if this was not the explicit intention of the course: more of a happenstance. An intentional pedagogy would leave a lot less to chance.

Not everyone wants to be transformed and nor should they. FE is a broad church and some people really do 'just' want to learn a new skill. It is time to move away from the dangerous idea that education must and should be transformational and that educators are the people who make it so. This is a fallacy, and a self-aggrandising one at that. Despite the claims of glossy prospectuses and outsized, outside Ofsted banners, transformation is not in the gift of the teacher, the college or the sector, nor does it follow a growth mindset (Dweck, 2017) as night follows day. Transformative experiences are supported by conditions, individuals, circumstance, openness to learning and cultural acceptance. As long as the idea that teachers can be transformational is ideologically incorporated, we remove the aspiration of emancipation away from individuals (and communities) and gateway it; furthermore, we set up educators to be measured against their supposedly transformational behaviours, perfectionist standards (Brown, 2015) that can never be met.

All of this creates a sector that sees perfection as 'normal': when did 'outstanding' stop meaning 'to stand out'? And when did good stop being good enough (Husband, 2017)? FE is fuelled by gratitude: of the student towards the teacher, of the teacher towards the institution that enables them to carry out their 'vocation'. Brown's (2015) lifetime of research into shame and vulnerability points the finger at perfectionist cultures for creating unhealthy workplaces, and the evidence around mental ill health in the teaching profession is irrefutable (e.g. see Glazzard and Bancroft, 2018). In increasingly over-bureaucratised cultures, the agency of all concerned is dangerously eroded and transformational potential is reduced to teaching by numbers – literally, in the case of fashionable approaches such as Lemov's (2015) not unproblematic *Teach Like a Champion*, currently finding a foothold in FE (Doxtdator, 2018).

Lacking definition, ignored, oppressed by expectations of perfection: FE internalises the Cinderella metaphor and is unable to articulate any sense of agency, including its own pedagogy. We literally can't speak our own language any more. The cultures and structures of FE will not fundamentally change until we develop a new lexicon, one that neither harps back to the past nor apes the language of neo-liberalism.

'Transformation' and empowerment

As we begin to explore potential links between transformation and empowerment, it is important to acknowledge that despite its popularity, transformation is not a value-neutral term. Transformation as a metaphor has a dark side that is not frequently discussed. It is possible to argue that individuals driven to extreme acts (violence, self-harm, oppression) could be said to have had transformational learning experiences that have convinced them that their actions are right and justified (Daley et al., 2015). Transformation through encounter with learning is not always positive, and there are plenty of educators out there who think that only 'other people' need to be transformed.

Transformation as a concept has been around educational literature for more than a century. Dewey wrote about 'the transformation of experience' (Illeris, 2018), and Mezirow picked up this thread, believing as he did in the capacity of every person to engage in meaningful dialogue with themselves *and others*. Although his vision has been transmuted into a focus on the individual in recent years, Mezirow's theories of transformative learning still encapsulate the struggle between education and the commodification of human beings (Mezirow, 2000). Addressing his concept of *perspective transformation* – 'a structural change in the way we see ourselves and our relationships' – he openly criticised competence-based education and accountability-focused systems in adult learning (Mezirow, 1978). Sadly, change has not flowed towards transformative ideas, but disappointingly away. As we have explored, the inevitability of this is seen as axiomatic – as is the conflation of economic growth with 'progress' (Bregman, 2016). Education for all, as long as we all want the same thing. It is little wonder that we cling onto those glimmers of potential change that emerge as transformational/tragic life stories. In an ideal world, we hope that those who have had transformative experiences through learning can go on to influence policy and practice, but this is not happening quickly enough to change the world in complex times (Wilson, 2015).

We all stand on the shoulders of giants, and Mezirow's inspiration Paulo Freire wrote of conscientisation: the need to name, challenge and confront oppressive relationships, whether they be personal or systematic. While the experiences of some individuals will undoubtedly be personally transformative, no organisation can truthfully claim to be the instigator of that. The problem is rooted in the tangled expectations of our profession: transformation, on the one hand, and accountability, on the other. Measurement of performance, leading to profit and financial sustainability, is now managerially more important than the educational experience itself. This culture is set at the very top of the ladder, manifest in posters displayed prominently at the Department for Education during 2017: 'If it can be measured, it can be monitored'. Culturally, if not economically, the trickle-down effect works.

Pedagogy: 'good help' in FE

Key questions

How can FE enable everyone to 'feel hopeful, identify their own purpose and confidently take action'?

Surveying the public sector as a whole, NESTA (2018) define 'good help' as supporting people to 'feel hopeful, identify their own purpose and confidently take action'. Recognisable in FE, 'bad help' is defined as 'undermining people's confidence, sense of purpose and independence' (p1). Where FE pedagogy is angled towards economic outcomes, it leads to 'bad help' learning cultures, where dependency finds a secure foothold. There is synchronicity between a 'bad help' approach and the 'tragic life story' culture.

We contend that 'pedagogy' – a mindful, intentional and theoretically grounded practice of teaching – is an essential prerequisite for 'good help' learning. We define pedagogy as both what happens in the classroom and the impact on students of what happens outside the classroom. In this sense, the idea of pedagogy as the art and science of learning and teaching (Illeris, 2018) is complemented by the idea of disposition, not in the sense of the passive 'natural' teacher, but in an active acknowledgement that pedagogy extends beyond actions. A meaningful pedagogy is only possible where the teacher has enough autonomy to exercise their judgement and does so in pursuit of creating a learning environment where each student can discover, identify and reinforce their own sense of purpose: good help.

Where organisational conditions are oppressive, this level of autonomy is unlikely, and as a conse-quence pedagogy becomes a shadow of itself, reduced to actions, 'tools' and outcomes.

We strongly resist being drawn into a false dichotomy of 'traditional' and 'progressive' approaches to pedagogy, which plays out so unhelpfully on Twitter and occasionally elsewhere. This damaging binary allows for no room to 'let newness in' (Rushdie, 1988) and anchors FE to a (possibly rose-tinted) past that has little relevance for a complex future. The uncertainties of now require new pedagogies that rethink past hegemonies, and educators need thinking time to determine these: impossible as a unicorn in some organisations. To return to Gramsci, this is an 'interregnum' for FE, as well as for much else. For too long, FE has been trying to fix itself in response to the exhausting whirl of policy changes, layering sticking plaster on sticking plaster until it resembles an unholy mess of entangled and half-understood imperatives. What's needed is a fundamental reimagining. We believe that the concept of 'good help' is as useful a place to start as any.

Purposeful pedagogies

Current pedagogies exist that can be repurposed to local contexts. Many of these flourish (where they can) outside the FE 'system', such as the ESOL (English for speakers of other languages) organisation English for Action, which employs a purposeful pedagogy, drawing on theories of participatory edu-cation that are not uninfluenced by Freire. Uniquely in ESOL, the professional network NATECLA provides a space for educators to nourish their practice outwith the organisation, providing up-to-date policy context alongside professional development and a campaigning voice. As long as organisations are driven not by pedagogy, but by the demands of a superstructural construct, such as capitalism, the language (structure, culture, mindset) is set from the top.

Anti-heroic leadership

One of the instigators of the NESTA (2018) 'good help' research is Richard Wilson, and his earlier work around distributed leadership, *The Anti-Hero* (Wilson, 2015), offers an alternative approach that is beginning to influence FE. Wilson's anti-heroes are thought leaders for complex times, people at the heart of an organisation who have more wriggle room than their economically obedient hierarchical leaders. In many English FE institutions, the anti-hero approach is gaining traction among educators positioned in the emergent, hierarchically central role of the advanced practitioner, or AP (Tyler et al., 2017). Working on projects that fall outside the organisation's core business, APs (in theory at least) have space to operate and amnesty from any 'mistakes' that follow taking measured risk. This is a vul-nerable place to be, in a perfectionist culture, but where these 'spaces to dance' (Daley et al., 2015) are carved out, and particularly where they can be harnessed to the student voice – highly valued in theory (NUS, 2017) – much might be possible.

Research constellations

In our view, theory without practice is certainly sterile, but practice without theory is mindless. Consequently, we argue that where educators own – and do – their own enquiry, based in practice and on collaborative critical reflection, pedagogies become more robust and student- (rather than compli-ance-) focused as they come from a source and point of original learning (e.g. see Drew et al., 2016).

A complication is that FE research has – perhaps inevitably – followed the money. Major policy shifts trail funded research programmes in their wake and a positivist turn in social science research has also contributed to a patchy landscape. In particular, what is referred to as the 'non-traditional' manifestations of FE (assuming colleges at the centre), including community learning and education in prisons, are beginning to show signs of lacking robust, contemporary theoretical underpinnings. More pervasive is a sense that any research culture there used to be in FE dimmed in recent years, if indeed the mid 1990s can still be deemed recent (e.g. see CLMH, 2018). Despite (a weak) inclusion in the English professional standards for FE educators – knowing about research rather than doing it (ETF, 2014), a research-focused culture within FE as a sector is some way from being mainstream in practice.

Fortunately, we are happy to report that a renaissance is taking hold. Driven by FE educators themselves and supported by 'fellow travellers' in higher education, a research movement is coalescing around various networks, conferences and publications such as ARPCE, LSRN and TELL (see the glossary at the end of this chapter), *Further Education and the Twelve Dancing Princesses* (Daley et al., 2015), and regional research meets. At the same time, professional development funding distributed via the Education and Training Foundation in England is encouraging practitioner research, as well as funding developmental projects for advanced practitioners (see above). Social media, particularly Twitter, connects and amplifies these 'constellations of practice' (Mycroft and Sidebottom, 2018).

Thinkers are our friends

Initial teacher education has some culpability in the anti-theory culture that has burdened further education in recent decades – and we write as teacher educators. Tired, outdated reading lists and easy theory tropes at best fail to inspire and at worst replicate education's inequalities. Where are the women on teacher education reading lists? Where are the writers of colour? Where, indeed, are the videos, research reports and podcasts that can inspire, engage and provide 'good science'? There is an urgent need to decolonise teacher education curricula and research (Patel, 2015). The FE workforce is as diverse as its student population. It is time this was reflected in its professional formation.

Resistance to 'theory' is also endemic among educators who have not traditionally been required to have higher-level qualifications and who may experience some defensive 'impostor syndrome' when asked to engage with dusty theories that seem alien to practice. A 'thinkers are our friends' approach assumes all parties (including the dusty theorists) are equal thinkers, creating personal theories of practice that only differ by how publicly available they are.

Diffractive practice

Finally, we wish to challenge the old 'reflective practice' axiom, which took a firm hold across education from the 1990s onwards. There's nothing wrong with reviewing one's practice in a critical, self-aware manner, particularly when that is connected with the practice of a personal ethics (Braidotti and Hlavajova, 2018). But how often is that the case? Reflection operates in isolation, holding up a mirror to the individual, with the potential to further pathologise the practice of the educator in a perfectionist culture.

A diffractive practice, rather like a kaleidoscope, brings in diverse perspectives of others (CLMH, 2018). A collaborative critical approach to reflection further invites a deepening of the thinking to move beyond review of actions to a searching of underlying values, principles, beliefs and assumptions.

Optical metaphors are not uncommon in education, and Barad (2007) defines diffraction as not just looking at what happened, but looking at the impact of what happened, in process with others, to bring in much-needed 'newness' to pedagogies struggling under the weight of a schizophrenic culture.

The time is now: what's next for FE?

Key questions

How can FE 'get up and get on with it'?

Given the challenges, the crisis of identity and the underfunding endemic in FE, you would be excused for thinking that the sector had been stunned into inaction, retreating to lick its metaphorical wounds and defend itself from attack. This is only partially the case. The sector (or sectors, if you see Northern Ireland, Scotland, England and Wales as the separate policy areas they are) has become entirely accustomed to flux, renewal and 'innovation'. Accustomed, however, does not mean accepting (Edward et al., 2007). At a glance, the perception that nothing ever stands still in FE is a mistake easily forgiven. In reality, despite endless waves of policy and regime change, much in FE stays constant, for good or ill. This may sound glib, but FE has students with the same needs as they ever did, educators with the same requirements and stakeholders with the same interests. It doesn't matter how policy approaches the issues; the fundamental function of FE (aka lifelong learning) remains that of enabling meaningful educational experiences for all who come through its doors.

It's a fool's errand to try to formulate any sort of plan that will have wholesale meaningful impact on a sector as diffuse as FE. The diversity of the sector is its issue and its strength. Although we have taken pains to show that FE can have a defined identity, there remain a great many individual organisations each with their own constellations of practice and specific cultures, and trying to legislate for this amorphous diversity inevitably leads to that sticking plaster mentality, an attempt to bandage injuries inflicted by relentless reform. What FE constellations do have in common is inertia: frozen like petrified deer in the face of existential threat. Foley (2013) channels Bergson's notion of petrification: 'The petrified are not easy to deal with. They have resolved to stop changing and so rage at the manifestations of change all around' (p41). Inertia presents in so many ways: obduracy, self-protection, a dogged commitment to personally held values, subversion and resistance to new ideas, but petrification has protected FE to the extent that it has held its form despite unimaginable provocation. Without it, much reform would have cut deeper and harder than it has. Inertia can and does act as a filter and renders pointless any further reform that stops short of fatal devastation.

However, it is time to get up and move on. This is a call to arms. The opposite of inertia is momentum, and in FE this takes the form of an affirmative sector-wide movement focused on robust self-owned evidence, which attempts to remove itself from the constraints of bureaucracy, endless reform and policy shift. A movement that attends to the constant and never-changing purpose of FE. Those working as educators know FE's value, its potential, and moreover its future.

This call to arms is directed at leaders and managers. A call to be bold and brave enough to redevelop autonomy and engage with alternative possibilities for the future. Engagement with the ideas outlined here does not mean abandoning all aspects of education for positive economic futures, but it does mean putting pedagogy first. We argue that the same measures can be achieved within a policy context aligned with the value of the human, not exclusively their potential economic worth. FE is not a means to an end, but a means within itself.

It is time to ditch the self-fulfilling prophecy that will inevitably consume any remaining aspirations of learning for the greater good and remove the pressure from FE. Let the sector develop its partnerships, pathways, methods and processes without continued reform. Repeated compliance is draining and remains stubbornly meaningless in the face of relentless, foundationless change. The language of marketing has no place within education, and those that espouse it have a whole world of commerce to plunder. Education only needs marketing when it is funded to promote competition. Continually weighing the pig without feeding it or giving it time to grow will make it lose weight. Continually starving FE and measuring it while blaming it for poor performance breeds resentment and failure. Educators deserve better, students deserve better and FE deserves better.

FE needs time and space to recover and regroup. We boldly call on policymakers to leave the sector alone for *three years* and see what it formulates in response to its obligations. Thinkers need time to think so that action can develop that is meaningful. This, of course, would inevitably mean that it steps out of line with the political cycle, and in the current climate that is unlikely to happen, so leaders from within the sector also need to answer the call. The idea of anti-heroic leadership is intensely appealing and further adds weight to the sense that ultimately the future of FE lies in its people.

We are caught in a round of endless, meaningless sticking plaster change. It is time to be incisive, to encourage FE's wounds to be exposed and allow time for them to heal. The cycle of victimhood needs to come to an end and the sector allowed to coalesce and speak for itself. In the course of our work, we meet countless bright, talented, frustrated FE people, and this convinces us that our profession has all the resources it needs to carry out this life-saving endeavour.

Glossary

ARPCE: Association for Research in Post-Compulsory Education

LSRN: Learning and Skills Research Network

PCET: Post-Compulsory Education and Training

TELL: Teacher Education in Lifelong Learning

References

Anderson, N. and Peart, S. (2016) Back on track: exploring how a further education college re-motivates learners to re-sit previously failed qualifications at GCSE. *Research in Post-Compulsory Education*, 21(3): 196–213.

Atkins, L. (2009) *Invisible Students, Impossible Dreams: Experiencing Vocational Education 14–19*. London: Trentham Books.

Avis, J. (2018) Socio-technical imaginary of the fourth industrial revolution and its implications for vocational education and training: a literature review. *Journal of Vocational Education and Training*, 70(3): 337–363.

Barad, K. (2007) *Meeting the University Halfway: Quantum Physics and the Entanglement of Meaning and Matter*. Durham, NC: Duke University Press.

Blunkett, D. (1990) *The Learning Age*. London: HMSO.

Boreham, N. (2010) A theory of collective competence: challenging the neo-liberal individualisation of performance at work. *British Journal of Educational Studies*, 52(1): 5–17.

Boroditsky, L. (2010) *How Language Shapes Thought*. Available at: http://longnow.org/seminars/02010/oct/26/how-language-shapes-thought/

Braidotti, R. and Hlavajova, M. (2018) *Posthuman Glossary*. London: Bloomsbury Academic.

Bregman, R. (2016) *Utopia for Realists*. London: Bloomsbury.

Brown, B. (2015) *Daring Greatly*. London: Penguin.

CLMH (2018) *Community Learning Mental Health Research Project*. Available at: https://mhfe.org.uk/clmh-pilots/

Coates, D.S. (2016) *Unlocking Potential: A Review of Education in Prisons*. London: The Stationery Office.

Coffield, F. (2014) *Beyond Bulimic Learning: Improving Teaching in Further Education*. London: Trentham.

Crisp, R. and Powell, R. (2016) Young people and UK labour market policy: a critique of 'employability' as a tool for understanding youth unemployment. *Urban Studies*, 54(8): 1784–1807.

Daley, M., Orr, K. and Petrie, J. (2015) *Further Education and the Twelve Dancing Princesses*. London: Trentham Books.

Daley, M., Orr, K. and Petrie, J. (eds) (2017) *The Principal: Power and Professionalism in FE*. London: Trentham.

Doxtdator, B. (2018) *Beyond Champions and Pirates*. Available at: www.longviewoneducation.org/beyond-champions-pirates/

Drew, V., Priestley, M. and Michael, M.K. (2016) Curriculum development through critical collaborative professional enquiry. *Journal of Professional Capital and Community*, 1(1): 92–106.

Dromey, J., McNeil, C. and Roberts, C. (2017) *Another Lost Decade? Building a Skills System for the Economy for the 2030s*. Available at: www.ippr.org/files/2017-07/another-lost-decade-skills-2030-july2017.pdf

Dweck, C. (2017) *Mindset: Changing the Way You Think to Fulfil Your Potential*, rev edn. New York: Random House.

Ecclestone, K. and Hayes, D. (2009) *The Dangerous Rise of Therapeutic Education*. London: Routledge.

Edward, S., Coffield, F., Steer, R. and Gregson, M. (2007) Endless change in the learning and skills sector: the impact on teaching staff. *Journal of Vocational Education and Training*, 57(2): 155–173.

Elliott, G. (1996) Educational management and the crisis of reform in further education. *Journal of Vocational Education & Training*, 48(1): 5–23.

ETF (2014) *Professional Standards for Teachers and Trainers in Education and Training (in England)*. Available at: www.et-foundation.co.uk/wp-content/uploads/2017/05/ETF_Professional_Standards_Overview_Poster_AW1.pdf

Foley, M. (2013) *Life Lessons from Bergson*. London: Pan Macmillan.

Glazzard, J. and Bancroft, K. (2018) *Meeting the Mental Health Needs of Learners Aged 11–18*. St Albans: Critical Publishing.

Graeber, D. (2018) *Bullshit Jobs: A Theory*. London: Penguin.

Husband, G. (2017) The renovation of Machiavellian innovation: a return to a celebration of the good. In M. Daley, K. Orr and J. Petrie (eds), *The Principal: Power and Professionalism in FE*. London: Trentham.

Husband, G. (2018) At last, we're defining the duck-billed platypus: further education sector identity and research. *Times Educational Supplement*, No. 5308, 13 July 2018.

Illeris, K. (2018) *Contemporary Theories of Learning*. London. Routledge.

Illsley, R. and Waller, R. (2017) Further education, future prosperity? The implications of marketisation on further education working practices. *Research in Post-Compulsory Education*, 22(4): 477–494.

Lemov, D. (2015) *Teach Like a Champion 2.0: 62 Techniques That Put Students on the Path to College*. San Francisco, CA: Jossey-Bass.

Mayo, P. (2009) The 'competence' discourse in education and the struggle for social agency and critical citizenship. *International Journal of Educational Policies*, 3(2): 5–16.

McMurray, S. (2019) The impact of funding cuts to further education colleges in Scotland. *Journal of Further and Higher Education*, 43(2): 201–219.

McWhorter, J. (2014) *The Language Hoax*. Oxford: Oxford University Press.

Mezirow, J. (1978) Perspective transformation. *Adult Education*, 28(2): 100–110.

Mezirow, J. (2000) *Learning as Transformation: Critical Perspectives on a Theory in Progress*. London: John Wiley.

Mycroft, L. (forthcoming) A world in miniature: the storytelling potential of research offcuts. *Journal of Post-Compulsory Education*, 24(2).

Mycroft, L. and Sidebottom, K. (2018) Constellations of practice. In P. Bennett and R. Smith (eds), *Identity and Resistance in Further Education*. London: Routledge.

NESTA (2018) *Good and Bad Help: How Purpose and Confidence Transform Lives*. Available at: www.nesta.org.uk/report/good-and-bad-help-how-purpose-and-confidence-transform-lives/

NUS (2017) *Students Shaping the Post-16 Skills Plan*. London: NUS.

O'Leary, M. (2016) *Reclaiming Lesson Observation*. London: Routledge.

Orr, K. (2018) Further education colleges in the United Kingdom: providing education for other people's children. In R. Latiner Raby and E.J. Valeau (eds), *Handbook of Comparative Studies on Community Colleges and Global Counterparts*. Cham: Springer.

Patel, L. (2015) *Decolonising Educational Research: From Ownership to Accountability*. London: Routledge.

Pellegrino, J.W. and Hilton M.L. (eds) (2012) *Education for Life and Work: Developing Transferable Knowledge and Skills in the 21st Century*. Washington, DC: National Academies Press.

Peters, B.G. (2017) What is so wicked about wicked problems? A conceptual analysis and a research program. *Policy and Society*, 36(3): 385–396.

Pinar, W. and Irwin, R. (2004) *Curriculum in a New Key: The Collected Works of Ted T. Aoki*. London: Routledge.

Rushdie, S. (1988) *The Satanic Verses*. New York: Random House.

Simmons, R. (2010) Globalisation, neo-liberalism and vocational learning: the case of English further education colleges. *Research in Post-Compulsory Education*, 15(4): 363–376.

Tyler, E., Marvell, R., Green, M., Martin, A., Williams, J. and Huxley, C. (2017) *Understanding the Role of Advanced Practitioners in English Further Education*. London: Institute for Employment Studies.

Wilson, R. (2015) *The Anti-Hero*. Available at: https://osca.co/publications/anti-hero-the-hidden-revolution-in-leadership-change/

INDEX